THE OLD COLONIAL SYSTEM

1660–1754

PART I. — VOL. I.

THE
OLD COLONIAL SYSTEM
1660–1754

BY

GEORGE LOUIS BEER

AUTHOR OF "BRITISH COLONIAL POLICY, 1754–1765," "THE ORIGINS
OF THE BRITISH COLONIAL SYSTEM, 1578–1660"

PART I
THE ESTABLISHMENT OF THE SYSTEM
1660–1688

IN TWO VOLUMES
VOL. I

Gloucester, Mass.
PETER SMITH
1958

Avec de la réflexion, des lectures et de l'habitude, on réussit par degrés à reproduire en soi-même des sentiments auxquels d'abord on était étranger; nous voyons qu'un autre homme, dans un autre temps, a dû sentir autrement que nous-mêmes; nous entrons dans ses vues, puis dans ses goûts; nous nous mettons à son point de vue, nous le comprenons, et, à mesure que nous le comprenons mieux, nous nous trouvons un peu moins sots.

H. Taine, Voyage en Italie, I, pp. 5, 6.

La storia, come tutti i fenomeni della vita, è *l'opera inconsapevole di sforzi* " *infinitamente piccoli* „; *compiuti disordinatamente da uomini singoli e da gruppi di uomini, quasi sempre per motivi immediati, il cui effetto definitivo trascende sempre la intenzione e la conoscenza dei contemporanei; e appena si rivela, qualche volta, alle generazioni seguenti.*

Guglielmo Ferrero,
Grandezza e Decadenza di Roma, I, pp. ix, x.

PREFACE

It is the purpose of this work as a whole to describe the establishment, development, and operation of the English colonial system from the days of its formal creation down to the period leading to its disintegration. The era of inchoate beginnings has been treated in the writer's " Origins of the British Colonial System, 1578–1660," and the transitional years preceding the troublous days of the American Revolution have been discussed in some detail in the writer's " British Colonial Policy, 1754–1765." Thus this work is not only unhampered by problems of origins, but it is to a great extent liberated from those controversial questions which ultimately were decided, if not solved, by the ordeal of battle.

The term "colonial system " has no precise connotation, and is susceptible of varying meanings of more or less ample extension. As employed here, it is synonymous with that complex system of regulations whose fundamental aim was to create a self-sufficient commercial empire of mutually complementary economic parts. An understanding of this system must rest primarily upon an analysis of the economic theories then current, mainly in so far as they found expression in the Acts of Trade and Navigation. But these laws by no means constituted the whole system. The scheme of imperial defence was a closely correlated part, and the English fiscal arrangements, as well as the method of regulating the slave-trade, were integrally connected with it. In addition, it will be essential to study carefully both the administrative machinery in England and that established in the colonies for the purpose of carrying into effect these various laws and regulations. For, obviously, the efficacy of a system cannot be gauged without a knowledge of the means and extent of its enforcement. Furthermore, in order to understand the operation of these regulations, it is essential to examine the political and economic development of the separate colonies, not, however, as independent processes of social evolution, but only to the extent that they were affected by English policy. Various fundamental phases of colonial development have consequently been kept in the dim background, and some even have been ignored. Thus, although the purpose is not to describe the economic genesis of the United States, and although the point of view is primarily the imperial one, the work is something more and also something less than merely an economic history of the old Empire. One of its chief aims is to ascertain precisely what the statesmen of the day sought to accomplish, what means they employed for their purposes, to what extent these instruments were adapted to the actual situation, and how the various parts of the Empire developed under these regulations.

It is a platitude scarcely worth mentioning that all historical facts should be approached without any preconceived ideas as to their meaning, but it is not sufficiently realized that economic data especially are liable to be distorted by the investigator's personal theory of social philosophy. In this work, the facts presented have not been weighed either in the scale of the free-trader or in that of the protectionist. In the form in which they are presented, they can be further interpreted by either school, and probably both will draw from them conclusions satisfactory to themselves. The material has purposely been treated in a purely historical manner. No attention, for instance, has been paid to such questions as that raised by Adam Smith, whether the diversion of British capital from the European to the colonial trade was a national disadvantage. Nor has an attempt been made to ascertain whether in reality there was such a diversion; and, if there were, whether it was a direct result of the laws of trade. Such questions are predominantly economic and to some extent academic. For our purposes it is merely necessary to see what the legislators and statesmen contemplated and if the desired results followed, dismissing all such purely hypothetical questions, whether the Empire would not have been better off without any attempts to mould its economic growth, or whether the actual results attained were not in despite of these efforts or at the expense of other and possibly more vital interests. No answer to such queries can carry universal conviction; and at the end of much argumentation, we would be just about where we started.

The authorities for this work are manifold in nature and origin. To a preponderant extent, it is based upon the Colonial State Papers in the Public Record Office in London. In the aggregate, considerable material of importance has also been derived from the Treasury, Admiralty, Domestic, and Foreign Papers in the same repository. A large number of the official documents — especially such as relate to the period under consideration in this section of the work — have been published more or less fully by the British Government in the various calendars, and a considerable number have appeared in such other collections as the New York Colonial Documents, the *Virginia Magazine of History and Biography*, and Lefroy's " Memorials of the Bermudas." In addition to the manuscript sources, these printed materials have been constantly used, but as a general rule the most important of the documents, both published and unpublished, have been consulted in their original form. The manuscript volumes of the Privy Council Register were also used before the publication of the calendar had rendered further recourse to them largely superfluous. Some invaluable information was also derived from the manuscripts in the British Museum, as well as from those in the Bodleian at Oxford. Naturally the English and colonial statutes, the Journals of the House of Lords and House of Commons, the reports of the British Historical Manuscripts Commission were continually used. Finally, the voluminous pamphlet literature of the day, the contemporary diaries, various collections of family papers, and other miscellaneous sources yielded some indispensable imformation.

In its entirety, this material forms an imposing mass, but it leaves many a detailed question unanswered. Moreover, its very bulk is embarrassing. As an eminent man of letters with a marked historical bent has said: "Quand un fait n'est connu que par un seul témoignage, on l'admet sans beaucoup d'hésitation. Les perplexités commencent lorsque les événements sont rapportés par deux ou plusieurs témoins; car leurs témoignages sont toujours contradictoires et toujours inconciliables." Had Anatole France ever investigated the economic history of the seventeenth-century English Empire, he would even more fully have appreciated the truth of his own words. The trace of deliberate exaggeration in them could then have been omitted. The statistics available for that period are not only most fragmentary, but they were gathered in a thoroughly unscientific manner. Accurate statistics are only of most recent date and are still far from general. Moreover, a considerable portion of the evidence is embodied in memorials and petitions from interested parties, and hence cannot be accepted at its face value. It has to be compared with documents emanating from opposing sources, and must then be studied in connection with other data in order to estimate the degree and extent of its credibility. Without some knowledge of their

origin, so as to be able to discount the personal equa-
tion, numbers of these documents would have to be
discarded as worthless. Even with the immeasurably
more complete means of information at the disposal of
the student of present economic problems, it is most
difficult to reach an agreement as to the precise facts.
This would seem a hopeless task when long past phe-
nomena are investigated. Still, the general course of
development in the old Empire, as well as many of the
subsidiary currents, can be traced with considerable
precision; and this after all is the essential matter.
Caution and care must, however, be observed at every
turn; and definite quantitative terms can be conscien-
tiously used only with a reservation of considerable
doubt.

Without entering the polemical lists, where the question whether or no history is an art or a science can
always count upon attracting intrepid opposing cham-
pions, it is obvious that the modern historian's method
of presentation must differ radically from that of the
artist. "A picture is finished," said one of the greatest
of modern painters, "when all trace of the means used
to bring about the end has disappeared." In these
days of critical scholarship, a history so constructed,
no matter how authoritative its sources were, would
have scant chance of escaping the fate of the still-born.
Hence full references have been given for virtually
every statement. In the foot-notes has also been printed
considerable illustrative material; and to this place

likewise has been relegated a mass of more or less technical matter, which will probably be of interest and importance to the critical student, but assuredly would not
appeal to the general reader. It was hoped in this
way to keep the text readable. For it is fully realized
that what Bishop Stubbs wrote about his own special
field of investigation is at least equally applicable to
this branch of historical work: it "cannot be mastered,
can scarcely be approached, — without an effort."

GEORGE LOUIS BEER.

New York City,
November 26, 1912.

CONTENTS

CHAPTER I

THE COLONIAL POLICY OF THE PERIOD . . . . . .   PAGE 1

An era of marked expansion — General policy of Charles
II and his advisers — Sir George Downing and William
Blathwayt — England's foreign and colonial trade — The
opposition to emigration leads to objections to colonization
— The answer of the imperialists — The transportation of
convicts and others — Governmental regulation of emigration — The economic advantages expected from colonization — The colony as a source of supply — The preference
for the plantation type of colony.

CHAPTER II

THE LAWS OF TRADE AND NAVIGATION AND IMPERIAL DE-
    FENCE   58

The Navigation Act of 1660 — The Staple Act of 1663
— The Plantation Duties of 1673 — Scotland under these
statutes — Ireland and the colonies — Temporary dispensations of the laws — The system of imperial defence — The
colonial garrisons — The West Indian buccaneers — The
Barbary pirates.

CHAPTER III

THE ENGLISH FISCAL SYSTEM AND IMPERIAL FINANCES   128

The tariff of 1660 — Its preferential treatment of English
colonial products — The prohibition to plant tobacco in
England and the efforts required to enforce it — The at-
tempt in 1671 to increase the sugar and tobacco duties —
The impost of 1685 and colonial opposition to it — The
Crown's dues in the colonies — The Restoration settlement

PAGE

in the Caribbee Islands — The four and a half per cent revenue and the opposition of Barbados to it — The Virginia quit-rents — The establishment of a permanent revenue in Virginia under the control and at the disposal of the Crown, and the attempt to do so in Jamaica — The appointment of Blathwayt as Auditor-General of the colonial revenues.

CHAPTER IV

CENTRAL AND LOCAL ADMINISTRATIVE MACHINERY   .   . 224

Parliament and Crown — The Privy Council and its Committees — The Secretaries of State — The Council for Foreign Plantations of 1660 — The Council for Trade of 1660 — Its revival in 1668 and that of the colonial council in 1670 — The Council for Trade and Plantations of 1672 — The Lords of Trade — The Admiralty and the Colonies — The Treasury and the Commissioners of the Customs — The Royal Governor — The naval officers — The collectors of the customs — The Surveyor General of the Customs — Quarrel between Giles Bland and Governor Berkeley of Virginia — The colonial admiralty courts — The use of the navy to suppress illegal trading.

CHAPTER V

THE SLAVE-TRADE AND THE PLANTATION COLONIES   .   . 316

Classification of the colonies according to their imperial value — The demand for slaves in the West Indies — The English African Company — Dutch opposition to its trade — The complaints of Barbados against the Company — Its reorganization in 1672 — Opposition of the West Indian colonies to the Royal African Company — Its attempts to supply Spanish America — The interlopers.

THE OLD COLONIAL SYSTEM

1660–1754

CHAPTER I

THE COLONIAL POLICY OF THE PERIOD

An era of marked expansion — General policy of Charles II and his advisers — Sir George Downing and William Blathwayt — England's foreign and colonial trade — The opposition to emigration leads to objections to colonization — The answer of the imperialists — The transportation of convicts and others — Governmental regulation of emigration — The economic advantages expected from colonization — The colony as a source of supply — The preference for the plantation type of colony.

THE normal development of every healthy and expanding state forms a series of alternating periods of internal readjustment and of external growth. The former are caused by the ever changing social conditions within the body politic and the ensuing more or less urgent necessity of bringing its institutions into harmony with the shifted balance of power. The latter inevitably result from the impact of state upon state in those competitive struggles and rivalries, either warlike or purely commercial, which constitute international history. Rarely does a state develop to a marked extent simultaneously in both directions, because in the stress of conflicting interests single-minded concentration can as a rule alone command success.

The establishment of the Commonwealth in England, following the collapse of the Stuart cause after the execution of Charles I, gave the nation a sorely needed respite from the internal strife that for nearly two generations had hampered its external development. The decade that was dominated by Cromwell's vigorous personality was marked by the devotion of keen attention to commercial and colonial expansion. It was clearly recognized that the commercial supremacy of the Dutch was a formidable obstacle in the path of England's economic development, and during the Interregnum considerable progress was made in overcoming this impediment.[1] X The Navigation Acts of 1650 and 1651, themselves based on earlier but less comprehensive precedents, gave a great impetus to English shipping. At the same time, with a view to increasing English sea power and commerce, considerable attention was devoted to colonial questions, and Jamaica and Nova Scotia were added to the over-sea dominions. Beyond furnishing valuable precedents, little, however, was actually accomplished either toward creating an efficient administrative machinery for governing the Empire, or toward developing a coherent system for regulating its commercial activities.[2] The position of the Cromwellian government was too insecure to permit thereof. X

X Such a system was created after the reëstablishment of the monarchy in 1660, when the fairly stable equilibrium within the body politic admitted the devotion of more undivided and closer attention to commercial and colonial matters. X

[1] See Beer, Origins of the British Colonial System, pp. 372 *et seq.*, and Beer, Cromwell's Policy in its Economic Aspects, in Pol. Science Quart., Vols. XVI, XVII.

[2] Beer, Origins, pp. 383 *et seq.*

Those varied forces, which ever since the days of Elizabeth,[1] had under untoward circumstances been steadily working for national growth — for sea power, commerce, and colonies — were then released from the trammels hitherto hampering their free action.

⊀ The Restoration was an era of marked expansion; the exuberant vitality of the age found its chief outlet in this direction. Commercial wars were waged with the sword or by means of hostile tariffs; foreign trade was prosecuted with unwonted vigor by large companies; in the Far East, in Africa and in America, new factories, trading settlements and colonies were added to the growing list of imperial outposts. It was a spontaneous national movement, based on the demands of the country's economic life, and in general enlisted the sincere and energetic support of the leading statesmen of the period from King Charles down.⊁ However notable was their divergence regarding internal questions, in this respect there certainly was substantial unanimity. Despite his hedonistic attitude toward life, his lazy, self-indulgent amiability, Charles II was an efficient man of affairs, with a clear insight into the fundamental causes of a nation's material prosperity. Hostility to his disingenuous and tortuous course in religious and constitutional questions, and to the highly discreditable nature of his diplomatic relations with France, has thrust into the obscure background the more enduring and laudable phases of his varied activities. As a discerning critic has well said,

[1] England's rise as a maritime power dates from this period. *Cf.* Brit. Mus., Lansdowne MSS. 691, f. 61.

"however much he might disregard the sentiments of his subjects, he never played fast and loose with their material interests." [1]   Charles II favored wise schemes of internal improvement, supported the commercial and colonial enterprises of the day, and in his general foreign policy sought to overthrow the Dutch commercial dominion. "Upon the king's first arrival in England," so writes his confidential adviser Clarendon, " he manifested a very great desire to improve the general traffick and trade of the kingdom, and upon all occasions conferred with the most active merchants upon it, and offered all he could contribute to the advancement thereof." [2]   His policy was largely dictated by the commercial and colonial interests of England.

Immediately after the Restoration, the new government was put to the test, and its decision was significant. In his treaty of 1656 with Spain, Charles II had agreed, in the event of recovering the crown of his ancestors, that he would return Jamaica and would aid Philip IV to reconquer Portu-

[1] Cunningham, Growth of English Industry and Commerce, Modern Times (ed. 1903) II, p. 194. Some weight should, however, be given to the following contemporary anecdote.   According to Bishop Burnet, "Coventry told lord Essex, that there was once a Plantation cause at the council board, and he was troubled to see the king espouse the worst side: and upon that he went to him, and told him in his ear that it was a vile cause which he was supporting. The king answered him, he had got good money for doing it."   Burnet, History of my own Time (ed. O. Airy) II, p. 111.

[2] Clarendon's Autobiography (Oxford, 1827) II, p. 231. In his speech in Parliament of September 13, 1660, Clarendon said that Charles II "doth consider the infinite Importance the Improvement of Trade must be to this Kingdom; and therefore His Majesty intends forthwith to establish a Council for Trade." Lords Journal XI, p. 175[b]. See also Clarendon's speech in December. Ibid. p. 237[a]; Parl. Hist. IV, p. 170.

gal. But when England had acclaimed him as her lawful king, Charles II, with the full support of the House of Commons,[1] absolutely refused to surrender Dunkirk and Jamaica, the chief fruits of Cromwell's ambitious policy.[2] At the same time, largely also for commercial reasons, steps were taken to strengthen still further the ties binding England and Portugal. In 1660 was proposed, and two years later was consummated, a marriage between Charles II and Catharine of Braganza, the sister of the King of Portugal. By the marriage treaty, England received Bombay in the East Indies, Tangier in northern Africa, and many important commercial concessions.

These two measures the retention of Jamaica and the Portuguese marriage — together with the refusal to comply with France's demand for the restitution of Nova Scotia,[3] distinctly implied the adoption and continuation of Cromwell's maritime policy.[4] Such a course was bound to bring England again into conflict with the Dutch, then the dominant maritime and commercial nation. The Dutch, said Shaftesbury in 1673, are "England's eternal enemy, both by interest and inclination."[5] The intensity of this

[1] Com. Journal VIII, p. 163.

[2] In his diary, Evelyn reports that on September 27, 1660, Charles "received the merchants' addresses in his closet, giving them assurances of his persisting to keep Jamaica." In answer to Spain's demand for its restitution and that of Dunkirk, the Privy Council on December 6, 1660, wrote to the Spanish Ambassador that Charles II did not find himself obliged "de rendre ces deux places de la Jamajque et Dunquerque." Evelyn, Sept. 27, 1660; P. C. Cal. I, p. 302.

[3] C. C. 1661–1668, nos. 225, 226, 240–243, 322, 323.

[4] Cf. Seeley, Growth of British Policy II, pp. 118, 128.

[5] Parl. Hist. IV, p. 506.

opposition of vital interests caused the two Dutch wars of
the reign, which paved the way for England's ultimate commercial supremacy.   The most prominent point of contention among others of equal, if not greater, fundamental
importance, concerned England's right to engage in the
African slave-trade, which the Dutch vigorously and even
violently denied.   These slaves were needed to develop the
sugar plantations in the West Indies, and thus this trade
was an integral part of the colonial movement.[1]   Charles II
had personally invested in this African enterprise,[2] and so
also had several other members of the royal family, conspicuously his cousin, Prince Rupert, and his brother, the
future James II, then Duke of York.   Rupert, moreover,
was the founder of the Hudson's Bay Company, and for a
number of years directed its activities.[3]   The future James
II had also invested in this undertaking and took a personal
part in its management.   He was likewise a stockholder
in the East India Company and in the Royal African Company.[4]   In addition to his connection with these chartered

[1] In 1695, a prominent Bristol merchant stated that the West Indian
and African trades were in his estimation "the most profitable of any we
drive, and (I) do joyn them together because of their dependance on each
other."   John Cary, An Essay on the State of England (Bristol, 1695),
p. 65.

[2] For his investment in the first African company of his reign, see Public
Record Office, Declared Accounts: Audit Office, Bundle 3, Roll 1; Pipe
Office, Roll 6.

[3] C. P. Lucas, Canada (Part I, New France), pp. 185, 186; W. R. Scott,
Joint-Stock Companies to 1720 II, pp. 228, 229; Beckles Willson, The
Great Company; A. C. Laut, The Conquest of the Great Northwest.

[4] Before his accession to the throne, James had £3000 stock in the East
India Co., £3000 stock in the Royal African Co., and £300 stock in the
Hudson's Bay Co.   Brit. Mus., Add. MSS. 15,896, p. 55.

companies, James was energetically engaged in developing his proprietary dominion of New York, on which he spent no inconsiderable sums of money, from which, as all previous experience in such enterprises had amply manifested, no adequate return could reasonably be anticipated except in the more or less distant future. Moreover, James's sincere interest in the concerns of the navy constitutes one of the few bright spots in his checkered career.[1]

The chief statesmen of the era were likewise keenly alive to the importance of colonial and commercial expansion. Administrative and executive authority centred in the Privy Council, which was composed both of members of the old Cromwellian group and of faithful adherents of Charles during his wanderings on the continent. The former, conspicuously prominent among them Shaftesbury, were naturally in favor of this movement. Shaftesbury was a vigorous opponent of the Dutch as the dominant commercial nation; he was the leading spirit in the settlement of the Carolinas, and in 1672 was placed at the head of the Council of Trade and Foreign Plantations, which directed the colonial policy of the government. But the royalist section of the Privy Council was, at least in this respect, fully in accord with the old Cromwellians. During their decade of exile, they had suffered much from the success of Cromwell's vigorous, if not wholly scrupulous, policy, which had

[1] In his speech of May 30, 1685, in the House of Lords, asking for additional revenue, James said: "But, above all, I must recommend to you the care of the Navy, the strength and glory of this Nation; that you will put it into such a condition, as may make us considered and respected abroad." Grey, Debates, 1667–1694, VIII, pp. 347, 348.

effectively deterred the continental powers from active aid in support of their master. The lesson was one not to be forgotten, especially by so intelligent a man as was the chief of these cavalier statesmen, Edward Hyde, Earl of Clarendon. Though cautious in his foreign policy,[1] he fully appreciated the value of the colonies, and was actively interested in their development and administration. In his autobiography Clarendon writes that, both before and after the Restoration, "he had used all the endeavours he could to prepare and dispose the king to a great esteem of his plantations, and to encourage the improvement of them by all the ways that could reasonably be proposed to him." [2]

Other leading statesmen of the day, such as Henry Bennet, Earl of Arlington, likewise devoted great attention to these questions, and in addition there was a group of minor states-

---

[1] In Parliament, Clarendon supported the Portuguese marriage even though Spain threatened war, saying that "whosoever is against the Match with Portugal is for the delivery of Dunkirk and Jamaica." Parl. Hist. IV, pp. 181 et seq. He was, however, anxious to avoid war with the Dutch. Bodleian, Clarendon MSS. 85, f. 430.

[2] Clarendon's Autobiography (Oxford, 1827) III, p. 407. In a speech in Parliament in 1662, Clarendon said : " How our neighbours and our rivals, who court one and the same mistress, trade and commerce, with all the world, are advanced in shipping, power, and an immoderate desire to engross the whole traffic of the universe, is notorious enough." Consequently, he said, England must spend large sums on the army and navy ; those who murmur at the expense of defending Dunkirk and the other new acquisitions, "which ought to be looked upon as jewels of an immense magnitude in the royal diadem, do not enough remember what we have lost by Dunkirk, and should always do if it were in an enemy's hands; nor duly consider the vast advantages those other dominions are like, by God's blessing, in short time, to bring to the trade, navigation, wealth, and honour of the king and kingdom." Parl. Hist. IV, p. 250.

men, politicians, and officials whose influence was most important. Prominent among them was Arlington's successor as Secretary of State, Sir Joseph Williamson, whose carefully compiled note-books testify to his methodical study and detailed knowledge of colonial questions.[1] But of these men the most influential by far was Sir George Downing, trained in New England, a nephew of the elder John Winthrop and the second on the list of Harvard's subsequent long roll of graduates. During his youth he had left Massachusetts for the West Indies,[2] and shortly afterwards appeared in England. Under Cromwell, he filled satisfactorily several responsible administrative and financial positions, and at the time of the Restoration was England's representative at the Hague. Abandoning his late associates, he succeeded in ingratiating himself with Charles II and was continued in his post in Holland. As a diplomat, he strenuously supported the English merchants in their acrimonious disputes with the Dutch, and was a strong advocate of war as the best way out of the existing *impasse*. In addition to his diplomatic work, Downing was very active in the fields of administration and legislation. From 1667 on, under his supervision as Secretary to the Commissioners, "the routine of Treasury business and Treasury bookkeeping was systematized and regulated in a remarkably thorough and able manner."[3] Later, as one of the Com-

[1] Sir Robert Southwell, however, said in 1680 that Williamson 'was not very attentive to the business of the Plantations.' C. C. 1677–1680, p. 469.

[2] Winthrop Papers I, p. 536.

[3] Cal. Treas. Books, 1660–1667, p. xliii.

missioners of the Customs, he was most influential in shaping the details of colonial policy and the actual course of administration.   But it was in legislation that his influence on the colonies was most potent.   In every one of that important series of statutes regulating colonial trade, his hand was apparently the one that guided Parliament.[1]

Downing's personal character, in so far as he was a time-server and had betrayed his former associates, the regicide refugees in Holland,[2] has been probably only too justly impugned, but there can be no question of his great ability and efficiency as a public servant.[3]   The following excerpt from a letter written by him in 1663 to Clarendon embodies the economic creed of the day.   "Be the Governm.ᵗ what it will," he held, "trade may be had if they give themselves to Encourage it, But it is not to be had in a day, nor by one

---

[1] The four chief laws affecting the colonies were 12 Ch. II, c. 18, 15 Ch. II, c. 7, 22 and 23 Ch. II, c. 26, and 25 Ch. II, c. 7.   For Downing's activity in connection with the Navigation Act of 1660, see Com. Journal VIII, pp. 120, 129, 142, 151, 153.   It was apparently due to him that the celebrated "enumerated commodities" clause was added to the statute.   The "Staple Act" of 1663 was also seemingly drafted by him.   Brit. Mus., Add. MSS. 22,920, ff. 11, 12.   Downing was also prominent in the passage of the Acts of 1671 and 1673.   Com. Journal IX, pp. 224, 237, 238, 252, 273, 275. On Downing's influence see also post, passim.

[2] In this connection Pepys said that Downing had acted "like a perfidious rogue," and that "all the world takes notice of him for a most ungrateful villaine for his pains."   Pepys, March 12 and 17, 1662.   On this see R. C. H. Catterall, Sir George Downing and the Regicides, in Am. Hist. Rev. XVII.

[3] When Pepys heard of Downing's appointment as Secretary to the Treasury, he wrote: "I think in my conscience they have done a great thing in it; for he is active and a man of business, and values himself upon having things do well under his hand; so that I am mightily pleased in their choice."   Pepys, May 27, 1667.

good act, but to be pursued from Step to Step." [1] In striving for this end, Downing displayed marked intellectual consistency and great constructive ability. To him, far more than to any other individual, is due the commercial system which was elaborated during the Restoration era for the regulation of the Empire's trade.

Finally, mention should be made of another official, William Blathwayt, who for thirty years was closely identified with colonial affairs. His influence was, however, by no means so fundamental as was that of Downing. Blathwayt had considerably less constructive ability and was active mainly in administration, while Downing powerfully influenced the underlying policy. By his industry and ability — Blathwayt was "very dexterous in business," records the diarist Evelyn [2] — he had risen from very moderate circumstances, [3] and in the course of time occupied simultaneously a number of lucrative posts. Among these was that of Auditor General of the colonies, which brought under his supervision the various colonial financial systems. Then, as Secretary to the Lords of Trade, he virtually created the routine administrative machinery of the colonial office in London, which was continued after 1696 by the Board of Trade, of which he was at the outset a prominent member.

In addition to these statesmen, politicians, and officials, there was a large body of courtiers, noblemen, merchants, and

[1] Hague, Dec. 25, 1663, Downing to Clarendon. Bodleian, Clarendon MSS. 107, f. 53[b].

[2] Evelyn, June 18, 1687.

[3] He was related to the Povey family, a number of whom held minor colonial positions.

traders who, partly for personal and partly for patriotic reasons, were instrumental in furthering this movement of expansion. Some devoted their attention to private commerce, others to the development of the great trading companies — preëminently those which had secured monopolies of the commerce with Africa and the East Indies. Closely affiliated with this body of men, and in many cases overlapping, was a group engaged in new colonial enterprises, such as the Carolinas and Jerseys, and in developing the resources of the existing plantations. The governing classes, composed mainly of the landed gentry, were working in close coöperation with these groups to further the commercial and colonial expansion of England. The ensuing national growth was on a conspicuously rapid scale.

It was fully realized at the time that England's development depended upon the possession of adequate naval strength, and that sea power was the fundamental factor upon which must be based the future commercial and colonial empire, of which the statesmen of the day had some inevitably indistinct, but prescient, visions. In his speech on the adjournment of Parliament in September of 1660, the Speaker said that the Act of Navigation "will enable your majesty to give the law to foreign princes abroad as your royal predecessors have done before you : and it is the only way to enlarge your majesty's dominions all over the world ; for so long as your majesty is master at sea your merchants will be welcome wherever they come ; and that is the easiest way of conquering." [1] The Restoration government zeal-

[1] Parl. Hist. IV, p. 120.

ously pursued this policy of fostering the development of sea power by measures discriminating against alien shipping. Despite some unavoidable concomitant disadvantages, the actual end attained coincided with the aims of those enacting these measures. To this notable extent the policy was unquestionably completely successful. Sir Josiah Child, one of the most intelligent men of affairs of the time, asserted that without the Navigation Act "we had not been Owners of one half of the Shiping, nor Trade, nor employed one half of the Sea-men which we do at present." [1] Under the protection of this measure the English mercantile marine approximately doubled itself between 1660 and 1688. [2] The royal navy also, but to a somewhat less noteworthy degree, showed considerable advance. [3]

This great increase in shipping naturally implied a cor-

---

[1] Child, A New Discourse of Trade (London, 1693), p. 91. The Navigation Act has been the subject of controversy from the day of its enactment until the present time. Later critics, under the influence of the free trade doctrine, have contended that the development of the English mercantile marine took place in spite of the law, or that it was at the expense of other interests equally, or possibly even more, important. Such criticism is largely academic ; it is ineffective and unconvincing, because it rests on a series of hypotheses that cannot be verified. The crucial point in judging the success of the policy is that certain means were adopted to attain a definite end and that the goal in view was actually reached.

[2] "As to our Stock in Shipping, old and experienc'd Merchants do all agree, that we had in 1688, near double the Tonnage of Trading Ships, to what we had *Anno* 1666." Charles Davenant, Discourses on the Public Revenue and on the Trade of England (London, 1698) II, p. 29.

[3] In 1660 the tonnage of the navy was 62,594, in 1688 it was 101,032. Davenant, *op. cit.* II, p. 29. The great increase in the English navy dated from the period of the French wars.

responding expansion in England's foreign commerce.[1] Shortly after the Restoration, London's foreign trade amounted to about six millions sterling, of which two-thirds were imports.[2] On this basis, the total foreign commerce of England was somewhat over eight and a quarter millions.[3] By the end of the century this figure had risen to nearly twelve and a half millions, and it was especially gratifying to the mercantilist mind that virtually this entire increase was in the exports. These had risen from about two and three-quarters to nearly seven millions.[4]

[1] Ships cleared outwards from England:

	English Tonnage	Foreign Tonnage	Total Tonnage
1663 (about) . .	95,266	47,634	142,900
1688	190,533	95,267	285,800
1697	144,264	100,524	244,788
1700 (about) . .	273,693	43,635	317,328

Cunningham, *op. cit.* II, p. 932, appendix F. See also the statistics in House of Lords MSS. (1695–1697) II, pp. 421, 422.

[2]

	Exports	Imports
1662–1663	£2,022,812	£4,016,019
1668–1669	£2,063,274	£4,196,139

C. O. 388/8, E 31; Brit. Mus., Sloane MSS. 2902, f. 118. Misselden estimated that in 1613 England's exports were £2,090,640 and the imports £2,141,151. The corresponding figures for 1622, as estimated by him, were £1,944,264 and £2,519,315. Misselden, The Circle of Commerce (London, 1623), pp. 120, 121, 127–129.

[3] *Cf.* W. R. Scott, Joint-Stock Companies to 1720 I, p. 266.

[4] The exports from England for the 4 years 3 months from Sept. 29, 1697, to Christmas, 1701, were £29,597,387. The total imports for the same

In this growing commerce, the trade with the American plantations — the colonial trade proper — was assuming an ever-increasing importance. During the first decade of the Restoration, it amounted to only about one-tenth of the whole.[1] Twenty years later this trade had increased from roughly £800,000 to £1,300,000,[2] and towards the end of the century it had considerably more than doubled itself. It then amounted to £1,750,000 and constituted one-seventh of England's total foreign commerce.[3]

period were £23,597,387. The annual averages were: exports £6,964,091, imports £5,486,941. C. O. 388/17, N 239. For the detailed statistics of these years, see House of Lords MSS. (1699–1702) IV, pp. 434, 435; Whitworth, State of the Trade of England (London, 1776), Part I, pp. 1–6.

[1]

EXPORTS FROM LONDON

	TOTAL	TO THE COLONIES
1662–1663	£2,022,812	£105,910
1668–1669	£2,063,274	£107,791

IMPORTS INTO LONDON

	TOTAL	FROM THE COLONIES
1662–1663	£4,016,019	£484,641
1668–1669	£4,196,139	£605,574

C. O. 388/8, E 31; Brit. Mus., Sloane MSS. 2902, f. 118.

[2] For the six years from 1683 to 1688, the average exports to the American colonies were £350,000, and the imports thence, including Newfoundland, were £950,000. Davenant, op. cit. II, p. 218.

[3] The average annual exports from England for the 4 years 3 months from Sept. 29, 1697, to Christmas, 1701, were £6,964,091, of which £753,404 went to the colonies, including therein Newfoundland. As regards imports, the corresponding figures were £5,486,941 and £1,013,086. For further details,

These proportions are in themselves not large, but the
rate of increase was a disproportionately striking one; and,
moreover, these bare figures by no means indicate the intrinsic importance to England of this branch of her commerce.   The men of the day argued in a circle of sea power,
commerce, and colonies.   Sea power enabled England to ex-
pand and to protect her foreign trade, while this increased
commerce, in turn, augmented her naval strength.[1]   The
argument in respect to colonies ran in the same unending
strain, and underlying both was the fundamental idea that
sea power was the essential factor.   Now, in proportion to its
volume, the colonial trade employed far more English shipping than did England's commerce with foreign countries.
In the first place, a considerable proportion of this foreign
commerce was conveyed in alien shipping,[2] while such vessels
were by the Navigation Act totally excluded from the colonial
trade.   Furthermore, not only were the colonial products as

see House of Lords MSS. (1699–1702) IV, pp. 434, 435; Whitworth, *op.
cit.* Part I, pp. 1–6.

[1] Early in the following century, Lord Haversham, in a speech before the
House of Lords, well expressed the current view. "Your Fleet and your
Trade," he said, "have so near a relation, and such mutual influence upon
each other, they cannot well be separated; your trade is the mother and
nurse of your seamen; your seamen are the life of your fleet, and your
fleet is the security and protection of your trade, and both together are the
wealth, strength, security and glory of Britain."   Parl. Hist. VI, p. 598.
A writer of earlier date put the question thus: "The undoubted Interest
of *England* is *Trade*, since it is that only which can make us either *Rich* or
Safe; for without a *powerful Navy*, we should be a *Prey* to our *Neighbours*,
and without *Trade*, we could neither have *Sea-Men* nor *Ships*."   A Letter
to Sir Thomas Osborn (London, 1672), p. 13.

[2] See *ante*, p. 14, note 1.

a rule bulky in relation to their first cost,[1] but in addition a vessel was usually able to make only one voyage a year to America, while two, three, and even more could be made from England to the European continental countries. Thus the colonial trade gave employment to far more shipping than its mere volume indicated.[2] In 1678, the Commissioners of the Customs reported to the Lords of Trade that "the Plantacon trade is one of the greatest Nurseries of the Shipping and Seamen of this Kingdome, and one of the greatest branches of its Trade."[3] Similarly, it was estimated in a memorial of the same year that "these Plantations, Newcastle Trade and the Fishery, make ¾ of all the Seamen in yᵉ Nation."[4]

[1] The rate of freight on tobacco from Virginia to England fluctuated greatly, and was naturally considerably higher in time of war than during peace. In the period under discussion the extreme limits seem to have been £5 5s. and £16 a ton. Bruce, Economic History of Virginia I, pp. 450–452. In a rough way, and naturally inversely, these amounts about equalled the fluctuating value in Virginia of the tobacco to be transported. The price of tobacco ranged approximately from ½d. to 2d. a pound. In 1671, it was calculated that the net proceeds received by the planter from 80 cwt. of raw sugar was £44 7s., while the freight to England thereon amounted to £18 8s. C. O. 31/2 ff. 54 et seq.

[2] During the year ending Sept. 29, 1677, there came to London from the English West Indies and the Bermudas alone 155 ships of 15,845 total tonnage. During the same year, the entries from London outwards to these colonies were 80 ships of 11,365 total tonnage. C. O. 1/42, 60 i, 60 ii; C. O. 324/4, ff. 58, 59. Cf. England's Guide to Industry (London, 1683), preface.

[3] C. O. 1/42, 60; C. O. 324/4, ff. 56–58.

[4] Brit. Mus., Egerton MSS. 2395, f. 574. Sir Josiah Child also pointed out that the trade of the English colonies in America was of great bulk and employed as much shipping as most of the trades of England. Child, A New Discourse of Trade (London, 1693), p. 164. Similarly, John Pollexfen stated that the colonial trade ought to be encouraged since it employed so

Thus the colonial trade was becoming of ever-increasing importance to the national development of England; its value was fully recognized, and even over-emphasized, at the time by both Englishmen [1] and foreigners.[2] The title of a contemporary pamphlet, "Plantation Work, the Work of this Generation," [3] is of considerable significance. The territorial acquisitions in America were, however, not prized as possible homes for an overflowing population in England, but virtually solely as feeders for English commerce. In the eyes of the English government, colonial expansion was a subordinate, though vital, part of the larger movement of commercial progress. This was a striking characteristic of Restoration thought, and naturally greatly influenced

many ships and seamen, for this trade and that to Newcastle have become "the chief support of our Navigation, and Nursery for Seamen." Pollex-fen, A Discourse of Trade, Coyn and Paper Credit (London, 1697), p. 86. In the first decade of the following century, a writer, with a marked tendency to exaggeration, even estimated that nearly two-thirds of English shipping was employed in the colonial trade. Neh. Grew, The Meanes of a most Ample Encrease of the Wealth and Strength of England, in Brit. Mus., Lansdowne MSS. 691, f. 61b.

[1] Thus one writer, after carefully analyzing the plantation trade, claimed that the colonies "doe not more if soe much depend upon the interest of England, as the interest of England doth depend upon them." Bodleian, Rawlinson MSS. A 478, f. 48.

[2] In 1671, the Venetian Ambassador in England, Pietro Mocenigo, wrote to his government: "Anco il negozio dell' America è in libertà di ogni suddito inglese a praticarlo, quale ogni giorno si avanza e si rende più florido, accresciutasi la coltura nella Giammaica, popolata l'isole di Barbada e di San Cristofero, e introdotta l'industria nelle provincie della Nuova Anglia, Virginia e Florida. Tale è il traffico dell' Inghilterra dilatato per tutto il mondo." Le Relazioni degli Stati Europei, Serie IV, Inghilterra (Venezia, 1863), p. 449.

[3] By W. L., published in London, 1682. See especially pp. 6–8.

colonial policy. When England first embarked on this career of expansion, under Elizabeth and James I, the prevailing view was radically different.[1] It was then generally thought that England was over-populated, and consequently colonization was advocated as a means for relieving this congestion. It was, however, gradually realized that this diagnosis was incorrect, and that emigration not only was no remedy for pauperism and its attendant evils, but might be a drain on the national strength. England's own resources were by no means fully developed, and the great progress in industry and commerce during the Restoration era afforded employment to increasing numbers. Furthermore, the necessity for a large population was emphasized by the international rivalries of the day. As these became more acute, and especially when it was realized that a struggle with France, whose population greatly exceeded that of England, was inevitable, a loss in inhabitants was regarded with considerable alarm and trepidation. Hence, from about the middle of the seventeenth century on, when England became engaged in a bitter contest with Holland, until the close of the period of the French wars, emigration was regarded as an inherently pernicious phenomenon, as a positive evil, which should be tolerated only in return for countervailing and greater advantages to be derived from the colonies. A private individual, like William Penn, primarily interested in the settlement of his own vast concession, might claim that "colonies are the Seeds of Nations, begun and nourish'd by the Care of wise and populous

[1] Beer, Origins, Chapter II.

Countries; as conceiving them best for the Increase of humane Stock, and beneficial for Commerce ";[1] but this by no means represented the attitude and purpose of the nation and its government. At this time England did not regard herself as the actual or prospective "Mother of Nations." That was a part at first forced upon her by the inexorable facts of colonial development, and assumed voluntarily only in the nineteenth century, when the completed industrial revolution had made necessary the possession both of over-sea homes for her swarming multitudes and of expanding markets for her busy factories. Diametrically opposed was the Restoration attitude.

According to the view then prevailing, the population of England was not only not redundant, but by no means equal to its productive capacity. People were wealth,[2] ran the argument, and hence it was even urged that immigration into England should be encouraged.[3] The Earl of Shaftesbury gave expression to these current views in a memorial on the decay of lands, rents, and trade, which he addressed to

[1] William Penn, The Benefit of Plantations, or Colonies, in Select Tracts relating to Colonies, p. 26; A. C. Myers, Narratives of Early Pennsylvania etc., p. 202.

[2] "All Kingdoms or Governments are Strong or Weak, Rich or Poor, according to the Plenty or Paucity of the People of that Government." The Irregular and Disorderly State of the Plantation-Trade (about 1694), in Am. Hist. Assoc. Report, 1892, p. 37.

[3] Samuel Fortrey, England's Interest and Improvement (Cambridge, 1663), pp. 4–13. Among the fundamental characteristics of mercantilism was "the exaggerated importance attached to the number of population and its density." Ugo Rabbeno, The American Commercial Policy (London, 1895), p. 27.

Charles II in about 1672.[1] "I Take it for granted," he said, "That the Strength & glory, of yor Matie and the wealth of yor Kingdoms, depends not Soe much on anything, on this Side of heauven, as on the multitude of yor Subjects, by whose mouths & backes, the fruits & Commoditys of yor Lands may haue a liberall Consumption." Abundant people, he added, are necessary for military purposes, and to increase the public revenue and the national manufactures, but of late England's population has fallen off by reason of the plague, wars, and emigration to America, and consequently land has decreased in value, while the cost of manufacturing has risen. As a remedy, he proposed, to encourage immigration, and to "Stopp the draine, that carrys away the Natiues from us." This suggestion was adopted by the government, which encouraged the immigration into England of foreign Protestants,[2] especially of French Huguenots. The settlement of these refugees from Louis XIV's religious persecution in London and elsewhere was facilitated by grants from the English government, which welcomed them as a valuable addition to the industrial population.[3] The change in opinion regarding this question inevitably involved a fresh consideration and a revised estimate of the economic value of colonies.

One of the ablest of the public men of the Restoration era,[4] Sir William Coventry, in his "Essay concerning the

[1] Shaftesbury MSS., Section X, in Public Record Office.
[2] *Cf.* S. P. Dom. Chas. II, Entry Book 36, ff. 327, 328.
[3] Cunningham, *op. cit.* I, pp. 327–331.
[4] Lodge, England, 1660–1702, pp. 66, 67.

Decay of Rents and their Remedies," written in about 1670, complained of "the long continued diverting of the Young and prolifick People to the Plantations."[1] At the same time, a well-known publicist, Roger Coke, maintained that "Ireland and our Plantations Rob us of all the growing Youth and Industry of the Nation, whereby it becomes week and feeble, and the Strength, as well as Trade, becomes decayed and diminished."[2] So general was this view that the imperialists of the day were put on the defensive, and were forced to answer these current charges.[3] In 1689, the representatives of Barbados in England found it necessary to publish a refutation of the charge that the colonies were weakening England. They skilfully pointed out that the population of a country depends upon its industrial development, and added "tis strange we should be thought to

[1] Brit. Mus., Sloane MSS. 3828, f. 205ᵇ.

[2] Roger Coke, A Discourse of Trade (London, 1670), p. 46. *Cf.* pp. 12, 13, 43. In 1667, Mr. Garroway said that the English colonies "have a constant supply out of *England*, which in time will drain us of people, as now Spain is, and will endanger our ruin, as now the *Indies* do *Spain*." Grey, Debates, 1667–1694, I, p. 40. Evelyn referred to "the ruinous numbers of our Men, daily flocking to the *American* Plantations, and from whence so few return." John Evelyn, Navigation and Commerce (London, 1674), p. 112. On this rare pamphlet, see the author's diary under date of August 19, 1674. For similar statements, see Carew Reynell, The True English Interest (London, 1674), p. 33 ; Britannia Languens (London, 1680), p. 176 ; England's Guide to Industry (London, 1683), preface.

[3] The proprietors of East New Jersey, when engaged in an attempt to attract Scottish settlers to their colony, took pains to assert that "the chief Reason against Forraign Plantations being the drawing too many Inhabitants out of the Nation, and so leaving the Countries at Home unfurnished of People" did not apply to Scotland, which could spare some of its population. A Brief Account of the Province of East-New-Jersey (Edinburgh, 1683), p. 3.

diminish the people of *England*, when we do, so much increase the Employments" there.[1]

In general, the defence of the colonial movement was conducted on these lines. Dalby Thomas, the author of an interesting account of the West Indies published in 1690, admitted that people were the wealth of a nation, but denied that the American colonies, by causing emigration from England, occasioned "the Decay both of the People and Riches of the Nation," because one laboring man in the West Indies was of more advantage to England than were a considerable number of his fellows at home.[2] Sir Francis Brewster maintained that it could not "be denied, however some may apprehend, but the Foreign Plantations add to the Strength and Treasure of the Nation, even in that of People, which is generally thought our Plantations abroad consume; but if it were considered, That by taking off one useless

[1] The Groans of the Plantations (London, 1689), pp. 26–29.

[2] Dalby Thomas, An Historical Account of the Rise and Growth of the *West-India* Colonies (London, 1690), in Harleian Miscellany II, pp. 342, 346, 363. Essentially the same argument was used by William Penn to "deny the vulgar Opinion against Plantations, that they weaken *England*." He claimed that the colonies had enriched the mother country in various ways: first, because the industry of those settling in them is worth more than if they had remained at home — "the Product of their Labour being in Commodities of a superiour Nature to those of this Country"; secondly, as more is produced in the colonies than can be consumed in England, this excess is exported to foreign nations, "which brings in Money, or the Growth of those Countries, which is the same Thing"; thirdly, by settling in the colonies, many have prospered and are able to buy far greater quantities of English manufactures than if they had remained at home; fourthly, the colonial trade employs a large number of ships. William Penn, *op. cit.* pp. 26–28; A. C. Myers, Narratives of Early Pennsylvania *etc.*, pp. 202–204.

person, for such generally go abroad, we add Twenty Blacks in the Labour and Manufactories of this Nation, that Mistake would be removed." [1]

John Cary, a prominent Bristol merchant and a writer on the economic questions of the day, as a preliminary to his discussion of colonial trade also considered it necessary to discuss the doubt raised by "many thoughtful men," whether the colonies had been of advantage to England.[2] These men, he said, urged that the colonies had drained England of multitudes of people, who might have been serviceable at home in improving husbandry and manufactures; and that, as its inhabitants are the wealth of a nation, England was the poorer to the extent of this emigration. Cary admitted that people were wealth, provided there was adequate employment for them, yet he claimed that the colonies were of distinct value to England, both as a market for English produce and as a source of supply.[3]

[1] Sir Francis Brewster, Essays on Trade and Navigation (London, 1695), p. 70. It was, however, contended by another writer that the labor of the same people in the English fisheries and manufactures would have produced a greater profit than that derived from the plantation commodities, sugar, tobacco, dyeing-stuffs, etc. raised by them. Moreover, had these people not emigrated, he maintained, they would have consumed more English produce, for England supplied the colonies with only a small part of their foodstuffs. The bulk, he asserted, came from Ireland and from the northern colonies, and as a result, he concluded, the colonial trade had during the past twenty years become increasingly disadvantageous to England. Britannia Languens (London, 1680), p. 173.

[2] John Cary, An Essay on the State of England in relation to its Trade (Bristol, 1695), pp. 65–67.

[3] Cary said that, in varying degrees, the colonies were advantageous to England, "as they take off our Product and Manufactures, supply us with

But without such compensating benefits, he wrote to a private correspondent, emigration would be like "opening a Vein in a Mans Body, & letting him bleed to death, wch might be of good use to his health if no more Blood was taken from him than he could well Spare."[1]

In another essay of about the same time, essentially the same views were expressed.[2]   Its author said that "a vulgar error has too much prevailed with some of our great men to the prejudice of those Plantations, and therein to the interest of England, viz. that the Colonies of the West Indies drains us of our people, in which consist our wealth and strength, and consequently we should be richer and greater without them."   This argument he answered by stating that the colonies had returned as many people as they had received, and by pointing out that, in addition, these possessions were of great economic advantage to England. "The labor of the people there is twice the value to England that it would be at home, both because the commodities are more profitable, and that it gives England a market

Commodities which may be either wrought up here, or Exported again, or prevent fetching things of the same Nature from other Princes for our home Consumption, employ our Poor, and encourage our Navigation; for I take *England* and all its Plantations to be one great Body, those being so many Limbs or Counties belonging to it, therefore when we consume their Growth we do as it were Spend the Fruits of our own Land, and what thereof we sell to our Neighbours for Bullion, or such Commodities as we must pay for therein, brings a second Profit to the Nation."

[1] Cary to Edmund Bohun, Jan. 31, 1696.   Brit. Mus., Add. MSS. 5540, f. 61.

[2] Considerations about the English Colonies in America, in MSS. of Duke of Buccleuch and Queensberry (H. M. C. 1903) II, pp. 735-737.

she could not otherwise have, both abroad and at home, to her great enrichment."

Similarly, Charles Davenant, in his well-known work on England's revenue and trade, discussed the two general objections to the colonies : first, that they are a retreat for men opposed to the established system in church and state ; secondly, "that they drein this Kingdom of People, the most Important Strength of any Nation."[1] In connection with this latter objection, Davenant called attention to the fact that, in spite of the colonies, England's population had greatly increased since 1600. He did not, however, deny the validity of this general argument against colonization, merely pointing out that in England this disadvantage had been more than counterbalanced by other factors. "Countries that take no Care to encourage an Accession of strangers," he freely admitted, "in Course of Time, will find Plantations of Pernicious Consequence." But this, he said, was not the case with England, which had added to its population a large number of Huguenot refugees. On the whole, he concluded that the colonies "are a spring of Wealth to this Nation, that they work for us, that their Treasure centers all here."

From this somewhat summary account of contemporary thought, it is apparent that in itself emigration to the plantations was in general deemed a decided evil, which could be condoned only if greater contervailing advantages were derived from the colonies. This phase of public opinion was naturally reflected in the views and attitude of the

[1] Davenant, *op. cit.* II, pp. 195–203.

government. In this connection may profitably be cited an episode which throws considerable light on the policy of the authorities. In 1679, a suggestion was made to the Carolina proprietors that a considerable number of Huguenots should be transported to their colony, where they could raise silk, oil, wine, and such other products as England was obliged to purchase from southern Europe. The Lords Proprietors, however, stated that they had already spent large sums of money and had brought the colony to so prosperous a condition that for years men had gone thither on their own account. Hence, the proprietors were not willing to incur this additional expense, but they pointed out that the proposition would be advantageous both to them and to England, because these French refugees were skilled in planting vineyards and olive trees and in the making of silk; and, if these industries were once successfully established in Carolina, other foreign Protestants would be attracted there.[1] The proposal appealed to the government, but before deciding to grant the desired assistance,[2] it referred the matter to the Commissioners of the Customs, as was usual when an expert opinion was wanted on financial or commercial questions.

As this board had not been informed whether these Huguenots were already in England or were still in France, their careful report of April 14, 1679,[3] contained alterna-

---

[1] C. C. 1677–1680, pp. 321, 328, 336.

[2] These Huguenots requested that two ships of the navy transport eighty families to Carolina, and that £2000 be reimbursed to them for their expenses out of the English customs on commodities imported from the proposed settlement. *Ibid.* pp. 340, 341.

[3] No. Ca. Col. Rec. I, p. 243.

tive advice, contingent upon the ascertainment of this fact. "We canot," they wrote, "advise that his ma^tie should give any Incouragement to any People who are settled in this Kingdome whether Natives or fforeigners to transport themselves from hence into any of his Maties Plantac̃ons or Ireland. On the contrary, we are of opinion that there are too many ffamilyes that do daylye Transport themselves both to the Plantac̃ons & to Ireland to the unpeopling & ruine of this Kingdome. And we are of opinion that means are rather to be used for the hindring then the promoting thereof; but if these ffamilies are now really in parts beyond the Seas, we think that the Encouraging of them to come over to goe to Carolina is a very good Work." This report was approved, and orders were given to provide two ships for the transportation of these Huguenots to Carolina, provided they had or should come to England for this specific purpose only.[1]

In view of this attitude, it would, indeed, not have been surprising if the government had restricted emigration to the colonies. Under the prevailing conditions, the problem was, however, not an urgent one. Although there was a steady stream of people flowing from England to America, it was of but insignificant dimensions,[2] and was composed in part

[1] C. C. 1677–1680, pp. 364, 366, 367, 428, 435, 455; P. C. Cal. I, pp. 825, 826.

[2] Reliable figures are unfortunately not available. Davenant estimated that the annual average emigration to the colonies amounted to 1800 people as against 300 returning yearly from them to England. Davenant, *op. cit.* II, p. 203. Those who opposed colonization as tending to weaken England were inclined grossly to over-estimate the number of emigrants. *Cf.* Carew Reynell, The True English Interest (London, 1674), pp. 7, 8.

of foreigners who had sought a merely temporary refuge in England. There was not sufficient economic pressure in England to cause a marked dislocation of population. Nor were conditions in the colonies so attractive that adventurous spirits were drawn there in large numbers by the confident expectation of bettering their social status. Emigration and subsequent settlement involved heavy expenses,[1] and the outcome was at best an uncertain one. Some especially energetic, or merely sanguine, Englishmen emigrated with such hopes, but a large proportion of those voluntarily leaving England did so for non-economic reasons. It was to escape the penalties of the English religious code that many Quakers left their homes and settled in New Jersey and Pennsylvania.

In addition, the English government systematically deported to the colonies many undesirable clements in its population — political prisoners, religious nonconformists, delinquents, and criminals.[2] Thus, in 1665, 126 Quakers in Newgate, as well as some others imprisoned elsewhere, were ordered to be transported to the colonies.[3] In 1666, 100 Irish rebels were deported to Barbados,[4] and in 1685, after the collapse of Monmouth's insurrection, 800 of his ad-

[1] The cost of transportation alone continued as formerly to be about £6. Brit. Mus., Egerton MSS. 2395 ff. 277 et seq.; A. C. Myers, Narratives of Early Pennsylvania, etc., pp. 194, 211. Cf. Beer, Origins, p. 49.

[2] J. D. Butler, in British Convicts shipped to American Colonies (Am. Hist. Rev. II), gives some interesting details, and shows that the convict element was of considerable proportions.

[3] P. C. Cal. I, pp. 393, 394, 402, 415, 417.

[4] MSS. of Earl of Egmont (H. M. C. 1909) II, p. 16.

herents were sent to forced labor in the same colony,[1] and some also were transported to Jamaica.[2]   Disorderly persons and convicts were regularly shipped to America.[3]   Virginia objected to this policy and secured exemption from it;[4] but, in 1684, St. Kitts sent to England a petition, which was granted, that the 300 malefactors "long since ordered" might finally be transported so as to strengthen the colony.[5] Many of these convicts were well adapted to their new life; in some, the very qualities that had brought them into difficulties with the complex civilization of England fitted them admirably for the primitive conditions in the colonies, where extreme individualism and independence were an advantage in the conflict with the more or less untamed forces of nature.

These various elements, voluntarily settling in America or forcibly located there, in part peopled the new colonies that

---

[1] G. M. Trevelyan, England under the Stuarts, p. 431.   See also C. C. 1685–1688, pp. 139, 140, 147–149, 651.

[2] Ibid. p. 201.

[3] Cf. P. C. Cal. I, pp. 370, 371; II, p. 36.

[4] Charles II, being informed by letters from Virginia that "great danger and disrepute is brought vpon that his Majestys Plantation by the frequent sending thither of ffellons and other Condemned Persons," for the prevention whereof Virginia had passed an order prohibiting such importation, on October 21, 1670, by Order in Council, directed that in future no felons nor convicts be sent to Virginia, but only to the other colonies.   P. C. Cal. I, p. 553.   See also Va. Mag. XIX, pp. 355, 356.

[5] P. C. Cal. II, pp. 68, 69.   Already in 1676 the English government had agreed to meet the expense involved in their transportation, and in 1677 Treasurer Danby instructed the sheriffs of London and Middlesex to deliver 300 convicts to a London merchant, who was to give bond to take them to St. Kitts.   Cal. Treas. Books, 1676–1679, p. 826; C. C. 1675–1676, pp. 335, 346, 347; P. C. Cal. I, pp. 708, 709.   See also C. C. 1677–1680, pp. 572, 573.

were founded in the Restoration era. But to some extent these territories, especially the Carolinas and the Jerseys, were settled by the surplus population of Barbados, the Bermudas, Virginia, and New England. The restless spirit of the people in some of the older colonies, the gradual displacement of white labor by the negro in the sugar plantations of the West Indies, the confined limits of the already more than adequately populated Bermudas, combined with the fact that by reproduction alone the population of these colonies was increasing rapidly, greatly facilitated and would in itself probably have led to this territorial extension of the Empire. The Atlantic seaboard, not the interior, was the line of least resistance for this expanding population.

In general, except in so far as the deportation of those deemed undesirable at home was concerned, the English government was naturally adverse to emigration from England.[1] It tried, however, to facilitate immigration into the colonies from Scotland and Ireland.[2] Yet the govern-

[1] As it was deemed important that Jamaica should be speedily settled, emigration to that colony was even encouraged. In 1661, a royal proclamation offered thirty acres of land to each settler and stated that "all Free persons shall have liberty without Interruption, to transport themselves and their Families, and any their Goods (except only Coyn and Bullions) from any of Our Dominions and Territories, to the said Island of Jamaica." When, in 1662, the new Governor, Lord Windsor, came to Jamaica, he brought this proclamation with him. British Royal Proclamations, 1603–1783 (Am. Antiqu. Soc. 1911), pp. 112–114; W. J. Gardner, A History of Jamaica (London, 1909), p. 51.

[2] The "Staple Act" of 1663, which prohibited the importation of European commodities into the colonies except from Fngland, specifically exempted from this prohibition servants from Ireland and Scotland. 15 Ch. II, c. 7, § v.

ment did not find it necessary, except in one respect, to adopt measures to restrict the slight spontaneous movement of emigration to the colonies.[1] One of the chief benefits expected from the Newfoundland fishery was the training and increase of seamen, and hence the crew of every English fishing vessel had to be composed in part of inexperienced and untrained men. If these seamen were allowed to settle in Newfoundland or to emigrate thence to the other colonies, the advantage of this country as "a nursery of seamen" would be greatly diminished. Hence, the English vessels going to Newfoundland for their annual fishing were obligated to bring their crews back to England and the emigration of seamen from Newfoundland to New England was strictly forbidden.[2]

While the extent of emigration did not necessitate the adoption of any comprehensive measures to check its course, in connection with it there developed certain evils which occasioned governmental interference and control. As a rule, in return for his passage to America, the emigrant agreed to work in semi-servitude for a term of years, usually five. On arrival in the colonies, the master or owner of the

[1] The officials who supervised emigration could, however, readily restrict the movement by creating obstacles. In 1682, Governor Lynch of Jamaica complained to the Lords of Trade that few or no servants came from England and that he was informed 'that my Lord Chief Justice will permit none to come, though they are willing and go to acknowledge it before the Magistrate as the law directs.' He asserted that the idle people, who did mischief in London, would prove beneficial in Jamaica. C. C. 1681–1685, p. 282.

[2] C. O. 195/2, f. 7; P. C. Cal. I, pp. 558–563; C. C. 1677–1680, pp. 600, 601; C. C. 1681–1685, p. 294. See *post*, Chapter X.

ship recouped himself by selling this temporary slave, euphemistically known as an indentured servant. Since the demand for labor in the colonies was very keen, this traffic was found most profitable, and inevitably led to many grave abuses. In 1660, it was said that "diuerse Children from their Parents, and Seruants from their Masters, are daylie inticed away, taken upp, and kept from their said Parents and Masters against their Wills, by Merchants, Planters, Commanders of Shipps, and Seamen trading to Virginia, Barbados, Charibee Islands and other parts of the West Indies, and their Factors and Agents, and shipped away to make Sale and Merchandize of." [1] Accordingly, in 1664, an office was created for registering the contracts of such persons as should go to the colonies as servants.[2] The evils complained of, however, still continued.[3] In addition to "spiriting," as this kidnapping and forcible transportation was popularly called, another abuse developed. Many persons, who had agreed to go to the colonies and had received money for so doing, afterwards pretended that they had been carried away against their will, and induced their friends to prosecute the merchants who had transported them.

[1] P. C. Cal. I, pp. 296, 297. See also Brit. Mus., Egerton MSS. 2395, ff. 277 et seq. The Council for Foreign Plantations, appointed in 1660, was instructed to consider how the colonies may best be supplied with servants, but that none should be forced to emigrate or be enticed away and that only such as were willing "to seeke better fortunes than they can meete with at home" should be encouraged. C. O. 1/14, 59, ff. 3, 4; N. Y. Col. Doc. III, pp. 34–36.

[2] P. C. Cal. I, p. 384.

[3] B. T. Journals 124 (Miscellanies, 1664–1674), ff. 1–19. For a case of "spiriting" in 1679, see P. C. Cal. I, p. 863.

As a result, in 1682, the office established in 1664 was abolished, and a more elaborate and effective method was inaugurated for controlling this system of contract labor.[1]

From the foregoing, it will be plainly apparent that one of the chief advantages originally anticipated from the colonial movement by the contemporaries of Hakluyt and Raleigh and by their successors under the first Stuarts had proven illusory. England no longer wanted over-sea dominions as homes for a population that was thought excessive, and had even veered to the opposite point and regarded colonies as an evil sapping the national strength to the extent that they attracted to them the inhabitants of the metropolis. Hence, there was a marked tendency in favor of the colonization of tropical and sub-tropical regions which could be advantageously exploited by a small white population superintending the labor of a large number of negro slaves. Thus Sir Josiah Child, in discussing the widespread view that the colonies had prejudiced England "by draining us of our People," conceded that, "people being Riches," emigration to America would be a distinct national loss, unless "the employment of those People abroad do cause the employment of so many more at home in their Mother Kingdoms."[2] He then pointed out that for one Englishman in the West Indies there were as a rule eight to ten negro slaves, and that, as their joint labor gave employment to four men in England, emigration to those colonies would increase the population of the mother country.

[1] P. C. Cal. II, pp. 41–43.

[2] Child, A New Discourse of Trade (London, 1693), p. 184.

On the other hand, according to him, ten men in the northern colonies, such as Massachusetts, did not employ one man in England.[1] Hence it followed inevitably that the southern continental and especially the island colonies were regarded with marked favor.

This attitude likewise was a direct consequence of the prevailing economic theory of colonization and of the actual course of colonial trade. ⋋ What exactly were these economic benefits that England expected to derive from the colonies in order to counteract any loss that might be suffered through emigration to them? As has already been pointed out, the colonial trade was highly valued as one of the main foundations of England's growing sea power. This view was more emphasized than it had been in the period of origins.[2] In addition, there were claimed certain specific fiscal and economic advantages. A curious idea prevailed extensively during the seventeenth century that the English customs duties on colonial produce were paid by the colonies and that they consequently contributed largely to the public revenue.[3] ⋌ Thus Clarendon tells us that, before the restoration of the kingship, he had become convinced of the value of the colonies and that "he had been confirmed in that

---

[1] *Ibid.* pp. 207, 208. Early in the following century, N. Grew, in the course of an essay on the economic condition of England, said that "the Transporting of People to our Plantations Should be Stinted. Whether with the Addition of their Blacks they may not Multiply Sufficiently to Answer the Trade we haue or may haue with them without sending them any more People or with fewer Sent I humbly Conceiue deserves to be Considered." Brit. Mus., Lansdowne MSS. 691, f. 108.

[2] Beer, Origins, pp. 73, 74.

[3] This idea was prominent before 1660. *Ibid.* pp. 201–203.

opinion and desire, as soon as he had a view of the entries in the custom house; by which he found what a great revenue accrued to the Crown from those plantations." [1] Many other writers also called attention to this supposed benefit. William Penn pointed out that each Virginia planter produced three thousand pounds of tobacco yearly which paid in England an import duty of £25, "an extraordinary Profit." [2] Similarly, the writer of "Some Observations about the Plantations" stated that the customs on tobacco and sugar, amounting yearly to £160,000, were paid by the colonies.[3]

It does not require much subtle or searching analysis to perceive that the reasoning leading to this conclusion was largely erroneous. In so far as was concerned that portion of the colonial products consumed in England, these duties were shifted to the English consumer, and affected the colonial producer only to the limited extent that they restricted the available demand by enhancing the retail price. This constituted the bulk of the customs revenue derived from the colonial trade, and unquestionably the same amount would have arisen if the tobacco and sugar had been imported from foreign countries instead of from the colonies. In addition, a considerable proportion of the colonial im-

---

[1] Clarendon's Autobiography (Oxford, 1827) III, p. 407.

[2] William Penn, *op. cit.* p. 27; A. C. Myers, Narratives of Early Pennsylvania *etc.*, p. 203.

[3] Brit. Mus., Add. MSS. 28,079, f. 85. See also Brit. Mus., Egerton MSS. 2395, f. 574. In his Discourse and View of Virginia, Governor Berkeley pointed out that one-quarter of the English customs revenue was derived from colonial goods. Egerton MSS. 2395, f. 357[b]. In the seventies this revenue amounted to about £600,000. W. R. Scott, *op. cit.* III, pp. 530, 531.

ports into England was again reëxported; in such cases the greater part of the English duties was repaid, on tobacco three-quarters, on sugar one-half. What remained in the Exchequer was not large in amount, but to this extent certainly the colonies contributed to England's public revenue. Likewise the small export duties levied in England on English goods shipped to the colonies were ultimately paid by the colonial consumer, as were also the customs duties collected on foreign goods in course of shipment *via* England to the colonies. But, in the main, this supposed advantage was fictitious. Delusions are, however, as effective in social evolution as are unassailable facts. The bulk of the revenue from the colonial trade was derived from the import duties on tobacco and sugar,[1] and this fact furnished an additional reason for favoring the plantation type of colony.

Apart from the greater stress laid on the colonial trade as a source of sea power, and apart from this somewhat higher estimate of its fiscal importance, the Restoration economic theory of colonization corresponded closely with that obtaining at the outset of the movement, under Elizabeth and her successors.[2] It was still deemed the primary function of the colony to furnish the metropolis with supplies not produced there, and which otherwise would have to be

---

[1] See an account of the customs paid in the year 1676–1677 on goods imported from:

Barbados and the Leeward Isles	£20,781
Jamaica	£ 3,500
Bermudas	£ 2,406
	£26,687

C. O. 1/42, 60 iii; C. O. 324/4, ff. 58, 59. For further details see *post*, Chapter III.

[2] Beer, Origins, Chapter III.

secured from foreign rivals in Europe. In other words,
the ideal colony was one which would have freed England
from the necessity of importing anything from her competitors.   In addition, the supplies obtained from the plantations were not to be entirely consumed in England, but
their surplus was to be exported to foreign countries to the
manifest advantage of the nation's trade balance.[1]   As far as
it was possible the colony was to differ from England in its
economic pursuits, producing nothing that interfered with
the fullest development of any English industry or trade.
It was to be the economic complement of the mother country,
both together constituting a self-sufficient commercial
empire.   It naturally followed that the colony was to
purchase its manufactures from England and thus employ
English labor.   But while its value as a market was fully
recognized,[2] chief stress was laid upon the colony as a source
of supply.[3]   "The ends of their first settlement," wrote
Cary, "were rather to provide Materials for the increasing our Trade at home, and keeping our people at work

[1] Without these reëxports of colonial produce, it was claimed, England's
balance of trade would have been an unfavorable one.   Bodleian, Rawlinson A 478, f. 48.

[2] Pollexfen pointed out that the colonies consumed large quantities of
English products and manufactures, as well as provisions and handicraft
wares, and supplied England with some goods for further manufacture and
others in great abundance, especially tobacco and sugar, for export to foreign nations.   John Pollexfen, A Discourse of Trade, Coyn and Paper
Credit (London, 1697), p. 86.

[3] Among the papers of William Bridgeman, Clerk of the Privy Council
toward the end of the seventeenth century (Evelyn, May 7, 1699; Dict.
of Nat. Biography: John Bridgeman), is an unsigned and undated memorial
on the plantation trade which, more than was customary, emphasized the

THE COLONIAL POLICY OF THE PERIOD

here." [1] This view was supported by the actual facts of the existing colonial trade.

The exports to the colonies were far less than the imports thence. In 1662–1663 the exports from London to the plantations were only £105,910, as opposed to imports of £484,641. Six years later, although these exports had remained at virtually the same figure — they were £107,791 — the imports had risen to £605,574.[2] The exports [3] were comparatively

value of the colonies as markets. Its author pointed out that England exported to other places but few manufactures, except woollens, and rarely many foreign commodities, while to the colonies were sent manufactures of wool, iron, brass, tin, lead, leather, silk, and also provisions and other necessaries, "which we cannot with any profitt carry into other Countryes." Nor, he added, do we export much less of foreign commodities than of our own. He wrote pessimistically about England's export trade in woollens, which he claimed was declining rapidly, and asserted that the colonies alone could compensate for this loss of foreign markets. Bodleian, Rawlinson A 478, f. 48.

[1] Brit. Mus., Add. MSS. 5540, f. 61. In his Discourse and View of Virginia, Governor Berkeley especially emphasized the importance of colonization in that "those comodities wee were wont to purchase at great rates and hazards, wee now purchase at half the usuall prices. Nor is this all, but we buy them wth our own manufactures, which here at home employ thousands of poor people." Brit. Mus., Egerton MSS. 2395, f. 357^b.

[2] C. O. 388/8, E 31; Brit. Mus., Sloane MSS. 2902, f. 118. It should be noted that these statistics were not compiled in a scientific manner, and should not be used for precise deductions. It is not even certain that these figures do not include the entire colonial trade of England. The great disparity between exports and imports was due mainly to the fact that the value of the imports included the charges in bringing the colonial goods to England. In addition, in the English exports was not included the important item of negro slaves sold to the colonies.

[3] They included a great variety of goods — textiles, medicines, provisions, liquors, books, candles, instruments, tools, hardware, clothing, etc. Details, with the exact quantities exported from England during the years 1662–1663 and 1668–1669, may be found in B. T. Trade Papers 4.

insignificant, and their economic importance was still further diminished by the fact that they included a considerable proportion of foreign goods reëxported from England.[1]

[1] This has, however, been questioned. W. R. Scott, *op. cit.* I, p. 266. In 1678, the Commissioners of the Customs reported that "ships bound from England to the plantacons do usually Carry great Quantities of all English Manufactures & Comodities as also Considerable quantities of forreign Goods imported into England, whereof halfe of the Custome upon Exportačon againe remaynes to the King." C. O. 1/40, 60; C. O. 324/4, ff. 56–58. In 1680, a pessimistic writer, with a marked tendency to exaggeration, complained that as a result of "the insufficiency of our home-Manufactures, and the *growing Luxury* of our *Planters* we are forced to send vast quantities (of foreign goods) thither already, particularly, *foreign Linnens of all sorts, Paper, Silks, and Wines of all sorts, Brandies,* and other things mentioned in the next Section, besides great quantities *of Wines* sent from the *Madera's,* paid by Bills of Exchange drawn on our Merchants in *Lisbon.*" Britannia Languens (London, 1680), pp. 163, 164. In the first decade of the following century, a writer stated: "Nor is there any Sort of Goods of our own Growth or Make or from abroad, but they are Exported to Some or other of your Majesties Plantations." Brit. Mus., Lansdowne MSS. 691, f. 61[b]. See also Bodleian, Rawlinson MSS. A 478, f. 48.

[2]

	IMPORTS INTO ENGLAND	
	From Sept. 29, 1662 to Sept. 29, 1663	From Sept. 29, 1668 to Sept. 29, 1669
Tobacco	7,367,140 lbs.	9,026,046 lbs.
Sugar: brown	130,000 cwt.	166,776 cwt.
white	16,000 cwt.	23,720 cwt.
Cotton-wool	7,500 bags	6,472 bags
Ginger	2,000 cwt.	3,318 cwt.
Cacao	1,200 cwt.	2,264 cwt.
Beaver	14,600 skins	13,900 skins
Otter	4,278 skins	6,271 skins
Buff-hides	4,202	5,276
Indigo	14,000 lbs.	16,000 lbs.
Fustic	4,334 cwt.	4,420 cwt.
Lignum-vitæ	1,088 cwt.	1,042 cwt.
Tortoise-shell	2,896 lbs.	3,292 lbs.
Granadilla	144 cwt.	skins £92 = 12 = 2.

B. T. Trade Papers 4.

The relatively large imports were virtually entirely composed of tobacco and sugar, the northern colonies contributing nothing but a few skins and furs.[1] During the following decades the imports into England still continued to be greatly in excess of the exports, though the disparity was decreasing. For the six years from 1683 to 1688, the average annual amounts were estimated at respectively £950,000 and £350,000.[2] At the beginning of the new century, the discrepancy, though still noteworthy, had still further decreased, the average imports being £995,288 as opposed to exports of £737,284.[3]

An analysis of this trade for one or two years [4] will disclose a curiously instructive state of affairs. Of England's total colonial trade of £1,638,086 in the year 1697–1698 about

[1] See footnote 2 on p. 40.

[2] Davenant, *op. cit.* II, p. 218.

[3] These are the averages for the 4 years and 3 months from Sept. 29, 1697, to Christmas, 1701. C. O. 388/17, N 239.

	ENGLAND'S IMPORTS FROM THE COLONIES	ENGLAND'S EXPORTS TO THEM
Sept. 29, 1696 to do. 1697	£588,502	£289,271
Sept. 29, 1697 to do. 1698	866,933	771,235
Sept. 29, 1698 to Xmas, 1698 . . .	170,345	239,378
Xmas, 1698 to Xmas, 1699	916,191	748,029
Xmas, 1699 to Xmas, 1700	1,226,701	682,414
Xmas, 1700 to Xmas, 1701	1,049,804	692,401
Xmas, 1701 to Xmas, 1702	813,756	444,809

These figures do not include Newfoundland.

House of Lords MSS. (1699–1702), IV, pp. 434, 435; C. O. 388/9, F. 61. These figures are also available in more detailed form in Sir Charles Whitworth, *op. cit.* Part I, pp. 1–6.

[4] See footnote 1 on p. 42.

seven-eighths, £1,420,207, was with the sugar and tobacco colonies.[1] The trade with the northern continental colonies — New England, New York, and Pennsylvania — amounted to only £172,191, less than 11 per cent of the

1

	Sept. 29, 1697 to Sept. 29, 1698		Christmas 1698 to Christmas 1699	
	Imports into England from	Exports from England to	Imports into England from	Exports from England to
Barbados	308,089	146,849	273,947	150,968
Nevis	54,748	14,547	74,857	16,477
Antigua	52,903	20,756	109,440	30,435
Montserrat	24,421	3,369	23,162	7,159
Jamaica	189,566	120,774	174,844	136,690
	629,727	306,295	656,250	341,729
Virginia and Maryland . .	174,052	310,133	198,115	205,074
	803,779	616,428	854,365	546,803
Bermudas	2,926	3,970	58	1,330
Bahamas	184			302
Hudson Bay	8,031	2,852	4,235	944
Carolina	9,265	18,460	12,362	11,399
Pennsylvania	2,720	10,701	4,540	17,062
New York	8,763	25,278	16,818	42,781
New England	31,254	93,475	26,660	127,277
Totals	866,922	771,164	919,038	747,898

House of Lords MSS. (1699–1702), IV, pp. 446, 447; B. T. Trade Papers 15, f. 267; Whitworth, *loc. cit.* The slight discrepancies between this table and the preceding one are due to the omissions of the fractions of a pound and to insignificant errors on the part of the original compiler.

[2] The exports to Virginia and Maryland were abnormally large in order to supply the deficiency of European supplies resulting from the war which ended in 1697. In 1696–1697 these exports were only £58,796 and in 1698–1699 £205,074. It was only toward the middle of the eighteenth century that these exports normally reached this figure of £300,000. Whitworth, *op. cit.* Part I, pp. 1–6, 51–56.

total. Of this amount, the exports were £129,454, which while not an insignificant quantity, was by no means an imposing one. Without taking into account the slaves purchased, Jamaica alone afforded just as big a market. The imports were only £42,737 and moreover consisted in part of tobacco, sugar, and other West Indian produce.[1] Furthermore, this small trade with the northern continental colonies between Maryland and Canada employed but little English shipping. Of the 226 ships sailing from England for the colonies in 1690–1691, only eight were bound for these colonies.[2] Their

[1] An analysis of the figures for 1698–1699 affords essentially the same result.

The total colonial trade amounted to	£1,666,936
That with the sugar colonies was	£ 997,979 (60% −)
That with the tobacco colonies was	£ 403,189 (24% +)
That with Pennsylvania, New York, and New England was	£ 235,138 (14% +)
That with the remaining colonies was	£ 30,630 (2% −)
	£1,666,936 (100%)

[2] In order that the navy should not suffer for want of seamen, during time of war permission had to be secured by mercantile vessels before departing from England. The following table of ships allowed to sail, dated Dec. 2, 1690, is of considerable interest:

DESTINATION	NO. OF SHIPS	TONNAGE	NO. OF SEAMEN
Virginia and Maryland	103	13,715	1,188
Barbados	71	9,198	761
Leeward Isles	23	1,710	205
Jamaica	20	2,720	237
Bermudas	1	20	5
New England	7	540	77
Pennsylvania	1	60	6
	226	27,963	2,479

commercial insignificance from the imperial standpoint
would be still further emphasized if in the total of the
colonial trade were included, as might legitimately be, the
English exports to Africa and the number of ships employed
in carrying slaves to the plantation colonies.[1]

From this brief analysis of England's colonial trade it is
apparent that the northern continental colonies in no degree
conformed to the ideal type and to virtually no extent contributed any of the advantages expected from colonization.
The favor with which the plantation type of colony was
regarded for other reasons was inevitably greatly strength-
ened by these facts. As this had important consequences

C. O. 324/5, f. 150. See also B. T. Trade Papers 12, ff. 58, 90. The
figures for the following year give the same general result:

West Indies	95 ships with 1858 men
Virginia and Maryland	76 ships with 1241 men
New England and New York	6 ships with 107 men
Other colonies	17 ships with 244 men
	194 ships 3450 men

B. T. Trade Papers 12, f. 138. See also similar figures for one month of
1681 in C. O. 5/1111, ff. 79, 80.

[1]   ENGLAND'S TRADE TO AFRICA

	IMPORTS	EXPORTS
1696–1697	£ 6,615	£ 13,435
1697–1698	2,496	70,587
1698–1699	19,225	96,295
1699–1700	26,888	155,793
1700–1701	21,074	133,499
1701–1702	31,295	96,052

Whitworth, *op. cit.* Part I, pp. 1–6.

both on the economic and on the political policy toward these dependencies, an account of contemporary thought on this subject should prove instructive. Those who were interested in developing the resources of the West Indies were naturally especially vehement in urging the cause of tropical colonization. The general argument was clearly expressed in a memorial [1] sent in 1671 to the Council of Foreign Plantations by one Andrew Orgill, who had lived in Barbados and subsequently became a prominent citizen of Jamaica.[2] He divided the existing colonies into two distinct classes,[3] of which one is "already, and will dayly grow more destructive to the trade of this Kingdome," because those colonies belonging to it do not produce sufficient commodities different from those of England, so as "to imploy the people that live there, but are forced to use our Trade to subsist by." The other group supply such commodities as cannot be produced in England, and if encouraged will be of infinite advantage, "because they are, as it were, new Trades

---

[1] B. T. Journals 124 (Miscellanies, 1664–1674), ff. 19–23.

[2] C. C. 1669–1674, p. 129; C. C. 1675–1676, p. 521; C. C. 1677–1680, pp. 55, 58, 146. Orgill was the inventor of a successful device for extracting the juice from the sugar cane. P. C. Cal. I, p. 647; Cal. Dom. 1675–1676, p. 493; Cal. Treas. Books, 1676–1679, p. 104.

[3] The anonymous author of a letter written in 1673 to Sir Robert Howard, on the subject of securing and improving the colonial trade, divided the colonies into four groups: (1) such whose produce is the same as that of Europe and which consequently are "diametrically opposite to the Interest of England"; (2) the tobacco plantations, whence is imported nearly all the tobacco consumed in England, and in whose interest "wee are so zealous as to prevent the growth thereof even in England"; (3) the not very important cotton, indigo, ginger, and cacao colonies; (4) the sugar colonies. C. O. 1/30, 10.

found out to employ great numbers of people." [1]   Consequently, Orgill argued, colonies of the first class — such as New England, which has the same products as England and competes with her, which builds ships and is bound to engage in manufacturing — should be discouraged, while those of the other type should be fostered.   This "may draw the Inhabitants from the first to this other, which if effected must be of infinite advantage to the trade and Navigation of this Kingdome." [2]

[1] These colonies "must be Supplyed with Clothes, and all kind of our Manifactoryes from hence, because their Countries are not capable of producing them, but of other rich Comodities gained with lesse Labour, which will beget great employment for his Maj[ties] Subjects here, and our Merchant shipps to export our Comodities to them, and import theirs to us."

[2] Orgill predicted that, as their population increased, Virginia and Maryland would become like New England, because the over-production of tobacco would force them to build ships and set up manufactures to clothe themselves.   "Tobacco," he said, "sometimes will doe noe more then pay the duty, and charge of bringing it to the market, therefore, they must eyther become very poor, or remove to a better place, or sett up our Trades and Manifactures for their Subsistance."   In order to prevent the increase of the continental colonies, he urged that inducements be offered to their people to remove to Jamaica, which produces "many very rich Comodities that grow not in Europe."   He said that fifteen hundred to sixteen hundred people in New England were ready to settle in Jamaica, provided liberty of conscience were assured to them.   The author of a contemporary "Treatise to prove England by its Trade and Commerce equivalent in Wealth and Strength to a far greater Territory" pointed out that in New England were large numbers of able-bodied Englishmen employed chiefly in the lowest form of agriculture, the breeding of cattle, and that Ireland could have contained all these people.   The other colonies, he said, while they do indeed plant commodities which will not grow so well in England, weaken themselves by living too scattered and grasping at more land than will suffice to produce "said Exotics."   As to the people of New England, he added, "I can but wish they were transplanted into old England or Ireland

Similar ideas were embodied in a memorial [1] presented to the government in 1674 by Ferdinando Gorges, who, in addition to his inherited rights to Maine, had important interests in the West Indies. As a member of that active and influential, and to a great extent unique, body, the Committee of Gentlemen Planters of Barbados in London, his expressed opinions were naturally somewhat tinged by personal bias. In this memorial he laid down the general rule, that "such plantations as are settled uppon the Continent of America or large Islands which doe Swallow upp greate numbers of people and by reason of Vast Tracts of Land are able to produce Both food and Rayment for thire livelyhood & requireth neither from their Mother Nation are Doubtless rather Injurious then profitable to this Kingdome." Leaving the general for the particular, he pointed out that these objections did not apply to Barbados and the Caribbee Islands; for Barbados, being managed by about 5000 Englishmen, who had purchased 70,000 negroes, is supplied with "a great part of their Provisions & all their Clothing household stuffe horses & necessaries from England to the Value of aboue Three hundred Thousand pounds p ann." Furthermore, these few Englishmen give employment to 200 ships and 6000 seamen, and together with the other West Indian colonies send yearly to England a native commodity, sugar, worth

(according to proposalls of their owne made w[th]in these 20 yeares)."   Brit. Mus., Add. MSS. 22,781, ff. 29, 30. This statement, in the same words, can also be found in England's Guide to Industry (London, 1683), p. 78.

[1] C. O. 1/31, 21 ; Brit. Mus., Egerton MSS. 2395, f. 490 ; C. C. 1669–1674, pp. 564, 565.

£600,000, "a great part whereof is yearly exported which is no small help to the Ballance of Trade of this Nation." Moreover, he continued, England's trade to Africa depends entirely on these colonies. Gorges's inevitable conclusion from these premises was that only colonies of the plantation type should be encouraged.

The same views, though generally in a less extreme form, were presented by the economic writers of the day.[1] In his celebrated essay on trade, Sir Josiah Child asserted that "New-England is the most prejudicial Plantation to this Kingdom," because its inhabitants produce the same commodities as England and compete with her in the fisheries. Besides, England buys from them only a few great masts, some furs and train-oil, whose yearly value is small, the bulk of the imports from New England consisting of sugar, cotton, and tobacco obtained from the other colonies in return for provisions which otherwise would be furnished by the mother country.[2] Similarly, in his valuable account of the colonies,[3] published in 1690, Dalby Thomas pointed out that New England did not plant any American commodities, except for their own use, but "by Tillage, Pasture, Fishing, Manufactures and Trade, they, to all Intents and Purposes

[1] According to one writer, "the Southern Plantations are the most advantageous to us. . . . For our North Colonies, as those of *New England*, and the rest afford only such Commodities as we have our selves, and so breed no good Commerce." Carew Reynell, The True English Interest (London, 1674), pp. 90, 91. See also p. 33.

[2] Child, A New Discourse of Trade (London, 1693), pp. 204–208.

[3] Dalby Thomas, An Historical Account of the Rise and Growth of the *West-India* Colonies (London, 1690), in Harleian Miscellany II, p. 360.

imitate *Old England*, and did formerly much, and in some Degree do now, supply the other Colonies with Provisions in Exchange for their Commodities. . . . But this cannot chuse but be allowed, that, if any Hands in the *Indies* be wrong employed for domestick Interest, it must be theirs, and those other Colonies, which settle with no other Prospect than the like Way of Living: Therefore, if any, such only should be neglected, and discouraged, who pursue a Method, that rivals our native Kingdom, and threatens, in Time, a total Independency thereupon. But, as this cannot be said of our Tobacco Colonies, much less is it to be feared from our Sugar Plantations."

John Cary,[1] likewise, stated that of all the plantations New England was of least advantage to England, for its inhabitants, being industrious, trade to the rest of the colonies, which they supply with provisions and other goods, and in return take their products to foreign markets and thus hurt the trade of England. To debar them from this trade in provisions to the southern colonies, he thought, would be inadvisable, but their exports thence should be strictly confined to England.[2] By these means England would become

[1] Cary, An Essay on the State of England in Relation to its Trade (Bristol, 1695), pp. 69, 70.

[2] Another writer complained that the northern colonies "hinder Trade to our Southern Plantations, by supplying *Barbadoes*, *Jamaica*, and the rest, with such things as we do: so that they take the bread out of our mouths, and are rather a disadvantage, than advantage to us." Carew Reynell, The True English Interest (London, 1674), pp. 90, 91. See also p. 33. Six years later, it was asserted that the Irish "furnish our *Foreign Plantations* with very much of their Butter, Cheese, Clothes, and other necessaries of the growth and product of *Ireland:* Considering which, and

the centre of imperial trade, "and standing like the Sun in the midst of its Plantations would not only refresh them, but also draw Profits from them."

Charles Davenant's views were exceptionally moderate. While recognizing the bad features inherent in colonies like New England, he maintained that the concomitant advantages outweighed them. He admitted the truth of the current charge that the northern colonies had drained England of the majority of those emigrating, and yet had yielded commodities of but scant value. "The Fact is so," he said, "but if it were otherwise, the Plantation Trade could not perhaps be carry'd on," for the southern colonies cannot feed themselves and, especially during war, are dependent on the northern colonies. It is true, he further conceded, that England could furnish these provisions, but, he added, perhaps only at such high prices as would retard the development of the sugar colonies. Besides, England exports to these northern colonies all kinds of manufactures, "Cloaths, and House-hold Furniture, much oftener renew'd, and thrice as good, as the same Number of People could afford to have at home." On the whole, his conclusion was that these colonies were advantageous, because, instead of sending provisions

that those of *New England* of late furnish the rest with *Flower, Bisket, Salt, Flesh, Fish* &c. (all which were formerly Exported from hence) we may expect our *Plantation-Trade* for *Sugar, Tobacco,* &c. must ere long be wholly driven with *Exported Money, or with foreign Goods bought with Exported Money.*" For this and other reasons, this pessimistic writer concluded that the colonies in general "may be Considered as the true Grounds and Causes of all our present Mischiefs." Britannia Languens (London, 1680), pp. 163, 164, 176.

to the southern plantations, England was thus enabled to send manufactures to the northern colonies.[1] His somewhat negatively favorable opinion of these colonies was, however, made contingent upon one crucial factor — that they obeyed the provisions of the colonial commercial code.[2] Similarly, in its report of December 23, 1697,[3] the Board of Trade called attention to the fact that from the American colonies were imported large quantities of sugar, tobacco, and other goods, exceeding much in value the merchandise exported to them, and that over one-half of these products was again exported, after having paid considerable duties in England. In general, however, they remarked that "althô the more Southern Colonies are much more beneficial to England than the Northern, yet being all contribute to the taking off great Quantities of Our Woollen Goods, other products, and handicraft Wares, & to maintain and encrease Our Navigation, and the Inhabitants being Your Majestys Subjects, We humbly conceive the Trade to and from those Colonies deserves the greatest Encouragement," and will be advantageous so long as the laws of trade and navigation are obeyed by them.

It is thus apparent that the northern continental colonies — Newfoundland of course excepted — diverged radically

[1] Charles Davenant, *op. cit.* II, p. 225. *Cf.* pp. 204, 205. Later he says: "We hope 'tis sufficiently prov'd, that the Plantations are Advantagious to *England*, and that the Southward and Northward Colonies, having such a mutual Dependance upon each other, all Circumstances considered, are almost equally important." *Ibid.* p. 230.

[2] *Ibid.* pp. 204–206.

[3] B. T. Trade Papers 23, ff. 130–170.

from the ideal type conceived by the seventeenth-century statesmen. Beyond some masts, a few furs, a small quantity of fish-oil and some vessels, these colonies produced nothing to send to England, with whom, on the other hand, they competed in a number of directions: in the carrying trade, in the fisheries, and in supplying the island colonies with food-stuffs. While they bought a considerable proportion of their European manufactures in England, this quantity was in itself not very large, and it was decidedly a moot question whether or no this fact counterbalanced the existing manifest disadvantages. Hence English statesmen looked askance at the development of New England. Moreover, its political recalcitrancy and disinclination to conform to the imperial commercial code imposed many irksome problems; and, even if these were settled in accordance with the wishes of the English government, the ensuing advantage was problematical. No matter what the outcome, England according to the current view seemed bound to lose. New England did not fit into the colonial scheme. Its entire elimination from the globe would probably have been welcomed. Yet, for many reasons, England could not afford to let the northern continental colonies renounce their allegiance. Under the prevailing conditions, political independence was for these colonies an impossibility; freedom from England inevitably implied subjection to some other European power, in this instance France. To England this would have meant an incalculable loss of prestige, and moreover, as a French colony, New England would have been an even more vexatious thorn in the side of the Empire, rendering insecure

the invaluable possessions to the north and south — Newfoundland, the nursery of seamen, and the tobacco colonies,
Maryland and Virginia.   Thus England clung to this region,
and even sanctioned its further settlement, not for any
clearly defined economic advantages, but in order to obviate
the greater negative losses resulting from its domination
by others.

At the Restoration in 1660, the English Empire was composed of several distinct groups of colonies, separated by
large primeval tracts, stretching along the sea-board from
Newfoundland to Florida.   In South America English
colonial enterprise was represented by Surinam.   In addition, there were in the Caribbean Sea a number of island
colonies whose resources were being rapidly exploited.   Farther north in the Atlantic were the Bermudas.   During the
Restoration era, instead of new acquisitions being made in
tropical regions, Lord Willoughby's colony of Surinam was
conquered by the Dutch and subsequently ceded to them by
treaty; all that England secured in this area was a doubtful
title to trade in Yucatan.   On the other hand, on the continent, while Nova Scotia was restored to France, the entire
region between New England and Maryland was settled, and
also the country south of Virginia.   Thus it would appear
that in the broad facts of territorial expansion the course
of events ran diametrically counter to the tendency toward
tropical colonization.   The favor with which the plantation
type of colony was regarded apparently found only a most
inadequate expression in the actual facts of colonial development.   To a certain extent this was true, for the English

government was unable to shape the actual development in accord with its desires. The English Empire was primarily a product of private initiative. From the very beginning there were present in it an inherent contradiction of purposes and two irreconcilable tendencies, which ultimately led to the American Revolution. The colonization of New England was not the result of a normal movement of expansion, but was rather a political and religious schism in the state. In consequence thereof there was planted on American soil a group of communities whose actual development, fostered by the conscious and unconscious aims of its members, tended steadily toward the formation of an organic body politic with interests distinct from those of the Empire. This was radically opposed to the aims of the Restoration statesmen and their successors.

But a mere recital of the bald facts of colonial expansion during the Restoration, without further examination of their real meaning, tends to an exaggeration of the divergence between the aims of the government and the actual results accomplished. The conquest of New York from the Dutch in 1664, leading directly to the settlement of the Jerseys and Pennsylvania, was undertaken by the English government partly for military reasons, in order to consolidate the existing colonies, and partly also to prevent the illegal trading in tobacco between the Dutch settlements and Virginia and Maryland, which lessened the economic value of these colonies to England.[1] In other words, one of the main

[1] C. O. 1/44, 59, ff. 53–55; N. Y. Col. Doc. III, pp. 44–49; C. C. 1661–1668, nos. 345, 357, 597, 605, 644. See *post*, Chapter XII.

ideas underlying this enterprise was to secure to England the fullest advantage from the possession of these tobacco colonies. Moreover, William Penn sought to develop in his dominion such commodities as England was obliged to purchase in southern Europe. "We hope," he wrote in 1685, "that good skill in our most Southern Parts will yield us several of the Straights Commodities, especially Oyle, Dates, Figgs, Almonds, Raisins and Currans."[1] In the actual course of imperial development, however, the most salient fact at the time was the settlement of Jamaica and the rapid rise of that colony and of the other West Indies to great wealth and prosperity. Nor should it be forgotten that the Carolinas were designed to be colonies of the plantation pattern, and that in South Carolina ultimately was developed the purest type of such a colony that existed on the continent.

In so far as policy was concerned, apart from actual achievement, the colonization of the Carolinas was of far greater significance than the conquest of New Netherland and its annexed territories. With a view to furthering the settlement of that region, the charter of 1663 for a limited period exempted certain products of the proposed colony from the English import duties.[2] The list included silks, wines, currants, oils, and olives, products that could be ob-

[1] A. C. Myers, Narratives of Early Pennsylvania etc., p. 265. On this subject and especially on Penn's attempts to introduce the production of wine, see ibid. pp. 207, 224, 241, 242, 287, 288.

[2] No. Ca. Col. Rec. I, p. 27 ; C. C. 1661–1668, no. 427. This exemption was repeated in the charter of 1665. No. Ca. Col. Rec. I, p. 108 ; C. C. 1661–1668, no. 1011.

tained by England only from the countries of southern Europe. It was hoped that the Carolinas would free England from such dependence on foreigners. Here again is manifest the stress that was laid on the colony as a source of supply.[1]

To the men of the day the very idea of uncontrolled commerce was totally foreign, and as the colonies to the extent that they drew upon the population of England were regarded as evils to be countenanced only in return for greater compensating advantages, it followed that a system of regulations would be created to secure these benefits to the metropolis. This relation is clearly expressed in the oft-quoted words of Sir Josiah Child. It was in connection with his discussion of emigration, wherein he adhered to the current view, that he said: "All Colonies and foreign Plantations do endamage their Mother-Kingdom, whereof the Trades of such Plantations are not confined to their said Mother Kingdom by good Laws and severe Execution of those Laws."[2] In a similar strain, John Cary wrote to a correspondent: "Please to note that all Plantations settled abroad out of our own People must needs be a Loss to this Kingdome except they are imployed there to Serve its

---

[1] In order to obtain settlers, the patentees turned to Barbados, stating that it was not the purpose of the new colony to raise sugar or tobacco, but wine, oil, currants, raisins, silk, *etc.*, "by means whereof the money of the nation that goes out for these things wilbe Keept in the Kinges Dominions and the planting part of the people imploy there time in planting those comodyties that will not injure nor overthrow the other plantations." So. Ca. Hist. Soc. Coll. V, pp. 13, 14; No. Ca. Col. Rec. I, pp. 46, 47; C. C. 1661–1668, no. 547.

[2] Child, *op. cit.* p. 183.

Interest." [1]   It would almost seem that the systematic commercial code of the Restoration era, which was based on the somewhat scattered, though definite, predecents of the former age, was an inevitable consequence of the change in attitude towards emigration, in consequence of which colonies were valued solely as sources of maritime and commercial strength.   The nature of these regulations was determined by the current economic theory of colonization and by the ultimate end in view, which was the creation of a powerful self-sufficient commercial empire, dominating the seas and controlling the course of foreign exchanges.

[1] Brit. Mus., Add. MSS. 5540, f. 61.   This direct connection is also plainly expressed in the Act of 1671, which prohibited the future shipment of the "enumerated goods" from the colonies to Ireland, because otherwise the advantages derived from the possession of colonies would be diverted from England, "although this kingdom hath, and doth daily suffer a great prejudice by the transporting great number of the people thereof to the said plantations, for the peopling of them."   22 and 23 Ch. II, c. 26, §§ x, xi.

CHAPTER II

THE LAWS OF TRADE AND NAVIGATION AND IMPERIAL DEFENCE

The Navigation Act of 1660 — The Staple Act of 1663 — The Plantation Duties of 1673 — Scotland under these statutes — Ireland and the colonies — Temporary dispensations of the laws — The system of imperial defence — The colonial garrisons — The West Indian buccaneers — The Barbary pirates.

SHORTLY after the reëstablishment of the monarchy in England, Parliament passed the famous Navigation Act of 1660, which was followed by so rapid a development of the English mercantile marine, that contemporary writers with feelings of profound admiration termed it the "Sea Magna Charta"[1] and the "Charta Maritima."[2] This important statute took less than a month to pass the House of Commons,[3] there being virtually no opposition, since the bill embodied principles that were then universally accepted, and which already formed part of England's traditional policy. In the first place, the Act discriminated in many ways against foreign shipping and in some specific instances, as in the colonial trade, absolutely prohibited its employment. In the second place, the law was designed to prevent foreigners

---

[1] Sir Francis Brewster, Essays on Trade and Navigation (London, 1695), p. 92.

[2] Josiah Child, *op. cit.* (ed. 1694), preface and p. 112.

[3] Com. Journal VIII, pp. 120, 129, 142, 151, 153.

from securing the benefit of the new sources of supply opened up by English colonization.×

The policy of protecting the national shipping from foreign competition was of most ancient date, and had been followed fairly consistently since mediæval times. It was as far back as the fourteenth century, in the reign of Richard II, that the first navigation act had been passed, and during the two following centuries a number of similar measures were enacted.[1] Under the first two Stuarts this policy had been somewhat intermittently enforced by royal orders and proclamations,[2] with the distinct purpose of making England a great maritime power.[3] During the Commonwealth, this policy was definitely embodied in the comprehensive statute of 1651. Subordinate to this policy of fostering the growth of the national mercantile marine by protective measures, and at the same time a logical outcome and an integral part thereof, was the practice of excluding foreigners from trading with the English colonies and of confining their export trade to the metropolis. Prior to the Restoration, these principles had already been applied in an unsystematic manner to the growing Empire in America and the West Indies.[4] The Order in Council of

[1] Beer, Commercial Policy of England toward the American Colonies, pp. 10–13.

[2] Beer, Origins, pp. 238–240.

[3] In 1635, the Venetian ambassador in England wrote: "È massima fondamentale di Stato in Inghilterra, d'invigilare sempre ad essere effettivamente più potente di tutt'i suoi vicini sul mare." Le Relazioni degli Stati Europei, Serie IV, Inghilterra (Venezia, 1863), p. 306.

[4] Beer, Origins, Chapters VII, VIII, XII.

1621,[1] prohibiting Virginia from exporting its produce to foreign countries, was subsequently expanded in scope to embrace the other colonies, except Newfoundland. In 1633, foreigners were forbidden to trade in Virginia,[2] and by the far-reaching Act of 1650 they were excluded from commercial intercourse with any and all of the colonies.

⸙ These two closely related policies were embodied in the Navigation Act of 1660. Its fundamental purpose was to foster the development of national strength by an increase of sea power and commerce. Inevitably, it amounted to an act of economic warfare against the Dutch. Despite their underlying racial sympathies and their common Protestantism, which had within the memory of living man emerged victorious from a severe struggle with the well-organized and still threatening forces of the Catholic Counter-Reformation, the English and Dutch were engaged in one of those bitter economic contests which constitute so great a part of modern international history. In the fisheries of northern Europe, in the trade to the Baltic which alone furnished the naval stores that were absolutely indispensable to the maritime powers, in the commerce with the spice islands of the Far East and with opulent India, in the slave-trade to Africa whose profits and whose apparent necessity dulled whatever moral aversion from the system that otherwise might have existed, the Dutch had for two generations stood directly in the path of England's ambitious plans for economic expansion. In addition, owing to lower freight rates, combined

[1] C. O. 5/1354, ff. 201, 202 ; P. C. Cal. I, pp. 48, 49.
[2] P . C. Cal. I, p. 192.

with more abundant capital and a more efficient system of credit, the Dutch monopolized to a marked degree the carrying trade and to a less extent the foreign commerce of Europe. Up to the Navigation Act of 1651, a considerable portion of England's foreign trade had been carried in Dutch bottoms. Moreover, during the anarchy of the Civil War, the Stuart regulations of colonial commerce had inevitably fallen into disregard, and as a result the Dutch merchants had secured an alarmingly large share of the trade with the English tobacco and sugar colonies.[1] The Act of 1650 had to some extent redressed this situation, but had not completely ousted the Dutch from what all European governments then regarded as an exclusive national preserve.[2] It was thus inevitable that the Dutch, as the leading commercial and maritime power, should suffer most from the protective measures embodied in the Navigation Act of 1660. Shortly after its passage, on October 1, 1660, the Venetian representative at the court of Charles II wrote to the Senate of his city-state that this Act would affect adversely all commercial centres, but particularly Holland and other northern countries, which had the largest commerce with England.[3]

In the regulation of England's European trade, the Navigation Act of 1660 was less rigid and stringent than had been

[1] Beer, Origins, pp. 352 et seq.

[2] Ibid. pp. 388 et seq.

[3] The Italians, he added, would be little affected, "ma Olandesi, Danesi, et altri Settentrionali son li più attacati, perche questi solevano portare gran parte delle Merci forestieri, e particolarm^te dall' Indie." Venetian Archives, Inghilterra, Dispacci al Senato 50, no. 257.

its predecessor passed in 1651.[1] (By means of prohibitions and discriminating duties, embodied in two rather obscurely worded clauses, which were supplemented by other legis-

[1] 12 Ch. II, c. 18, § viii provided that no goods of the growth or manufacture of Russia, no masts, timber or boards, salt, pitch, tar, resin, hemp, flax, raisins, figs, prunes, olive-oils, no grain or corn, sugar, potashes, wines, vinegar, spirits or brandy could be imported into England and Ireland, except in ships belonging to the people thereof, whose master and three-quarters of whose crew were English. Furthermore, no currants or commodities of the Turkish Empire could be imported into England and Ireland except in English-built shipping navigated as above, or in ships of the place of production or of the ports whence the goods could only or usually had been transported. The subsequent clause somewhat mitigated this prohibition. Section ix provided that all wines of the growth of France or Germany, if imported in ships not belonging to those places, should pay aliens' duties; and similarly, that all Spanish, Portuguese, Madeira, Canary wines, and all the commodities mentioned in the preceding clause were subject to the payment of these additional duties, if imported in other than legally navigated English shipping. These aliens' duties, dating back to mediæval times (Gerard Malynes, Consuetudo, vel Lex Mercatoria (3d ed., London, 1686), p. 139; Laws, Ordinances, and Institutions of the Admiralty of Great Britain (London, 1767) I, p. 307; Atton and Holland, The King's Customs (New York, 1908), pp. 13, 112, 321) were considerably amplified by the "Old Subsidy" of 1660. (12 Ch. II, c. 4, §§ i, ii and the annexed Book of Rates.) They constituted a marked discrimination against foreign shipping. In 1677, the Commissioners of the Customs reported that these additional duties amounted "in a manner to a prohibition." (Cal. Dom. 1677–1678, pp. 470, 472.) Under these regulations, however, Holland could still remain the *entrepôt* for a large number of European goods consumed in England. Therefore, it was further provided in 1662 that no wines other than Rhenish, no spicery, grocery, tobacco, potash, pitch, tar, salt, resin, boards, timber, olive-oil could be imported from the Netherlands or Germany in any ship whatsoever. (13 & 14 Ch. II, c. 11, § xxiii.) The complexity of these regulations naturally caused many difficulties of interpretation. See John Reeves, History of the Law of Shipping and Navigation (Dublin, 1792) and D. O. McGovney, The Navigation Acts as applied to European Trade, in Am. Hist. Rev. IX, pp. 725–734.

lation, English shipping was given a marked advantage over its competitors in the importation of European commodities into England and Ireland.   Furthermore, foreign ships were excluded from the English and Irish coastwise trades,[1] and fish caught in such vessels was subjected to the payment of onerous duties.[2] ⁊

In so far as the history of the development of the old colonial system is concerned, these regulations of England's European, coasting, and fishing trades have only an indirect importance, except in that it was distinctly provided that ships built in the colonies were to enjoy the same privileges as those of England and Ireland.[3] Similarly, to be legally navigated, the master and three-quarters of the crew had to be English, which term naturally included such subjects as resided in the colonies. The Navigation Act protected and encouraged equally the domestic and the colonial mercantile marine. This was a cardinal maxim in English policy, departed from in only one insignificant instance,[4] while

---

[1] The coast district included Ireland, England, Wales, Berwick-on-Tweed, Guernsey and Jersey.   12 Ch. II, c. 18, § vi.   Wherever England is mentioned in this exposition of the laws, the term is intended to include also Wales and Berwick-on-Tweed.

[2] 12 Ch. II, c. 18 § v.   The provisions against foreign fish were made much more rigorous by 15 Ch. II, c. 7, §§ xvi, xvii, and 18 Ch. II, c. 2, § ii.

[3] 12 Ch. II, c. 18, § vii.

[4] The Act of 1673 for encouraging the Greenland whale fishery provided that whale-fins and train-oil caught and imported in English ships were to be duty free.   If imported and caught in colonial vessels, oil was to pay 6s. a ton and whale-fins 50s.   If caught in colonial, but imported in English vessels, these duties were one-half.   If caught in foreign vessels, these respective duties were £9 and £18.   25 Ch. II, c. 7, § i.   For the working of this act, see C. O. 194/8, O 46.   At one time also, an incorrect interpreta-

a number of the colonies persistently discriminated against English shipping.[1] (Thanks to this virtual parity of treatment, colonial vessels, after taking their fish to the Mediterranean ports, were able to sail thence with European products to England.)

(As regards the produce of the non-English parts of America, Africa, and Asia, the Navigation Act provided that such goods could not be imported into England or Ireland except in English, Irish, or colonial ships, legally navigated, and then only from their place of growth and production or from such ports whence they had usually been shipped.[2] A subsequent clause somewhat modified this, and made it legal to import in English vessels from Spain and Portugal the products of the colonial possessions of these two countries.[3] The direct intent of this regulation was to prevent the products of the foreign colonies, especially those of the Dutch in the Orient, from being imported into England in foreign shipping. But, as English ships were generally not allowed access to these foreign possessions, their produce was by these clauses virtually debarred from the English and Irish markets to the manifest advantage of the English colonies.[4]

tion of the law threatened to a minor extent to discriminate against colonial shipping. See *post*, Chapter VIII.

[1] See *post*, Chapters III, XI.

[2] 12 Ch. II, c. 18, §§ iii, iv. See also §§ xii, xiii.

[3] These products could also be imported from the Azores, Canaries, and Madeiras. *Ibid.* § xiv.

[4] Under the tariff of 1660, sarsaparilla had to pay a duty of 2*d.* a pound, but if imported directly from the place of growth in English shipping only one-

As regards the colonial trade proper, the Navigation Act provided that no goods could be imported into or exported from any of the English possessions in America, Africa, or Asia but in vessels belonging to the people of England or Ireland, or in such as had been built in and belonged to "any said plantations." The master and at least three-quarters of the crew of these ships had to be English.[1] As the vessels engaged in certain branches of England's European trade had to be of both English build and ownership in order not to incur the penalty of the onerous aliens' duties, the colonial trade was in this respect somewhat less restricted.[2] This

third of this duty was payable. Some sarsaparilla was imported from Jamaica, but it not being clear that it was of the production of that colony, the question of the amount of customs payable was submitted to Sir William Jones, Solicitor-General from 1673 to 1675 and Attorney-General from 1675 to 1679. Jones decided that, if this sarsaparilla was not of the growth of Jamaica, it must pay the full duties, on the ground that America was of vast extent, and "as much Navigation may be used by bringing it from one part of America to another as from some part of America home." Brit. Mus., Add. MSS. 30,218, ff. 64^b, 65. In 1717, an English ship imported into England some foreign colonial cocoa-nuts from New York and Barbados, and the question arose whether or no said ship and the cocoa-nuts were liable to forfeiture. The Attorney-General, Sir Edward Northey, held that, as these cocoa-nuts were the produce of the Spanish colonies where Englishmen were not permitted to trade, and as, both before and after 1660, they had always been imported into England from the English colonies, this method of importation was legal. Other authorities disagreed with him, and considered the forfeiture valid. Brit. Mus., Hargrave MSS. 275, f. 65^b; Add. MSS. 8832, ff. 308, 309.

[1] Under exceptional circumstances, this provision as regards the crew was not rigidly insisted upon. Cf. Treas. Books, Out-Letters, Customs 11, ff. 19, 20; Cal. Treas. Books, 1676–1679, Jan. 31, 1677.

[2] For an instance in 1660 of a foreign-built ship in the colonial trade, see Brit. Mus., Add. MSS. 5489, f. 61.

led to some dissatisfaction,[1] and accordingly, in 1662, Parliament enacted that no foreign-built ships, except those bought before October 1st of that year, should enjoy the privileges of an English-owned ship, although navigated and owned by Englishmen, but that all these vessels should be deemed alien and as such their cargoes should be subject to the additional customs duties.[2] This

[1] In 1662, the elder Brethren of Trinity House were asked to "give an opinion whether we have ships enough of our own to drive our own trade, or in case there be not, what time is fit to be allowed for buying, or building of them, and whether they do not esteem it advantageous for this nation to forbid any foreign built ships after the prefixt time." They replied that the shipping of England was more than enough for carrying on the existing trade, and that the buying of foreign ships would be disadvantageous. MSS. of Trinity House (H. M. C. VIII, 1), p. 251[a].

[2] 13 & 14 Ch. II, c. 11, § vi; Com. Journal VIII, pp. 347, 353, 354, 383, 384, 390–392; Brit. Mus., Add. MSS. 30,218, ff. 27, 28. Hence, while foreign-built vessels bought after 1662 could legally engage in the colonial trade, their cargoes had to pay the aliens' duties. See Northey's decision of 1706, in Brit. Mus., Hargrave MSS. 141, ff. 35[b], 36. Cf. also P. C. Cal. I, pp. 824, 825; Va. Mag. XX, p. 250. The Staple Act somewhat restricted this right, providing that no commodities of the growth or production of Europe could be imported into the colonies except in English-built ships or in such as had been bought before Oct. 1, 1662. 15 Ch. II, c. 7, § vi. For an instance in 1677 of the exaction of the aliens' duties on some sugars imported from Barbados into London in the ship *Success* of Bristol, see Cal. Treas. Books, 1676–1679, pp. 625, 626. Danby subsequently ordered the restitution of these duties, as he intended to order this vessel entered on the register of free ships. *Ibid.* These duties were in themselves sufficiently high to drive practically all unfree ships from the colonial trade, but in addition the English government in 1685, apparently without legal warrant, ordered the seizure in the colonies of "all vessels belonging to strangers and forreine vessells not made free" found trading there. C. O. 324/4, f. 142; P. C. Cal. II, p. 81; C. C. 1685–1688, p. 27. See also P. C. Cal. II, pp. 86, 87. In 1686, the *O'Brien*, an Irish ship bound for Jamaica, was seized on the high seas and

provision practically barred all foreign ships purchased after 1662 from the colonial trade, though in some instances the owners were able to induce the government to place them on the free list.[1] Ships purchased by the colonies from foreigners were also treated as unfree, and no provision was made for naturalizing alien vessels condemned in the colonial courts.[2]

subsequently condemned in the Nevis Admiralty Court as an unfree bottom. At the trial unanswerable evidence was introduced to the effect that the vessel had originally been of foreign build, but that it had been rebuilt in Ireland. According to the owner's statement she was "not a free ship although in Reallity ought to be, being Cast away in this Countrey (Ireland) and Rebuilt here." C. O. 1/57, 51; C. O. 1/58, 83 i-viii; C. C. 1685–1688, pp. 257, 263, 264. As a result of these conditions, the number of foreign-built ships engaged in the colonial trade steadily decreased. Of 51 ships loading enumerated commodities in Barbados from April 14, 1678, to Oct. 14, 1679, as many as 12 were of foreign build. Of 115 ships entering in the same colony from March 25, 1688, to June 25, 1688, only 5 were foreign-built. All the 55 vessels entering there from Aug. 12, 1690, to Nov. 12, 1690, were English-built. C. O. 33/13, nos. 1 et seq. The legal difficulty was definitely settled by the administrative statute of 1696, which absolutely debarred foreign-built vessels from the colonial trade. 7 & 8 W. III, c. 22, § ii. A complaint made at that time against this specific provision of the new law indicates clearly that such ships were still to some extent employed in the colonial trade. House of Lords MSS. (1695–1697) II, p. 233.

[1] On Nov. 24, 1685, Treasurer Rochester ordered the Commissioners of Customs to continue in force the warrants that Charles II had issued to a number of ships exempting their cargoes from the aliens' duties, as their withdrawal would be very injurious to the plantation trade. Treas. Books, Out-Letters, Customs 10, ff. 74, 75.

[2] In 1672, Sir Charles Wheler wrote to the Council of Trade that the Dutch derived good profits from selling shallops to the Leeward Islands, of which he was Governor, and that the Act of Navigation obliged him to seize such vessels without giving him any power to naturalize them after condemnation. C. O. 1/28, 9; C. C. 1669–1674, p. 328. In 1683, a Scotch vessel trading to Pennsylvania was seized and condemned in Pennsylvania.

As the lack of such a provision was found highly inconvenient, a custom established itself in some of the colonies, especially in Jamaica, of considering foreign-built vessels condemned in the local admiralty courts and subsequently bought by Englishmen as "free in all parts between the Tropicks." [1] When this matter was brought to the attention of the English government, it was referred to the Commissioners of the Customs, who reported in 1687 that this practice was without any legal warrant and that such certificates of freedom as had been issued by the Governor of Jamaica should be revoked.[2] Though contrary to the

Its new owners then imported in it into England some sugar and molasses from Barbados and, subsequently, a cargo of lumber from Norway. The English customs officials seized the vessel as forfeited under the Act of Navigation. But on the protest of the owners, it was discharged on payment of the aliens' duties on the cargoes of both voyages. Treas. Books, Out-Letters, Customs 10, ff. 177, 178.

[1] In 1686, Lieutenant-Governor Molesworth of Jamacia wrote that this was a "long allow'd practice," in whose favor much could be said, and that "a Certificat vnder the Gov^{rs} hand & seal of the Island (according ye vsuall form) hath been for many years accounted among vs a tantamount to the making of a Ship free in all parts between the Tropicks." C. O. 138/5, ff. 199–219; C. C. 1685–1688, pp. 272–275.

[2] In 1686, Captain Talbot of H. M. S. *Falcon* had seized such a ship as unfree. This vessel had originally come from Cadiz to Jamaica, where it was condemned in the Admiralty Court. It was then purchased by some local merchants and was used in the logwood trade between Jamaica and Campeachy. On the trial of Talbot's seizure, the Judge of the Jamaica Admiralty Court on a technical legal point, not germane to the question here under discussion, ordered the release of the vessel and its cargo. Captain Talbot appealed to England, and in 1687 the Commissioners of the Customs reported on this case that, by collusion and fraud, foreign-built ships were thus made free in the colonies. On information mainly derived from Molesworth's despatches, they further stated that foreign ships were

letter of the law, vessels in distress belonging to friendly foreign nations were, however, allowed to refit in the English colonies and to purchase there such supplies as were indispensable, as well as to sell sufficient goods to cover these expenses.[1] The penalty imposed upon unfree bottoms trading to the colonies was forfeiture of the vessel and its cargo as well.[2] To render these regulations more

tried in the colonial courts on the information of the owner; they were then condemned and appraised at an exceedingly low valuation. Of this amount the owner, as informer, was entitled to one-third and to him also the Governor ceded his third. Thus these ships were made free within the tropics by paying to the Crown only one-third of an exceedingly low appraisal. The Commissioners then pointed out that this distinction, that is of freedom within the tropics and not elsewhere, was without any legal basis, and advised that such certificates, of which they understood about twenty were outstanding, be called in, but only slowly so as not to dislocate the logwood trade of Jamaica. C. O. 138/5, ff. 199–219, 326–333; C. O. 1/58, 64, 64i; C. O. 1/60, 28, 40, 40i; C. C. 1685–1688, pp. 255, 272–275, 303, 356, 357, 361.

[1] A provision to this effect was usually introduced in the international treaties. C. C. 1685–1688, pp. 383, 384; Haring, The Buccaneers in the West Indies, p. 197. In the instructions issued in 1663 to Governor Willoughby of Barbados was a clause permitting the giving of "Wood and Water and such Ships provision, as the Subjects of any Nation in amity with Vs, shall stand in need of." P. C. Cal. I, p. 359. For such an instance in 1671, see C. C. 1669–1674, p. 155. In 1672, Lieutenant-Governor Lynch of Jamaica allowed a Dutchman driven by stress of weather to that island to sell as many negroes as were required to refit his ship. Ibid. p. 323. As a rule, the colonial authorities carefully reported the details of such cases to the English government so as to protect themselves against charges of countenancing illegal trade. On the privileges accorded to English ships seeking aid in the French colonies, see S. L. Mims, Colbert's West India Policy, pp. 199, 200.

[2] One-third of such forfeitures was apportioned to the Crown, one-third to the Governor of the colony in case the ships were seized where the law had been violated (otherwise this share also went to the Crown), and one-third belonged to the seizer or informer. But in case the offending vessel

effective the statute of 1660 further prohibited all aliens
from acting as merchants or factors in the colonies.[1]

was seized by a ship of the royal navy, one-half went to the Crown and one-
half to the officers of the royal navy to be apportioned among them according to the rules for the division of prizes. This naturally led to some disputes between the officers of the navy and the governors. See, e.g., C. O.
1/26, 79, 79i, ii; C. C. 1669–1674, p. 233.

[1] 12 Ch. II, c. 18, § ii. Foreigners, who had become naturalized or had
been made denizens, enjoyed the privileges to which natural-born subjects
of the Crown were entitled. Cf. C. C. 1675–1676, pp. 144, 147. As a number of foreigners had settled in the colonies, some means had to be devised
for conferring these rights other than by naturalization by Act of Parliament
or by the issue of letters of denization by the Crown. Accordingly, naturalization laws were passed by some of the colonial legislatures and the
governors also on their own authority bestowed the privileges of an English
subject on foreigners within their jurisdiction. Such naturalization conferred the rights of an English subject within the specific colony and
enabled an alien to act as a merchant there. But immediately the question arose, whether such naturalization were valid in the other dominions.
This was a difficult problem, which even to this day has not been satisfactorily solved. See E. B. Sargant, British Citizenship (London, 1912).
English practice varied. Thus in 1671, the ship of a Jewish resident of
New York, although provided with a pass from Governor Lovelace of that
colony, was condemned in Jamaica on the ground that the owner was
not a denizen. This decision was, however, reversed in England. C. C.
1669–1674, pp. 434–436, 453. In 1682, the English government took a
diametrically opposite position. In that year a New England vessel was
seized in St. Kitts because a native of France was a part owner. As this
Frenchman had received letters of naturalization from Governor Culpeper
of Virginia, Governor Stapleton of the Leeward Islands deferred the execution of the sentence of condemnation and wrote to England for instructions.
Acting on the opinion of Chief Justice North, that naturalization in any
colony was only local, the Lords of Trade ordered the condemnation carried
into effect. C. C. 1681–1685, pp. 198, 211, 243, 250, 258, 346; P. C. Cal.
II, p. 38; Blathwayt, Journal I, f. 102. In 1691, a similar case called for
decision. A Dutch merchant of New York petitioned the government,
stating that he and his fellows in that colony had since 1664 regarded them-

These provisions of the Navigation Act of 1660, though much more elaborate in form, in their general effect merely reproduced the earlier Stuart regulations and that of the Act of 1650 prohibiting foreigners from trading to the English colonies. At the last moment, however, apparently under the inspiration of Downing, was added a provision with distinctly original features.[1] The policy of confining the colonial export trade to England had already been unequivocally adopted by the first Stuarts. During the anarchy of the Civil War their regulations had fallen into desuetude and, except in isolated, sporadic instances, had not been revived by the Interregnum authorities.[2] This regulation was now elaborated in a form far more definite and scientific than the earlier precedents upon which it was based. The belated clause in the Act of Navigation

selves as "free subjects of England," but that some of the officers of the customs in England had demanded aliens' duties on goods imported by them. In pursuance of a report of the Customs board, the Treasury ordered that these merchants should enjoy the same privileges as any other subjects. Treas. Books, Out-Letters, Customs 12, f. 309. Foreigners seeking a new home in the colonies had to meet these facts. In 1685, some Huguenots, who were about to sail from England for New York, were warned by the government that their French-built ship and their goods would be seized if they proceeded to the English colonies, and that, being aliens, they could not become merchants or factors there under pain of forfeiture of their entire property. *Ibid.* 10, f. 54. On this entire subject, see Chalmers, Political Annals (London, 1780), pp. 316, 317; W. A. Shaw, Denizations and Naturalizations of Aliens (Huguenot Society of London Publ. Vol. XVIII); Carpenter, Naturalization in England and the American Colonies (Am. Hist. Rev. IX, pp. 288–304); Start, Naturalization in the English Colonies of America (Am. Hist. Assoc. 1893, pp. 317–339).

[1] 12 Ch. II, c. 18, § xviii; Com. Journal VIII, pp. 120, 129, 142, 151.
[2] Beer, Origins, pp. 400–403.

provided that, under penalty of forfeiture of the offending vessel and its cargo,[1] no sugar, tobacco, cotton-wool, indigo, ginger, fustic or other dyeing-woods produced in the English colonies could be shipped elsewhere than to England, Ireland or some other English colony.[2]

With the exception of tobacco, of which the chief producers were Virginia and Maryland, the commodities enumerated in this list — whence the policy is commonly known as that of enumeration — were exclusively the produce of the West Indies. No one of the typical products of the New England colonies was enumerated for the obvious reason that, with insignificant exceptions, they could not be imported on a commercially profitable basis; and, even if it had been otherwise, England did not want them, as they ran parallel to English products and hence their importation would have injured English industries. The exotic commodities which England did not produce were enumerated, because England required them in order to become economically independent of her competing European rivals, and also to sell to them whatever surplus

[1] According to a legal opinion given in 1698, if a ship took any of the enumerated goods to a foreign port, both the vessel and its cargo were subject to forfeiture in case the enumeration bond had been given in England, but if the bond had been given in the colonies, then only the amount stipulated therein could be claimed as a penalty.   Brit. Mus., Add. MSS. 9747, f. 107.

[2] When shipped to England, these commodities had to be actually landed and had to pay the English customs as well as a number of petty charges, such as town-dues and wharfage.   Only then could they be reshipped to foreign markets.   C. O. 324/4, ff. 191–206; C. C. 1685–1688, pp. 175–177.

might remain after the English consumption had been supplied. In both ways would the nation's balance of trade be fortified and its economic welfare advanced. The policy of enumeration was the clearest possible expression of the current economic creed.

In order to make this regulation effective, ships intending to sail to the colonies from England or Ireland were first required to give bonds, either of £1000 or of £2000 contingent upon their tonnage, to carry these enumerated commodities to England or Ireland.[1] On the other hand, vessels arriving in the colonies from any other place were obliged to give bonds in like amounts there to take these products either to England or Ireland, *or to some other English colony.* This difference between these two kinds of bonds was distinctly favorable to colonial ships. If strictly enforced, it would have given them a virtual monopoly of the intercolonial trade, since the terms of their bonds debarred most English ships trading to America from taking the enumerated commodities from one colony to another.[2] As a matter of fact,

---

[1] 12 Ch. II, c. 18, § xix. In the colonies, certificates that such bonds had been given in England or Ireland had to be produced to the proper authorities. For these certificates, see C. O. 1/56, nos. 29, 30, 30i.

[2] In his notes of 1676, after reciting the terms of the bonds given by English ships trading to the colonies, Sir Joseph Williamson wrote: 'It shall seem an English ship going from hence cannot trade from one plantation to another; or on lading in any plantation she must either produce a certificate of such a bond having been enacted into here in England, or must then enter into such a bond to the Governor to carry the goods to England or some other of the plantations (so by this clause it should seem such an English ship may trade directly from one Plantation to another. *Qu.* how this consists with the first clause?).' C. C. 1675–1676, p. 381.

for approximately the first twenty-five years after 1660, no special stress was placed upon this distinction,[1] which seems to have been the result of careless legislation rather than of deliberate intent, and English vessels did extensively engage in the intercolonial trade.[2] Towards the end of the Restoration period, when in every respect a more rigid and meticulous enforcement of the law in the colonies was demanded by the home government, this distinction in the two kinds of bonds was, however, strictly insisted upon.[3]

[1] In 1672, the Lords of the Treasury wrote to the Governors of Barbados, Jamaica, and Virginia to seize six specific ships that had left England without giving bonds, in case they should arrive within their respective jurisdictions. But in the same year the King wrote to the West Indian Governors to enforce the laws of trade; and, in case any ships should arrive from England without having given bond there, they were instructed not to permit them to lade any enumerated goods without first taking bond from them. Cal. Treas. Books, 1669–1672, p. 1232; ibid. 1672–1675, pp. 15, 16.

[2] An examination of some of the naval office lists of the period, defective and incomplete though they are, shows conclusively that English vessels did not abide by the strict letter of the law. In a list of 1678–1679, of 51 ships arriving in Barbados, 43 had given bonds in England, and 8, which had not sailed from England, gave bonds in the colony. Yet of these 51 vessels only 32 were bound directly for England, though all had on board enumerated commodities. C. O. 33/13, no. 1 (Barbados Naval Office Lists, 1678–1703). An account of the 25 Ch. II, c. 7 duties paid in Barbados at about the same time shows that 27 ships were bound for the other colonies, of which 7 belonged to England and 20 to the colonies. Ibid. no. 2. In 1679–1680, of 50 ships lading enumerated commodities in this colony, 13 had given bonds in the plantations. Of these 50, only 4 belonged to the colonies, yet a considerable number were bound for New England, New York, Virginia, Maryland, etc. C. O. 33/14, no. 1. See also the subsequent accounts in this and the preceding volume. The above facts show clearly that English ships were at this time able to engage in the intercolonial trade.

[3] In 1685, Captain Allen, R. N., who was employed in suppressing illegal trade in Virginia and Maryland, asked for further instructions on several

×The Navigation Act of 1660 introduced no fundamentally new principle in the regulation of colonial trade. For the exclusion of foreigners from commerce with the English plantations and for the restriction of their export trade to the metropolis, ample precedents could be found in former

questions about which he was in doubt. One concerned his duty in regard to a number of English-built ships that had cleared in England for the Madeiras or Cape Verde Islands, but had come to the colonies without having given bond in England. The report of the Commissioners of the Customs, which was approved by the Lord Treasurer and the Privy Council, instructed him that "no Ship coming from any part of the World, except from one Plantation to another, or from his Majestys Islands or Territorys in Asia, Africa or America, is to be permitted to enter into any Bond whatever in the Plantations but it they take in any Goods there, both the said ship and Goods are become forfeitable, and ought to be seized and prosecuted accordingly." P. C. Cal. II, pp. 85–88. This distinction was also clearly emphasized in the trade instructions issued in 1686 to Sir Edmund Andros. In case any ship should arrive in New England with enumerated commodities, he was to see if bond had been duly given, and if not, he was to seize the vessel and cargo. If bond had been given, he was to examine it to see if its condition was to come to England alone, or to England or some other English colony. In the former case he was to forbid the vessel to unload. C. O. 5/904, ff. 330–332. Similarly, the instructions issued in 1686 by the Surveyor General of the Customs in the colonies, Patrick Mein, to the Virginia collectors stated that no enumerated goods were to be laden on any vessel coming from England until a certificate should have been produced of a bond given in England to carry these goods there; but, in case the ship should come from any other place, bond was to be given to carry these products to England or to some other English colony. C. O. 1/59, 34, § 9. Cf. also C. O. 5/903, f. 106. In reply to one of the charges made by Captain Crofts, R. N., against the Virginia administration, the Governor, Lord Howard of Effingham, at this time stated that no one of the Council, except Bacon, was engaged in trade, but that some were part owners of London ships, *which fact did not concern the one-penny duty.* He meant by this that English ships were prevented by the terms of their bonds from taking tobacco to another colony. C. O. 1/62, 20 ii.

English practice. The effect of the Act was to give English, Irish, and colonial shipping a monopoly of the carrying trade within the Empire, and to make England the staple for tobacco and the West Indian products.[x] Under this law, however, English merchants, and even those of alien nationality, could send foreign manufactures and other commodities from the various states in Europe in English shipping to the colonies. In this way, the colonial trade would to some extent be taken out of the hands of English merchants and the value of the colonies as markets for England lessened. In order to obviate this, Parliament in 1663 passed an additional law, whose preamble[1] outlines concisely, but clearly, its underlying motives. Such direct trade from the continent of Europe was in the future forbidden in order to maintain "a greater correspondence and kindness" between the colonies and England and for "keeping them in a firmer dependance upon it, and rendring them yet more beneficial and advantagious unto it in the further imployment and increase of English shipping and seamen, vent of English woolen and other manufactures and commodities, rendring the navigation to and from the same more safe and cheap, and making this kingdom a staple, not only of the commodities of those plantations, but also of the commodities of other countries and places, for the supplying of them." An analysis of this condensed statement will show that the motives, though mainly economic, were also partly political and military. The obvious economic advantages were an increase in the business of the English merchants, with prob-

[1] 15 Ch II, c. 7, § v.

ably an enlarged consumption of English manufactures by the colonies; more employment for English shipping on account of the indirect voyages resulting from the law; and also a larger customs revenue, since European products shipped to the colonies through England would in the process have to pay some duties.[1] As a result of the ensuing closer commercial relations, the political ties binding the colonies to the mother country would inevitably become closer. Finally, the trade to the colonies, instead of being carried on from scattered points on the continent, would become centralized in a few clearly marked trade-routes radiating from England. This would be an immense military advantage and would greatly facilitate England's onerous task of defending this trade from pirate or enemy.

Accordingly, the "Staple Act" of 1663 prohibited, under the same severe penalties as were imposed by the Navigation Act of 1660, the importation into the colonies of any European commodities that had not been laden and shipped in England.[2] Goods whose importation into England for

[1] This fiscal advantage was not very marked, as these duties were insignificant. It is not mentioned in the Act of 1663, but a subsequent statute summarizes the reasons for the policy of enumeration and that of the staple, stating that otherwise the trade of the colonies would "in a great measure be diverted from hence, and carried elsewhere, his Majestys customs and other revenues much lessened, and this kingdom not continue a staple of the said commodities of the said plantations, nor that vent for the future of the victual and other native commodities of this kingdom." 22 & 23 Ch. II, c. 26, §§ x, xi.

[2] As in the case of the enumerated commodities, before they could be reëxported from England, these foreign goods had to be actually landed in England. This provision was, however, not always strictly enforced and, in consequence, in 1676 the English customs officials were instructed to see

consumption there was strictly forbidden could, however, be shipped to the colonies; for otherwise, the authorities said, they would be "debarred of all such comodities." [1] From the rigor of the law were also excepted certain articles, whose inclusion in the prohibition would have been obviously detrimental to the welfare of the colonies. Thus salt for the Newfoundland and New England fisheries was exempted, in order not to hamper in any way these industries in their competition with England's foreign rivals for the markets of southern Europe. [2] Similarly, horses and provisions [3] were allowed to be exported directly from Scotland and Ireland to the colonies, mainly in order not to raise the cost of the production of sugar and other commodities in the West Indies. Finally, wine of the Madeiras and Azores, possessions of England's ally, Portugal, could be shipped directly from these places. This last clause was somewhat obscurely worded, so that it was not clear whether or no Parliament had intended to include as well the wines

that these goods were "entirely unladen and actually put on shore." In 1679, renewed orders to this effect were issued. Cal. Treas. Books, 1676–1679, p. 206; Treas. Books, Out-Letters, Customs 5, f. 30. The object, of course, was to ensure full payment of the English customs duties.

[1] Cal. Treas. Books, 1660–1667, pp. 620, 621.

[2] In 1687, some London merchants requested permission to ship salt directly from Europe to Virginia for use in a fishery that they proposed to establish there. The matter was referred to the Treasury and by them to the Customs, who recommended granting the request, but for one voyage only, as an experiment, with proper safeguards to prevent any violation of the other provisions of the commercial system. This report was approved, and the petition was granted. P. C. Cal. II, pp. 102, 103. Cf. Treas. Books, Out-Letters, Customs 11, ff. 100, 101.

[3] And also servants.

of the Canaries, which belonged to Spain. Regarding this moot point many and bitter were the disputes, attaining a political significance totally incommensurate with its intrinsic economic importance, and still remaining not definitely decided when the American Revolution rendered unnecessary all further argument.[1]

[1] The Act of 1663 does not specifically name the Canaries, but enumerates the Madeiras and Western Islands of Azores. The Navigation Act of 1660, however, mentions the "Western Islands, commonly called Azores, or Madera or Canary islands." Thus there was some reason for holding that Parliament had intended to include the Canaries. But, apart from the intent of the legislature, the crux of the question was whether these islands formed part of Africa or of Europe. If they were held to belong geographically to Africa, which was the more natural view, the direct importation of wine from them into the colonies would still have been perfectly legal, even if mention of the Canaries had been intentionally omitted from the Act of 1663. In 1706, Sir Edward Northey, then Attorney-General, held that the Canaries formed part of Africa. Brit. Mus., Hargrave MSS. 141, ff. 35 b, 36. During the Restoration period, however, the English government consistently maintained that the importation of wine from the Canaries into the colonies was illegal. The royal proclamation of Nov. 24, 1675, enjoining the enforcement of the trade laws, especially the Staple Act of 1663, mentioned among the commodities exempted wines only from the Madeiras and from the Western Islands or Azores. British Royal Proclamation, 1603–1783 (Am. Antiqu. Soc., 1911), pp. 126–128. A not inconsiderable part of Randolph's complaints against Massachusetts concerned this trade. See post, Chapter XI. In 1686, came before the English government the case of a vessel condemned by the New England Admiralty Court for importing Canary wines. The Commissioners of the Customs reported that in construction and practice these islands were considered to be in Europe, though at times placed in the maps of Africa. They further added that, although the Madeiras were also geographically in Africa, yet the Act of 1663 supposed them to be in Europe, as otherwise it would not have specifically excepted their wines. Moreover, they said, Spain did not consider the Canaries as a colony, but as a part of itself, and hence foreigners were allowed to trade there. As, however, the master of the vessel in question was ignorant of his transgression, and for

In the course of a few years it was found that, in the actual working of the enumeration clauses of the Act of Navigation, there developed certain definite inconveniences, for which a remedy was deemed desirable. When imported into England, these commodities paid duties, but, when shipped to another colony, either no or very slight customs were levied by the local authorities and none of course by England, and thus the colonial consumer fared much better than his fellow in the mother country. Moreover, when reëxported from England, only a part of the duties collected there was repaid, and consequently such goods were under some disadvantage in competing in foreign markets with those shipped there directly from the colonies in violation of the law.[1] The latter was a very important consideration, and was brought to the attention of Parliament by some merchants engaged in the Virginia trade, who complained "that New England men did carry much tobaccoe & other Commoditys of the Growth of the plantations to New England, & from thence did carry them to fforraigne nations, whereby they could undersell them & Lessen his ma[ties] Customes."[2]

other reasons as well, the Commissioners advised its release. The Attorney-General, Sir Robert Sawyer, did not agree with this report, stating that the Canaries were a part of Africa, and that the law must be construed in accordance with the geographical facts. Accordingly, Governor Andros was instructed to discharge the seizure and the bond given to abide by the decision of the case in England. Blathwayt, Journal I, ff. 201–203, 210. See also Goodrick, Randolph VI, p. 195.

[1] 25 Ch. II, c. 7, § ii, explicitly gives these as the two reasons for the duties imposed thereby.

[2] This statement and the following facts regarding the passage of the law are derived from a letter of Edward Thornburgh, on behalf of the Com-

Upon learning of this complaint, the Committee of Gentlemen Planters, who looked after the interests of Barbados in England, appeared before the parliamentary committee having this matter under consideration. They assured this body that all the sugar exported from the West Indies to New England (except what was consumed there) was ultimately brought to England, and that it was impossible for the New England traders to ship it to Spain and Portugal, where the English product was prohibited, or to France, because of the high impost there. These Barbadians likewise pointed out how necessary to them was their trade with New England, and further "Possessed seuerall Parliam^t men how impracticable it was for them to Lay a tax on those that had noe members in theire house." [1] Parliament, however, was not converted by these arguments, and early in 1673[2] passed a law laying export duties on the enumerated products when shipped to another colony.[3] The Act provided that, if any vessel should lade any of

mittee of Gentlemen Planters, to the Barbados Assembly, dated April 1, 1673. C. O. 31/2, ff. 123, 124; C. C. 1669–1674, p. 475. In "Some Observations about the Plantations," it was also said that these 1673 duties were "wholly made in reference to New-England." Brit. Mus., Add. MSS. 28,079, f. 85.

[1] They pointed out "the great necessity the Sugar Plantations had of a trade with them for Boards timber pipstaues horses & fish, & that they could not mainetaine theire buildings, nor send home theire Sugars, nor make aboue halfe that quantity without a Supply of those things from New England."

[2] These duties are occasionally referred to as those of 1672. The bill was, however, agreed to by the House of Lords on March 29, 1673. Com. Journal IX, p. 281.

[3] 25 Ch. II, c. 7, § ii.

these commodities, and also cocoa-nuts,[1] without first giving bond to take them to England and nowhere else, then there should be paid certain duties, which were roughly based on those imposed by the English tariff of 1660, generally known as the Old Subsidy.[2] Of these duties by far the most important were those on tobacco and sugar,[3] which were the

[1] Although sometimes so stated, cocoa-nuts were not placed on the enumerated list by the statute. A duty of 1d. a lb. was merely imposed if they were exported elsewhere than to England. This error even crops up in unexpected quarters. In the draft instructions for the customs officials in America, prepared by the Customs Board and sent by them in 1697 to the House of Lords, appears on the margin of § 3 a list of the enumerated commodities in which were included cocoa-nuts. House of Lords MSS. (1695–1697), II, p. 473. Elsewhere this list is correctly given. *Ibid.* p. 17.

[2]

	PLANTATION DUTIES OF 1673	ENGLISH DUTIES OF 1660
Sugar: white *per cwt.*	5s.	5s.
brown and muscovado *per cwt.*	1s. 6d.	1s. 6d.
Tobacco *per lb.*	1d.	2d.[a]
Cotton-wool *per lb.*	$\frac{1}{2}$d.	free
Indigo *per lb.*	2d.	$\frac{5}{12}$d.
Ginger *per cwt.*	1s.	1s.
Logwood *per cwt*[b]	£5	——
Fustic and other dyeing-woods *per cwt.*	6d.	3d.
Cocoa-nuts *per lb.*	1d.	2s. 6d. *per cwt.*

[a] The subsidy of 1660 itself imposed a duty of only 1d., but in the Book of Rates of 1660 provision was made for an additional duty of 1d.

[b] It was presumably an error for £5 a ton. 13 & 14 Ch. II, c. 11, §§ xxvi, xxvii, allowed the importation of logwood into England, and imposed a duty of £5 a ton. It may be mentioned that Charles II granted the revenue from these logwood duties in England to Nell Gwyn for twenty-one years from Sept. 29, 1683 on. Treas. Books, Out-Letters, Customs 8, ff. 239, 273; 10, f. 36.

[3] *Cf.* C. O. 29/3, 7.

only commodities entering extensively into intercolonial commerce. The sugar duties were the same as those of the English tariff of 1660; on raw sugar, the most important variety, they amounted to one shilling and sixpence the hundredweight, a not inconsiderable tax. On tobacco the duty imposed was one-penny a pound, which was only one-half of the English customs of 1660, possibly because the legislators overlooked the additional duty of one-penny imposed at the same time in the Book of Rates annexed to the statute.

Though distinctly in the form of a revenue bill, the main purpose of this law was to render unprofitable violations of the enumeration clauses of the Act of 1660.[1] Some revenue of but insignificant size, it is true, was naturally derived from it, but this was an incidental feature.[2] Even

[1] Forty years after its passage, the question arose whether these duties were payable on some sugar shipped from St. Christopher to Nevis for trans-shipment to England. In support of the affirmative, it was argued that the Leeward Islands were distinct colonies, each under a lieutenant-governor with separate assemblies, although in extraordinary cases the governor-general could call a general assembly, capable of making laws binding all the islands. April 28, 1715, the Attorney-General, Sir Edward Northey, gave his opinion that the intent of the law was to impose the duties when the goods were shipped from colony to colony for sale, but not if merely for further trans-shipment, and that consequently these duties were not payable in the case before him. Brit. Mus., Hargrave MSS. 275, f. 39ᵇ; Add. MSS. 8,832, ff. 245–249. However equitable this decision, it grossly misrepresented the purposes of the law.

[2] The earliest original colonial account that I have seen is one from Barbados, giving the details of the collection of £63 from 27 vessels during the latter half of 1679. The destination of these vessels was, to Virginia 10, to New England 9, to Carolina 4, to New York 2, to the Bermudas 1, and to Newfoundland 1. C. O. 33/13, 2. There is extant, however, an account pre-

when these duties were paid, the goods were still subject to the enumeration regulation and could not be reshipped from the intermediate colony directly to foreign markets. The wording of the law was somewhat ambiguous on this point, but the English government ruled decisively in favor of this interpretation,[1] and all question was definitely removed by a clause in the great administrative statute of 1696.[2]

These three Acts of Parliament — the Navigation Act of 1660, the Staple Act of 1663, and that of 1673 imposing the Plantation Duties — constitute the economic framework of the old colonial system. They have hitherto been consid-

pared by the Comptroller-General of the Customs in England in 1679, giving in detail the quantities of these commodities, with the duties paid thereon in each West Indian island during the year beginning Sept. 29, 1677. In submitting this account, the Comptroller stated that no accounts had hitherto come from New England, and that those from Virginia, Antigua, and some of the other colonies were still in the hands of the Auditor. The major portion of these commodities consisted of 962,166 lbs. of sugar shipped mainly to New England and Virginia, on which about £640 must have been collected. 57,409 lbs. of cotton were shipped, virtually all to New England, on which the duty amounted to about £120. Brit. Mus., Add. MSS. 8133ᶜ, f. 237; C. O. 1/43, 180.

[1] In 1676, in consequence of a complaint that some New England merchants were violating the enumeration clauses, this point was submitted to the Attorney-General by the Lords of Trade. In reply, Sir William Jones stated that these goods were still subject to the enumeration clauses of the Act of 1660. C. O. 5/903, f. 106; C. O. 324/4, ff. 29, 30; C. C. 1675–1676, pp. 337, 350; Chalmers, Political Annals (London, 1780), pp. 319, 323, 324. The officials in America were instructed so to interpret and enforce the law. N. Y. Col. Doc. III, p. 384; Mass. Hist. Soc. Coll., 3d series, VII, pp. 132, 133.

[2] 7 & 8 W. III, c. 22, § viii; House of Lords MSS. (1695–1697) II, p. 478. Hence, as often as these goods were shipped from colony to colony, so often were these duties payable.

ered solely with reference to England and the colonies; it remains now to see what provision was made for regulating the trade between the English colonies and Scotland and Ireland. On the Restoration, the union of the three kingdoms in the British Isles that had been effected by Cromwell, and which in the eyes of some constitutes one of his two chief titles to everlasting fame,[1] was again dissolved. Scotland again became a separate kingdom, united to England only by virtue of a common sovereign, and Ireland once more reverted to its status of a subordinate principality.

As the American colonies were dominions of the English Crown, it is not surprising that free intercourse between them and Scotland was not allowed.[2] The Navigation Act of 1660 treated Scottish ships as unfree,[3] and excluded them

---

[1] Cf. John Morley, Cromwell, p. 466; Seeley, British Policy II, p. 103; Goldwin Smith, The United Kingdom, II, p. 21.

[2] It should also be pointed out that the enumerated articles could not be imported into the Channel Islands and that European goods could not be shipped directly from them to the colonies. The States of Jersey desired some modification of the law, but this was refused as no adequate means could be devised to prevent the enumerated goods from being shipped from that island to foreign ports. The law was, however, occasionally evaded, and some seizures were made in consequence thereof. P. C. Register Charles II, XI, ff. 159, 160, 178; P. C. Cal. I, pp. 568–570, 574, 587, 588, 657–659, 666, 748, 749; C. C. 1675–1676, pp. 358, 359; C. O. 388/5, 420; Cal. Treas. Books, 1669–1672, pp. 1011, 1027, 1030, 1034, 1170. The Isle of Man was likewise outside of the English fiscal barriers and the same regulations applied to it.

[3] It was, however, provided by 12 Ch. II, c. 18, § xvi, that aliens' duties should not be levied on corn and salt of Scottish production, or on fish caught and cured by Scotsmen and imported by them directly in Scottish-built ships, whereof the master and three-quarters of the mariners were subjects of Charles II. Cf. Cal. Treas. Books, 1660–1667, p. 325.

from the colonial trade. Under it the enumerated articles could not be shipped directly from the colonies to Scotland; and, furthermore, the Staple Act of 1663 prohibited the direct shipment from Scotland to the colonies of anything but servants, horses, and provisions.

In consequence of some remonstrances from Scotland,[1] the Privy Council on August 30, 1661, temporarily suspended the Navigation Act in so far as it applied to that kingdom, and ordered the officers of the customs to investigate this question.[2] On October 30, 1661,[3] they reported that the suspension of the Navigation Act in favor of Scotland would greatly injure the English customs by freeing many goods from the payment of the aliens' duties.   Moreover, they said, it would give Scotland liberty to trade to the colonies, "which are absolutely English which will bring infinite losse to his Majestie and as much prejudice to the English Subject." For the Scottish merchants, they pointed out, could not be effectively bound to bring the colonial products to England and Ireland, but would either ship them directly to foreign countries or make Scotland "the Magazine" for their supply "and leaue this Nation to its home Consumption." They concluded with the significantly typical statement that "the Plantacons are his Maties Indies wthout charge to him raised & Supported by the English Subjects who imploy aboue 200 Saile of good Ships every yeare, breed

---

[1] Cal. Dom. 1661–1662, p. 74.

[2] P. C. Cal. I, p. 318.

[3] S. P. Dom. Charles II, XLIV, no. 12.   That part of the report referring to the colonial trade is in P. C. Cal. I, pp. 319, 320.   An outline is in C. C. 1661–1668, no. 178, and in Cal. Dom. 1661–1662, p. 135.

abundance of Marin[rs] and begin to grow into Commodities of great Value and esteeme, and though Some of them Continue in Tobacco yet upon the Returne hither it Smells well, and paies more Custome to his Ma[tie] than the East Indies four times ouer."

This adverse report was referred by the Privy Council to a special committee,[1] and as they fully supported its conclusions,[2] on November 22, 1661, an order was issued abrogating the temporary suspension of the preceding August and again subjecting Scotland and her shipping to the pains and penalties of the Navigation Act.[3] Scotland's retort to England's exclusive policy had been the passage in 1661 of her own Navigation Act, directly modelled on that of England.[4] This law contained a clause exempting English and Irish vessels, provided in return Scottish ships should receive similarly favorable treatment from England. On England

---

[1] Cal. Dom. 1661–1662, pp. 135, 136.

[2] On Nov. 18, 1661, Treasurer Southampton and Lord Ashley reported to the King: "If the liberty allowed by the Order of Councell were fit to be granted to the Scotch nation it could only be done by Act of Parliament . . . and those noble lords of the Scotch nation which first petitioned for the liberty did onely pray that their suite might by your Majesty be recommended to the Parliament. Concerning the liberty itselfe petitioned for, we find it contrary to the maine end of the Act of Parliament which aimed at the increase of English shipping and employment of English mariners." Moreover, they said, such a liberty would decrease the customs revenue, for even in the proposition made by the Earls of Lauderdale and Crawford, that five or six Scottish ships might have freedom to trade to the colonies and return thence to Scotland, "your Majesties Customes might be concerned thereby near 20,000 l. by the yeare." Cal. Treas. Books, 1660–1667, pp. 305, 306.

[3] P. C. Cal. I, pp. 318–320; Cal. Treas. Books, 1660–1667, p. 325.

[4] Acts of Parliament of Scotland (1820), VII, p. 257.

refusing to concede this point, the Scottish law was enforced,[1] but it was naturally ineffective in securing more liberal treatment, since Scotland's economic resources were not only in themselves meagre, but also still largely undeveloped, and hence its trade offered but few attractions to the English merchants in comparison with that to the American plantations.

While Scottish ships were thus excluded from the colonial trade, in a few exceptional and sporadic instances the Crown used its much-questioned authority to dispense with the law in their favor. In 1663 and in 1664, one John Browne, who held a patent for erecting a sugar refinery in Scotland, was granted licenses to trade to the colonies with four Scottish ships, provided they returned directly to Scotland or England.[2] In 1669, with a view to stimulating the development of New York, permission was given to two Scottish ships, with such persons as should desire to settle there, to trade between that colony and Scotland, provided no colonial products whatsoever were carried to the dominions of any foreign prince.[3] The Farmers of the Customs forthwith complained that this order was ambiguous and would allow these vessels to take the enumerated goods to any of the King's dominions; that these ships might injure the English customs revenue to the extent of £7000 yearly and that the permission was in direct opposition to

[1] Theodora Keith, Commercial Relations of England and Scotland, 1603–1707, p. 115.

[2] Brit. Mus., Add. MSS. 35,125, f. 74; C. C. 1661–1668, nos. 543, 848, 867.

[3] P. C. Cal. I, p. 512; N. Y. Col. Doc. III, p. 180; C. C. 1669–1674, p. 13.

three Acts of Parliament. They, therefore, prayed for its revocation, unless these ships should first touch at an English port, there pay the customs and enter into a bond not to carry any colonial goods elsewhere than to England or the other colonies.[1] In reply, it was stated that the design of the Duke of York in securing this permission was merely to transport planters to New York, and that, while the desired bond regarding the return voyage would be conceded, no Scottish ship could possibly, without ruin to the adventurers, touch at an English port on her outward voyage, 'by reason of demurrage on contrary winds or other accidents.'[2] Accordingly, the permission was modified, and permission was granted to two Scottish vessels to sail to New York with not less than four hundred planters, provided they took with them only commodities of England, Scotland, or Ireland and returned from New York either to some other English colony or to England.[3]

While Scotland was debarred to a great extent, and her ships entirely, from direct trade with the English colonies,[4] Scotsmen as subjects of Charles II could legally settle in the colonies and trade there on the same terms as English-

[1] N. Y. Col. Doc. III, pp. 180, 181; C. C. 1669–1674, p. 16.

[2] N. Y. Col. Doc. III, pp. 181, 182; C. C. 1669–1674, pp. 16, 17.

[3] P. C. Cal. I, pp. 516, 517. A letter from New York, dated Dec. 31, 1669, states that these long expected ships had not yet arrived. C. C. 1669–1674, p. 47.

[4] In an age of such poor means of communication, there was naturally some evasion of the law. In 1678, Danby approved of the proposal of the Commissioners of the Customs to send a correspondent to Scotland to give an account of such ships as might come there directly from the English colonies. Cal. Treas. Books, 1676–1679, p. 1000.

men. For some time, however, this right was not fully
conceded. It rested on a well-established principle of the
English common law. Shortly after the accession of James I
to the throne of England, the law officers gave it as their opinion that, by the common law, Scotsmen born after that date
were Englishmen in the fullest sense of the term. "They
were born within the King's allegiance, and they must be
regarded as his subjects, as far as his dominions extended." [1]
This view was fully sustained in 1608 by the court in the
well-known "Calvin's Case." [2] According to this decision,
Scotsmen serving on an English vessel would not make it
unfree under the terms of the Navigation Act of 1660, which
provided that the master and three-quarters of the crew of
a legally qualified ship had to be English. The English
Parliament's answer to the Scottish Navigation Act of 1661
was the insertion of a clause in the Statute of Frauds in the
Customs of 1662, providing that "any of his Majesty's
subjects of England, Ireland, and his plantations, are to be
accounted English, and no others." [3]

According to the modern doctrine of parliamentary
sovereignty, this clause unquestionably superseded the
common law principle applicable to the case, and would
effectually have barred Scotsmen from service on English
ships, since it would have subjected them to the severe
penalties imposed on vessels with alien crews. But the
jurists of the day did not hold that Parliament was om-

[1] S. R. Gardiner, England, 1603–1642, I, p. 326.
[2] *Ibid.* pp. 355, 356.
[3] 13 & 14 Ch. II, c. 11, § vi.

nipotent.[1] For some time the point at issue was not definitely decided, and occasionally a ship was seized on account of its Scottish crew,[2] but toward the end of the century it was finally established that the common law principle, and not the statute, was the law of the land.[3]

As Ireland, unlike Scotland, was not a sister kingdom whose rank, theoretically at least, was coördinate with that of England, its treatment under the colonial system was radically different.[4] The Navigation Act of 1660 placed

[1] *Cf.* C. H. McIlwain, The High Court of Parliament and its Supremacy.

[2] In 1670, Nicholas Bake wrote to Williamson, complaining that a ship had been seized and condemned in Barbados, on pretence that she was not manned with the required proportion ot Englishmen, the Scotsmen in her crew not being held to be such. He added that these Scotsmen 'take it wondrous unkind to be thus debarred the liberty of subjects. Many wish there were not this nice distinction between the nations.' C. O. 1/25, 17; C. C. 1669–1674, pp. 59, 60. In 1687, George Muschamp, the South Carolina Collector, also seized a ship on this ground. C. O. 1/60, 19; C. O. 324/5, ff. 2–4. In 1683, Governor Cranfield of New Hampshire wrote to Blathwayt: "Here are severall Scots men that inhabitt and are great interlopers and bring in quantities of goods underhand from Scotland." He requested the ruling of the Attorney-General on the legality of Scotsmen acting as merchants or factors in the colonies, stating that they claimed this right on the ground that they were born within the King's allegiance. Goodrick, Randolph VI, pp. 130–133.

[3] In 1698, the Solicitor-General, Sir John Hawles, held that a Scotsman must be accounted an Englishman within the Acts of Navigation despite this clause in the Act of 1662. Whatever the intent of Parliament might have been, he said, since by law a man born in Scotland is a subject of England, and since the two kingdoms, while they remain united, are accounted but one nation as to matters of privilege, "ye above Clause will not exclude a Scotsman from the priviledge of an English Subject." Brit. Mus., Add. MSS. 30,218, ff. 249^b–250^b. *Cf.* Chalmers, Political Annals, p. 258.

[4] A brief synopsis of this subject is in the MSS. of Marquess of Lothian (H.M.C. 1905), pp. 301–304.

Irish ships on an equal footing with those of England and the colonies,[1] and it was likewise fully conceded that Irishmen, being subjects of Charles II, could under the law constitute part or the whole of the crew of a legally manned English vessel.[2] Moreover, it was distinctly provided that the enumerated articles, and naturally all other colonial products as well, could be shipped directly from the colonies to Ireland. Thus, at the outset Ireland enjoyed the same privileges in the colonial trade as did England, or any one of the English colonies.[3] This liberal treatment was a result of an ill-defined tendency to regard Ireland as one of England's foreign plantations. Such a view was, however, at variance with the actual facts, for Ireland's status was a hybrid one. In addition to being an English plantation, that country was also a rival, though subject, kingdom with economic interests distinct from those of England. Hence some of the privileges at first freely conceded to Ireland as a colony pure and simple were subsequently withdrawn from the competing kingdom.

The Staple Act of 1663 prohibited the direct exportation from Ireland to the colonies of anything but servants, horses, and provisions.[4] As foodstuffs constituted the bulk of Ireland's exports, this prohibition was of no especial eco-

---

[1] 12 Ch. II, c. 18, §§ i, iii, v, vi, viii. See also the legal opinion of Sir William Jones, in Brit. Mus., Add. MSS. 30,218, f. 36.

[2] 13 & 14 Ch. II, c. 11, § vi.

[3] Conversely, Ireland was also subjected to the same restrictions as was England. An Act of 1660 prohibited the growing of tobacco in both England and Ireland. 12 Ch. II, c. 34.

[4] 15 Ch. II, c. 7, § v.

nomic significance.[1]   Another clause in this Act, however, was of greater importance, because it might be interpreted to mean that in future the enumerated goods could not be imported directly into Ireland from the colonies.[2]   But, as very frequently happened at the time, this clause was obscurely worded and the purpose of the legislature was far from clear.   All doubts were removed, however, by an Act of Parliament passed in 1671,[3] which specifically provided that in future these enumerated articles could not be shipped directly from the colonies to Ireland.[4]

The representatives of Barbados in London had vigorously opposed the passage of this law, which in the form that it first passed the House of Commons would have prevented the

[1] In 1683, Ireland's total exports were £570,342, of which £44,862 went to the colonies.   Brit. Mus., Sloane MSS. 2902, f. 137.

[2] Clause ix provided that any officer of the customs in England, allowing these enumerated goods to be carried to any place before they had been landed in England, should forfeit his place.

[3] Sir George Downing was also prominently connected with the passage of this law.   See especially Com. Journal IX, pp. 213, 214, 224, 226, 237, 238.   On Oct. 31, 1670, Downing wrote to Sir John Shaw: "Please send to my house to-morrow the bill for Plantation trade and against planting tobacco.   To-morrow being holiday I shall have leisure to look it over."   See also his letter of Dec. 5, 1670, about this matter.   Cal. Treas. Books, 1669–1672, pp. 679, 698.

[4] 22 & 23 Ch. II, c. 26, §§ x, xi, stated that the intent of clause ix in the Act of 1663 was that the enumerated goods could no longer be sent directly to Ireland, but that as this right under the Act of 1660 had not been expressly repealed, these commodities continued to be shipped there to the manifest disadvantage of England, in that the colonial trade "would thereby in a great measure be diverted from hence, and carried elsewhere, his Majesty's customs and other revenues much lessened, and this kingdom not continue a staple of the said commodities, nor that vent for the future of the victual and other native commodities of this kingdom."

importation of provisions into the West Indies not only from Ireland, but from New England as well. Owing to their efforts, these far-reaching clauses were omitted by the House of Lords.[1] The chief trade affected by the Act of 1671 was, however, not that of the West Indies, but that with Virginia and Maryland, for Ireland consumed a quantity of tobacco totally disproportionate to its wealth and population.[2] The complaints of the Irish merchants were voiced by the Lord-Lieutenant, the Earl of Essex, who wrote in 1672 to Arlington that the great decay in Ireland's trade was primarily due to this law.[3] His proposal for its modification was vigorously opposed by the English Commissioners of the Customs, who reported that, according to the usual

[1] On Dec. 6, 1671, the Assembly of Barbados wrote to the Committee of Gentlemen Planters in London, that they had heard of a recent Act of Parliament which prohibited the direct shipment of their sugars to Ireland; they had given little credit to this report, but if such a law were in agitation, the committee should try to prevent its passage. C. O. 31/2, ff. 87–91; C. C. 1669–1674, p. 284. In reply, the Gentlemen Planters wrote on June 12, 1672, that this matter had been regulated during the last session of Parliament, and that, though they were in constant attendance, the bill had passed the House of Commons without their knowledge, "butt before itt passed the house of Lords wee putt in many objections to itt, and gott seuerall Clauses of itt left out & altered, which would have wholy excluded a Supply of Provisions not onely from Ireland, but New England & other places allsoe, which was as much, as was possible to be Done." C. O. 31/2, ff. 100, 101; C. C. 1669–1674, p. 369.

[2] "The one luxury of all persons was tobacco, and Petty estimated that two-sevenths of a man's whole expenditure in food went in purchasing this article." A. E. Murray, Commercial Relations between England and Ireland, p. 20.

[3] "Before this Act this Kingdome had setled a considerable Trade thither of Beef, Butter, and Tallow, and other commodities wth wch this country abounds." Essex Papers (Camden Society, 1890) I, pp. 35, 36.

practice, the trade of the English colonies was reserved to their mother country, and that to permit even a limited amount of unrestricted trade between them and Ireland would be prejudicial to England, "for by such an allowance y⁰ Kingdome of Ireland will have yᵉ oportunity of vending not only their owne manufactures, but those also of other parts of Europe in yᵉ Plantačons, when only those of England were before sold." [1] This report was approved by the government and Essex's proposal was rejected.[2]

More than such firm adherence to principles on the part of the English government was required to secure the enforcement of this law in Ireland, where public opinion was hostile. The English Treasury appointed a representative in Ireland to prevent the landing of enumerated goods from the colonies,[3] and the Irish customs officials were especially instructed not to permit such illegal practices.[4] But the law was only very imperfectly enforced.[5] The enumeration of tobacco was extensively evaded by vessels from the

---

[1] *Ibid.* I, pp. 54–56.

[2] Cal. Treas. Books, 1672–1675, pp. 72, 73. Essex based his plea for permission for twenty Irish ships to trade freely to the colonies on Ireland's sufferings as a result of the war. In addition to informing him of the adverse report of the Commissioners of the Customs, Treasurer Clifford emphasized the fact that England was bearing the entire burden of the Dutch war.

[3] *Ibid.* 1669–1672, p. 1280. In 1678, Danby appointed four men to ferret out infractions of this law. *Ibid.* 1676–1679, p. 1046. See also Treas. Books, Out-Letters, Customs 5, ff. 14, 42, 63–65.

[4] Cal. Treas. Books, 1669–1672, p. 1197; *ibid.* 1672–1675, p. 367.

[5] In 1673, Treasurer Clifford enumerated nine ships that had sailed from the colonies (four from New England, one from Antigua, one from Montserrat, two from Nevis, and one from Virginia) directly to Ireland with such prohibited goods. *Ibid.* 1672–1675, p. 35.

colonies sailing directly to Irish ports under "pretences of Shipwrack and other fraudulent Devices." As the Farmers of the Irish Revenue connived at these frauds,[1] the English government was helpless until it was held that the English Admiralty had authority to seize the offending vessels in Ireland.[2] During the years 1678 to 1680, a large number of vessels were seized in Ireland on warrants of the English Admiralty for importing tobacco directly from the colonies.[3]

[1] The English merchants complained that, although tobacco could not be legally imported into Ireland from the colonies, "nevertheless they of Ireland and New England and some from Virginia have and do come, by consent and without any seizure, for none can make a seizure but the Custom House officers, who in Ireland are the farmers' servants and dare not seize, it being their masters' interest to have all they can brought there." Cal. Dom. 1676–1677, pp. 586, 587.

[2] The opinion of the Attorney-General, Sir William Jones, may be found in Brit. Mus., Add. MSS. 30,218, ff. 40, 41. See also P. C. Register Charles II, XV, f. 119; B. T. Trade Papers 11, 189; P. C. Cal. I, pp. 845, 846; Cal. Treas. Books, 1676–1679, p. 170. In 1686, the Commissioners of the Irish Revenue stated ' that while the law was in force during the nine years already mentioned, all the plantation goods were imported direct into Ireland as freely as when the trade was open by the Navigation Act.' This statement is grossly exaggerated, and was made with the direct purpose of securing a repeal of the law. C. O. 324/4, ff. 183–191; C. C. 1685–1688, pp. 152, 153.

[3] These ships were chiefly Irish. Records of the trials of approximately 25 are extant. Nearly all of this tobacco came directly from Virginia and Maryland; only a small quantity was imported from Antigua. Virtually no sugar was imported in these vessels. Details may be found in Public Record Office, Admiralty High Court, Libels 118, ff. 89, 91, 112–114; 119, ff. 1, 2, 16, 17, 39, 41, 62, 63, 71, 80, 97–99, 104, 124, 145, 148, 167, 170, 173, 188; 120, ff. 19, 61, 105. One of the most interesting cases concerned the *Providence* of London, belonging to Colonel John Curtis (? Custis) of Virginia, which had landed 300 hogsheads of tobacco in Ireland toward the end of 1678. *Ibid.* 119, ff. 101, 176; 120, f. 23; Ormonde MSS. (H.M.C. 1906), New Series IV, pp. 304, 305.

Immediately thereafter the state of affairs again changed. The Act of 1671 prohibiting the direct shipment of the enumerated colonial products to Ireland contained a clause limiting its duration to nine years. Its date of expiration fell at a time when England was in a whirl of frenzied excitement in consequence of the "Popish Plot" and the subsequent abortive proposal to exclude James, Duke of York, from the succession to the throne. Apparently as a result of its absorption in these heated questions, Parliament inadvertently failed to make any provision for the continuation of the Act of 1671. Accordingly, from 1680 on, all colonial commodities could again be freely shipped directly to Ireland. A curious and entirely unanticipated state of affairs now resulted, for in the meanwhile the Act of 1673 had been passed imposing export duties on the enumerated articles, unless the condition of the bond was to ship them to England only. On the expiration of the Act of 1671, the law regulating the terms of these bonds was that of 1660, which provided that all vessels sailing from England to the colonies should give security to bring these products to England or Ireland. If the English vessels engaged in this trade should give such bonds, according to the terms of the law of 1673, the export duties imposed thereby would then become due on all these products laden by them, even if they were shipped to England. In order to obviate this unforeseen result, which would greatly have hampered English trade, early in 1681 an Order in Council was issued, allowing these vessels to give bonds omitting the word Ireland, in which case the duties would not be payable.

The order, however, not only did not provide any remedy for the Irish colonial trade, but distinctly stated that these duties of 1673 were payable on the enumerated products when shipped either to Ireland or to the English colonies.[1]

Thus, while the enumerated goods could, after the expiration of the Act of 1671, be shipped directly to Ireland, according to the letter of another law, the plantation duties of 1673 then became due thereon. Although the law on this point was plain, yet the result was mainly fortuitous and was apparently not the intent of the legislature. Hence it is not surprising that there ensued in the colonies, especially in Maryland, some difficulties based on a misunderstanding of the law and a natural reluctance to pay taxes whose validity was plainly open to question on other than purely legal grounds.

In Maryland, the proprietor, Lord Baltimore, was engaged at this time in a characteristic quarrel with the English customs officials, one of whom, Nicholas Badcock,[2] wrote on May 26, 1681,[3] to the Commissioners of the Customs that four ships had arrived from England with certificates of having given bonds containing the word Ireland, and that accordingly he had demanded the 1673 duties on the tobacco laden on them, which he claimed would amount to at least £2500. Payment thereof, he further wrote, was refused, with the support of Lord Baltimore and the Maryland

[1] C. O. 1/46, 97; C. O. 324/4, ff. 130–135; P. C. Cal. II, pp. 15, 16; C. C. 1681–1685, p. 9.

[2] He was Surveyor and Comptroller of the Customs, and subordinate to the Collector. C. C. 1681–1685, p. 164.

[3] C. O. 1/146, 150; C. C. 1681–1685, pp. 58, 59.

Council, who told him not to meddle in this matter. Baltimore was apparently sincere in his attitude, being pardonably ignorant of the law. His letter of June 7, 1681,[1] to Lord Anglesey shows a complete failure to grasp the point at issue.[2] The English government carefully investigated the charges of Badcock, and decided to reprimand Baltimore severely and to order him to pay the £2500, which it was claimed the revenue had lost by his interference.[3] Accordingly, on February 8, 1682, the Secretary of State, in the name of Charles II, wrote a vigorous letter, calling Baltimore sharply to account for obstructing the revenue officers and threatening him with legal proceedings against his charter.[4] In reply, Baltimore wrote to Sir Leoline Jenkins, then Secretary of State, that he was very much troubled at the King's letter, and that the difficulty was due to his ignorance of the law and to Badcock's wilfully con-

[1] C. C. 1681–1685, p. 67.

[2] On July 10, 1681, Nicholas Badcock again wrote to the Commissioners of the Customs, saying that he was about to seize the tobacco in question, on which these duties had not been paid, but had been deterred by threats of the Governor and Council. C. O. 5/723, ff. 61–65; C. C. 1681–1685, p. 85.

[3] C. O. 391/3, f. 317; C. C. 1681–1685, pp. 151, 157. On behalf of the Commissioners of the Customs, Sir George Downing attended the Lords of Trade, and informed them that Lord Baltimore was in error and that the plantation duty of 1d. was payable on tobacco shipped from Maryland to Ireland. On Dec. 14, 1681, the Maryland Collector of the Customs, Christopher Rousby, with whom Baltimore was engaged in a serious quarrel, wrote to a member of the colonial Council, that Baltimore's behavior toward Badcock in this matter of the 1d. duty had been very much resented by the Lords of the Privy Council. C. C. 1681–1685, pp. 159, 160.

[4] P. C. Cal. II, pp. 28–31; C. C. 1681–1685, pp. 195, 196.

cealing both the instructions he had received from the Commissioners of the Customs and the Order in Council of 1681 enjoining the payment of the plantation duties on shipments to Ireland.[1]

In this connection the English government renewed its orders for the collection of the 1673 plantation duties in such cases.[2] The colonial customs service was, however, not effectively organized, and as a result the payment of these duties was extensively evaded.[3] In order to put a stop to this, the English government issued orders to seize the enumerated goods in Ireland in case the duties thereon had not been paid.[4] The Commissioners of the Irish Revenue thereupon suggested that it would be found more advantageous if, in lieu of the export duties payable in the colonies, one-half thereof should be collected in Ireland and remitted to the English Exchequer. This suggestion met with approval, and the colonial governors were then instructed to

[1] C. C. 1681–1685, pp. 232, 233. *Cf.* pp. 241, 242.

[2] The Maryland Collector of the Customs, Christopher Rousby, was instructed by the Customs and the Treasury to collect these duties when the bond mentioned Ireland. C. C. 1681–1685, pp. 159, 160.

[3] July 24, 1682, the Lords of the Treasury wrote to the Earl of Arran, Lord Deputy of Ireland, that the Commissioners of the Customs had informed them that several ships had sailed from the colonies to Ireland without paying the 1673 duties and that, as a remedy therefor, they had appointed Mr. Charles Horne to inspect and look after the plantation trade of Ireland. Ormonde MSS. (H.M.C. 1911), New Series VI, pp. 404, 405.

[4] "My Lord Treasurer Sent to the Lord Lieut of Ireland the opinions of the four Barons of the Exchequer, Attorney and Solicitor Generall, that the Enumerated Goods coming from the Plantations without having paid the Plantation Duty might be seized and Recovered in Ireland, and Orders were given to all Officers accordingly." C. O. 1/58, 84.

desist from collecting the 1673 duties on tobacco exported to Ireland.[1]

This arrangement had been in effect only a very short time,[2] when, much to the annoyance of the Irish merchants,[3] Parliament in 1685 revived the Act of 1671 prohibiting the direct exportation of these enumerated goods to Ireland.[4] Owing to their complaints, the Irish government worked actively to have the law changed. On February 15, 1686,[5] the Commissioners of the Irish Revenue wrote to the Lord-Lieutenant, stating that the half duty collected in Ireland on the enumerated colonial products had during the last six months of 1685 amounted to £5170, which was more than the entire sum that had been collected in all the colonies during ten years on account of the plantation duties. Consequently, they argued, that this arrangement was far more advantageous to England than was the total prohibition which had just been revived and which had never been effectively enforced. Moreover, they claimed that the revival of the law of 1671 would deprive Ireland of her entire colonial commerce, on account both of the additional hazard

[1] *Ibid.;* C. O. 324/4, ff. 183–191; C. C. 1685–1688, pp. 152, 153.

[2] *Cf.* Treas. Books, Out-Letters, Customs 10, f. 50.

[3] "The merchants in this country (Ireland) are much dejected at the revival of the act prohibiting them to trade directly to the Plantations, and especially at the prohibition of carrying hides and tallow into England." July 14, 1685, Sir John Perceval to Sir Robert Southwell. MSS. of Earl of Egmont (H.M.C. 1909) II, p. 157. *Cf.* p. 155.

[4] Com. Journal IX, p. 682; 1 Jac. II, c. 17. This law was subsequently continued and virtually made perpetual. 4 & 5 W. & M. c. 24; 11 & 12 W. III, c. 13, § ii; 5 Geo. I, c. 11, § xix.

[5] C. O. 324/4, ff. 183–191; C. C. 1685–1688, pp. 152, 153.

and time required by an indirect trade through England, and the expense and formalities necessitated in passing through the English customs. The Lord-Lieutenant, the Earl of Clarendon, sent this memorial, which he had ordered prepared in consequence of the complaints of the Irish merchants, to the English Lord Treasurer, and in his accompanying letter heartily supported its recommendations as advantageous both to England and to Ireland. He wrote that he had heard the English debates on this subject, 'which were not as ingenuous as I could have wished, or as such debates ought to be,' and suggested that the King dispense with the law for a year or two, as a trial, in order to see if the English revenue would suffer at all.[1]

This recommendation laid stress only on the fiscal side of the subject and ignored entirely the broader question of colonial policy. This phase of the subject was strongly emphasized by the English Commissioners of the Customs,[2] to whom the Irish memorial had been submitted for report. They brushed aside the question of revenue and pointed out that 'the true interest of England, as is also the usage of all nations, is to keep the Plantation-trade to herself.'[3] After answering in detail the Irish arguments, some of which were grossly exaggerated, they concluded their adverse report with the general statement, that the position of Ireland and its cheap provisions gave the Irish merchants a great advantage, so much so that, if they were allowed to

[1] C. O. 324/4, ff. 178–183 ; C. C. 1685–1688, pp. 160, 161.
[2] Sir Dudley North was at this time a prominent member of the board.
[3] C. O. 324/4, ff. 207–213 ; C. C. 1685–1688, pp. 166, 167.

trade on equal terms with those of England, they would in all probability deprive that kingdom in a great measure of its flourishing trade with its own colonies.

In reply, the Irish Commissioners prepared another detailed memorial,[1] again laying most stress on the fiscal side of the question and showing conclusively that the English revenue would to no extent whatsoever suffer from their proposal. They also claimed that there was no conceivable likelihood of Ireland drawing the plantation trade away from England and that the prohibition to import the enumerated articles directly into Ireland was of absolutely no benefit to England, but placed an unnecessary and onerous burden on the Irish merchants. This memorial was skilfully composed, but whatever chance of impartial consideration its able arguments might otherwise have had was lost by the tactless introduction of some direct charges of corruption against English customs officials in Bristol and in some other out-ports. The Commissioners of the Customs were plainly annoyed at these accusations, and in their final report of May 12, 1686,[2] refused to budge from their former opinion, stating that the entire body of the plantation laws was under their care and control, and that it was their business to correspond with the officials in England and in the colonies and to maintain a uniform and efficient system. This duty, they claimed, they could not perform, 'nor be responsible for it, if so great and near a kingdom as Ireland be freely let into the trade and suffered to trade directly with the

[1] C. O. 324/4, ff. 191–206; C. C. 1685–1688, pp. 175–177.
[2] C. O. 324/4, ff. 213–218; C. C. 1685–1688, pp. 187, 188.

Colonies.' The Lords of Trade accepted this report, and fresh orders were issued for the enforcement of the Act of 1671.[1]

During this controversy, the Earl of Clarendon had suggested that the King should, as an experiment, temporarily dispense with the Act of 1671, and cited an instance as a precedent for the legality of such action. In the constitutional disputes under the last two Stuarts this right of the Crown to dispense with the execution of Acts of Parliament figured prominently, but, in general, it was used sparingly in connection with the laws of trade and navigation.[2] Although it was directly contrary to the law, the government authorized Spanish vessels to trade to the English West Indies for slaves.[3] This power was, however, used on a comprehensive scale only during the two Dutch

[1] C. O. 324/4, f. 225; C. C. 1685–1688, pp. 204, 207, 264; P. C. Cal. II, p. 92. At this time were reported a number of evasions of the law. C. C. 1685–1688, p. 171; P. C. Cal. II, pp. 86, 87.

[2] In 1663, on reading a petition and some complaints about violations of the Navigation Act, the House of Commons resolved that His Majesty be desired to issue a proclamation for the effectual observance of this law "without any Dispensation or Contrivance whatsoever," whereby the Act may be violated, and to recall such dispensations if any had been granted. Com. Journal VIII, pp. 521, 522. As has already been pointed out, especial privileges were on a few occasions granted to Scotsmen. See *ante*, p. 88. In 1661, in connection with the case of three foreign Jews, who had resided in Barbados and were recommended to Charles II by the King of Denmark, the Council for Foreign Plantations reported on the whole question of allowing Jews to trade in the colonies. The Council left the larger question open, but advised giving a special license to these three men to reside in any English colony. C. C. 1661–1668, no. 140. On becoming English subjects, foreigners were of course allowed to trade in the colonies.

[3] See *post*, Chapter V.

wars, when the demands of the navy for men [1] made it advisable to permit English merchants to employ foreign seamen and ships. On March 6, 1665, an Order in Council was issued, dispensing with the Navigation Act in certain branches of the European trade, and allowing the employment by English merchants of foreign ships navigated by foreigners in the colonial trade.[2] On the conclusion of the war, in 1667, this dispensation was revoked;[3] but in 1672, on the outbreak of fresh hostilities with the Dutch, it was again issued [4] and remained in force until the conclusion of peace.[5]

[1] During peace the navy employed 3000 to 4000 seamen, but in 1665, 30,000 were needed. Pepys Diary, Jan. 15, 1665.

[2] The dispensation did not extend to the enumeration clauses or to the Staple Act of 1663. P. C. Register Charles II, V, ff. 68, 83; C. O. 324/4, ff. 219–224; P. C. Cal. I, pp. 392, 393, 403, 404. Cf. also Cal. Treas. Books, 1660–1667, p. 714. For some instances of foreign ships being employed in this trade, see C. C. 1661–1668, nos. 1459, 1469, 1544; P. C. Cal. I, pp. 466–474. On Feb. 28, 1665, the Farmer of the Customs had reported that the Act of Navigation ought not to be dispensed with in the colonial trade, as it would give the French and other foreigners too much insight into it. The French, they said, had already begun to inquire busily and had imitated the English by planting tobacco in France, besides developing their own plantations in the West Indies. C. C. 1661–1668, no. 947.

[3] P. C. Cal. I, p. 434; British Royal Proclamations, 1603–1783 (Am. Antiqu. Soc. 1911), pp. 114–116.

[4] P. C. Register Charles II, X, ff. 237, 238; C. O. 140/3, ff. 323–325; P. C. Cal. I, pp. 576, 577; C. C. 1669–1674, p. 414. See also S. P. Dom. Ch. II, Entry Book 36, ff. 327, 328; P. C. Cal. I, p. 633; C. C. 1669–1674, p. 553.

[5] P. C. Cal. I, p. 599. Cf. pp. 612–614. The proclamation of March 11, 1674, recalled this dispensation. British Royal Proclamations, 1603–1783 (Am. Antiqu. Soc. 1911), pp. 119, 120.

The various Acts of Parliament, whose provisions, inter-pretation, and development have been described, constituted the economic framework of the old colonial system, which for nearly two centuries regulated the course of trade in the British Empire.   They were a direct expression of the current economic theory of colonization, and their aim was to secure to England the fullest possible benefits from the possession of over-sea dominions.   The primary function of the colony was to foster the development of English sea power, commerce, and industry.   But, apart from its eco-nomic aims, it was realized that this system of regulating imperial trade possessed other distinct advantages.   It inevitably led to the limitation of commerce to a few well-defined routes, and thus greatly facilitated the task of protection.   Furthermore, it was perceived that the closer the commercial relations between colony and metropolis, the more firmly knit would become the political ties bind-ing them together.   Thus Charles Davenant pointed out that 'the Bent and Design of the Navigation Act was to make those Colonies as much dependant as possible upon their Mother-Country,' and that any continued violations thereof would have dangerous consequences which could not easily be cured.   For, he said, if the colonies should fall into trading independently of England, in course of time, they might erect themselves into independent commonwealths, which ultimately we should not be able to master ; "by which means the Plantations, which now are a main Branch of our Wealth, may become a Strength to be turn'd against us." [1]

[1] Davenant, *op. cit.* II, pp. 85, 86.

Such a system of rigid control over the commerce of dependent communities was the current practice of all colonizing nations. It necessarily implied the subordination of the colony's economic interests to those of the metropolis, and as a result in theory at least, if not always fully in practice, it is repugnant to modern economic, political, and ethical ideas. But these modern ideas are largely the result of changed conditions and were totally inapplicable in the seventeenth century, when they would have seemed, and correctly so, merely the vagaries of an unpractical utopian out of touch with the forces that were making history. In general, the economists of the day supported with substantial unanimity the principles upon which the system was based, and even those with the most liberal tendencies did not question their application.[1] England sanctioned the movement of expansion; and, although it was mainly the work of private enterprise, she had in so doing to assume many onerous burdens, but with the distinct purpose of gaining in return specific benefits. It would have been deemed the height of folly to leave colonial trade unfettered and to allow foreign

[1] The four writers of the period holding the most liberal views regarding trade were Sir Josiah Child, Charles Davenant, Nicholas Barbon, and Sir Dudley North. W. J. Ashley, Surveys Historic and Economic, pp. 268, 269. Of these, Child and Davenant were staunch upholders of the colonial system. Barbon and North did not directly discuss this question, but from their general underlying views, especially those of North, it might be inferred that in some respects at least their approval would have been withheld. Bauer, "Barbon," in Palgrave's Dict. of Pol. Economy; Pfeiffer, "Barbon," in Revue d'Histoire des Doctrines Économiques et Sociales IV, pp. 63 *et seq.;* Dudley North, Discourses upon Trade (London, 1691); Roger North, Lives of the Norths (London, 1826) I, pp. 351, 352.

rivals to reap where England had sown and where she was still obliged to expend considerable energy in preventing the intrusion of lawless marauders and well-organized enemies. The system was by no means one-sided and did not appear to be so to the men of the day. As compensation for the restrictions on the trade of the colonies, England protected them and gave such of their products as were needed and wanted a monopoly of the home market.

The chief positive burden which England assumed was that of imperial defence, in return for which it was considered justifiable to restrict and mould the economic life of the colonies. At various times during the Restoration period considerable trouble was experienced with New England, whose recalcitrant attitude toward imperial control threatened to dislocate the colonial system before it was even established. In 1675, when matters were nearing a crisis, was prepared an able memorial, evidently by Robert Mason, the proprietor of New Hampshire, wherein was clearly expressed the prevailing view regarding the respective rights and duties of metropolis and colony.[1] This paper urged the government to send to New England commissioners, who should 'endeavor to show the advantages which may arise to them by a better confidence and correspondence with England and by their cheerful submission to those ordinary duties, customs, and regulations, which are set upon trade in all other His Majesty's dominions, colonies, and plantations.' These commissioners were further to

[1] C. O. 1/34, nos. 68, 69; C. O. 5/903, ff. 9–13; C. C. 1675–1676, pp. 222–224. *Cf.* C. O. 1/18, 46; C. C. 1661–1668, no. 706.

point out how inconsistent exemption from these rules
would be with the fact that the King of England "in all
Treaties, and by his Fleets at Sea takes New-England into
the Common Protection, and provides for its Safety as
belonging to this Crowne, and may therefore expect some
Measure out of the benefitt that arises to them in their
Trade by their being English and happy subjects of this
Crowne."

This same idea was also clearly expressed by John Cary,
who asserted that, under a properly regulated system of
colonial trade, England "standing like the Sun in the midst
of its Plantations would not only refresh them, but also
draw Profits from them; and indeed it's a matter of
exact Justice it should be so, for from hence it is Fleets of
Ships and Regiments of Soldiers are frequently sent for
their Defence, at the charge of the Inhabitants of this
Kingdom, besides the equal Benefit the Inhabitants there
receive with us from the Advantages expected by the Issue
of this War, the Security of Religion, Liberty, and Property,
towards the Charge whereof they contribute little though a
way may and ought to be found out to make them pay more,
by such insensible Methods as are both rational and prac-
ticable." [1]

---

[1] John Cary, An Essay on the State of England (Bristol, 1695), pp. 70,
71. Cary repeated these views in a letter dated Jan. 31, 1696, and
addressed to a correspondent, who had objected to his proposal to treat
Ireland's trade like that of the colonies. He pointed out that all nations
pursued a similar policy toward their colonies, and that England was entitled to some return from the fact that they were defended and secured at
her expense. Brit. Mus., Add. MSS. 5540, ff. 59–61.

As the burden of imperial defence fell upon England, it could also be argued conversely that, whenever there was a conflict of interest between colony and metropolis, the former should necessarily be subordinated to the latter. For the heart of the Empire, England, had to be considered before all else, since upon its sound condition depended the very existence of the colonies. Without the active and potential support of England, they would have been at the mercy of other European powers, and would unquestionably have been converted into dependencies of Holland, Spain, or France, with the inevitable loss of their characteristic institutions and civilization. Hence, even from the colonial standpoint, there was a vital necessity of having a prosperous and powerful metropolis able to hold its protecting ægis over them. Shortly after the Restoration, Sir John Wolstenholme, one of the Farmers of the Customs, wrote to Massachusetts, expressing his gratification at their declared readiness to obey the laws of trade and navigation, which tend "so much to advance his Majestys service and the true English interest, wherein I conceave the English plantations are as much concerned, if wayed with judgment and discretion, as ourselves here; for if we doe not maintaine here the honour and reputation of his Majesty and the nation which must be by our navigation and shipping, which are our walls, the plantations will be subject to be devoured by straingers."[1] Similarly, John Cary, the Bristol merchant whose opinions have been often cited in this work, wrote to a correspondent in Antigua:

[1] Hutchinson Papers II, p. 108.

"The true Interest of England is its Trade; if this receives a Baffle, England is neither able to Support its Self, nor the Plantations that depend upon it, & then consequently they must crumble into So many distinct independ.̣ Govern^{ts} & thereby becoming weak will be a Prey to any Stronger Power wch shall attacque them." [1]

From the very nature of the Empire's political organization it followed inevitably that the main burden of its defence had to be assumed by England. As was said in 1683, "small divided remote Governments being seldom able to defend themselves, the Burthen of the Protecting them all, must lye upon the chiefest Kingdom of *England.* . . . In case of war with forraign Nations, *England* commonly beareth the whole Burthen and charge, whereby many in *England* are utterly undone." [2] Up to 1689, when began the Second Hundred Years' War with France, this task of protecting the Empire was not an especially arduous one. Yet even during these comparatively peaceful years, there were several important naval wars — with the United

---

[1] Brit. Mus., Add. MSS. 5540, f. 76.

[2] England's Guide to Industry (London, 1683), pp. 75–77. The author of this ingenious booklet maintained that the chief impediment to England's greatness was the existence of distinct governments, divided from one another by customs barriers, in England, Scotland, Ireland, the Channel Islands, the Isle of Man, and the various colonies. "There is no doubt," he said, "that the same people far and wide dispersed must spend more upon their Government and Protection than the same living compactly." His policy of unification would apparently have implied the abrogation of the laws of trade, for in his opinion it was a "dammage" to England's trade with Barbados and the other colonies that goods should be enumerated. *Ibid.* pp. 75–78.

Provinces, Spain, and France. International rivalry was acute, and the colonizing maritime powers were watching one another most jealously and closely.[1] Thus, during both peace and war, the burden of defence was far from a negligible one. While England did not shirk the task and, despite much muddling, performed it without encountering any irretrievable disasters, she expected the colonies not to remain supine, but to do their share. What exactly this share was could naturally not be precisely determined at this, or at any future, time; and ultimately, one hundred years later, it was upon the rock of imperial defence that the loosely constructed, unseaworthy old Empire shattered itself.[2] But prior to the troublous days preceding the American Revolution, there existed a general, though necessarily somewhat vague, understanding of the respective duties of metropolis and colony in matters of defence. The understanding that obtained in the eighteenth century was not based upon theoretical considerations, but had evolved empirically in actual practice. Many of the precedents upon which it was based date from the experiences of the Restoration period.

It was at that time clearly realized that the safety of the

[1] The French Ambassador in England sent to his government copies of the various state papers illustrating English policy and practice, such as the Act of Navigation of 1660 and other statutes, the commission and instructions of the Council of Foreign Plantations of 1660 and also those of the Council of Trade of the same year, the Carolina charter, various commissions issued to colonial officials, *etc.* Paris, Archives des Affaires Étrangères, Correspondance Politique Angleterre 74, f. 379; 88, f. 65; 105, ff. 205, 207, 220–230; 110, ff. 297 *et seq.*

[2] See Beer, British Colonial Policy, 1754–1765.

Empire depended upon adequate sea power. 'Those who are masters at sea in those parts may upon occasion take all these islands,' wrote the author of a contemporary account of the Leeward Islands.[1] During time of war, the English navy was active in colonial waters, but it was by no means large enough to afford complete protection. Under the circumstances, such episodes as the French conquest of the Leeward Islands and the successful Dutch raid on the merchantmen in Virginia waters during the war of 1665 to 1667 are not surprising. The colonies were able to be of very little assistance in these naval wars, but it should not be forgotten that the reconquest of the Leeward Islands was largely due to the energy of Barbados and its public-spirited governors, the two Lords Willoughby. Moreover, Massachusetts not only contributed supplies to this Barbadian expedition, but at the same time made a valuable present of masts to the royal navy.[2] The Jamaica buccaneers likewise were an important factor in inducing Spain to make peace on terms satisfactory to England. During times of peace, ships of the navy were also at various periods stationed in America, some in the West Indies and others in Chesapeake Bay and at Boston, for the purpose of protecting the colonies and of suppressing piracy and illegal trade.

During this period no extensive land operations were carried on, and hence there was no need for active colonial coöperation. The proposed expedition against Canada, planned by the English military authorities in the war of

[1] C. O. 1/42, 36; C. C. 1677-1680, pp. 222, 223.
[2] See *post*, Chapter XI.

1665–1667, did not, however, enlist any support from the New England colonies, who claimed that the season was too far advanced for a successful campaign.[1] In general, England assumed without hesitation the duty of naval protection and also full responsibility for military operations during war with a European power. Whatever questions arose as to the respective obligations of metropolis and colonies concerned the protection of the colonies during time of peace. England consistently sought to limit her obligations to defending the colonies against European powers and to make the colonies assume full responsibility for defence against the Indians.[2] Hence, as far as it was possible, the number and size of the permanent garrisons in America was limited. The condition of affairs, however, was such that some soldiers had to be maintained in the colonies at the expense of the English Exchequer.

Of the permanent military establishment, the greater part was located in the West Indies, which were most exposed to sudden onslaught from England's rivals. For a number of years a considerable force was stationed in Barbados,[3] and until toward the end of the period a garrison

[1] See *post*, Chapter XI.

[2] In 1681, Lord Culpeper suggested 'the uniting of all the King's subjects in America to help each other in case of foreign enemies, rebellions, and Indians, in such proportions as the King shall direct'; and in particular that 'no war or peace with Indians should be made without the knowledge and assent of the Governor and Council of Virginia, the only Colony that the King can call his own.' C. C. 1681–1685, pp. 127, 128. Later, the first part of this statesman-like proposal was adopted by the English government.

[3] In 1670, Barbados asked that Sir Tobias Bridge's regiment be disbanded, as it was of no use in time of peace. C. O. 31/2, f. 1; C. C. 1669–1674, pp. 116–117.

was maintained in Jamaica at the expense of the English Exchequer.[1]   In St. Kitts, where France also had a colony, a small force was permanently established.[2]   Similarly, on account of the danger of French invasion, a regular garrison was stationed in New York, but the English government paid only part of this expense, contributing £1000 yearly to the Duke of York for this purpose.[3]   For several years after Bacon's rebellion — the force sent from England for its suppression, it was asserted, cost the English taxpayer more than £100,000 [4] — a body of regular soldiers was also maintained in Virginia.[5]   In the aggregate, this expense, though by no means inconsiderable,[6] was not for-

[1] In 1662, the yearly charge of the troops in Jamaica was £3539.   P. C. Cal. I, p. 328.

[2] The annual charge of these two foot-companies was £2778 and in addition £700 was paid to their commander, Colonel William Stapleton, who was also the Governor of St. Kitts and the other Leeward Islands.   Cal. Treas. Books, 1676–1679, pp. 57, 140, 141, 519, 524, 525; Blathwayt, Journal I, ff. 109, 110; P. C. Cal. I, pp. 627–629.

[3] Cal. Treas. Books 1669–1672, pp. 466, 475, 640, 657, 662, 708; ibid. 1672–1675, p. 113; ibid. 1676–1679, pp. 313, 425, 652, 1183.   See post, p. 119.

[4] C. C. 1681–1685, pp. 130, 131.

[5] For different reasons a small force was also posted in Boston during the government of Andros.

[6]   COLONIAL MILITARY ESTABLISHMENT IN 1679

Leeward Islands: two companies		£2778
Jamaica: major-general	£ 300	
maintenance of forts	£ 600	
two companies	£3327	£4227
New York: allowance for forts and garrisons	. . . .	£1000
Virginia: major-general	£ 300	
maintenance of forts	£ 600	
two companies and sundries £3911	. . . .	£4811
		£12,816

midable, and in addition it was in part defrayed by revenue derived directly from the colonies,[1] but it was met grudgingly and borne with exceedingly bad grace by the English government, which was always hovering on the verge of insolvency.

The pay of the soldiers was chronically in arrear, and in general, but more specifically in St. Kitts, the colonial garrisons were neglected by the home authorities. The treatment of the soldiers in St. Kitts was inexcusably outrageous. In 1675, it was reported that the two companies in this colony were in very bad shape, being incomplete as to numbers and not having received any pay for three years, "so that they are naked and have onely Subsisted by the Charity of the Planters, and the care of their Colonell," while the French forces on the island were well paid and clothed.[2] The Privy Council ordered this rectified, but within a few years the same conditions again existed.[3] In 1681, Colonel William Stapleton complained that the pay of his soldiers was three years in arrear, and that, as his credit was exhausted, he could no longer support them. This gallant soldier added that it would be more pleasing to him to disband them, than to see English soldiers starving and naked, while those of the French on the other side of the frontier were amply fed and well accoutred.[4] When, in 1687,

---

P. C. Register Charles II, XV, ff. 90, 150; C. O. 1/43, 70; C. O. 324/4, ff. 63 et seq.; P. C. Cal. I, pp. 837, 846–848; Brit. Mus., Add. MSS. 10,119, f. 52; C. C. 1677–1680, pp. 382, 383.

[1] See post, p. 119.
[2] P. C. Cal. I, pp. 627–629.
[3] Cf. C. C. 1677–1680, pp. 244, 245.
[4] C. C. 1681–1685, pp. 95, 96. Cf. p. 140.

the new Governor, Sir Nathaniel Johnson, arrived, he was shocked at the condition of the garrison. A number of the soldiers were too old for service; in general, their arms were in bad order, their clothes were miserable, and their pay was four years in arrear.[1]

It was the policy of the English government to shift the expense of these garrisons to the colonies, as soon as their finances were in such shape that they could bear it. When Virginia had recovered from Bacon's rebellion, most of the English troops sent to suppress this disturbance were withdrawn, but a small force was retained in the colony. As in St. Kitts, the pay of these soldiers was soon in arrear,[2] and in 1681 it was proposed to disband them. The Governor, Lord Culpeper, opposed this suggestion, pointing out that the West Indies did not need garrisons, as they had little to fear while England was master at sea, but that in Virginia not only were the Indians a constant source of danger, but the unsettled state of the neighboring colonies, Maryland and North Carolina, made it necessary to retain the force there.[3]

Virginia was at this time facing an economic crisis due to the abnormally low price of tobacco resulting from over-production.[4] In view of the ensuing unrest, which it was

[1] C. C. 1685–1688, p. 414.
[2] Va. Mag. XIV, pp. 359–361; C. C. 1681–1685, pp. 127, 128.
[3] On this occasion, he stated that 'the north part of Carolina has always been dangerous to Virginia, being the resort of the scum and refuse of America, and as yet almost without the face of Government.' C. C. 1681–1685, pp. 130, 131.
[4] *Ibid.*

feared might culminate in an uprising, it was urged also by others, in addition to Lord Culpeper, that the garrison should be retained.[1] The Lords of Trade were convinced by these arguments, but their recommendation for the retention of the two foot-companies was overruled by the Privy Council, which ordered that their pay cease from Christmas of 1681 on, and that they be disbanded unless Virginia were willing to assume this charge.[2] As the colony decided that, 'in its present necessitous state,' this outlay would be too heavy, the troops were finally disbanded in the late spring of 1862.[3]

In 1680, it was also determined to withdraw the garrison that had been in Jamaica ever since Cromwell's conquest, as it was thought that the colony was fully able to bear this burden.[4] When the news of this contemplated step reached Jamaica, Sir Henry Morgan, then in charge of the colony, wrote to Secretary Jenkins that the two companies were absolutely essential and were daily used in capturing fugitive and rebellious slaves and in reducing pirates.[5] The government, however, adhered to its decision and the troops were disbanded.[6]

Thus, from 1682 on, the only permanent garrisons in the

[1] C. C. 1681–1685, p. 134.

[2] *Ibid.* pp. 135, 142.

[3] *Ibid.* pp. 175, 228, 229, 237, 238, 240, 241, 245. In 1683, when this question came up again, the Lords of Trade decided that no garrison should be kept in Virginia unless without expense to the King. *Ibid.* p. 506.

[4] C. C. 1677–1680, p. 624.

[5] C. C. 1681-1685, pp. 102, 103.

[6] *Ibid.* p. 205.

colonies, apart from the troops sent over with Andros in order to facilitate the political reorganization of New England, were those in St. Kitts and in New York.   These were retained on account of the dangerous proximity of the French. The former were paid by the English Exchequer, but out of funds derived from the four and a half per cent export duties in the Caribbee Islands.[1]   To the cost of the latter £1000 was contributed by the English Treasury,[2] but when the northern colonies were consolidated under Andros, it was the intention that this charge should be paid out of the revenue arising in "the Dominion of New England."[3]   From this time on, England resolutely refused to support garrisons in such of the colonies as could themselves stand this expense. It was only under exceptional circumstances and under the stress of absolute necessity, that any English forces whatsoever were permanently maintained in America.   This remained the practice until 1763, when conditions had so fundamentally altered that the precedent established under the Restoration had to be abandoned.   The attempt of the English government at that time to secure from the colonies a part of the funds needed to maintain the large force required in America precipitated the disruption of the old Empire.

In addition to supporting these temporary and permanent garrisons, the Restoration government, when sufficiently urged by the importunities of the colonies, sent them supplies

[1] Brit. Mus., Add. MSS. 15,896, ff. 62, 66.

[2] Of this annual allowance, £6750 was apparently still unpaid at the time of the accession of James II.   Brit. Mus., Add. MSS. 15,896, f. 54.

[3] C. O. 5/904, ff. 409, 410.

of warlike stores [1] — arms, cannon, powder, shot, and whatever else was needed in the fortifications or by the local militia.[2] In some instances also, especially in Jamaica, England spent considerable sums on the colonial fortifications,[3] and in general supervised their location and construction in the royal provinces. In one instance, at least, in the location of the fort in Virginia during the second of England's Dutch wars, colonial knowledge of the facts was with grievous consequences overridden at Whitehall.[4]

In addition to the duty of protecting the colonies against organized foes, England was also obliged to police the high-

---

[1] In 1686, the newly appointed Governor of Jamaica, the Duke of Albemarle, said that this charge had always been borne by the King. C. C. 1685–1688, p. 202.

[2] An Account of all the Ordnance, etc., delivered to the Colonies since 1660, dated Office of the Ordnance, May 22, 1677.

Bahamas, 1672 . . . . £	95
Barbados, 1664/8	8695
Bermudas, 1666/73	255
Carolina, 1664/71	546
New England, 1664	2438
Hudson Bay, 1670	27
Jamaica, 1660/76	18,923
Leeward Islands, 1665/72	3463
Virginia, 1665/76	5626
New York, 1666/74	2159
Africa, 1660/1671	2010
	£44,237

C. O. 1/40, 71. During the following eight years the value of such supplies sent to the colonies was £4780. C. O. 324/4, ff. 117–120.

[3] On Jamaica, see P. C. Cal. I, pp. 299–303, 307, 324–327, 375. In 1679, Charles II gave Stapleton £1500 for fortifying the Leeward Islands. Blathwayt, Journal I, ff. 109, 110.

[4] Osgood, American Colonies III, pp. 254–258.

ways of commerce then infested with pirates of diverse
stripes and nationalities. Of these numerous scourges of
peaceful traders, the two most important groups were the
Barbary corsairs and the West Indian buccaneers.[1] The
Caribbean swarmed both with pirates and with nearly
equally lawless privateers, who, on the strength of commissions from the local authorities, — French, Dutch,
Spanish, and English, — preyed to some extent indiscrimi-
nately on commerce. But Spain suffered most severely
from their activities. Up to 1670, when was concluded
the war with Spain begun by Cromwell, England used these
buccaneers freely in attacks upon the Spanish colonies and
their commerce. But after that date, England consistently
exerted herself to suppress these privateers, a number of
whom turned pirates. Considerable difficulty was encountered, for the dragon's teeth sown by England herself
in the decade from 1660 to 1670 had yielded their inevitable
crop of desperate and lawless freebooters. In order to
subdue them, vessels of the navy had to be permanently
established in the West Indies, and in 1687 a special squadron under Sir Robert Holmes was sent with this object to
the Caribbean.[2] As a result of the continual activity of
these frigates, piracy in these waters, if not fully suppressed,
was at least so disciplined that the trade thence with Europe
and with the continental colonies could be carried on in
comparative safety.

[1] See *post*, Chapter VII.
[2] C. C. 1685–1688, pp. 421, 467, 488; British Royal Proclamations,
1603–1783 (Am. Antiqu. Soc., 1911), pp. 140–142.

The military operations carried on against the other pirate group, the Barbary corsairs, were on a much more extensive scale,[1] and were of equal, if not greater, value to the colonies, especially to those on the continent that were engaged in active trade to the Mediterranean. After the expulsion of the Moors from Spain in 1492, there followed over three centuries of desultory naval fighting between the forces of the Cross and the Crescent.[2] It was one phase of the perennial conflict between the irreconcilable East and West, during which those who were so unfortunate as to be captured by their foes were treated with revolting cruelty. The Mohammedan was forced to ply the oars in the galleys of the Mediterranean nations, the Christian became a slave in the household or shop of an unsympathetic master in Tripoli or Algiers.[3]

The extent and destructive nature of the operations of these corsairs of Algiers, Tunis, and Tripoli rendered navigation in European waters very hazardous. The Mediterranean, on which was their base of operations, was naturally most affected, but their activity extended even to the English Channel. In 1677, a direct voyage from Ireland to France was on their account deemed one of considerable

---

[1] See J. S. Corbett, England in the Mediterranean.

[2] See for the early stages of this conflict E. H. Currey, Sea Wolves of the Mediterranean.

[3] The Carolina proprietor, Seth Sothell, who was taken prisoner in 1679, complained that he was forced by his captors to "carry Morter, Brick and stone for the Masons with a heavy Chaine of Nine links, each linke two inches and halfe thick upon his legg besides Bolt and Shackle." P. C. Cal. II, p. 3.

hazard.[1] A petition of 1679 from the wives and relatives of one hundred and sixty-one English captives in Algiers stated that some of them had been "taken in thirteen Virginia ships, even at the mouth of the Channel." [2] In the same year, Seth Sothell, one of the Carolina proprietors, when on his way to assume the government of their northern settlement, was taken prisoner by the Algerines.[3] In 1680, Governor Bradstreet of Massachusetts gave as one of the reasons for the colony's delay in sending to England accredited representatives, that 'the great hazard of the seas creates a backwardness in persons most suitable to be employed as agents, for we have already lost five or six of our vessels by Turkish pirates, and many of our inhabitants continue in miserable captivity among them.' [4] In this very year, for fear of these pirates, the captains of most of the sugar ships in Barbados resolved to sail

[1] June 16, 1677, Sir Robert Southwell wrote to Lady Perceval: "Touching your voyage into France, you seem now to point at going directly (from Ireland), but truly considering the rovers that are now at sea, and even the Algerines that lie off the Lands End, who are neither of them very civil, though we be in friendship withal, I cannot approve of your going from Ireland into France by sea, and therefore you must needs choose this way (by England), where the road is plain." MSS. of Earl of Egmont (H.M.C. 1909) II, p. 67.

[2] House of Lords MSS. 1678–1688 (H.M.C. 1887), p. 137.

[3] C. C. 1677–1680, p. 326; P. C. Cal. I, p. 838. See also Playfair, The Scourge of Christendom, p. 131. In 1680, William Harris, a prominent New Englander, was also taken prisoner by the Algerines. C. C. 1677–1680, pp. 589, 590.

[4] *Ibid.* p. 549. Among the obstructions to the colony's trade enumerated by Bradstreet in 1680 was mentioned the activity of these Algerines. C. O. 1/44, 61 i.

for England by the circuitous route north of Ireland and Scotland.[1]

These scattered, but significant, facts show plainly how great was the danger from these corsairs, even though England was energetically endeavoring to suppress their depredations and had, in fact, concluded a series of treaties promising immunity to English ships.[2] In 1662, was concluded a treaty with Algiers, which provided that English ships, either furnished with admiralty passes or the major part of whose crew was English, should not be molested. The Algerines did not, however, abide by their treaty obligations, and for the next twenty-five years periodic violations thereof were followed by fresh treaties of substantially the same tenor, each one secured by armed force.   Such treaties and subsidiary agreements were secured from Algiers in 1664, 1668, 1669, 1671, 1682, 1683, and 1686. Substantially the same were England's relations with the other Barbary states.[3]

In addition to the naval force required virtually permanently in the Mediterranean in order to secure any respect whatsoever for these agreements, England during the frequent intervals of more or less active hostilities had to protect her merchant vessels.   In 1678, the Admiralty was instructed to send a number of men-of-war to ply off the mouth of the Channel in order to protect the Virginia

[1] C. C. 1677–1680, pp. 532, 533.

[2] England's relations with Algiers are described in Playfair, *op. cit.* pp. 78–152.

[3] Treaties and agreements were concluded with Tunis in 1662, and with Tripoli in 1662 and 1676.

tobacco ships from the "Pyrats of Argier who may probably
lye in waite for them."[1]   The following year, on account of
the "present Warr with the Turks and their Strength," an
exceptionally strong convoy had to be appointed for the
Newfoundland fleet sailing with fish to the Mediterranean
ports.[2]

The treaties with these states granted immunity to all
ships belonging to subjects of Charles II and thus included
colonial vessels.   Such English ships were to go free, if
provided with an Admiralty pass or if the majority of their
seamen were English subjects.[3]   Careful regulations were
prepared for the issue of these passes,[4] so that they should
not fall into the hands of foreigners, who would then benefit
by England's naval successes.   At this time, no rules were as
yet prepared for the issue of Algerine passes in the colonies,[5]

[1] P. C. Cal. I, p. 809.

[2] *Ibid.* pp. 816, 817, 821, 822.

[3] See §§ ii, iii, and iv of treaty of 1671 with Algiers.   The Tripoli treaty
of 1676 contained the same clauses.   Public Record Office, State Papers
Foreign, Treaties, Barbary States 9, 10.

[4] Col. Entry Book 96, ff. 26–29, 54; P. C. Register Charles II, XII, ff.
157–159; British Royal Proclamations, 1603–1783 (Am. Antiqu. Soc. 1911),
pp. 129, 130.

[5] Cal. Dom. 1676–1677, p. 521.   In 1678, on the petition of a London
merchant owning a New England built ship then at Boston, Massachusetts, to the effect that he "dares not stirre without his Majestyes pass,
to protect her against the Turkes," the Privy Council ordered the Admiralty
to issue the requested pass, although the case was one not provided for under
the rules.   P. C. Cal. I, p. 796.   In 1683, Governor Cranfield of New
Hampshire wrote to the Lords of Trade for authority to issue Algerine
passes.   C. C. 1681–1685, pp. 368–369.   In the same year, Randolph wrote
to Blathwayt that it was "desired by some Merc^{ts} in Boston that they
might haue the benefitt of Algeere Passes for such of their ships as carry

because in general there was no real necessity for such a provision, and more specifically in so far as New England was concerned, because of the slight control England was able to exercise over the colonies there.[1] But under the other clauses of the treaties with these powers, colonial vessels were exempted from capture and molestation, provided the majority of their crews were English.[2]

The comparative immunity from these corsairs secured by England was of great importance to her commerce and to that of the colonies. It was only by dint of repeated expeditions and hostile demonstrations with bombardments of their towns and naval engagements, that the Barbary states were forced to treat the English flag with some semblance of respect. Other European nations did not fare so well, for unless absolutely compelled by overwhelming force, these North African powers would not make peace with all Christendom and thus lose a chief source of their revenues.[3] Thanks to its political connection with England,

fish from us to the Streights" and requested that a number of blank passes be sent to New England. Goodrick, Randolph VI, p. 147.

[1] C. C. 1677–1680, pp. 15, 16; Cal. Dom. 1676–1677, p. 521. See *post*, Chapter XI.

[2] There was, however, a distinct advantage in having a pass, because then the vessel was not subjected to examination by the corsairs. Moreover, at one time the Turks seized all ships not provided with passes on the strength of the English proclamation of 1675, which apparently required all English vessels to secure these documents. Cal. Dom. 1677–1678, pp. 470–472.

[3] " The Algerines were shy of contracting too many alliances, lest there should be no nation to prey upon, and we read of a solemn debate in the Divan to decide which nation should be broken with, inasmuch as the slave masters were becoming bankrupt from the pacific relations of the State." Stanley Lane-Poole, the Story of the Barbary Corsairs, p. 270.

Massachusetts was able to ship with comparative safety the products of its fishery — the colony's basic industry — to the Mediterranean markets. As a result of these treaties also, the crops of the tobacco and sugar planters could be brought in relative security to Europe.

In the eyes of the statesmen and publicists of the day, England was fully justified in restricting colonial commerce in return for the burden assumed in defending and policing the Empire. If there existed any doubts on this point, they were more than quieted by the preferential treatment accorded to colonial products in the English market. While the enumerated articles could not be shipped to any place in Europe but England, in return competing commodities of foreign nations were virtually excluded from this market. The reciprocal nature of the old colonial system is manifest not only in the scheme of imperial defence, but to an even more marked degree in the preferential features of England's fiscal system.

CHAPTER III

THE ENGLISH FISCAL SYSTEM AND IMPERIAL FINANCES

The tariff of 1660 — Its preferential treatment of English colonial products — The prohibition to plant tobacco in England and the efforts required to enforce it — The attempt in 1671 to increase the sugar and tobacco duties — The impost of 1685 and colonial opposition to it — The Crown's dues in the colonies — The Restoration settlement in the Caribbee Islands — The four and a half per cent revenue and the opposition of Barbados to it — The Virginia quit-rents — The establishment of a permanent revenue in Virginia under the control and at the disposal of the Crown, and the attempt to do so in Jamaica — The appointment of Blathwayt as Auditor-General of the colonial revenues.

FROM the very outset of the colonial movement it was clearly understood that the proposed settlements in America were to be outside the English fiscal barriers, and that merchandise exported to the colonies or imported from them should pay the English customs duties. If the colonial trade had been left completely uncontrolled, the colonies would still necessarily have been more or less affected by these duties, but the English fiscal regulations would not have been integrally connected with the colonial system proper. The enumeration clauses and the Staple Act of 1663, however, perforce subjected a number of colonial products, and also many articles consumed in the colonies, to the English customs. These duties in many ways affected the economic development of the colonies, and formed an important part of the old colonial system. Without some knowledge of their nature, scope, and purpose, it is impossible fully to understand the economics or the politics of the old Empire.

In 1660, the most important of the preceding laws imposing taxes on imports and exports were consolidated in one statute, generally termed the "Old Subsidy."[1] In this Act, Parliament granted to Charles II for life a subsidy of tonnage and poundage. The former was a specific duty of varying amounts on wines imported; the poundage was equivalent to 5 per cent on all imports and exports[2] according to their fixed value as given in the "Book of Rates," which formed an integral part of the statute.[3] As the goods were at the time rather arbitrarily appraised,

[1] 12 Ch. II, c. 4.

[2] According to the statute, these duties were imposed on imports and exports both of the realm *and its dominions*, and hence their collection in the colonies would have been legal. Although this fact was not lost sight of, no general attempt was made to enforce the law. In one exceptional instance, however, these duties were ordered collected. In 1663, Charles II granted permission to Spanish ships to trade to the English West Indies for negroes, provided: 1, that whatever goods were imported or exported in these ships should pay in the colonies "the same duties of Tonnage and Poundage as is now established by Law in this Our Kingdome of England"; 2, that on every negro thus exported, except such as had been contracted for in England by the Royal African Company, there should be paid a duty of ten pieces of eight. P. C. Register Charles II, III, ff. 336–338; P. C. Cal. I, pp. 345–349. Such export duties on negroes were frequently collected, but I have seen no evidence of the collection of the tonnage and poundage.

[3] By mistaking these valuations for the actual duties imposed, Professor Channing grossly misjudges the effect of the tobacco duties on Virginia. Edward Channing, A History of the United States II, p. 12.

and as, in addition, it was not attempted subsequently to make these valuations correspond with the ensuing radical market fluctuations, these duties were by no means even approximately equivalent to 5 per cent. Thus, while the rating of colonial raw sugar was at the time somewhat under its duty-paid market value in England, in the next decade it was considerably in excess thereof.[1] Moreover, as far as colonial tobacco was concerned, there was apparently no attempt whatsoever at a correct appraisal. Colonial tobacco was valued at twenty pence a pound, when it could be freely bought in Virginia and Maryland for from one-penny to twopence, and sold in England, after paying duties, freight, and other charges, for from four to five pence.[2] Thus, while nominally a system of *ad valorem* rates, actually the tariff was one of specific duties.

In general, the Old Subsidy imposed this 5 per cent tax on all English produce and manufactures exported to the colonies as well as elsewhere. These export duties were, however, of but slight importance in imperial history. In a report on colonial trade prepared in 1678 for the Lords of Trade, the Commissioners of the Customs stated that these duties amounted to but little, "the Comodities of this

---

[1] Colonial raw sugar was rated at 30s. the cwt., refined at £5. Prior to 1667, before the great increase in the sugar output of the French colonies began to make itself seriously felt, the prices in England were respectively 40s. and £5. In 1670 and the following years, they were roughly 22s. to 23s., and 45s. to 70s. In Barbados, the price of raw sugar was in 1670 about 12s., and the English duty of 1s. 6d. was thus at that time equivalent to 12½ per cent on the colonial value. C. O. 1/26, 57; C. O. 31/2, ff. 54 *et seq.*; Brit. Mus., Egerton MSS. 2395, ff. 639–641.

[2] Brit. Mus., Harleian MSS. 1238, ff. 20–22.

Kingdome being but low rated in the Book of Rates." [1]
Moreover, apart from their slight extent, the incidence of
these taxes varied with the specific circumstances of each
case. At this time England was still predominantly an
agricultural country and normally exported foodstuffs to
the colonies. Such commodities had to pay these export
duties, which naturally to some extent lessened England's
ability to compete with the provision colonies in supplying
the West Indies. Apart from all other circumstances of
the case, such taxes in themselves were to this extent of
benefit to the northern continental colonies. [2] In such instances these export duties were, in general, almost entirely
paid by the English farmer. [3] Similarly in other cases, in
which colonial and English goods came into competition —

---

[1] C. O. 1/42, 60. In 1671, the customs officials had estimated these export duties at about £30,000. House of Lords MSS., H.M.C. IX, Part II,
p. 10[b]. This estimate cannot, however, be reconciled with the extant
accounts of exports to the colonies.

[2] Exactly opposite in effect would be the payment of bounties on the
exportation of corn from England. Prior to 1689, such bounties were in
force only during the years 1673 to 1678. N. S. B. Gras, The Corn Bounty
Experiment of Charles II, in Quarterly Journal of Economics XXIV, pp.
419–421.

[3] Wheat, rye, peas, beans, barley, malt, oats, beef, pork, bacon, butter,
cheese, and candles could be exported only when under certain prices, and
then only on payment of the export duties. 12 Ch. II, c. 4, § xi. These
prices were subsequently changed, and ten years later this price restriction
on exportation was removed. 15 Ch. II, c. 7, § ii; 22 Ch. II, c. 13, §§ i, iv.
Immediately after the Revolution of 1688/9, Parliament even gave bounties
on the exportation of these grains — rye, malt, barley, and wheat. 1 W.
& M. sess. 1, c. 12. "For nearly a century England was made by the
Corn Laws a corn-exporting country." R. E. Prothero, in Social England IV,
p. 444.

such as hats, shoes, and clothing — these export duties
could not in their entirety be shifted to the colonial consumer. Whenever there was direct or indirect competition
between the products of the metropolis and the colony,
this feature of the English fiscal system hampered English
industry and benefited that of the colonies. But in other
instances, where there was no such competition, these
export duties unquestionably raised the price at which
the commodities were sold in the colonies.[1]

Far more important to the colonies than these export
duties was the treatment accorded to their imports into
England. In connection with the export duties only some
slight favors were conceded to the colonies,[2] but the import

[1] Of interest and importance to the colonies was the removal of some of
the previous prohibitions to export certain commodities, such as iron, arms,
saddles, geldings, oxen, *etc.* 12 Ch. II, c. 4, § x. These prohibitions dated
back to mediæval times and had as a rule been waived in the colonial
charters of the first half of the seventeenth century. Beer, Origins, pp.
105, 106. The exportation of some articles, such as tin and tobacco-pipe
clay, still continued to be forbidden. Cal. Treas. Book, 1660–1667, p. 155;
Carkesse, The Act of Tonnage and Poundage (London, 1726), pp. 765 *et seq.*

[2] By the Act of 1660 the export duties on geldings and nags shipped to
the colonies were only half the regular duties. These duties were, however,
very high, and in 1663 the House of Commons recommended the Crown to
give leave to accommodate the colonies with such horses as they might require. Accordingly, Charles II issued a proclamation giving "free Liberty
for transportation of Horses into any of his Majesties Plantations " without payment of duties, on license being first obtained. Com. Journal VIII,
pp. 532, 533; P. C. Register, Charles II, III, ff. 491, 495; P. C. Cal. I, pp.
367, 368. For these licenses and the subsequent history of this subject, see
P. C. Cal. I, pp. 346, 437, 451, 489, 531; C. C. 1669–1674, pp. 32, 41, 44;
22 Ch. II, c. 13, § viii. An Act of 1663 lowered the duties on such coals as
should be exported to the colonies. In 1669, on the ground that Barbados
was in want of wood to boil its sugars and hence needed Newcastle or Welsh

duties were so adjusted as to give many colonial products marked advantages over those of foreign nations. The tariff of 1660 rated English colonial ginger, indigo, cotton, sugar, and tobacco much lower than the foreign competing products. Ginger of the East Indies was valued at three shillings a pound, that of the West Indies at one shilling fourpence, and that of the English colonies at only a trifle over twopence.[1] Foreign indigo was valued at three shillings fourpence a pound, as opposed to one shilling for the English product. Foreign cotton paid fourpence a pound, while that of the English plantations was free. Spanish and other

coal, it was suggested that the English export duties on coal be discontinued, and also those on all other shipments to Barbados. The law was, however, not changed. 15 Ch. II, c. 7; 9 Anne, c. 6; Carkesse, *op. cit.* p. cxiii; Treas. Books, Out-Letters, Customs 12, f. 383; C. C. 1699, pp. 590, 591. Arms were occasionally allowed to be shipped to the colonies free of duties. Treas. Books, Out-Letters, Customs 5, f. 25; 9, f. 91. For an instance of the relaxation of the law in favor of some malt intended for shipment to Virginia, see Cal. Treas. Books, 1660–1667, pp. 159, 160, 289. The Hudson's Bay Company was also favored by the government. In 1681, the Company was granted permission to export "their Clothes, Provisions, Victuals Arms Ammunition Implements & Materials necessary for the Maintaining & defence of their forts, Colonies and factorys" customs free, as did the African and East India Companies. Treas. Books, Out-Letters, Customs 5, ff. 317–318. *Cf.* f. 21. A number of the colonial governors, such as Lord Culpeper, Sir Richard Dutton, and the Duke of Albermarle, when departing for their posts, were allowed to ship their supplies and those of their retinues free of duty. *Ibid.* 5, ff. 37, 289; 11, ff. 42, 43. Tools for the use of the planters in the Carolinas and Bahamas could also be exported free of customs. No. Ca. Col. Rec. I, pp. 27, 108; Cal. Treas. Books, 1669–1672, p. 1343.

[1] On the duties on ginger, see Treas. Books, Out-Letters, Customs 8, f. 4; P. C. Cal. II, pp. 191, 192. This exceedingly low duty on English colonial ginger was not in the original law, but was added later by the Treasury.

foreign tobacco was charged with sixpence a pound, as against only twopence collected from the English colonial commodity.[1] On unrefined English sugar the duty was one shilling sixpence a hundredweight, as against four shillings on the foreign product. On refined sugar the differential, while marked, was considerably less. English refined paid five shillings the hundredweight, the foreign product seven shillings fourpence.[2]

It will be noticed that the commodities to which preferential treatment was accorded were those on the enumerated list, which came from the West Indies and the tobacco colonies on the continent. None of the products of New England were either enumerated or given such treatment, because they were not wanted or because they were so bulky in nature that they could not stand the cost of carriage across the Atlantic. In this latter class were naval stores and lumber, in which case far more heroic measures than differential duties would have been necessary in order to make possible colonial exports to England. Nor could the grain and provisions of the northern colonies find a market

---

[1] Foreign tobacco was valued at 10s. a pound, on which 5 per cent amounted to 6d. English colonial tobacco was valued at 1s. 8d., on which the duty was 1d., but an additional duty of 1d. was also charged thereon.

[2] The classification of the various grades of sugar in the Act of 1660 was not clear or exhaustive, which fact led to some difficulties. In 1667, it was agreed between the Farmers of the Customs and the Barbados merchants, that sugars of and below the grade of the finest Brazilian muscovado should be considered unrefined and all others white or refined. Cal. Treas. Books, 1667–1668, pp. 146, 147. See also C. O. 1/22, 20; C. C. 1661–1668, no. 1679; Brit. Mus., Stowe MSS. 324, ff. 4 et seq.; Egerton MSS. 2395, ff. 629 et seq.

in the mother country, for England was still able to sell foodstuffs in competition with her colonies in neutral markets.[1]   But even if such importations into England had been feasible, this trade would not have been countenanced. England was still largely agricultural, and the dominant landed interest had inserted in the tariff of 1660 very high import duties on wheat, rye, beans, barley, and malt.[2] These duties were not aimed at the colonies, such imports from them being then virtually impossible.   They were followed by other measures, likewise not directed against the colonies, but at Ireland, prohibiting the importation into England of cattle, sheep, swine, beef, pork, and bacon.[3]

The preferential treatment of the enumerated products in the tariff of 1660 was of great advantage to the colonies

[1]   EXPORTS OF PROVISIONS FROM ENGLAND TO THE COLONIES

	1662–1663		1668–1669
Butter, firkins	239	. . . .	470
Beer, tuns	234	. . . .	757
Beef, barrels	12		
Candles, dozens	206	. . . .	1810
Cheese, cwt.	294	. . . .	226
Hops, cwt.	17		
Malt, quarters	496		
Wheat meal, quarters	60	. . . .	94
Oatmeal, bushels	111	. . . .	32
Peas, quarters	14		
Apples, bushels	12		

B. T. Trade Papers 4.

[2] See also 15 Ch. II, c. 7, § iii ; 22 Ch. II, c. 13.   For details, see H. Saxby, British Customs (London, 1757), pp. 111–114.

[3] 15 Ch. II, c. 7 ; 18 Ch. II, c. 2 ; 20 Ch. II, c. 7.   For details, see Murray, Commercial Relations between England and Ireland, pp. 24 *et seq.*

interested, and gave their products a virtual monopoly of the English market. In the year 1687–1688, 168,807 pounds of indigo were imported into London from the English West Indies, as contrasted with 27,038 from elsewhere.[1] In the same year only 16,000 pounds of Spanish tobacco passed through the London custom-house, while nearly 15,000,000 pounds came from the English colonies.[2] Similarly, with the exception of a relatively small quantity of highly refined Brazilian sugar, the English market was virtually entirely supplied by the English West Indies.[3]

This preferential system, with its ensuing monopoly, and

[1] C. C. 1699, pp. 606.

[2]

TOBACCO IMPORTED INTO LONDON

	Spanish	English Colonial
1685–1686	26,940 lbs.	14,514,513 lbs.
1686–1687	4,797 lbs.	14,067,177 lbs.
1687–1688	16,180 lbs.	14,874,359 lbs.

Brit. Mus., Sloane MSS. 1815, f. 35. In 1660, and presumably later as well, some Spanish tobacco was also smuggled into England. Com. Journal VIII, p. 124; Cal. Treas. Books, 1660–1667, pp. 54, 56. On the importation of Spanish tobacco in 1661, see also Portland MSS. (H.M.C. 1893) II, p. 143.

[3] Bodleian, Rawlinson A 478, f. 63; House of Lords MSS., H.M.C. IX, Part II, p. 11[b]. In the eighteenth century, foreign sugars were extensively shipped as English from the continental colonies to England, thus evading the higher duties. Beer, British Colonial Policy, 1754–1765, p. 247. The earliest case of this nature, which I have seen, occurred shortly after the Restoration, when an English ship freighted in Brazil three hundred chests of sugar, then took in the rest of her cargo at Barbados, "and so paste in England for a shipe which brought all her Loadinge from his Ma[ties] plantations." Public Record Office, State Papers Foreign, Portugal 5, ff. 190, 191.

the enumeration of these products must be considered together. The advantages conferred by one were held to counterbalance the restrictions imposed by the other. They were two clauses in what had originally been an actual bargain between metropolis and colony. In 1623, the Virginia Company and that of the Bermudas offered to ship all their tobacco to England, provided in return they were granted a virtual monopoly of the home market.[1] This proposition had been accepted. As then, so now in 1660, the restriction of colonial exports to England was more or less counterbalanced by the exceptional treatment received there.

Except in so far as these import duties decreased consumption in England and thus lessened the demand for the colonial products, they were shifted to the English consumer. But only a part of the enumerated goods imported into England was consumed there. A considerable portion was reshipped to neutral markets, where they competed with similar products of the Spanish, Portuguese, Dutch, and French colonies. The duties on this portion would unquestionably be borne by the colonial planter. Moreover, under the Staple Act of 1663, foreign European goods could be shipped to the colonies only through England, where they paid duties. Thus the effect of the laws of trade and navigation in combination with the English fiscal system was virtually to impose a direct tax on the colonial producer and consumer. In these cases, however, a special arrangement greatly lessened the extent of these duties. In general, on all goods, whether colonial or foreign, reshipped from Eng-

[1] Beer, Origins, p. 132.

land within a specified period of reasonable length,[1] one-half of the duties was refunded. The amount accruing to the Exchequer was thus two and a half per cent of the value of the commodities as stated in the Book of Rates. In the case of colonial tobacco — the most important item — not only was half of the subsidy repaid, but also the entire additional duty of one-penny; the amount remaining in the English Treasury on Virginia tobacco reëxported from England to foreign markets was thus only a half-penny a pound.

Of the enumerated colonial products the only one which could be grown successfully in England was tobacco. Hence the preferential duties were not sufficient to give colonial tobacco a monopoly of the English market; if this were desired, additional measures would be required. In 1620, in consideration of the Virginia Company agreeing to pay import duties on tobacco, which, while lower than those on the Spanish product, were in excess of what it was obliged to pay by its charter, James I issued a proclamation prohibiting the growing of tobacco in England.[2] Subsequently, a number of other proclamations of like tenor, and extending the prohibition to Ireland, were published. This Stuart prohibition, which could never be fully carried into effect, was continued by the Interregnum government and was vigorously, if not completely, enforced.[3] A variety of motives,

[1] By the Act of 1660 a year was allowed, if such goods were reshipped by an English merchant; if by an alien, nine months. The period was subsequently further extended.

[2] Beer, Origins, pp. 112, 113, and Chapter VI.

[3] *Ibid.* pp. 403–408.

prominent among them the desire to foster the welfare of the colonies, underlay this policy, which was fully adopted by the Restoration government.

In 1660, Parliament passed an Act prohibiting under severe penalties the growing of tobacco in England and Ireland, except only in very small quantities for scientific and medicinal purposes.[1] As was customary, the preamble of the statute succinctly summarized the actuating causes of the measure. It stated that, after considering how important the colonies were and how necessary it was that they be defended and encouraged, since they employed a quantity of shipping, were a good market, and supplied England with commodities formerly purchased of foreigners at dearer rates; and as tobacco was one of their principal products, while that grown in England was not so wholesome and besides diminished the customs, therefore Parliament enacted this prohibition.[2] Thus the chief grounds upon which the policy was based were economic; the formerly so prevalent moral opposition to the use of the narcotic had virtually entirely disappeared.

[1] 12 Ch. II, c. 34; Com. Journal VIII, pp. 194, 197, 212; House of Lords MSS., H.M.C. VII, Part I, p. 135. The prohibition naturally included Wales, but also extended to Guernsey and Jersey.

[2] In his speech to the King, at the end of the session, in December of 1660, the Speaker of the House of Commons said, in reference to this Act, that the climate of England was so cold that tobacco never came to maturity, that when manufactured it rotted quickly, and that the physicians agreed that it was unwholesome. Besides, he said, the planting of tobacco in England would lessen the customs, destroy the plantations, discourage navigation and shipping, "which are the walls and bulwarks of your majesty's kingdom." Parl. Hist. IV, pp. 164 et seq.

It was found extremely difficult to enforce this law, primarily because the industry was most profitable. In a number of the counties of southwestern England, the farmers were very successful with this crop and were exceedingly loath to abandon it. Parliamentary prohibitions, though accompanied by heavy fines, were hopelessly inadequate; more energetic measures were necessary to uproot the industry. Early in 1661, on the advice of the Council of Foreign Plantations,[1] a proclamation was issued enjoining the strict execution of the parliamentary prohibition against growing tobacco.[2] As this was found ineffective, on April 30, 1662, the Privy Council instructed the High Sheriff of Gloucestershire — the centre of the English tobacco district — to pluck up, destroy, and burn the tobacco grown and planted there.[3] Similar letters were also sent to the high sheriffs and justices of the peace of the adjoining counties, Worcester and Hereford.[4] The law, however, was not fully enforced. On July 13, 1662,[5] the Privy Council took the High Sheriff of Gloucestershire to task for gross neglect in "that there is very much Tobacco growing in that County that remaines undestroyed." Recourse had even to be

[1] C. C. 1661–1668, no. 32.

[2] P. C. Register Charles II, II, ff. 146, 171; P. C. Cal. I, p. 303; Brit. Mus., Egerton MSS. 2543, f. 33.

[3] P. C. Register Charles II, II, f. 622; P. C. Cal. I, p. 330. On May 10, 1662, Secretary Nicholas wrote to this sheriff that the King, hearing that he had not left town and considering that it was then the season for planting tobacco, wished him at once to repair to his county, so as to put in execution the commands formerly given him. Cal. Dom. 1661–1662, p. 367.

[4] P. C. Cal. I, p. 330 n.

[5] *Ibid.*

had to the militia in order to gain some respect for the law.[1]

Those chiefly affected by the incomplete enforcement of the prohibition complained to the government. In 1662, Sir William Berkeley, the Governor of Virginia, and others interested in that colony and in Maryland, prayed that royal commands be issued to the sheriffs to put the Act in full execution.[2] The Farmers of the Customs were also concerned, for the planting of tobacco in England by so much diminished the imports thereof and with it the customs revenue. Accordingly, in 1663, more energetic measures were adopted. Parliament increased the penalties imposed on those growing tobacco,[3] and the Privy Council wrote to the sheriffs of the counties of Gloucester, Worcester, Hereford, Monmouth, and Oxford that great quantities of tobacco were still planted, and required them to aid the Surveyor General of the Farmers of the Customs, and such persons as he should see fit to employ, in destroying this crop. By his commission this officer was empowered to demand assistance from the sheriffs, justices of the peace, mayors, bailiffs, constables, "and all other his Majesty's officers both Civil and Military."[4] But, instead of contracting, the area of production was spreading both to the East and to the West.

---

[1] On Aug. 6, 1662, a correspondent wrote from Bristol to the Marquis of Newcastle that the militia was to appear that month to destroy the tobacco, in which many there were interested. Portland MSS. (H.M.C. 1893) II, p. 144.

[2] C. C. 1661–1668, no. 358.

[3] 15 Ch. II, c. 7, § xviii. The Act stated that, despite the law of 1660, the English tobacco crop had increased.

[4] P. C. Cal. I, p. 367.

In order to control the situation, the government now found it necessary to employ the army. In the spring of 1664, the Privy Council wrote to the High Sheriff of Gloucestershire to destroy all the tobacco planted, especially that near the town of Winchcomb, where the enforcement of the law had always been most strenuously resisted.[1] At the same time, the Lord-Lieutenant of the county was instructed to assist the sheriff with the necessary horse.[2] As tobacco continued to be grown, particularly in the vicinity of the towns of Winchcomb in Gloucestershire and Evesham in Worcestershire, where the sheriff had been opposed and was unable to carry the prohibition into effect, the government two months later ordered the Duke of Albemarle to send a troop of horse of the Earl of Oxford's regiment to assist Thomas Fownes, who had been commissioned to destroy this tobacco.[3] The following year, 1665, these instructions to Albemarle were repeated.[4] Yet, in 1666, the Privy Council received information, that great preparations were being made and that much new ground was in readiness for the planting of tobacco, and again ordered the High Sheriff of Gloucestershire to proceed against the law-breakers.[5] Strenuous opposition was encountered, culminating in riots in Winchcomb and Cheltenham, where the people said "that they would loose their Liues rather then obey the Lawes in that case provided."[6]

---

[1] Beer, Origins, pp. 405–407.

[2] P. C. Register Charles II, IV, ff. 56, 57; P. C. Cal. I, p. 377.

[3] P. C. Register Charles II, IV, f. 117; P. C. Cal. I, pp. 379, 380.

[4] P. C. Register Charles II, V, f. 165.

[5] P. C. Register Charles II, V, f. 377; P. C. Cal. I, pp. 408, 409.

[6] P. C. Register Charles II, V, f. 397; P. C. Cal. I, pp. 410, 411, 416.

Similar difficulties continued throughout 1667 and 1668.[1] In 1667, the Farmers of the Customs complained of the quantity of tobacco planted and of the laxity of the local officials in enforcing the law.[2] As some of the justices of the peace were unwilling to obey the Privy Council's order for the destruction of this tobacco, a troop of 120 horse-guards was sent to Gloucestershire in the summer of 1667 to assist the sheriff.[3] In 1668, the Farmers of the Customs were again active in trying to secure the enforcement of the law, and obtained the coöperation of the Treasury.[4] Yet it would appear that not only was the planting of tobacco not stopped, but that it was increasing and spreading in England. Thus, in 1668, the Privy Council sent letters ordering the destruction of the tobacco plants not only to the sheriffs and justices of the peace of the five counties already mentioned — Gloucester, Worcester, Hereford, Oxford, and Monmouth — but also to those of the adjacent counties of Warwick, Salop, and Flint, as well as to those of the more remote and widely separated, Essex and York.[5]

But the planting of tobacco still continued. In 1671, in

---

[1] P. C. Register Charles II, VI, ff. 62, 507, 527, 528, 530, 532, 539, 547, 550, 552, 561, 563; P. C. Cal. I, pp. 430, 431.

[2] Cal. Treas. Books, 1667–1668, pp. 42, 59, 225.

[3] Fleming MSS. (H.M.C. 1890), p. 52. See also Pepys, Sept. 19, 1667.

[4] Cal. Treas. Books, 1667–1668, pp. 356, 521, 592.

[5] P. C. Register Charles II, VII, f. 361; P. C. Cal. I, p. 473. On Sept. 9, 1668, a list of the violators of the law in Yorkshire was read and referred to the Farmers of the Customs. P. C. Register Charles II, VIII, f. 5. Other counties subsequently referred to as growing tobacco were Lincoln, Nottingham, and Wilts. P. C. Register Charles II, XII, ff. 80, 81, 363; *ibid.* XVI, ff. 32, 312, 525.

order to make the prohibition more effective, Parliament granted greater authority to the local officials, such as constables, bailiffs, and tithing-men;[1] and, in the same year, another proclamation had to be issued with renewed orders to destroy the prohibited crop.[2] In 1672, since great preparations had been made for growing tobacco in the counties of Gloucester, Wilts, Hereford, and Worcester, to the great prejudice, as was alleged, of navigation, the customs and the colonies, the Privy Council again was forced to take steps to secure the destruction of the plants.[3] Throughout the following decade the course of events was essentially the same. Every year commissions had to be issued to enforce the law in the recalcitrant counties, and troops of horse had to be sent to assist in the work and to force the farmers to submit.[4] In 1682, or thereabout, Winchcomb was referred to as "the now famed town . . . because of their late planting tobacco and the soldiers coming hither yearly to destroy it, but now here is little or none planted."[5] From about this time on much less is heard of violations of the law, and hence presumably it was fairly effectively enforced. But until 1690 it was necessary to commission special officials to

[1] 22 & 23 Ch. II, c. 26, §§ i, ii.

[2] P. C. Register Charles II, VII, f. 361; P. C. Cal. I, p. 473.

[3] P. C. Register Charles II, X, f. 297. See also Cal. Treas. Books, 1669–1672, p. 1232.

[4] P. C. Register Charles II, XI, ff. 67, 68, 262, 462; ibid. XII, ff. 80, 81, 363; ibid. XVI, ff. 32, 312; P. C. Cal. I, pp. 592, 611, 630, 631, 667, 726, 783; ibid. II, pp. 7, 20, 21, 35; H.M.C. IX, Part II, p. 450ᵃ; Cal. Treas. Books, 1672–1675, pp. 482, 483; ibid. 1676–1679, pp. 330, 346, 588; Cal. Dom. 1677–1678, p. 363.

[5] Portland MSS. (H.M.C. 1893) II, p. 302.

destroy any tobacco planted,[1] and that date may be regarded as marking the final extinction of this flourishing industry.

The first prohibition against English tobacco was issued in 1620, and thus it took seventy years of more or less constant effort and energetic measures to uproot this industry. This in itself is adequate proof of the fitness of England for the crop and of the extent of the sacrifice demanded from the English farmers. It was not alone these farmers who objected to the prohibition. In 1674, Carew Reynell, a contemporary economic writer of considerable knowledge and ability, maintained that "that which would bring infinite wealth to this Nation (if the Law would permit it) is the planting of Tobacco. . . . Before the severity of the Laws against its planting, it went well forward, and would still, if it were reversed. . . . For by relation there were above six thousand Plantations of it, in *Gloucestershire, Devonshire, Sommersetshire, and Oxfordshire:* all the objections that are against it, cannot vye with the advantages that it produces." The entire South of England, he further asserted, was adapted to its production; and, in the opinion of some, the tobacco was better than the colonial, though others held it to be inferior. Nor did Reynell agree with those who maintained that a repeal of the prohibition would adversely affect the English customs revenue and mercantile marine. To the natural suggestion that such a reversal of policy

---

[1] P. C. Register Charles II, XVI, f. 525; *ibid.* James II, I, f. 177; III, f. 158; P. C. Cal. II, pp. 36, 135. Giles Dowle, who was especially employed in this work, received a salary of £80, which in 1685 was ordered inserted in the regular establishment. Treas. Books, Out-Letters, Customs 8, ff. 111, 209; 10, f. 58.

would injure Virginia, he replied: "What though it should, we are bound to look to our selves at home first." Moreover, he continued, "it were better, if that *New-England* and *Virginia* both, if possible, were remov'd farther towards the South, for then they would consume our own Commodities, and might meet with store of Silver and riches, whereas now they have little necessary Trade for us, possessing only such things as we have." It would be far better, he further argued, if Virginia would desist from growing tobacco, "they living but poorly on it," and should plant instead mulberry trees, vines, and olives as was already being done in Carolina.[1]

Such arguments did not, however, influence the government, and the prohibition was enforced. While a desire to promote the prosperity of the colonies was not the sole motive, it was a very prominent one;[2] and at all events they were the direct and immediate beneficiaries of the measure. In forming an estimate of the old colonial system this fact should not be undervalued or ignored. No law reg-

[1] Carew Reynell, The True English Interest (London, 1674), pp. 32–35.

[2] Even the Treasury, which was naturally mainly interested in the fact that the planting of tobacco in England diminished the customs revenue, emphasized this point. In its instructions for the enforcement of the law, sent in 1668, it was said that the English industry was "to the greate discouragement of trade, destrucion of his Ma^tles plantations and lessening of his Ma^tles Revenue of ye Customs." Treas. Books, Out-Letters, Customs I, f. 121. In 1674, Treasurer Latimer (the future Danby) stated that the violations of this prohibition resulted in "the apparent loss of the King's Customs, the discouragement of the Plantations in America, and the great prejudice of the trade and navigation of the realm." Cal. Treas. Books, 1672–1675, pp. 482, 483. *Cf.* also House of Lords MSS., H.M.C. VIII, Part I, p. 139^a.

ulating colonial trade demanded from the over-sea dominions direct sacrifices in any way commensurate with those that the farmers of southwestern England were forced to bear.[1]

The Old Subsidy of 1660 formed the basis of the English customs revenue. During the period of the protracted and costly French wars, following the Revolution of 1688/9, other subsidies, either partial or full ones, were granted by Parliament, until under the first Hanoverians the import duties in general amounted to three complete subsidies. Thus, apart from the tonnage duties on wine and other specific taxes, these duties were at that time equivalent to fifteen per cent of the rated value of the commodities imported. In addition, on various occasions, special imposts were voted by Parliament. During the reign of Charles II, abortive attempts were made to impose such additional duties on colonial products, and finally, on the accession of James II, a heavy tax was laid on tobacco and sugar.

In his colonial, as well as in his foreign policy, Charles II was hampered by financial difficulties, which were not of his own creation.[2] The immoderate demands of his female favorites and the extravagance of the luxurious Court were by no means the primary causes of the grave fiscal disorders

[1] Naturally it should be remembered that this English industry prospered under the protection of very high duties, and that presumably English tobacco could not have competed on equal terms with that of Virginia and Maryland.

[2] "Charles was driven into the arms of Louis XIV simply by his financial distress — a distress which was brought upon him more by the irony of events and by sins of omission of his faithful Commons than by any sins of commission of his own." W. A. Shaw, in Cal. Treas. Books, 1660–1667, p. xlii.

of the reign. The estimates of the revenue granted by
Parliament in 1660 were far in excess of the actual yield,
and the income was hopelessly inadequate for the legitimate
expenditures of the government.[1] The ultimate result was
the virtual declaration of insolvency by the government in
1672, known as the "Stop of the Exchequer."[2]

A year before this, in 1671, an unsuccessful attempt had
been made in Parliament to lay additional import duties on
tobacco and sugar, and a bill to this effect was passed by the
House of Commons.   In this bill, the new duties on English
colonial tobacco were one and a half pence a pound, as opposed to fourpence on the foreign product.[3]   A petition
against these additional duties was presented on behalf of
the merchants, importers, and planters of tobacco,[4] stating
that this important trade would be greatly injured thereby.
The petitioners asserted that their industry employed 140
ships and bred many mariners, that it gave England a good
market for her manufactures, that the customs on tobacco
amounted yearly to £100,000, and finally that the proposed
additional duties would divert the trade to the Dutch.   In
addition, the customs officials, while maintaining that the
proposed taxes would not lessen the consumption of tobacco
in England, pointed out, not only that such high duties
would stimulate smuggling, with which they were already
considerably troubled, but also that even under existing

---

[1] *Ibid*. pp. xxvi, xxvii.
[2] Evelyn, March 12, 1672.
[3] House of Lords MSS., H.M.C. IX, Part II, p. 8[a].
[4] *Ibid*. p. 10[b].

conditions the tobacco trade was far from prosperous.[1]   The House of Commons, however, remained unmoved by these arguments and passed the additional duties.[2]   That the bill ultimately failed of being enacted was due to the opposition to the proposed new taxes on sugar.

The tobacco duties aroused slight opposition in comparison with the sugar schedule, which affected a number of diverse and conflicting interests and could not be arranged to the satisfaction of all.   The ensuing heated discussions furnished one of the few occasions, such as in 1731–1733 and in 1764–1766, when colonial matters occupied the centre of the parliamentary stage.   Apart from the consumer, who is usually mute when such questions vitally affecting him are discussed, the chief interests concerned in the proposed additional duties on sugar were: (1) the merchants trading to

---

[1] *Ibid.* p. 10[b].   These views were partially confirmed by a memorial of this year, wherein it was maintained that the tobacco trade was grossly mismanaged.   In agreement with the general statement of the customs officials, it was asserted that last year many merchants had lost heavily on their importations of tobacco.   Hence, it was argued, if the duties were further increased, the trade would be ruined and many other mischiefs would follow; "most of them have beene made manifest in the Virginia Merchants reasons, therefore here omitted."   The writer of this memorial then gave several instances of gross frauds in the tobacco duties perpetrated with the collusion of the English customs officials, and proposed: (1) that all tobacco be landed at London, and that none be sent thence in an unmanufactured state, unless it were exported; (2) that the importer be allowed time to pay the duties and that they be repaid in full on exportation.   Under these conditions, he thought that even an additional duty of 4d. would not be harmful.   Brit. Mus., Harleian MSS. 1238, ff. 20–22.

[2] On the strength of these arguments against the proposed duties, the Committee in charge, by a vote of 18 to 4, reduced the additional duty from 1½d. to 1d., but the House negatived this amendment.

Portugal and their allies, the English woollen manufacturers;
(2) the English sugar refiners; (3) the English merchants
trading to the West Indies; (4) and the colonial sugar planters.   Each one of these four distinct groups was active in
furthering its own special interests.

As a result of the combined effects of Portugal's restrictive
colonial system [1] and of the preferential treatment accorded
to English colonial products in the tariff of 1660, the shipments of Brazilian sugar to England at this time amounted
to only 2000 chests (costing £40,000), whereas formerly
16,000 chests had been imported. [2]   This sugar bought in
Portugal was very highly refined and sold in the English
market for from £3 to £3 10s. the hundredweight, whereas
the price of the English refined sugars, which in general were
coarser, was only 45 to 50 shillings.   Hence it was maintained that, if additional duties were imposed, those on
Portuguese refined sugars should in equity be at least pro-
portionately higher. [3]   But England at this time had a con-

---

[1] Brazilian sugars had first to be landed in Portugal, and were subjected
to heavy taxes before reaching the foreign market.

[2] These and the subsequent facts about this Portuguese trade are derived
from two memorials prepared during the controversy.   One is in Bodleian,
Rawlinson A 478, f. 63; House of Lords MSS., H.M.C. IX, Part II, p. 11[b];
C. C. 1669–1674, p. 215.   The other is in House of Lords MSS., H.M.C.
IX, Part II, p. 12[b].

[3] The colonial interests asserted that owing to natural conditions —
low, fertile grounds, cheap horses, cattle, and negroes, abundant water carriage and water power for grinding — sugar could be produced 30 per cent
more cheaply in Brazil than in the English West Indies.   If the additional
duty were the same on Portuguese as on English refined sugar, they claimed,
it would "ruine the English Sugar Trade, and the Guiny Trade that depends
on it, which alone vents more of our manufactures, than doth Portugal."

siderable export trade to Portugal in woollens and other commodities, which, it was so alleged, employed 150 ships and amounted yearly to £350,000. The merchants engaged therein claimed that a further heavy tax on Portuguese sugar would cripple their trade and throw it into the hands of the French and Dutch.[1]

The English refiners were also directly interested in the proposed new duties. As a consequence of the great expansion of sugar planting in the English West Indies, sugar refining in England had become an important industry. In 1671, it was said, there were thirty refineries as opposed to only six, twenty years prior thereto.[2] In addition, in Barbados, but in none of the other colonies, a small quantity of sugar was refined and a considerably larger quantity was somewhat improved. When imported into England, this partially refined sugar paid only the same duties as the raw product.[3] Under the tariff of 1660, English colonial refined

[1] The colonial interests showed that England, as it was, imported but little Brazilian sugar, and hence maintained that England's export trade to Portugal was not dependent on the sugar imports thence. They further contended that only about one-quarter of the sugar bought by English merchants in Portugal was shipped to England, the bulk being carried in English vessels to other markets.

[2] The colonial interests asserted that there were only twelve refiners in England in 1671. These and the subsequent facts are derived from various memorials prepared during the controversy: C. O. 31/2, ff. 50 *et seq.*; *ibid.* ff. 54 *et seq.*; Bodleian, Rawlinson A 478, f. 63; House of Lords MSS., H.M.C. IX, Part II, p. 12[b]; C. C. 1669–1674, pp. 215, 216. Professor E. R. A. Seligman has in his remarkable library a contemporary broadsheet giving the case of the English refiners and the planters' answer.

[3] The various grades of sugar made in Barbados were: (1) Muscovados, which was simply the juice of the cane boiled to a consistency and put into

sugar paid duties of five shillings the hundredweight, as opposed to one shilling and sixpence on the raw and partially refined commodity. The ratio was thus three and one-third to one. The object of the English refiners was to have this ratio maintained and even enlarged, so that refined sugar could not be profitably imported from the colonies; and they also wanted partially refined sugars imported from the colonies to pay higher duties than the raw product. With this object in view, various calculations were prepared by them to demonstrate that it took at least four pounds of raw sugar to make one of refined. This was exaggerated, and so also was the opposing contention of the colonial interests to the effect that only two pounds of brown were required to make one of white.[1]   It was further maintained on

pots, the molasses or syrup being then drawn off; (2) Sun-dried was made in the same way, but was subsequently dried in the sun for from six to eight hours; (3) Clayed was muscovado with the molasses washed from the grain. When taken from the pot, the clayed sugar was divided into two kinds, of which a small portion was white and the balance brown. All these grades, except the small quantity of white sugar, paid duties in England of only 1s. 6d. the cwt. Brit. Mus., Egerton MSS. 2395, ff. 640, 641. The English refiners stated that, in 1669, 8338 tons of brown and only 118 tons of white sugar were imported. House of Lords MSS., H.M.C. IX, Part II, p. 12[b]. In one of the colonial memorials, it was asserted that two-thirds of the planters in Barbados improved their sugars and that the rest could not make both ends meet. This was a gross exaggeration, unless the term "improved" was meant to include the most rudimentary processes of partial refining. Twenty years later it was stated that one-quarter of the imports from Barbados consisted of clayed or purged sugars. Brit. Mus., Stowe MSS. 324, f. 8.

[1] In 1670–1671, the price of refined sugar in England varied according to the quality from 45s. to 70s., while that of the raw article was about 23s. C. O. 31/2, ff. 54 et seq.; Bodleian, Rawlinson A 478, f. 63; House of Lords MSS., H.M.C. IX, Part II, p. 13[a].

behalf of the colonies that, if the proposed additional duties were based on a ratio of four to one, the English refiners would not only have so overwhelming an advantage over those in the colonies that they would be able to engross the entire white sugar trade, but, as the only buyers of brown sugar, they would also be able to set the price for it 'to the utter undoing of the sugar colonies.' In addition to wanting this liberal differential, the English sugar manufacturers desired a large drawback paid on the exportation of their product, as under existing conditions they could not compete in neutral markets with the continental refiners, who were able to secure English raw sugar more cheaply than they could. The English refiners paid the full duty on this raw sugar and received no drawback on the refined product exported by them, while one-half of the duties on raw sugar was refunded when it was reëxported from England to foreign markets.[1]

The English merchants engaged in the West Indian trade at this time actively supported the English refiners, mainly because the refining of sugar in the colonies would have lessened the amount of freight available for their ships.[2] On their part, the colonies opposed any additional tax on

[1] In 1680, it was pointed out that, as a result of this drawback system, the Dutch were able to secure English sugars and dyeing stuffs more cheaply than could the manufacturers in England, and hence had been enabled "to set up and beat us out of the Forreign Trade of *baked sugars*, of which they bake and vend above 20 times the quantity the *English* do; so do they now use the greatest part of our *Dying Stuffs*, gaining near as much, if not more, by these manufactures than the raw materials yield the *English*." Britannia Languens (London, 1680), p. 174.

[2] They also prepared a number of memorials: C. O. 1/26, 58; C. O. 31/2, ff. 54 *et seq.*; C. C. 1669–1674, p. 216.

their produce, wanted prohibitory duties on all foreign sugars, and sought to secure only a small differential between the refined and the raw product so that they could compete with the English refiners.[1]

As is seemingly inevitable in such controversies, these various groups, with their conflicting interests, issued misleading and inaccurate memorials and statements, omitting damaging facts and over-emphasizing favorable ones. The interests of the West Indies were ably represented in England by the Committee of Gentlemen Planters of Barbados, among whom were such influential men as Sir Peter Colleton, who was also connected with the Carolinas, and Ferdinando Gorges, the proprietor of Maine. When, in the fall of 1670, the scheme for an additional tax on sugar was broached, this committee presented a carefully prepared memorial to the Council for Plantations, and also submitted the same facts to Parliament. They maintained[2] that, prior to 1666, the English West Indies (Jamaica excluded) had employed annually 400 English ships with over 10,000 seamen and had produced a native commodity worth over £800,000 yearly to the nation. This sugar, they stated, had contributed largely to the English customs revenue, and one-half of it

[1] On Dec. 14, 1670, the representatives of Barbados in England wrote to the colony that 'Parliament is now laying a very heavy imposition on sugars, which is like to put the ratio in favour of Portugal and the refiners of England, which the writers are labouring to withstand.' C. C. 1669–1674, p. 141.

[2] C. O. 389/5, ff. 12–14; C. C. 1669–1674, pp. 129, 130, 214, 215; C. O. 1/26, 57; House of Lords MSS., H.M.C. IX, Part II, pp. 11a–11b; Brit. Mus., Egerton MSS., 2395, ff. 638 et seq.; Bodleian, Rawlinson A 478, f. 63.

had been again reshipped from England to foreign markets. The planter's gain, they contended, had been small, while the advantages to England had been important, though "till of late the Plantations never cost his Matie or his Predecessors anything for their maintenance or preservation." Up to 1666, they continued, the French had made very little sugar in the West Indies, but in that and the following year they captured the English part of St. Kitts and also Antigua and Montserrat, and seized in these islands over 15,000 negroes and materials for 150 sugar works, amounting in value to £400,000, which they carried to their own colonies. As a result, the memorialists said, the French sugar output had greatly increased and their islands had become strong and populous. Moreover, being desirous of becoming great at sea and of gaining supremacy in the sugar trade, France was encouraging her colonies, and among other measures had imposed virtually prohibitive duties on English sugars. In consequence, the French West Indies were prospering and had "become terrible to the English Inhabitants in that part of the World," while the English sugar islands were declining. Their sugar had fallen greatly in value, and their planters were emigrating to foreign colonies. From these premises the irresistible conclusion was drawn that the English plantations were in no way able to bear a further imposition on their sugars, since it "alwaies falls vpon the Planters," but that rather, after the example of France, a higher duty should be laid on the foreign product.[1]

---

[1] In 1664 and 1665, Colbert imposed very high duties on foreign refined sugars, which led to the rapid development of the French refining industry.

The gist of this doleful memorial, which grossly exaggerated the relative economic condition of the French and
English West Indies, as well as other vital facts, was that
no further tax should be imposed on English sugars, while
the small quantity of Portuguese refined sugar imported
should be totally excluded by a prohibitive duty.[1] In their
efforts in the House of Commons, these representatives of
Barbados came into conflict with the English refiners who
wanted the schedule so arranged that sugars could not be

In 1665 also, French raw sugars were given preferential treatment over those
of foreign countries, but by this *arrêt* no distinction was made between the
various grades of French colonial sugars, and all, whether refined or unrefined, had to pay a uniform duty of 4 livres per cwt. Under this arrangement it was far more advantageous to refine sugar in the colonies than in
France, and a considerable industry was established in them. The French
refiners complained of the handicap imposed upon them, and accordingly
in 1682 the duty on colonial refined sugar was raised to 8 livres, and two years
later the establishment of new refineries in the islands was prohibited.
S. L. Mims, Colbert's West India Policy, pp. 263–279. The ratio adopted
was thus two to one, but it took from two and a half to three pounds of raw
sugar to make one of refined. Thus these duties still gave an advantage to
the colonial refiners, in addition to the initial one that they enjoyed from the
fact that they had to pay the freight to France on only the refined product,
while their French competitors had to pay these charges on the bulky raw
product. Apart from the differences in cost of labor and capital, which
naturally were fundamental, it would appear that the ratio adopted by the
English government in 1660 would in other respects have placed the colonial and European refiner on a parity.

[1] On April 20, 1671, the Barbados Assembly wrote to the Gentlemen
Planters in London, thanking them for their great pains and endeavors to
prevent the new impost on sugar, and instructing them to keep up the opposition, but that, if the new tax could not be prevented, they should then
labor as much as was possible to have it doubled on foreign sugars, so that
only those from the English colonies could be imported. C. O. 31/2, f. 29;
C. C. 1669–1674, p. 199.

profitably refined in the colonies.[1]   The additional schedule
at first suggested was one farthing a pound on raw and one
penny on white sugars from the English colonies, as opposed
to twopence on those of foreign production.   In view of
the discrimination against Portuguese sugars, the Barbados
Committee was not much dissatisfied and was willing to
accept the proposed schedule.   But the merchants trading
to Portugal objected and, on showing how advantageous
was their trade, secured a reduction of the duty on foreign
refined sugars to one-penny.   The English refiners, supported
by the English merchants trading to Barbados, then suggested that a duty of one half-penny a pound be imposed
on a new class of "clayed" sugars.   This would have been
levied on the partially refined sugars made in Barbados,
which hitherto had paid the same duties as raw sugar.[2]
To this the Committee of Planters objected, and urged that,
if a new duty had to be placed on sugar, the English colonial product should receive preferential treatment.   They
also insisted that refining in the colonies should not be discouraged by high duties.   "In this," they wrote to the
Barbados Assembly "we were vehemently opposed by the
Refine[rs] and our merchants who alleadged, that white Sugar
was the Interest of not aboue five Planters & that to Discourage the making of itt in the Plantacõns was the Interest

---

[1] On May 1, 1671, this Committee sent a detailed account of the proceedings in Parliament to the Barbados Assembly.   Barbados Assembly Journal,
1670–1683: C. O. 31/2, ff. 45–76; C. C. 1669–1674, pp. 212–214.

[2] The English refiners stated that 4½ lbs. of brown equalled in value 1 lb.
of white sugar, and that 3 lbs. of brown equalled 1 lb. of clayed sugar.   House
of Lords MSS., H.M.C. IX, Part II, p. 12[b].   *Cf. ibid*. p. 13[a].

of England & the Generallity of ye planters." As the House of Commons found the Barbados Committee thus flatly contradicted by the West India merchants, of whom some had lived in that colony, it accepted the schedule before it and passed the bill.[1]

The Barbados Committee, knowing, so they wrote, "the Lords to bee men unconcerned & of more discerning Judgem[t] than the Generallity of the Commons," continued the fight when the measure reached the upper house. They handed in a memorial, and so did the other interested parties — the Lisbon traders, the English refiners, and the merchants trading to Barbados. The Governor of Barbados, William, Lord Willoughby of Parham, vigorously supported the planters, and the House of Lords was induced to reduce the duty on English white sugars from one-penny to two and a half farthings [2] and to omit the new class of partially refined sugars.[3] So amended, the bill was returned to the House of Commons, which "flew into a heate and voted the Lords had noe righte to abate of any ayd Graunted to the King & sent them that message." Various conferences followed, in which each house adhered to its position, and on the King proroguing Parliament, the bill fell.[4] This was the famous

[1] The full schedule is in House of Lords MSS., H.M.C. IX, Part II, p. 8[a]. In order to encourage sugar refining in England, large drawbacks were also granted on the exportation of white sugars.

[2] The Lords adopted the ratio between refined and raw sugar of $2\frac{1}{2}$ to 1, the Commons that of 4 to 1.

[3] These amendments are in House of Lords MSS., H.M.C. IX, Part II, p. 10[a].

[4] See also Com. Journal IX, pp. 238–240; F. R. Harris, Edward, Earl of Sandwich.

precedent so often cited during the constitutional controversies about the British budget of 1909.

Owing to this dispute between the two Houses, the attempt
to impose additional duties on tobacco and sugar failed in
1671. But the question was not definitely tabled. When
sending the details of what had happened to the colony, the
Barbados Committee wrote that it was necessary to get
the English merchants trading to the West Indies interested
in their 'improved sugars,' in order to separate them from
the refiners, because, if united, these two groups might be
too powerful, should Parliament again take up this measure.
Moreover, they added that the King was not pleased with
the loss of the bill, which was occasioned wholly by the dispute about sugar. On hearing of the failure of the bill,
the Barbados Assembly wrote to Lord Willoughby, thanking
him for his work in the House of Lords, and asserting that
the colony would be ruined if a further tax were imposed
on their sugar, unless that on the foreign product were at
the same time doubled.[1] They likewise wrote to the
Gentlemen Planters in London to continue their efforts at
the next parliamentary session, and enclosed a petition to
the King which asserted that Barbados was already in a
declining state.[2]

During the following fourteen years the project was kept
alive, and a number of memorials opposed and advocated
various schemes for additional duties on tobacco and sugar.[3]

[1] C. O. 31/2, ff. 41–45, 86, 87; C. C. 1669–1674, pp. 231, 283.
[2] C. O. 31/2, ff. 87–91; C. C. 1669–1674, pp. 283, 284.
[3] "The Virginia Trade Stated," evidently of 1677, opposed the imposition
of further duties on tobacco, using the old arguments and especially empha-

Nothing, however, was done until the accession of James II, in 1685, when Parliament granted for eight years heavy additional duties on tobacco and sugar.[1] The bill was devised by one of the ablest men of the day, the economist Sir Dudley North, then one of the Commissioners of the Customs, and was vigorously supported by him in the House of Commons. It aroused great opposition there,[2] and also outside of Parliament, from the merchants, retailers and consumers, "as if the utter ruin of all the plantations was to follow; and all trading from thence, and all dealing whatever in those commodities, were all to be confounded at one single stroke."[3] The additional duty imposed on English colonial tobacco was threepence a pound, as opposed to sixpence additional laid on the foreign product. Thus,

---

sizing the prevailing depression in the tobacco trade. C. O. 1/41, 142. In 1673, an anonymous writer discussed the question of the sugar duties. C. O. 1/30, 10; C. C. 1669–1674, pp. 469, 470. See also the two memorials in Brit. Mus., Egerton MSS. 2395, ff. 636; ff. 640, 641.

[1] 1 Jac. II, c. 4; Com. Journal IX, pp. 724, 733, 737, 738; Egmont MSS. (H.M.C. 1909) II, p. 155.

[2] It "made a greater stir, and had more opposition in parliament, than any later revenue or supply bill ever had; and, upon voting the supply, and charging it so to be levied, it was cried out upon as if it had been a surrender of liberty and property." Roger North, Lives of the Norths (London, 1826) II, p. 122. Sir John Reresby states that the proposed taxes were "much opposed" by many members of the House of Commons, who had direct or indirect interests in the colonies. They argued that these taxes would handicap the English colonies in competing with the French. Reresby replied that, if the rates were so high as to discourage consumption in England, this might happen; but, if the colonies sold as much as formerly, these additional duties "could neither prejudice our plantations or navigation." The Memoirs of Sir John Reresby (ed. Cartwright), pp. 330, 331.

[3] Roger North, op. cit. III, pp. 161–164.

under the Acts of 1660 and 1685, the total duty on colonial tobacco was fivepence and that on foreign tobacco one shilling the pound.[1] The sugar schedule was more complicated, but likewise contained the same preferential treatment of English colonial products. Muscovado or raw sugar paid additional duties of one farthing a pound, if English; of two farthings, if foreign. White or refined sugar from the English colonies was subjected to an additional duty of three farthings, as opposed to five farthings imposed on that of foreign production.[2]

In order to prevent any diminution of the sale of tobacco and sugar in the international markets, on the reëxportation of these commodities from England, the additional duties were refunded in their entirety.[3] It was the design of Par-

---

[1] This additional duty on tobacco was opposed on the grounds: (1) that the trade was depressed, the existing charges being already "more than often times the Commodity yielded"; (2) that these high duties would encourage smuggling and would lessen English consumption, experience showing that, the higher the tax, the less the revenue; (3) that these duties would stimulate the production of tobacco in Germany, France, and Holland and would tempt the traders to violate the enumeration of tobacco; (4) that necessity would force the colonies to use their lands for raising provisions and would oblige them to make manufactures hitherto obtained from England. Brit. Mus., Harleian MSS. 1238, f. 2.

[2] Moreover, foreign loaf sugar had to pay an additional duty of threepence a pound. The additional duty of three farthings was imposed on English sugar "fitt for Common use or Spending." As some muscovado sugars were fit for consumption, the question arose if they were in consequence liable to this higher duty. The Attorney-General, Sir Thomas Powys, decided in 1687 that it was clearly the intention of Parliament that the extra duty on all English muscovado sugars should be only one farthing. Brit. Mus., Add. MSS. 30,218, f. 134.

[3] The importer got possession of the goods on giving security for the duty, and, if the goods had not been sold or exported within eighteen months,

liament in imposing these taxes that they should be wholly borne by the consumer in England, the "consumptioner" as the statute called him, and not at all by the planter or importer. With this idea in view, a curiously naïve scheme was devised. The additional duties were not made payable by the importer — he merely gave security for their ultimate payment — but by the first buyer on receipt of the goods.[1] On June 26, 1685, a circular letter was sent in the King's name to the various colonial Governors, informing them of the new duties and stating that, as they were "not laid on the Planter or Merchant, but only upon the Retailer, Consumptioner, or Shopkeeper, wee are well assured (they) will not be inconvenient or burthensome to our Subjects under Yo[r] Government."[2]

The impost of 1685 aroused considerable hostile feeling in some of the colonies,[3] especially in Barbados, which was in the forefront of every movement of opposition to England's economic measures. The Virginia Assembly sent an address, in which the Council and Governor, how-

he had to pay the duty. 1 Jac. II, c. 4, § x. The period during which the tobacco could be reëxported was subsequently extended to three years. 7 Geo. I, stat. 1, c. 21, § x. Large allowances were made for cash payment of the duties and for damage and shrinkage while the goods were in the importers' hands. 1 Jac. II, c. 4, §§ viii, ix; C. C. 1685–1688, pp. 71, 98, 99; C. O. 1/56, 67.

[1] For the administrative features, see Treas. Books, Out-Letters, Customs 10, ff. 36, 38, 40–42, 45, 50, 56, 112, 126. This cumbersome system was abandoned in 1696. 7 & 8 W. III, c. 10, § iii.

[2] C. O. 31/3, ff. 135–137, 141–143; C. C. 1681–1685, p. 59.

[3] Randolph wrote that he feared it was injuring New England, whose trade to the colonies directly affected had decayed very much since its imposition. Goodrick, Randolph VI, p. 235.

ever, refused to join, praying the King to dispense with the
new duty on account of the low price of tobacco, and asserting that the tax, 'though designed to fall on the retailer and
consumer, would surely fall on the planter.'[1]   At the same
time, the Governor, Lord Howard of Effingham, wrote that
"the late Additional Imposition on Tobacco has so dis-
turbed the Planters here, either by the not right apprehend-
ing the Act, or by their fears that their Diana and Sole
Commodity will Downe and Come to nothing that it is
difficult to persuade them otherwise."[2]

On August 29, 1685,[3] before the exact terms of the law
were known in Jamaica, Lieutenant-Governor Hender
Molesworth wrote to William Blathwayt that the additional
duties would greatly discourage planting and would throw
land out of cultivation.   Not knowing that these duties
were to be refunded on reëxportation of the commodities
from England, he claimed that the result would be that English sugars would be unable to compete in foreign markets
with those of the Portuguese, Dutch, and French possessions.[4]   A month later, however, after the provisions of the
law were fully known, Molesworth wrote that his former
criticisms were based on a misapprehension and that, in
his opinion, the additional duties would in the main be

[1] C. C. 1685–1688, pp. 116, 117.

[2] Nov. 14, 1685, Howard to Blathwayt.   Blathwayt, Journal I, f.
184.

[3] C. C. 1685–1688, p. 84.

[4] 'The short of it is,' he wrote, 'that Virginia receives a mortal stab,
Barbados and the Islands fall into a hectic fever, and Jamaica into a consumption.'

shifted to the consumer and would not fall upon the planter.[1]

The opposition from Barbados was more persistent and better organized. On September 14, 1865,[2] the Assembly, Council, and Deputy-Governor of the colony wrote to the Lords of Trade, stating that the island was heavily in debt and that the sugar industry was not profitable. Consequently, they could not stand the additional duty, which they claimed to know by woeful experience would fall upon the producer and not upon the consumer, as was intended.[3] They also enclosed a detailed memorial showing the great cost of producing sugar and its relatively low market value, as a result of which they claimed that Barbados was in a deplorable state.[4]　Letters were also sent by the Assembly to

---

[1] 'I find that the additional duty on sugar is much otherwise than we apprehended.　We believed that it was to be paid on all imported sugar without exception; but, considering that it is only to be paid on what is expended in England, and that our exported sugars are free from it, I incline to the opinion that it will fall chiefly on the expender.'　C. C. 1685–1688, p. 96.

[2] C. C. 1685–1688, pp. 93, 94.

[3] They stated that since the beginning of the year sugar had declined in price from 13s. 6d. and 14s. to 8s. the cwt.

[4] They asserted that the annual cost of a plantation of 100 acres, figuring interest at 5 per cent on the capital invested in the land, buildings, and machinery, making allowance for wear and tear, and including the cost of labor and running expenses, as well as the parochial taxes, amounted to £745 10s.　Such a plantation would yield yearly only £400 of raw sugar (figuring the price at 10s. a cwt.) and £140 of rum and molasses.　Thus there was a deficit of about £200, which they asserted had hitherto been avoided by "claying" their sugars.　This clayed sugar, they claimed, was not worth twice as much as muscovado or raw sugar, but the new duties thereon were three times as high and consequently they would no longer be

William Blathwayt, the influential Secretary of the Lords of Trade, to the Governor of Barbados, Sir Richard Dutton — then in England answering charges against him — and to Sir Peter Colleton of the Committee of Gentlemen Planters, asking their support for this address.[1] About a month later, the Deputy-Governor of Barbados, Edwyn Stede, wrote to the Lords of Trade, acknowledging receipt of the King's letter to the effect that it was the intent that these duties should be paid by the consumer, but stoutly maintaining that it was found 'by experience of sales, both here and in England, that the duty falls on the planter, and will continue to do so unless, by your great wisdom, some means be found to moderate it.'[2]

These complaints from Virginia and Barbados were referred to the Commissioners of the Customs, who reported that they contained nothing that they had not already frequently heard from the London merchants; that it was 'the abundance of sugar and tobacco, not the duty, that brings them evil;' and, accordingly, they recommended that no change should be made in the duty for at least a year.[3] To this the Lords of Trade agreed.[4]

able to "clay" their sugar. They then claimed that the result would be equally disastrous if they shipped their raw sugar to England for sale there, and that the new duties would still further reduce the price of sugar in Barbados from 10s. to 7s. a cwt.   C. O. 31/3, ff. 120 *et seq.*

[1] C. C. 1681–1685, p. 95.

[2] He added that the people were mostly in debt and under great affliction, in consequence of a very poor crop and the great mortality among their negroes and servants due to smallpox. *Ibid.* p. 109.

[3] C. C. 1685–1688, pp. 125, 127, 141, 147.

[4] *Ibid.* p. 202.

There was no necessity for the cumbersome method of paying these duties in order that they should be shifted to the consumer. As Hender Molesworth said, 'it ought to fall out so by natural course of trade,'[1] since these new duties were not imposed on that portion of the crops sold in foreign markets. It was the price in this international market that regulated the amount received by the planter for his entire product. The only way in which these duties could adversely affect the colonies was by lessening consumption in England. To some degree this must have been the result, but its extent was apparently not important. In the case of tobacco, upon which the new duties were relatively much higher than were those on sugar, they also led to the adulteration of the article in England [2] and likewise probably stimulated smuggling, both of which reacted unfavorably on the planter. The disadvantages to the colonies were, however, slight in comparison with the renewal of the preferential treatment of their produce.

These new taxes produced a comparatively large revenue; from 1688 to 1692 it averaged about £122,000 yearly, of which £90,000 was derived from the tobacco impost.[3] These duties were thus most satisfactory from the financial

[1] C. C. 1685–1688, p. 96.

[2] The stalks or stems, which weighed about 20 per cent of the tobacco, were soaked, pressed flat, and then cut and mixed with the leaf tobacco. Brit. Mus., Harleian MSS. 1238, f. 29.

[3] Brit. Mus., Stowe MSS. 324, f. 64; *ibid.* 316, ff. 3, 4. The importations of tobacco into England at this time were from fourteen to nineteen million pounds annually, the impost being paid on about one-half only, as the balance was reëxported to foreign markets. Brit. Mus., Harleian MSS. 1238, f. 31; Sloane MSS. 1815, f. 35; C. O. 5/1305, 54–56.

standpoint, and furthermore they were easy to collect. It could not reasonably be expected that so large a revenue would be abandoned, unless it were clear that these duties hampered the development of the colonies, especially as their produce was granted a monopoly of the English market. This, of course, could not be demonstrated. Ever since that time tobacco has been a most fruitful source of income to the British Exchequer.[1] The tobacco trade quickly adjusted itself to the new conditions, and Virginia and Maryland soon forgot about these new duties. But Barbados, always energetically active, continued the agitation and as those who represented its interests in England had considerable influence, the sugar duties were not continued on their expiration in 1693, while those on tobacco were prolonged and ultimately made perpetual.[2]

Thus the English tariffs were so constructed that the most important of the colonial products had a monopoly of the English market. During the course of their enforced trans-shipment through England, these enumerated articles also paid some duties to the English Exchequer. On raw sugar they amounted to ninepence the hundredweight, which was not onerous,[3] but on tobacco the duty was one

---

[1] "No other product that enters into commerce is taxed so heavily as tobacco. England levies a tax of 77 cents per pound when it contains 10 per cent of moisture; 85 cents per pound, when there is less than this amount. This is from twelve to fifteen hundred per cent on the prices which the farmers receive." Shelfer, Tobacco, in Am. Econ. Assoc. 3d series, V, 1, p. 142. This statement refers to American tobacco, and was written before 1904; since then the duties have been increased.

[2] 2 W. & M. sess. 2, c. 5; 4 & 5 W. & M. c. 15; 9 Anne, c. 21.

[3] The value of sugar in Barbados in 1670 was about 12s. a cwt.

half-penny the pound, which was considerable in proportion to the value of tobacco in the colonies.[1]   Furthermore,
some duties were retained on European goods shipped from
England to the plantations.   In effect, these were equivalent
to direct taxes on the colonies; and, while not of great importance, they were not negligible from a revenue standpoint.   The half-penny on tobacco was the chief source of
revenue, and amounted on an average to about £15,000
yearly just prior to the Revolution of 1688/9.[2]   In 1676,
this half subsidy on sugar was estimated at £5000 a year
and amounted to about the same sum a decade later.[3]   In
addition to this indirect method of taxing the colonies, Parliament in 1673 had also imposed duties on the intercolonial
trade.   At the time, some objection was made to this law on
the ground that it violated the principle of no taxation without representation; its purpose, however, was not to raise
a revenue, but to regulate imperial trade.   Incidentally
thereto it did produce a gross income of about £1000, of
which the bulk, however, was used in its collection.[4]

In addition to this instance of direct taxation by the Act
of 1673, whose actual fiscal importance was slight in comparison with its potential legal significance, some revenue was

---

[1] The price of tobacco in Virginia averaged about $1\frac{1}{2}d.$ the pound.

[2] The available statistical material is scanty and unreliable.   This statement is based upon a comparative study of a number of documents, of which
the chief are Brit. Mus., Harleian MSS. 1238, ff. 2, 31; Sloane MSS. 1815,
f. 35; C. O. 5/1305, nos. 54–56.

[3] Cal. Dom. 1676–1677, p. 464; The Irregular and Disorderly State of
the Plantation-Trade, in Am. Hist. Assoc. Report (1892), p. 38.

[4] See *ante*, p. 83, and *post*, Chapter IV.

derived on other grounds from colonial sources. The early colonial charters, as a rule, provided that one-fifth of whatever gold and silver might be obtained should be reserved to the Crown. In addition, the colonial proprietors were bound by their letters patent to make some annual acknowledgment of English suzerainty. Thus Lord Baltimore was obliged by his charter to deliver every year at Windsor Castle "two Indian arrows of those parts." No gold or silver was, however, found in the colonies; and the picturesque feudal acknowledgments were intended to be only symbolically significant and, besides, they were generally ignored.[1] In addition, the Crown as such was also entitled to certain rights and royalties. Fines, forfeitures, and escheats in the royal provinces, goods seized from pirates[2] and a portion of what was recovered from wrecks belonged to it. At one time the question of the Crown's share of wrecks became very prominent. In 1686, a small company was formed in England to recover treasure from wrecks, and William Phipps was sent by it to try his luck with a sunken Spanish ship off Hispaniola. The following year, the expedition returned to England with about £250,000, of which the Crown received £20,872 in settlement of its one-tenth share.[3] The news of this vast treasure-trove spread

[1] Blathwayt, Journal II, ff. 44–53. Among the receipts of the Exchequer, however, are £66 for 1682–1683, £40 for 1683–1684, and £93 for 1685–1686, as rent of Carolina. W. R. Scott, Joint-Stock Companies III, pp. 532, 533.

[2] C. O. 1/61, 42; C. C. 1685–1688, pp. 10, 11, 15, 29, 36, 47, 122, 255, 340.

[3] W. R. Scott, Joint-Stock Companies II, pp. 485, 486; III, pp. 536–539.

quickly in America, and from nearly all the colonies vessels flocked to the scene of action. A considerable amount of treasure was recovered, £50,000 being brought to the Bermudas alone. Acting upon the precedent established in England, the various colonial governors demanded one-tenth of this treasure as the Crown's share. While they were engaged in a largely unsuccessful attempt to collect these dues, orders were received from England that payment of one-half of what was secured by the wreckers should be made to the Crown. This aroused a storm of protest; and, as it was impossible to enforce this claim, in 1688 the government receded from its untenable position and instructed the Governors to demand only one-tenth as the Crown's share.[1] Searching for wrecked treasure was, however, in the long run a very precarious and speculative occupation, and naturally but little income was derived by the Crown from this source.

As in the case of wrecks, a certain proportion of prizes of war taken at sea was legally due to the King, and another share also to the Lord High Admiral. These were the Crown's fifteenths and the Admiralty's tenths,[2] but even in Jamaica, which was the centre of privateering, these dues were 'but a small matter.'[3] In addition, one-third or one-half — depending upon the nature of the case — of all forfeitures for

---

[1] Blathwayt, Journal I, ff. 244–248; C. O. 1/60, 88; Goodrick, Randolph VI, pp. 229, 240, 249; C. C. 1685–1688, pp. 391–393, 421, 455, 480, 489–494, 505, 506, 508, 509, 518, 519, 524, 529, 530, 538, 543, 551, 560.

[2] C. C. 1661–1668, no. 1138; *ibid.* 1669–1674, pp. 145–147.

[3] C. C. 1669–1674, p. 95.

violations of the Acts of Trade and Navigation was apportioned to the Crown, and under the charter of the Royal African Company the King was also entitled to one-half of all condemnations for violation of this Company's trade monopoly.[1] In general, this miscellaneous revenue was of but slight importance and besides it was, as a rule, devoted to colonial purposes.[2] Only in Barbados was this "casual revenue," as it was there called, of any fiscal importance. Here a special officer, who was also the Collector of the Customs, was entrusted with its collection; and, in 1687, £2500 was remitted to England, representing the proceeds of this revenue for the preceding four years.[3]

In addition to these rights and royalties, as successor to some of the colonial proprietors, the Crown was entitled to the revenue that would have accrued to them as lords of their domains. In Virginia and in the Caribbee Islands, especially, these rights were very important. In 1627, a few years after some small English settlements had been founded in Barbados and in St. Kitts, the most important of the West Indian islands, not colonized by Spain, were granted by charter to James Hay, first Earl of Carlisle. Their economic development was at the outset comparatively

---

[1] Blathwayt, Journal I, ff. 67, 79, 295. The same applied to forfeitures for violations of the monopoly of the Hudson's Bay Company.

[2] The casual revenue in Jamaica arising from fines, forfeitures, escheats, etc., and also that from the quit-rents, was applied to the uses of the colony. Blathwayt, Journal I, ff. 378-381.

[3] In 1682, Edwyn Stede was appointed receiver of the rents, revenues, prizes, fines, escheats, forfeitures, etc., arising to the Crown in Barbados. Ibid. I, ff. 108, 109, 258, 378-381.

slow, as the chief product was tobacco, in which they were at a considerable disadvantage in competing with Virginia.[1] The introduction of the sugar-cane during the period of the Civil War, however, led to an era of phenomenal growth and prosperity, especially in Barbados, which in a few years became by far the richest of the English colonies.[2] "The like Improvem:," a contemporary said, "was neuer made by any people vnder the Sonne." [3]

During the Civil War in England, the proprietary rights of the royalist Earl of Carlisle, son of the original patentee, were sequestrated, but in 1645, on his submission to Parliament, they were restored. In the same year, these islands were decreed in chancery to the creditors of the spendthrift first Earl in payment of debts amounting to £37,000. Two years later, in 1647, the proprietor leased his rights, subject to these claims of his father's creditors, for twenty-one years to Francis, Lord Willoughby of Parham.[4] On the execution of Charles I in 1649, Barbados abandoned its attempt to preserve a neutral attitude toward the struggle in

---

[1] "At the beginning all the foreign Inhabitants of the Caribbies apply'd themselves wholly to the culture of Tobacco, whereby they made a shift to get a competent livelihood; but afterwards the abundance that was made bringing down the price of it, they have in several places employ'd themselves in the planting of Sugar-canes, Ginger, and Indico." The History of Barbados, St Christophers, etc., trans. by J. Davies (London, 1666), p. 187. Cf. Beer, Origins, pp. 264, 265.

[2] The sugar-cane was said to have been originally introduced into Barbados from Brazil by one Peeter Brower of North Holland, but came to no perfection until 1645. Brit. Mus., Sloane MSS. 2662, ff. 54^b, 70.

[3] Brit. Mus., Egerton MSS. 2543, f. 123.

[4] Cal. Treas. Papers, 1557–1696, p. 12.

England and openly proclaimed the rights of his son, the future Charles II. But in 1652, after a stout resistance, the island was obliged to surrender to a strong parliamentary force. The proprietary system of Lord Willoughby was thereupon extinguished and a parliamentary Governor was appointed. The same course of events followed in the other West Indian colonies.

On the restoration of the monarchy in England, the question naturally arose what should be done with these islands. In England, the lands confiscated during the Interregnum were restored to their original owners. Should the same policy be adopted towards the proprietary rights in the West Indies? In favor of restitution were the Earl of Carlisle, as proprietor, and Lord Willoughby, the lease-holder, and naturally also the creditors of the original patentee. Opposed to them were the planters and colonists, and also the merchants engaged in trading to the sugar islands.[1]

In the early summer of 1660, Charles II recognized the rights of Lord Willoughby under the Carlisle patent of 1627, and directed the inhabitants of the West Indies to yield obedience to his government.[2] This was merely a provisional disposition of the matter, and in the meanwhile the government continued to investigate the case and to give hearings to the interested parties.[3] The Committee of

[1] C. C. 1574–1660, p. 482.

[2] *Ibid.* p. 483; Brit. Mus., Egerton MSS. 2395, f. 267.

[3] C. O. 1/14, 20; P. C. Cal. I, pp. 296, 297; C. C. 1574–1660, pp. 483, 484, 486, 488.

the Privy Council reported, however, on August 20, 1660, that Lord Willoughby should be restored to the rights of which he had been dispossessed by the 'illegal power of Cromwell.'[1] This report was approved, and Willoughby proceeded successfully to reëstablish the proprietary authority in Barbados and in the Leeward Islands.[2]

But those opposed to this settlement continued to agitate and succeeded in having the question reopened. They were aided by the fact that it was already recognized that these semi-feudal proprietary colonies were difficult to manage, and that from the imperial standpoint it would be advisable to convert them into crown colonies under the immediate control of the English government.[3] Early in 1661, the Privy Council ordered all who pretended to any interest in or title to the Caribbee Islands to deliver to the Attorney-General "their severall and respective Proprietyes" and to attend the board with their counsel.[4] As a result of this reëxamination of the case, the decision of the preceding year was reversed; and on March 28, 1661,

[1] C. C. 1574–1660, p. 489.

[2] *Ibid.* pp. 490, 494, 496; Brit. Mus., Egerton MSS. 2395, ff. 305, 329.

[3] In his overtures advising the creation of a council for foreign plantations, Thomas Povey urged that "such Collonies, as are the Proprietie of perticular Persons, or of Corporations may bee reduced as neare as can bee to the Same Method and Proportion with the rest; with as little Dissatisfaction or Iniurie to the Persons concerned, as may be." Brit. Mus., Egerton MSS. 2395, f. 273. In a memorial of the same time, such grants as those of Charles I to Carlisle were opposed. It was stated therein that Charles II had been surprised into reinstating Willoughby, and he was urged to appoint a Governor himself. Brit. Mus., Egerton MSS. 2543, f. 123.

[4] P. C. Cal. I, pp. 304, 305; C. C. 1661–1668, no. 36.

Sir William Morice, "his Majesties Principall Secretary of State," was ordered to notify Barbados "that the proprietors-ship of the said Island is invested in his Majestie." [1] Shortly thereafter, Lord Willoughby was appointed Governor of the colony by the Crown. [2]

The revocation of the Carlisle charter abolished only the powers of government granted therein, but left intact the patentee's property rights and the revenue to which he was entitled as grantor of the lands. There were diverse claims on this revenue, and only in 1663, after prolonged negotiations, was this matter definitely settled. It was then provided [3] that the annual profits arising to the Crown from the Caribbee Islands should be divided into two equal parts, of which one should go to Lord Willoughby during the six remaining years of his lease, but thereafter should "be entirely reserved in his Majesties dispose towards the support of the Government of the said Islands, and to such other purposes as his Majestie shall please to assigne the same." The second half was charged with the payment of two annuities; a temporary one of £500 to the Earl of Marlborough, whose grandfather had had a grant covering Barbados prior to that of Carlisle, [4] and a perpetual one of £1000 to the Earl of Kinnoul, who had succeeded to the Earl of Carlisle's

[1] P. C. Cal. I, pp. 305, 306.

[2] C. C. 1661–1668, nos. 80, 83.

[3] Cal. Treas. Papers, 1557–1696, pp. 12–14; P. C. Cal. I, pp. 362–365; C. C. 1661–1668, no. 482; Brit. Mus., Sloane MSS. 2441, ff. 7, 8. *Cf.* also C. C. 1699, p. 588.

[4] The annuity was transferred in 1665. C. C. 1661–1668, no. 1432.

rights.[1] After the payment of these two annuities, the balance of this second half of the revenue was to go to the creditors of the first Earl of Carlisle, who had not received "the least part of their Debts or Interest since his death." They, in return, agreed to cancel one-third of the amount due them, which reduced their claims to about £25,000. After the payment of this indebtedness, the "Second Moyety" of this revenue was also to revert to the Crown. Thus, ultimately the entire revenue, subject only to the Kinnoul annuity of £1000, would be at the disposal of the King.

Having thus apportioned the prospective income arising from the Caribbee Islands, it now remained to establish a permanent revenue in the place of the proprietary dues. With this object in view, the royal Governor, Lord Willoughby, who was departing for the West Indies, received careful instructions from the government. He was ordered to make these colonies "sensible that some Returne of Profitt, as well as Duty ought to be made Vs for our continuall and unwearied care of them," and he was authorized, if necessary, to employ part of the anticipated revenue in fortifying the colonies.[2]

Barbados was kept informed of the course of these protracted negotiations in England, and, while more than satisfied with the definite abolition of the proprietary charter, was naturally anxious to make the best terms possible as regards the revenue that should be paid to the Crown.

[1] Kinnoul was to receive £500 yearly up to 1670 and thereafter £1000 in perpetuity. *Cf.* Cal. Treas. Books, 1676–1679, Nov. 13, 1676.

[2] P. C. Cal. I, pp. 357, 358.

During the agitation for the revocation of the charter, the colony stated its willingness to pay to the King as much as had formerly been paid to the Earl of Carlisle, and at this time some in the island proposed an export duty of four per cent.[1] But in the summer of 1661, the President of the Council and the Council proposed to the Assembly to petition the King against this four per cent proposition and "to beseech his Majesty that hee will not put vs into a worse condition then formerly wee were in (wee growing poorer and our ground every day decaying) but that we may hold our lands as heretofore we did" on free and common socage tenure, paying the impost of two and four per cent, as was agreed between the Assembly and the proprietor. The Assembly, while approving, would not concur, as it did not consider a time, when the King's commands were daily expected, appropriate for such a petition.[2] Accordingly, on July 10, 1661, the President and Council wrote in their

---

[1] C. O. 1/15, 52; C. C. 1661–1668, no. 83.

[2] C. O. 1/15, 69; C. O. 31/1, 53; C. C. 1661–1668, no. 127. The Assembly was dissolved, and in a declaration to the people giving the reasons for this dissolution, the President and Council stated that a letter had recently been received from Sir James Drax to the effect that efforts were being made to induce the King to lay a tax on Barbados, "itt being not only the maintenance of the Government and all other publique charge but the paying of four out of Every Hundred of all Comodityes made and transported to his Ma^{tye}," which it was claimed would produce £25,000 yearly. The declaration stated that it was proposed to establish this tax by Act of Parliament, and urged quick action, for, if it were thus enacted, "it would bee hard getting of it repealed." Nothing was said about the illegality of such a parliamentary tax. Journal of Barbados Council, 1660–1686: C. O. 31/1, ff. 56, 57. The following year the colony, however, petitioned " that noe tax bee layd without the consent of the freeholders." *Ibid.* ff. 76, 77.

own names only to the Secretary of State, saying that they feared that the wealth of the colony had been grossly exaggerated and that proposals had been made to raise taxes greater than the people could bear. They therefore prayed the King not to impose the proposed four per cent tax and begged that they might not be obliged to pay any more than they had formerly done to the proprietor.[1]

The tactical weakness of Barbados in the approaching contest lay in the uncertainty of the land titles of many of the planters. In numerous cases they were defective and of doubtful legality. Above all things the colony desired that this be rectified, and that the existing grants should be confirmed. In 1662, they had petitioned the King that Parliament should pass a law removing all uncertainty from their land titles.[2] With this powerful and convincing argument at his disposal,[3] Willoughby arrived in Barbados in the midsummer of 1663 with the object of creating the desired revenue and of establishing crown government in the colony. The colonial executive had hitherto been appointed by him as leaseholder under the charter, and the Assembly

---

[1] C. O. 1/15, 70; Brit. Mus., Egerton MSS. 2395, ff. 305 *et seq.;* C. C. 1661–1668, no. 129.

[2] They wanted "Tenure in Soccage to bee held of the King &c paying Such an acknowledgem.[t] as the Governor Counsell and Assembly shall agree vnto." C. O. 31/1, 76, 77.

[3] Article xi of Willoughby's instructions reads : "Since it seemes requisite, that the Occupiers and Possessors of Land need further Confirmation from Vs, We giue you full Power as from Vs, further to graunt and confirme the same for such Consideration, and under such Covenants, Conditions and Reservations, as betweene you and the respectiue Parties shall be agreed on." P. C. Cal. I, p. 359.

had been convened on the same authority. Summoning this proprietary Assembly, Willoughby laid before it his instructions, in order, as he wrote, 'to avoid the delay of calling together a new one, which might be done if the present Assembly should not answer his Majesty's expectations.' [1] Thanks to his popularity in the island and by dint of great exertions, Willoughby [2] induced this Assembly in September of 1663 to pass the famous four and a half per cent export duty Act, which played a most prominent part in the future relations of the colony and England. [3] In the spring of

[1] C. O. 1/17, 78; C. C. 1661–1668, no. 561.

[2] On Aug. 25, 1663, Governor Willoughby addressed the Council and Assembly and said that Charles II "had been at very great charge in purchasing to himselfe" the Earl of Carlisle's patent, and that "although hee had been offered in England from some Gentlemen very large Sumes of money for his Revenue" here, yet he had refused it and to show his good will to the colony had left it to them to do what was requisite. C. O. 31/1, ff. 80, 81.

[3] There are two accounts available of what happened in Barbados. One stated that, when Willoughby arrived in Barbados, he published his royal commission as Governor and proclaimed that all powers derived from Carlisle's patent were null and void. Despite this, he summoned the old Assembly that had been elected under this patent. This body at first refused to act as an assembly, but being threatened and told that what they did would have no validity, but would merely be used as an argument with the legal Assembly to be convened subsequently, they were prevailed upon to pass the 4½ per cent Act. Brit. Mus., Stowe MSS. 324, ff. 4 et seq.; C. O. 1/22, 20; C. C. 1661–1668, no. 1679. At the time of the passage of the law, William Povey wrote to his influential brother, Thomas, in England, that Willoughby's "former just affable & noble Governm.ᵗ amongst these people" had won their affections and that no other person would have pleased them. He was able to secure the 4½ per cent Act, which may be thought a small matter in England, but is very considerable for this poor island that is still deeply in debt. "Indeed his Lord.ᵖ.ᵖ hath taken a very greate deale of paines in driueing this bargain for he hath been up early & downe late in advizeing & considering how to make out his Ma.ᵗⁱᵉˢ

the following year, the four Leeward Islands — St. Kitts, Nevis, Montserrat, and Antigua — followed suit and passed similar laws.   In 1665,[1] these five measures were confirmed by an Order in Council, and thus could not be repealed either by the colonial legislatures or by the Crown separately.

The wording of the Barbados law [2] was somewhat ambiguous, and its conflicting interpretations led to prolonged friction between the colony and England.   The Act first recited that Charles I had granted the island to Carlisle, but that the reigning King had acquired these proprietary rights and had appointed Willoughby as Governor with full power to assure to the people all their lands.   It then stated that many planters had lost the proprietary deeds, grants, and warrants for their land, and that many were in quiet possession without being able to prove their titles.   For the "quieting" these possessions, and as a remedy for the onerous dues formerly paid to the proprietor,[3] it was accordingly enacted that all those owning land according to the laws

intrest against y^e Allegations of y^e Planter, he hath spent three weekes in debate with y^e Assembly, vntill himselfe & they were allmost tired, y^e result at Last is y^t all Comodities of y^e growth of this Island shall" pay $4\frac{1}{2}$ per cent.   Brit. Mus., Egerton MSS. 2395, f. 383.

[1] C. O. 29/1, ff. 122, 147; C. O. 324/1, ff. 285–287; C. C. 1661–1668, no. 981;   P. C. Cal. I, p. 396.

[2] C. O. 29/1, ff. 47–50; C. O. 30/1 (Acts of Barbados, 1643–1672), pp. 55–57.

[3] The law stated that "the acknowledgment of forty pounds of Cotton *per* head, and other taxes and compositions formerly raised to the Earl of Carlisle was held very heavy."   In 1684, it was stated that the freeholders formerly held their lands of Carlisle under the acknowledgment of 40 lbs. of cotton per poll, and since then from the Crown on a free and common socage tenure.   Brit. Mus., Sloane MSS. 2441, ff. 11, 12.

and customs of Barbados should have their titles confirmed and made valid, and that all arrears of the proprietary dues and all such taxes in the future should be void, and that the lands should be held in free and common socage. The law then stated that nothing conduced more to the peace and prosperity of any place than the fact that the public revenue was in some proportion to "the public charges and expences; and also well weighing the great charges that there must be of necessity, in the maintaining the honour and dignity of His Majesty's Authority here; the public meetings of the Council; the reparation of the Forts; the building a Session's house and a Prison; and all other public charges incumbent on the Government," granted to the Crown an export duty of four and a half per cent on all dead produce of the island.

The exact intention of the lawmakers is not explicitly stated, nor is it clearly implied. The colony held that the entire revenue derived from these duties should be solely appropriated to the public services of the island enumerated in the Act, and that, only in case of a deficiency, should they be obliged to impose additional taxes. This view was consistently held by Barbados until, after one hundred and seventy-five years of incessant wrangling, the law was ultimately repealed.[1] The English government claimed that the revenue was granted in return for the confirmation of

---

[1] In the edition of the Barbados laws used, the editor says that this revenue was never applied to the purposes for which it had been granted, except in so far as the Governor's "English salary" of £2000 was paid out of it. C. O. 30/1, p. 58.

the existing land titles and the abolition of all proprietary dues;[1] that it belonged to the Crown, as successor to the proprietor, subject of course to the settlement made in 1663, but that otherwise it could be disposed of as it saw fit. The English government held that the ordinary public expenses of the colony, except the salary of the royal Governor, should be met by other taxes raised by the colony, and that this revenue should be used only to help the colony in special emergencies. Already in 1663, Willoughby had been instructed, if necessary, to apply part of this revenue towards fortifying the island. The contention of the English government derives some indirect support from the fact that the four Acts passed in 1664 in the Leeward Islands explicitly stated that the revenue was granted by them in return for the confirmation of their estates and the abolition of the proprietary dues.[2] On the other hand, from virtually the very outset, Barbados repudiated this interpretation and insisted upon its own construction of the law. Its very ambiguity was probably a direct result of the conflicting and not clearly expressed aims of Governor Willoughby and the Assembly which passed it. Apparently, neither Willoughby nor the legislature was perfectly ingenuous, and at the time each accepted the bill, just because it was susceptible of these divergent interpretations in harmony with their respective distinct purposes.

[1] In one of Williamson's note-books is a memorandum to the effect that Willoughby had secured this revenue 'on condition that all the planters, &c., should hold thenceforth all their lands in free soccage.' C. C. 1675–1676, p. 155.

[2] C. O. 324/1, ff. 295, 302, 310, 318.

Willoughby soon found himself in grave difficulties over this revenue. On the one side, he was importuned by the long-suffering creditors of Carlisle who clamored for their share;[1] on the other, he was beset by the colony, which claimed that the revenue should be entirely devoted to its public services. The Governor's troubles were greatly intensified in 1665 by the war with the Dutch. The English West Indies, especially the Leeward Islands, which still were joined with Barbados in one government, were inadequately fortified and also poorly protected by the English navy, and hence suffered severely from the French, who as allies of the Dutch had been drawn into the war. While recognizing the urgent necessity of strengthening the island's own fortifications, the Barbados Assembly refused to pass a satisfactory measure for raising the needed funds,[2] claiming that this should be provided for out of the four and a half per cent revenue.[3]

[1] These creditors claimed that Willoughby had converted their share of the revenue to his own uses. This the Governor vigorously denied and asked that his accounts be audited in England. C. C. 1661–1668, no. 992. In 1665, the English government appointed a special official to receive the share allotted to the creditors. P. C. Cal. I, pp. 394–396, 414.

[2] In his letter of July 5, 1665, Willoughby begged the King to allow him to use the $4\frac{1}{2}$ per cent revenue for building forts and maintaining men to defend them, as he had no other means of meeting these expenses. C. O. 1/19, 77; C. C. 1661–1668, no. 1017.

[3] Finally, in 1666, the Assembly passed a bill for raising a large amount of sugar 'to be disposed of by three of their own members . . . excluding the Governor and Council from all knowledge of the uses of this great levy.' This bill Willoughby refused to pass. C. C. 1661–1668, no. 1185. See also Brit. Mus., Sloane MSS. 2662, ff. 57 et seq. of the reversed side of the volume, and C. C. 1661–1668, nos. 1017, 1018, 1121, 1167. In 1667, how-

In this emergency, Willoughby, like most men of strong character and marked ability, would not allow himself to be fettered by his instructions, but used the entire four and a half per cent revenue for aggressive and defensive measures against the allied enemy. Unfortunately in 1666, while engaged in an expedition for the recovery of St. Kitts, Willoughby's vessel was wrecked by a hurricane, and he himself was drowned.[1]

His brother William succeeded to the barony and to the government of the Caribbee Islands. At this time the four and a half per cent revenue amounted to about £6000 yearly,[2] and as William, Lord Willoughby, wrote to the Privy Council in 1667, it had been pledged by his predecessor for materials for this war for some years to come, despite the fact that it had been found insufficient to meet 'the excessive charge' of supplying the fleet and maintaining the regiment sent from England. 'So that,' he continued, 'unless his Majesty issue satisfaction from his own exchequer,' he knew not where the necessary funds could be obtained, as the colony had already contributed very liberally.[3] Soon thereafter, however, the Treaty of Breda of 1667 restored peace and did away with the necessity of most of this heavy expenditure. But the English regiment, that of Sir Tobias Bridge, was continued in the West Indies, and as during the war it was again ordered that it be paid out of the four and

ever, Barbados made a large grant to fit out an expedition for the relief of the Leeward Islands. C. C. 1661–1668, nos. 1565, 1576.

[1] *Ibid.* nos. 1330–1333.

[2] *Ibid.* no. 1633.

[3] *Ibid.* no. 1648.

a half per cent revenue.[1]   Even for this purpose the revenue was hopelessly inadequate.[2]   The accounts at this time were in the greatest confusion,[3] and the revenue was heavily in debt;[4] the creditors of the Earl of Carlisle had so far received nothing,[5] and the annuities granted to the successors of the original proprietors of the islands had not been paid.[6] Thus the arrangement made in 1663 had not been carried out in any particular.[7]   On the other hand, in practice at least, the English government had been forced to grant the colony's demand, for virtually the entire revenue was devoted to its defence.   Barbados was, however, far from satisfied and continued its complaints.[8]

[1] It was to be paid out of that part of the revenue "which is designed to be employed for the support of the Government of that Island." P. C. Cal· I, pp. 470, 477, 480–482.   On this subject, see also C. C. 1685–1688, p. 634.

[2] C. C. 1661–1668, no. 1854; C. C. 1669–1674, pp. 57, 58.

[3] C. C. 1661–1668, no. 1803; P. C. Cal. I, pp. 492, 493; Cal. Treas. Books, 1669–1672, pp. 153, 154.

[4] C. C. 1661–1668, no. 1836; Cal. Treas. Papers, 1557–1696, pp. 12–14; Cal. Treas. Books, 1669–1672, pp. 443, 1059, 1060, 1077.

[5] In 1665, Willoughby stated that part of this revenue had been paid to the creditors, but they denied this.   C. C. 1661–1668, no. 992; P. C. Cal. I, pp. 394–396.   In 1668, the creditors complained that they had not received any part of the sum due them and that their representative had not been admitted as Comptroller of the Customs, as had been ordered. P. C. Cal. I, pp. 394–396, 450, 451; Cal. Treas. Papers, 1557–1696, pp. 12–14.

[6] P. C. Cal. I, pp. 539, 540; Cal. Treas. Papers, 1557–1696, pp. 12–14.

[7] In 1668, Willoughby wrote to the King that he would be able to see by the accounts sent home that this revenue 'is not sufficient to do all things, and that as yet the Governor has had nothing towards his support.'   C. C. 1661–1668, no. 1801.

[8] In 1668, the representatives of Barbados set forth the heavy burden of this tax, 'imposed by an assembly illegally convened,' and prayed that

In 1670, the four and a half per cent revenue in Barbados was farmed for seven years at a yearly rental of £7000, and that in the Leeward Islands for the same term for £700 yearly.[1] Barbados was greatly dissatisfied with this arrangement, as it was feared that it meant a permanent diversion of the revenue to England.[2]   Like his brother Francis, William, Lord Willoughby, always vigorously upheld the economic interests of the colony, and was outspoken in his opposition.[3] In an able memorial on the subject,[4] he fully adopted the colonial contention and, after reciting the terms of the Act of 1663, said that Barbados would be displeased at seeing what they had raised for themselves shipped to England. Furthermore, he pointed out, that during the recent war "the 4½ p Cent being applyed all to the publique use and the Creditt it had were principall means at that time of

it might be commuted for a cash sum or converted into some reasonable rate on sugar in England. C. C. 1661–1668, no. 1816. In 1669, Nicholas Blake said that this tax was pernicious and very vexatious and also suggested that in its place an additional customs duty be levied in England. C. C. 1699, p. 592.   In this year, Barbados addressed the King complaining of the use of this revenue for other purposes than those for which it had been intended, and asserting their inability to maintain their government, forts, and other charges, "wch ought to be defrayed out of that said Imposition."   Brit. Mus., Egerton MSS. 2395, f. 465.

   [1] Treas. Books, Out-Letters, Customs 2, ff. 211, 212; Blathwayt, Journal I, ff. 81–84; P. C. Cal. I, pp. 537–539; Brit. Mus., Egerton MSS. 2395, f. 417; Brit. Mus., Sloane MSS. 2441, f. 15^b; Brit. Mus., Add. MSS. 10,119, f. 42; H.M.C. XV, 2, p. 14; C. C. 1675–1676, p. 349.   In 1664, it had already been proposed to farm this revenue. C. C. 1661–1668, no. 873.

   [2] C. O. 31/2, f. 1; C. C. 1669–1674, pp. 116, 117, 155, 224.

   [3] C. C. 1669–1674, p. 81.

   [4] C. O. 29/1, ff. 122–124.

preserving this Island and the rest." With this revenue farmed, he claimed, Barbados would in the future be without money or credit to meet sudden emergencies.[1]

The English government ordered that the rent derived from the farms should be first devoted to the support of the forces stationed in these colonies and to the payment of their arrears, and then to the satisfaction of such persons to whom money was due for public services during the recent war there.[2] The cumbersome settlement of 1663 was virtually repudiated, and the admittedly legitimate claims of the Carlisle creditors were calmly ignored. Apparently they never received a farthing of their dues. Moreover, the farmers found their contract an unprofitable one, and made a number of claims for large allowances on account of war, plague, hurricane, and other unavoidable factors.[3] Many of these had to be conceded, and thus the

---

[1] "As for Antigua, Montserrat, and the rest of the Leeward Islands Except Nevis," he further wrote, "if they should at present be Farmed, in all probability it would totally ruine those Islands and so discourage the Planters, as to driue them to quitt the Island, and consequently instead of inuiting many of his Ma^{ts} Subjects from the French and Dutch (whom these Warrs haue driuen thither) force them off, and besides the King would Lett that which he knows not the value of, for if they prosper (as being encouraged they are like to do) the $4\frac{1}{2}$ p Cent may in a short time exceede Barbados."

[2] P. C. Cal. I, pp. 538, 539; Cal. Treas. Books, 1669–1672, p. 707. *Cf.* P. C. Cal. I, pp. 547, 552. In 1670, Sir Tobias Bridge's regiment was recalled and disbanded, which greatly reduced the charges on this revenue. C. C. 1669–1674, p. 224; Cal. Treas. Papers, 1557–1696, p. 13.

[3] In order to encourage the development of the English colony in St. Kitts, the Crown had also remitted the payment of the $4\frac{1}{2}$ per cent there during the first three years of Stapleton's government, from 1672 to 1675. C. C. 1677–1680, p. 573.

English government by no means obtained the full rental agreed upon. Of the £53,900 due for the seven years, the farmers in 1684 had paid only about £21,000.[1] In 1677, when these farms expired, they were renewed for another seven years, but at the reduced rental of £5300; on account of this contract, only £22,000 had been paid in 1684.[2] In this year was prepared a lengthy report, showing in detail that this revenue had in no way answered the expectations of those interested in it, that it was greatly in arrear, and that the system of farming it was far from satisfactory.[3] Moreover, the tax and its method of collection[4] were extremely

[1] Of the balance, the government in 1684 claimed only £10,481, whereof the farmers craved that £4800 be allowed them.

[2] On these farms, see Cal. Treas. Papers, 1557–1696, p. 14; Cal. Treas. Books, 1676–1679, pp. 6, 11, 12, 16, 60, 61, 421, 423, 424, 477, 774, 775, 836, 961, 1280, 1300; Public Record Office, Declared Accounts of Pipe Office, Customs Rolls 1254–1256; Blathwayt, Journal I, ff. 81, 82; Brit. Mus., Sloane MSS. 2441, f. 15; Brit. Mus., Add. MSS. 28,089, f. 41.

[3] Cal. Treas. Papers, 1557–1696, pp. 13–15. This report was made as a result of the demands of the Carlisle creditors and other claimants for satisfaction.

[4] Brit. Mus., Add. MSS. 28,089, ff. 43–45. In 1675, Barbados complained about the method of collecting this tax and found an able advocate in the Governor, Sir Jonathan Atkins, who was even more fearlessly outspoken in upholding the ecomomic interests of the colony than had been his predecessors, the Willoughbys. This complaint arose from the fact that, while hitherto a certain fixed sum had been paid for each cask of sugar, the farmers of the duties had ordered the casks weighed, claiming that the planters had gradually enlarged their size and were thus paying much less than was in reality due. The planters denied that there had been any fraud and said that hitherto "there was never any Duty more cheerfully paid" than this, but that weighing the casks was most inconvenient and expensive. The English government, as was usual, carefully investigated the matter. At a hearing held in 1676, the farmers of the 4½ per cent

unpopular in Barbados, and had led to incessant complaints during the fourteen years of the farm. Although the revenue was entirely devoted to the public concerns of these islands,[1]

revenue stated that in Barbados the casks of sugar had been raised in size from 1200 to 1600 pounds. This was denied by the Gentlemen Planters, and the matter was then referred to the Treasury, which was just negotiating a renewal of the farm. The Commissioners of the Customs thereupon reported that, unless there had been great abuses, the farmers would not have gone to the trouble of weighing the casks. C. O. 31/2, ff. 177–181 ; C. O. 391/1, f. 240 ; C. C. 1675–1676, pp. 210, 303, 474, 475, 478, 482 ; C. C. 1677–1680, pp. 6, 7. In 1673, instructions had been sent to Willoughby in Barbados and to Stapleton in the Leeward Islands to cause all sugars exported to be weighed as insisted upon by the farmers. Cal. Treas. Books, 1672–1675, p. 100. When, in 1684, the English government undertook the management of this revenue, the commissioners entrusted with its collection were similarly instructed. Treas. Books, Out-Letters, Customs 9, ff. 43–48, § vi.

[1] In 1682, the Lords of Trade reported that they had examined the petition of the Carlisle creditors and the case of many others who had claims against the 4½ per cent revenue, and that they found that this duty was already charged with the arrears and pay of the two foot-companies in these islands and of the royal officials there, so that for years to come there would be nothing to spare beyond the yearly cost and necessary support of the government, "for wch this Revenue was granted unto your M^{ty} " C. O. 29/3, ff. 130, 131 ; C. C. 1681–1685, p. 268. In 1672, the Nevis Assembly refused to grant a salary to Sir Charles Wheler, the first Governor-in-Chief of the Leeward Islands, on the ground that the 4½ per cent revenue was in lieu of all dues whatsoever payable to the Crown. They finally offered him a salary, 'but to none after him.' Wheler refused to agree to a law 'with an exclusive bar to the rights of succeeding Governors.' C. C. 1669–1674, pp. 337–339. In 1680, the King ordered £1500 out of the 4½ per cent revenue to be paid to Governor Stapleton for erecting forts in the Leeward Islands. C. C. 1677–1680, p. 475 ; P. C. Cal. I, pp. 870, 871. According to the establishment settled by the English government in 1679, the Governor of Barbados received a salary of £800, the Governor of the Leeward Islands one of £700, and the cost of the two foot-companies located in these islands was £2778 yearly. P. C. Register Charles II, XV, f. 150 ;

there was a chronic fear, especially in Bardados, that it would be otherwise employed.[1]

Accordingly in 1684, when the farm expired, the collection of this duty was turned over to the Lords of the Treasury and was by them entrusted to their subordinate board, the Commissioners of the Customs.[2] But at the same time, in deference to the oft-expressed wishes of Barbados, it was determined to allow the colonies to commute it into another tax more agreeable to them, but also payable to the Crown.[3] Instead of availing itself of this offer,

P. C. Cal. I, pp. 846, 847; C. O. 324/4, ff. 63 *et seq.* *Cf.* Brit. Mus., Add. MSS. 10,119, f. 52. In the three years, 1681 to 1683, £9971 was paid for the garrison in the Leeward Islands. Brit. Mus., Add. MSS. 15,896, f. 54.

[1] In 1671, the Barbados Assembly wrote to the Gentlemen Planters in London complaining that, while hitherto this revenue had been 'employed for the most part to the ends mentioned' in the Act granting it, the collectors appointed by the farmers refused to disburse anything for these purposes; and that, as a result, the forts would speedily decay, the prison was useless, and many public concerns were neglected. The Committee of Gentlemen Planters did not, however, press this complaint, as they thought it inopportune to do so when the English Treasury was all but bankrupt. C. O. 31/2, ff. 26–29, 87–94, 100, 101; C. C. 1669–1674, pp. 199–201, 283, 284, 369. At this time, the Provost Marshal General of the colony, Edwyn Stede, reported that the prison was so dilapidated that no prisoners could be secured therein, and that the Assembly had refused to repair it, stating that this expense should be charged to the 4½ per cent revenue. P. C. Cal. I, p. 572. In 1673, Sir Peter Colleton, then acting Governor of Barbados, said that, unless the Crown would assist the colony out of the 4½ per cent revenue, he could not see how the public charges could be met. C. O. 1/31, 43; C. C. 1669–1674, ff. 498, 499. See also C. O. 31/2, ff. 165, 172; C. C. 1675–1676, p. 193.

[2] Brit. Mus., Sloane MSS. 2441, f. 15[b].

[3] In order to obviate the inconvenient method of collecting these duties, Barbados in 1679 had offered to undertake their farm. In 1680, the Assembly instructed the Gentlemen Planters to endeavor to secure the commutation

Barbados proposed to farm the tax for a period of years at an annual rent of £6000.[1] The Governor of the colony, Sir Richard Dutton, who was apparently justly accused of having been bribed by the Assembly to lend his valuable support to this project, wrote strongly in its favor.[2] But at the same time the newly appointed collectors of this revenue in Barbados informed their superior officials in England, the Commissioners of the Customs, that they hoped in their first year to make the duties worth from £8000 to 10,000.[3] Accordingly, this board reported adversely on the Barbados offer, and it was rejected.[4]

Under this new management the four and a half per cent revenue showed from the outset somewhat better results,[5] and

of this tax into an import duty in England, and, if this could not be arranged, to contract for the farm on the best possible terms. Accordingly, in 1681, the King offered the colonies the opportunity of commuting this tax into one more to their liking. Montserrat, alone of the Leeward Islands, stated its willingness to pay an equivalent sum; the three other islands answered that they desired no alteration. The Barbados Assembly at first was willing to grant the Crown a revenue of £5000, arising from duties on imported wines and liquors, which they stated was £1000 more than the King had received from Barbados' share of the 4½ per cent. A bill to this effect, however, failed to pass, as it was insinuated that the King would grant this revenue to his rapacious mistress, Louise de Keroualle, Duchess of Portsmouth. C. O. 31/2, ff. 339-341; C. O. 29/3, ff. 72-75; C. C. 1677-1680, pp. 352, 517, 518; C. C. 1681-1685, pp. 15, 16, 30, 69, 73-75, 90.

[1] C. C. 1685-1688, pp. 8, 17.

[2] *Ibid.* pp. 21, 37, 38, 109.

[3] *Ibid.* pp. 9, 26.

[4] *Ibid.* pp. 56, 59, 64.

[5] The Exchequer received on this account £8260 in 1686-1687, £5000 in 1687-1688. Brit. Mus., Add. MSS. 10,119, f. 215.

later, after the Revolution of 1688/9, when the method of collection was better organized, it produced a considerable income, which the English government disposed of at its pleasure.   But up to that time it had by no means sufficed for the payment of the salaries of the governors of Barbados and the Leeward Islands and for the support of the St. Kitts garrison.[1]   As a result, the other legitimate claims on this revenue remained unsatisfied.   The annuity, which had been granted to the Earl of Kinnoul in consideration for the surrender of his unquestionably valid proprietary rights, was not paid from this source, but had to be defrayed by the Exchequer.[2]   Barbados was, however, far from satisfied. Apart from aught else, the bulk of the revenue was collected there, but was devoted to the pay of the forces in St. Kitts. The duty was regarded in the island as a distinct grievance, to which it was hoped that the new government of William and Mary would give redress.

As in the West Indies, so in Virginia, the Crown had succeeded to the rights of the proprietor; in this case, it was the London Company, whose charter had been revoked in 1624.   In its fruitless efforts to obtain some return on the capital invested in the undertaking, this colonizing body had granted land to settlers in Virginia, subject to the payment of an annual rent of two shillings for every hundred acres.   This system was continued when the Crown assumed

[1] The actual income from 1670 to 1684 was approximately £3000 yearly, while these charges amounted to about £4300.

[2] It was, however, not paid in full.   Cal. Treas. Papers, 1557–1696, pp. 13–15; Cal. Treas. Books, 1669–1672, pp. 707, 1216, 1304; *ibid.* 1676–1679, Nov. 13 and 28, 1676; Letters of Sir Joseph Williamson (Camden Society, 1874) I, p. 40.

the administration of the colony, but the few desultory attempts made by the first Stuarts to collect these quit-rents met with virtually no success.[1] In 1662, however, the Restoration government instructed Governor Berkeley to see that the quit-rents were justly and fairly levied.[2] At this time, these dues should have been paid on about one million acres, which would have meant an annual income of £1000.[3] But as an Act of the local legislature allowed the payment of the quit-rents in tobacco at the excessive rate of twopence a pound,[4] this revenue, granted that it could have been collected, would have been considerably less than this sum.[5] Not only did the planters resist the payment of these moderate dues, but in addition whatever revenue was collected was claimed by Henry Norwood, who in 1650 had been appointed Treasurer of Virginia by Charles II.[6] The situation was further com-

---

[1] Bruce, Economic History of Virginia I, pp. 556 et seq.; Beer, Origins, pp. 321, 322.

[2] C. C. 1661–1668, no. 368; Va. Mag. III, pp. 15–20.

[3] Va. Mag. III, pp. 42–47.

[4] Act xxxvi of 1661, Hening II, p. 31. Cf. p. 99.

[5] In 1662, Governor Berkeley said that the current price of tobacco was one penny the pound. Brit. Mus., Egerton MSS. 2395, f. 356.

[6] Force Tracts III, no. 10, pp. 49, 50; Va. Mag. XIV, p. 268. In 1671, Berkeley said that this was the only revenue that the King had in Virginia, but that he had given it away to a "deserving servant Coll. Henry Norwood." C. O. 1/26, 77i. Norwood claimed that his predecessor as Treasurer, Claiborne, had received the quit-rents without account by virtue of his office, and that he likewise was not accountable for this revenue. The English Treasury, however, decided against this ill-founded contention. Blathwayt, Journal I, pp. 93–95. In this connection it may be pointed out that, in September of 1649, Charles II granted to Sir John

plicated, when in 1669 the Earl of St. Albans, Lord Berkeley, and others secured the grant of the large tract of land included within the rivers Potomac and Rappahannock and Chesapeake Bay. In this extensive region, known as the Northern Neck, these proprietors were made lords of the soil and were authorized to grant land and to collect quit-rents from it.[1] Four years later, in 1673, Charles II granted for thirty-one years to the Earl of Arlington and Lord Culpeper all of Virginia, together with the rents reserved in any prior grants, and empowered them to convey any part of these lands to settlers, reserving the customary quit-rents for themselves.[2]

Hitherto Virginia had paid but slight attention to the quit-rent system. The rents had been virtually ignored, and the Crown had derived no revenue from this source.[3] It was realized, however, that private individuals would be more energetic in enforcing their legal rights, and for this reason, as well as for more vital ones, Virginia protested most emphatically against these grants. In consequence

Berkeley and Sir William Davenant the office of Treasurer of Virginia, and that shortly thereafter Davenant was appointed to this office, "in the absence of" Berkeley, Claiborne being "affected to the Parliam.ᵗ" Pepys MSS. (H.M.C. 1911), pp. 284, 302. Davenant, however, did not exercise the functions of this office.

[1] Patent Rolls, 21 Ch. II, Part 4.

[2] Hening II, pp. 427, 428, 519, 568–578; C. C. 1669–1674, p. 334; Blathwayt, Journal II, f. 403.

[3] When opposing the St. Albans and Culpeper grants, the Virginia agents stated in 1675 that, "though there is a Quit rent reserved to the Crown of one shilling for every 50 Acres Yet that hath not nor can be paid in money for want of Coyne, and is in itselfe soe inconsiderable that it hath never been paid into the Exchequ.ᵣ" C. O. 1/34, 101, 102.

thereof, the colony succeeded in securing a promise from Charles II, that he would take the quit-rent revenue into his own hands and apply it to the public services of the colony.[1]

The political disturbances in Virginia and the time consumed in its settlement after Bacon's rebellion occasioned some delay in carrying into effect this promise, and then followed prolonged negotiations with Lord Culpeper, to whom Lord Arlington had conveyed his interest in the patent of 1673.[2] Although Culpeper had never been able to enforce his valuable rights under this grant, he refused to surrender them without adequate compensation.[3] Finally in 1684, in return for a pension of £600 a year, payable during the still unexpired twenty years of his lease, Culpeper resigned his patent of 1673, as well as some other claims on

[1] P. C. Cal. I, p. 810. See also C. C. 1681–1685, p. 100; P. C. Cal. II, pp. 21, 22.

[2] Hening II, pp. 521, 578–583.

[3] In 1679, Virginia petitioned Charles II for a remission of the arrears of these rents, and for their future appropriation to the defence of the colony. In reply, Lord Culpeper, then Governor of Virginia, was instructed to state that the King had been carefully considering this matter, and would shortly give "such orders as shall consist with our service, and the ease of our people there." Va. Mag. XIV, pp. 359–361. In 1680, Culpeper wrote to the Lords of Trade that he had issued a proclamation for the collection of the quit-rents, but that as yet he had not received any particular account of them and feared that the low price of tobacco and the cost of collection would make them inconsiderable. C. C. 1681–1685, p. 154. In 1683, Culpeper stated that 'the non-payment of quit-rents has done great mischief. The only remedy is to cause the quit-rents reserved to be paid by large holders in specie, and by others in produce, that they may throw up the land that they cannot turn to account and leave it open for others.' In other words, he proposed to use these rents as a tax on undeveloped land. *Ibid.* p. 497; Va. Mag. III, pp. 225–238.

the Crown.[1] This annuity was a charge on the English Exchequer, and thus upon the English taxpayer was ultimately shifted the burden of Charles's ill-advised liberality towards his favorites.

In the same year in which this agreement was concluded, an Order in Council definitely ordered the application of this quit-rent revenue to the uses of Virginia.[2] At the same time, Charles II wrote to Lord Howard of Effingham, the Governor of Virginia, informing him of this agreement and instructing him to collect these rents in coin and not in tobacco, as had been optional under the Virginia law of 1661.[3] Hitherto that had been the customary method of paying such of these rents as could be collected,[4] but the established rate of twopence a pound was greatly in excess of the value of the inferior tobacco usually tendered for these dues. The colony's gratification at the successful outcome of its strug-

[1] Blathwayt, Journal I, ff. 11, 124, 125, 128, 129; C. C. 1681–1685, pp. 347, 348, 547, 660; Va. Hist. Register III, p. 183; C. O. 1/52, 56; Va. Mag. XIX, pp. 2, 3. In 1683, the Virginia Council had begged the King to give Culpeper 'just compensation' for his patent and to apply the quit-rents to the use of the colony, 'which will be a great relief and a help towards a fund for meeting emergencies.' C. C. 1681–1685, p. 425; Hening II, pp. 561–563. Cf. C. C. 1681–1685, pp. 623, 637, 639, 640, 747.

[2] Blathwayt, Journal I, ff. 378–381.

[3] C. C. 1681–1685, p. 670; Hening II, pp. 521, 522; Va. Hist. Register III, p. 183.

[4] Among the requests of York County in 1677 was one, to the effect that the quit-rents should be paid in tobacco at 2d. a pound, as had been customary for many years. To this the Commissioners, who had been sent to pacify Virginia, replied: "It was neuer paid otherwis, but this left to the Right Honourable the Lord Treasurer being part of his Majesties revenues but neuer yet accompted for into the cheque." C. O. 1/39, 92, 93.

gle was somewhat marred by this order for the payment of the rents in coin, and also by the fact that the quit-rents of the Northern Neck of Virginia were not included in this settlement.[1]

In 1685, the colony thanked the King for appropriating the quit-rents to the uses of the colony, but entreated him to allow those living in the Northern Neck to share in this bounty.[2] At the same time, the Assembly requested the Governor to accept tobacco in payment of these rents, since coin could not readily be obtained.[3] In reply, the Governor expressed surprise at such a request, in view of the fact that this revenue was to be applied to the public services of the colony, but agreed to give orders for the acceptance of tobacco in cases where money was scarce.[4] The English government was, however, firm on this point, and insisted that payment be made in money.[5] Nor was anything done towards buying out the firmly established interest of the patentees of 1669 in the Northern Neck.

[1] C. C. 1681–1685, p. 734. *Cf.* Va. Mag. VIII, pp. 177–179. Regarding these rents in the Northern Neck, Culpeper stated in 1683 that "the Thing hath been soe fully Setled, & Quietly Enjoyed that the Assembly Sent Agents to purchase the Same, and diverse of the Planters Inhabitants & others have Since bought Severall Quitt=Rents and other Parts thereof, to them and Their Heirs for ever." C. O. 1/52, 56. Culpeper had acquired the rights of the patentees of 1669, and in 1688 letters patent were issued confirming this grant. From Culpeper it descended to the Fairfax family. Va. Mag. XV, pp. 392–399; Va. Hist. Register III, p. 183.

[2] C. C. 1685–1688, pp. 5, 32. *Cf.* pp. 179, 180.

[3] *Ibid.* p. 119.

[4] *Ibid.* The Assembly then repeated its request and received the same answer. *Ibid.* p. 121.

[5] *Ibid.* pp. 185, 271, 279.

Under this new arrangement, the quit-rents were more systematically collected, and began to yield a regular income, which in the course of time became of not inconsiderable size. During the reign of James II, however, it averaged only about £850 yearly.[1] This small revenue was allowed to accumulate as a fund for such special emergencies as might arise in the colony. Thus, in 1685, the English Treasury authorized Governor Howard to apply £519 from it to the discharge of the debt of Virginia's regular revenue, which had been insufficient to meet the expenses of the colony's administration.[2]

Like the four and a half per cent revenue in the West Indies, the receipts from these quit-rents were regarded as something entirely distinct and apart from the ordinary revenue of the colony. They were looked upon in England as property that had devolved upon the Crown as successor to the proprietor. If the King appropriated them to the uses of the colony, this act was regarded as one of royal bounty. As in the case of the West Indian export duties,

VIRGINIA QUIT-RENT REVENUE

1684	. . . .	£ 574
1685	. . . .	£1029
1686	. . . .	£ 899
1687	. . . .	£ 836
1688	. . . .	£ 679
1689	. . . .	£ 685
1690	. . . .	£ 747

[1] Blathwayt, Journal II, f. 244. The sheriffs collected the rents and deducted 10 per cent for their services. The Auditor then received them from the sheriffs and was allowed 7½ per cent for his work. Va. Hist. Register III, p. 185.

[2] Blathwayt, Journal I, ff. 172, 181.

the colony had no control over the funds derived from this source. Nor could the royal governors draw upon them. All payments from this revenue had to be specifically authorized by warrants drawn in England.[1] Such a fund, under the sole control of the English government, could be developed into an effective instrument of political restraint, and could be advantageously used for some invaluable objects, whose merits were apt to escape the restricted vision of the provincial legislatures.

In addition to acquiring the rights of the patentees of the Caribbee Islands and of Virginia, the Crown was also the legal successor of the proprietors of the Bermudas and of New York. In neither of these cases, however, was there created at this time a substantial independent income accruing to the Crown. The Bermuda Company had tried to enforce a monopoly of the commerce of the islands belonging to it, and had also imposed on the colony's crop of tobacco a tax of one-penny a pound, which they claimed was employed for their public services and for those of the colony.[2] The settlers in the Bermudas complained bitterly and incessantly about this restrictive policy of the Company, and after years of agitation and denunciation, in 1684, its charter was finally revoked.[3] As a result, the Crown fell heir to

---

[1] In 1688, James II declared that this quit-rent revenue should be applied "to the Benefit and better Support of the Government of that colony according to such warrants as should from time to time be issued by His Maj'ty." Va. Hist. Register III, p. 183.

[2] Lefroy, Bermudas II, pp. 429-433; C. C. 1677-1680, pp. 393, 394.

[3] C. C. 1681-1685, pp. 676, 738.

the rights of the defunct Company. The English government, with almost incomprehensible stupidity, then decided
to continue its predecessor's obnoxious trade regulations,
regardless of the fact that they had been the fundamental
cause of the colony's discontent and of the ensuing successful
agitation against the Company's charter. During the preceding régime, the colony's crop of tobacco could be exported
only in the "magazine ship," belonging to the Company.
An attempt was made to continue this regulation, but, as it
proved burdensome and could not be enforced, it had to be
definitely abandoned in 1688.[1] Similarly, the government
tried to continue the Company's duty of one-penny a pound
on tobacco. In 1684, it was estimated that this duty, if it
were fully collected, would yield yearly from £1600 to £1800.[2]
The people in the colony, however, resolutely refused to
pay this tax, and consequently this claim also had to be
abandoned by the government.[3] In addition to these two
sources of profit, the Bermuda Company had derived an
income from the land, of which it had retained possession,
and from the whale fishery. It was figured that, under
good administration, these public lands would yield £600
yearly, and the royalties on the whale fishery £100.[4] The
Bermudas were, however, extremely independent, even to
the verge of lawlessness, and likewise frustrated all attempts

[1] C. O. 1/58, 75; C. O. 1/60, 88 vii; C. O. 1/62, 36; C. C. 1685–1688,
pp. 174, 175, 179, 185, 213, 222, 258, 259, 359, 392–395, 519, 529, 551, 568,
597.

[2] C. C. 1681–1685, pp. 663, 664.

[3] *Ibid.* 1685–1688, pp. 49, 101, 157, 394.

[4] *Ibid.* 1681–1685, pp. 663, 664; *ibid.* 1685–1688, pp. 258, 259.

to collect an adequate income from these sources.[1] In 1686, Sir Robert Robinson was appointed Governor of the colony with a salary of £400, of which £240 was to be paid by the English Exchequer, and £100 was to come from the royalties on whales and £60 from the Crown lands.[2] But from these last two sources, Robinson wrote in 1687, that he would be able to secure respectively only £15 and £25.[3] Thus the Crown was unable to establish an independent revenue in the Bermudas, as it had done in the Caribbee Islands, and the salary of the Governor had to be defrayed in large part by the English Treasury.

When, in 1685, James II succeeded to the Crown, New York by this fact became a royal province. As proprietor, James had derived no income from the colony, since its revenue as a rule fell short of the expenses of administration. The great bulk of this revenue was derived from import and export duties. In addition, some of the land had been granted on condition of the payment of inconsiderable quit-rents, which were, however, inefficiently collected.[4] As royal Governor, Dongan induced many to pay these rents, and in some instances he also succeeded in increasing the amount payable under the original grant.[5] The start thus made was, however, only a false one, for it

---

[1] C. C. 1685–1688, pp. 48–51, 295.

[2] C. O. 1/58, 75; C. C. 1685–1688, pp. 258, 259.

[3] C. O. 1/60, 88.

[4] N. Y. Col. Doc. III, pp. 260–262; C. O. 155/1, ff. 18–33; C. C. 1677–1680, pp. 237, 238.

[5] N. Y. Col. Doc. III, p. 401; C. C. 1685–1688, pp. 330, 331.

was only seventy years later that the New York quit-rents yielded a revenue of any importance.[1]

From the foregoing it is apparent that, prior to 1689, the English Treasury derived virtually no direct income from the colonies, and that the revenue which accrued to the Crown in its various capacities was practically in its entirety devoted to colonial purposes. But, if the colonies were but a most insignificant source of direct profit to the Exchequer and to the Crown, they were at the same time, apart from the cost of imperial defence, but a slight and constantly diminishing fiscal burden. It was the steadfast policy of the English government that each colony should ultimately raise the funds for its own local expenses. By the end of the Restoration period this had been practically effected.

From the imperial standpoint the English colonies were divided into two distinct groups, the so-called "proprieties" and the royal provinces. The former, whether of the corporation or proprietary type, inevitably had to develop their own fiscal systems, since they were subordinate jurisdictions with nearly complete powers of local self-government. However significant their various fiscal regulations may be for the student of the economic development of the United States, they have in themselves but slight imperial importance. Very little control was, or could be, exercised by England over the manner in which these semi-independent communities raised the funds for their local needs. In the crown colonies it was naturally far otherwise. Until the

[1] C. O. 5/216, f. 8.

end of the reign of Charles II, the only colony of this type on the continent was Virginia, while in the Caribbean Sea were Jamaica, Barbados, and the Leeward Islands. In all of these colonies were a number of officials appointed by the Crown, and inevitably the question arose: Who was to pay the salaries of these governors, secretaries, and judges? It was, however, realized that these officials, especially the governors, would become dependent upon the colonial assemblies granting their salaries, unless there were established permanent revenues, which the Crown was free to use for such purposes. Hence it became the aim of the English government to induce the royal provinces to grant to the Crown perpetual revenues, which could be disposed of in its discretion for the public services of the colony. In Barbados and in the Leeward Islands, this result had been attained by the four and a half per cent duty. But this revenue had been granted under especial circumstances, such as did not obtain in the other colonies. Moreover, it was remitted to England and paid out by warrants drawn there on the English Exchequer; and, in addition, the English government did not feel bound to devote these funds to the immediate services of the colonies whence they were derived. Unless in return for exceptional considerations, such as the English government was able to offer only in the case of the Caribbee Islands, no colonial legislature would be willing to grant a revenue of this nature. Hence, the revenues granted to the Crown in Virginia and Jamaica were kept in the colonies, and could be used solely for their public services. Unlike the four and a half per cent, they were not included in the receipts of the English Exchequer, but were treated purely as the revenues of the respective colonies. Permanent revenues of even this nature were, however, not readily granted by the colonies, and the English government was only partially successful in its efforts towards this end.

During the reign of Charles I, the Governor of Virginia had received a salary from the English Exchequer, but under the Commonwealth the colony itself had made this provision.[1] After the Restoration, the English government made some temporary arrangement for remunerating Sir William Berkeley's services as Governor;[2] but already in 1662 the Council for Foreign Plantations discussed this question, and decided that Virginia 'should bear its own charge and no longer be burthensome to the Crown.'[3] Accordingly, Governor Berkeley was instructed to take his salary of £1000 out of the Virginia export duty of two shillings on every hogshead of tobacco.[4] These duties were collected by officials appointed by the Assembly and accountable to it,[5] and yielded an adequate revenue. As instructed, Berkeley took

[1] Beer, Origins, pp. 320, 321, 367.

[2] In 1661, a warrant was issued for the payment of £2000 to Berkeley 'out of duties and customs arising from the next ship from Virginia in recompense for his services as Governor.' C. C. 1661–1668, no. 171; Cal. Treas. Books, 1660–1667, p. 296.

[3] C. C. 1661–1668, no. 345.

[4] *Ibid.* no. 368.

[5] Hening II, pp. 130–132. In case the tobacco was exported to any place but the English dominions in Europe, the duty was 10s. *Ibid.* pp. 133, 134. In 1662, a number of English traders complained about this export duty and the tonnage dues. C. C. 1661–1668, no. 352.

his salary from this source, and from it also were paid the members of the Council.[1]

Although there was no friction — as Governor Berkeley completely dominated the legislature, there could be none — this financial system was not wholly satisfactory to the English government, because the revenue was neither a permanent one, nor at its disposal and under its immediate control. In 1679, was made a comprehensive and careful investigation of the budgets and financial systems of the crown colonies,[2] and as a result it was determined to establish in Virginia and in Jamaica perpetual revenues. In 1680, Lord Culpeper, the Governor of Virginia, brought to the colony a law to this effect drafted by the Lords of Trade,[3] with instructions to secure its enactment by the local legislature.[4] After encountering considerable difficulty, he finally succeeded in so doing. At the first reading, the Assembly unanimously rejected this English-made bill, but ultimately passed it with equal unanimity, but only after having added

[1] The Virginia Assembly made Berkeley a regular additional allowance of £200 out of this revenue. In the seventies, it amounted to about £2500 yearly, of which the Governor received from £1200 to £1400 and the Council from £200 to £250. C. O. 1/26, 77 i; C. C. 1669–1674, p. 508; C. O. 1/34, 103; Hening II, pp. 314, 315. The salary of Berkeley's successors, Lords Culpeper and Howard of Effingham was £2000. C. C. 1681–1685, p. 479.

[2] P. C. Register Charles II, XV, ff. 90, 150; C. O. 1/43, 70; C. O. 324/4, ff. 63 *et seq.;* P. C. Cal. I, pp. 837, 846–848.

[3] P. C. Cal. I, p. 818. In Virginia, as in Jamaica, but on a much less extensive scale than there, an attempt was made at this time to introduce the Poynings' system of legislation in force in Ireland. *Ibid.* pp. 809 *et seq.*

[4] Va. Mag. XIV, pp. 360–366.

two clauses, which produced considerable trouble.[1] This Act[2] granted in perpetuity to the Crown, to be disposed of and to be received by it, the revenue arising from export duties of two shillings on every hogshead of tobacco,[3] from tonnage dues of one shilling threepence a ton, and from a poll-tax of sixpence on every immigrant. The clauses, which the Assembly had insisted upon adding to the English draft, exempted Virginia owned or built shipping from the payment of these taxes.

In the Virginia statute book could be found a number of similar laws discriminating against English shipping.[4] Hitherto, these had passed unnoticed in England, but such was not likely to be their good fortune now, since only shortly before this attention had been directed to this subject by

---

[1] Va. Mag. XIV, pp. 366, 367; C. C. 1677–1680, pp. 555, 568; *ibid.* 1681–1685, p. 153.

[2] Hening II, pp. 466–469.

[3] In case the tobacco were exported in bulk, each 500 pounds had to pay 2s. An Act of 1677 had already contained this provision. Hening II, p. 413.·

[4] An Act of 1662 exempted vessels wholly owned by Virginians from the payment of the 2s. and 10s. export duties, and an Act of 1669 granted them similar exemption from the castle dues. Hening II, pp. 135, 136, 272. By the Act of 1677, however, this exemption was to apply only to ships wholly built in Virginia and entirely belonging to its inhabitants. *Ibid.* p. 387. The perpetual revenue Act of 1680 did not mention the Act of 1677, but provided that the privileges granted by the Acts of 1662 and 1669 should remain in full force. Culpeper wrote in 1681 that the exemption granted to Virginia-owned vessels was inserted through a mistake, but that the exemption granted to Virginia-built vessels, 'notwithstanding your Lordships' opinion to the contrary, I still think most fitting (at least for a time), and it will, I am confident, be insisted on by the next, and by every subsequent Assembly in Virginia.' C. C. 1681–1685, p. 153.

the insertion of a similarly objectionable proviso in the Jamaica revenue law. The Lords of Trade 'very much disliked' the clauses granting exceptional privileges to Virginia ships, and accordingly recommended that these should be disallowed by the King, while in other respects the revenue law should be confirmed.[1] On the strength of their report, an Order in Council to this effect was issued on October 14, 1680;[2] and on the same day, the Lords of Trade wrote to Culpeper that they esteemed 'it not only irregular but inequitable, that ships owned in Virginia should receive more encouragement than those of others of the King's subjects.'[3]

The course of action adopted by the government was of more than questionable legality. A Virginia law could be disallowed by the Crown, but could not be partially confirmed and partially vetoed. Having secured a permanent revenue in the colony, the English government wisely would not run the risk of disallowing the entire Act, for it was extremely doubtful if such a measure could be secured from any other Assembly. On the other hand, the colony would naturally not pass a special bill repealing the privileges granted to vessels owned or built in Virginia, as these had been the indispensable conditions upon which the Act had originally been agreed to.[4] Thus, in return for a permanent revenue, which in general was ample for its specific

[1] C. C. 1677–1680, p. 612.
[2] P. C. Cal. II, p. 11.
[3] C. C. 1677–1680, p. 614.
[4] Va. Mag. XIV, pp. 367, 368; C. C. 1677–1680, p. 555.

purposes,[1] the English government was obliged to acquiesce in Virginia's discrimination against English shipping.[2] Although this preferential treatment did not lead to a rapid growth of the colony's mercantile marine, and hence its adverse effects on English shipping were only slight, the situation was one that could not but be galling to the imperial government, whose general policy was so largely based on the development of England's sea power.

The favorite colonial project of the Restoration statesmen was the development of Jamaica, the chief fruit of Cromwell's imperialistic policy. To this colony great attention was devoted and upon it money was spent by the government with an unwontedly lavish hand. In addition to appropriating comparatively large sums for the settlement and defence of Jamaica,[3] the English Exchequer assumed in 1663 the annual charge of £2500 for the island's ordinary establishment, of which the Governor's salary absorbed £1000.[4] Some steps were, however, also taken to create an independent revenue in the colony. The Governors

---

[1] At this time, the revenue amounted to about £3000 yearly. Blathwayt, Journal I, p. 46. In the year 1688–1689 the receipts were £3631. For details of this revenue and its disposition that year, see Va. Hist. Register III, p. 187.

[2] The Virginia Act of 1684, imposing duties on imported wines and liquors, exempted from their payment such of these commodities as were owned by Virginians and imported in vessels, either built in or belonging to Virginia. Hening III, pp. 23, 38.

[3] Cal. Treas. Books, 1660–1667, pp. 259, 267, 303, 362, 534, 617.

[4] *Ibid.* pp. 589, 667, 685, 720; C. C. 1661–1668, nos. 616, 656, 664; P. C. Cal. I, pp. 484, 485. In 1672, Sir Thomas Lynch induced the Assembly to raise his salary to £1500. C. C. 1669–1674, p. 335.

were instructed in 1662 and in 1664 to reserve for the Crown suitable rents in the land grants.[1] Other sources of income were also tapped. In 1670, the revenue arising from duties on wines and liquors, tonnage dues on shipping, licenses to sell ale, quit-rents, fines, and forfeitures amounted to £1900, while the necessary disbursements for the support of the government were almost double this amount.[2]

At this time the conclusion was reached in England, that the colony was able to defray its own expenses and that the yearly allowance of £2500 from the English Exchequer should be stopped.[3] This decision was, however, premature and could not be carried into effect. In 1673, Lieutenant-Governor Lynch wrote to the Council for Plantations,[4] that the revenue of Jamaica amounted to but £1800, while the charges of government were about twice this sum, and that, while he had hopes of its improvement, it would not for some time answer the needs of the colony. 'Young colonies,' he added, 'like tender plants, should be cherished and dealt easily with, it being better to put soil to their roots than to pluck too early fruit.'

Four years later, however, the English government, pressed by its own money difficulties, had definitely arrived

[1] C. C. 1661–1668, nos. 259, 664. The quit-rents established in Jamaica were not uniform as in Virginia. C. C. 1675–1676, pp. 342–344.

[2] C. C. 1669–1674, p. 95. This revenue was collected by royal officials. *Ibid.;* P. C. Cal. I, pp. 667, 668.

[3] C. O. 138/1, f. 113; C. C. 1669–1674, p. 306. This amount was divided as follows: £1000 to the Governor, £600 to the Deputy-Governor, £300 to the Major-General, and £600 for the maintenance of the forts. Cal. Treas. Books, 1672–1675, p. 575.

[4] C. O. 1/30, 19; C. C. 1669–1674, p. 477. *Cf.* C. C. 1669–1674, p. 504.

at the conclusion that Jamaica was prosperous enough to be fully self-supporting, and that its finances should be placed on a firm basis. At the same time was attempted an interesting constitutional experiment, whose success would have profoundly affected the Empire's future. In Jamaica had been established virtually the same governmental system as in Barbados and Virginia. The Governor, Lord Vaughan, had been empowered to summon an Assembly of the freeholders, who, with the advice and consent of the Governor and Council, had authority to make laws for the colony.[1] After some deliberation, it was decided in 1677 to change this system, and to introduce that prevailing in Ireland under Poynings' law of 1494.[2] Under this Act, the Irish Parliament had authority to pass only such bills as were submitted to it by the Crown and the English Privy Council. The report of the Lords of Trade in favor of this constitutional change in Jamaica was approved,[3] and

---

[1] These laws were to be in force for two years, unless disallowed by the Crown, and no longer, unless confirmed by it.   P. C. Cal. I, pp. 744–747.

[2] H. A. L. Fisher, England, 1485–1547, p. 60.   In 1679, the Lords of Trade said that this change in Jamaica was made on account of "the irregular, violent, and unwarrantable Proceedings of the Assembly."   P. C. Cal. I, p. 827.

[3] They recommended that "for the future no Legislative Assembly be called without your Majestys speciall Directions; but that upon Emergencys, the Governor do acquaint your Majesty by Letters with the Necessity of calling such an Assembly, and pray your Majestys consent and Directions for their meeting.   And at the same time do present unto your Majesty a scheme of such Acts as he shall thinke fit and necessary, that your Majesty may take the same into consideration, and returne them in the forme wherein your Majesty shall thinke fit, that they be enacted."   P. C. Cal. I, p. 745.   See also C. O. 391/2, f. 27 ; C. C. 1677–1680, pp. 67, 68.

Lord Carlisle, who was appointed Governor in succession to Lord Vaughan,[1] was instructed to introduce this new system. Among the laws prepared in England for submission to the Jamaica legislature was one granting a perpetual revenue to the Crown. This proposed revenue bill was carefully drafted.

The Lords of Trade had been instructed to prepare such a bill on the general model of the revenue law transmitted from Jamaica two years before this.[2] They carefully discussed the matter and, as was usual, sought the expert advice of the Commissioners of the Customs,[3] who suggested some alterations in the draft submitted to them. This board objected to the high duties on beer, spirits, and cider, as these commodities were imported mainly from England, and they protested against the special privileges granted to Jamaica vessels, since "Ships built in any of his Ma[ties] Plantacons are as free in England as ships built att London."[4] The bill was finally put into satisfactory shape, and, with other laws, was taken to Jamaica in 1678 by the Earl of Carlisle for enactment by the colonial legislature.[5]

---

[1] Brit. Mus., Add. MSS. 25,120, ff. 110, 111, 115.

[2] P. C. Cal. I, p. 744; C. C. 1677–1680, p. 178.

[3] C. C. 1677–1680, pp. 179, 180. The Lords of Trade considered Sir Thomas Lynch's Act of 1672 and that passed under Lord Vaughan. In the latter they found several 'dangerous innovations,' such as the appointment of a collector by it, in the place of the receiver appointed by the Crown. They decided that the revenue should be received by the crown officer.

[4] C. O. 1/41, 126; C. C. 1677–1680, p. 193.

[5] Out of this revenue, Carlisle was instructed to take a salary of £2000, and he was also allowed one-third of the fines, forfeitures, and escheats. C. C. 1677–1680, p. 230. See also P. C. Cal. I, pp. 761–763.

It was extremely unlikely that Jamaica would submit, at least without a severe struggle, to such an abridgment of its liberties as was implied in the contemplated new constitutional system.   As in all the colonies, the people here were very sensitive to anything that seemed to be, or was, in violation of an Englishman's traditional rights.   It is not surprising that Lord Carlisle was completely unable to accomplish his well-nigh impossible task.   The Assembly objected to the Poynings' system as impracticable, on account of Jamaica's remoteness from England, and because it rendered the Governor absolute.   The revenue bill was rejected, because it was perpetual, and for fear that the funds arising from it might be diverted to other than its intended purposes.[1]

The English government was, however, not disposed to yield without further effort.   Lord Carlisle was instructed to call another Assembly and, in case this body also rejected the laws transmitted from England, it was decided that he should be given such ample powers to govern the colony, as Governor Doyley had had, before a legislature had been

[1] P. C. Cal. I, pp. 826–833; C. C. 1677–1680, pp. 367–369. In 1679, Carlisle wrote to the Lords of Trade that the Assembly feared that this revenue 'would be in danger of being diverted like the four-and-a-half per cent in Barbadoes.' C. C. 1677–1680, p. 379. In this connection, the Lords of Trade reported that it could not be diverted, "since Provision is thereby expressly made that the same shall be for the better Support of that Government.   Besides that it is not suitable to the Duty and Modesty of Subjects to suspect Your Majestys Justice or Care for the Government of that Colony whose Settlement and Preservation has been most particularly carried on by your Majesty's tender regard and by the great Expence of your own Treasure." P. C. Cal. I, p. 829.

erected in Jamaica.[1] This new Assembly met, but, as Lord Carlisle had prophesied, it was not of a more amenable disposition than its predecessor, and likewise refused to pass the English-made laws submitted to it.[2] The Jamaica situation was naturally carefully studied in England,[3] and finally, in the fall of 1680, the government wisely receded from its untenable position and decided that, as theretofore, Jamaica should enjoy in matters of legislation the same privileges as did Barbados.[4] Lord Carlisle was instructed [5] to summon the Assembly, and, after announcing this decision, to endeavor to procure the passage of a perpetual revenue law according to the draft sent from England, from

---

[1] P. C. Cal. I, p. 833.

[2] C. C. 1677–1680, pp. 441–445. Before this news reached England, Sir Thomas Lynch, who had been very successful as Lieutenant-Governor of Jamaica, was consulted by the Lords of Trade and made a spirited and able defence of the colony, strongly condemning the attempt to change its constitution. He said: "It's probable the Assembly will reject the Laws thus offer'd them. Its certain there's an absolute necessity of a Revenue, for the publick charge is great and the debts many. It's possible the Council may joyn with my Lord to Order ye Laws for ye Governm^t to bee continued: but I verily believe they will not continue ye Revenue-Bill, for that they think belongs peculiar to ye Assembly. And if they did doe it, it would not bee without process; and I doubt the Judges &c. would quit, and Jurys constantly give against ye Officers. It would be ye Same or worse if any order went hence to that purpose, and give strange ombrage to the rest of the Colonies." C. O. 1/43, 172; C. C. 1677–1680, pp. 456–458.

[3] On Jan. 18, 1680, Secretary Coventry wrote to Carlisle: "The Truth is we are so very much imployed in our Transactions here at home that we cannot with that leisure debate the Affaires of the Plantations as we could when you were here, but yet a good deal of time hath been allotted to Jamaica." Brit. Mus., Add. MSS. 25,120, f. 151.

[4] C. C. 1677–1680, p. 622.

[5] C. O. 138/3, ff. 447 et seq.; C. C. 1677–1680, pp. 624, 625.

which no material deviations were to be permitted. Ample assurance was given that not only this revenue, but also that from the quit-rents, would be exclusively and entirely devoted to the public services of Jamaica.[1] Thus, in return for a satisfactory law, the Crown was willing to abandon its rights to the quit-rents, which were based on the fact that the King was the original lord of the soil.[2] Furthermore, Carlisle was forbidden to give his assent to any law exempting Jamaica vessels from dues payable by other English ships.[3] In his private instructions, accompanying these public ones, the Governor was authorized to consent to a revenue bill of not less than seven years' duration, provided a perpetual one were not obtainable.

[1] C. O. 138/3, ff. 448, 449.

[2] When, in 1677, the Lords of Trade first took up this question of the Jamaica revenue, they ordered that a search should be made in the instructions to Governor Modyford and elsewhere, in order to find out what evidence there was to justify the disposal of the quit-rents to the uses of the colony. C. O. 391/2, f. 27; C. C. 1677–1680, pp. 67, 68. In Jamaica, as opposed to Virginia, New York, and the Carolinas, the quit-rents formed part of the purely colonial revenue.

[3] C. O. 138/3, f. 452. During this prolonged controversy, Jamaica was forced in 1679 to pass a temporary revenue law, one clause of which aroused the ire of the English government, because it discriminated against English shipping. On Jan. 16, 1680, the Lords of Trade wrote to Carlisle, that they were much surprised at the clause exempting Jamaica ships from the taxes, as it had been expressly omitted in the draft sent by them, on the advice of the Commissioners of the Customs to the effect "that there might bee noe difference made between the Shipping of the built of any other His Maties Plantations, or the Shipping of the built or propriety of this Kingdome trading to and from Jamaica and the Shipping of that Island." C. O. 138/3, ff. 344–358; C. C. 1677–1680, p. 470. In reply, Carlisle wrote that the Assembly had insisted on this clause. C. C. 1677–1680, p. 518.

The main object in view was to make Jamaica self-support-ing, and thus to lessen the burden on England's far from over-flowing Treasury.[1]   In anticipation of the proposed revenue, an order was issued that the garrison in Jamaica be dis-banded and taken off the establishment, that the yearly allowance of £600 by the Exchequer for maintaining the forts in the colony be discontinued, and that the salaries paid from the same source to the Governor and his deputy be retrenched.[2]

Although completely victorious in the main constitu-tional struggle, and as a result in the enjoyment of the same full representative institutions as the other royal provinces, Jamaica was by no means ready to comply with the English government's wishes regarding a revenue bill.   As Carlisle had returned to England, the management of this matter devolved upon the Deputy-Governor, Sir Henry Morgan, then commonly called "Panama Morgan," on account of his successful buccaneering exploits on the Spanish Main. In the summer of 1681, Morgan wrote to the Lords of Trade

[1]
THE JAMAICA ESTABLISHMENT IN 1679

Governor	. . .	£1000
Deputy-Governor	.	£ 600
Major-General	. .	£ 300
Allowance for forts	.	£ 600
Garrison	. . .	£3327
		£5827

P. C. Cal. I, pp. 837, 846–848.

[2] C. O. 138/3, ff. 441, 442.   Carlisle's interest in the escheats, fines, and forfeitures of the colony was also stopped.   In 1681, the offices of Lieu-tenant-Governor and Major-General were discontinued and the two com-panies of soldiers were disbanded.   C. C. 1681–1685, pp. 97, 98, 102, 103, 113, 205.

that the Assembly would meet soon again, but that he feared it would not grant a perpetual revenue.[1] His doubts were fully justified. After considerable delay, the Assembly passed a revenue bill of only two years' duration, but Morgan induced them to rescind this and to pass another for seven years. This Act obliged the Governors to give a yearly account of the disposal of the revenue to the Assembly. This provision would have made the annual meeting of the legislature automatic, without the necessity of the Crown or the Governor summoning it, and naturally was considered highly prejudicial to the royal prerogative.[2] Furthermore, the Assembly tacked to the revenue bill a number of other measures, thus giving the English government no option but to confirm or to disallow one and all.[3] The Assembly too shrewdly argued that England, in her anxiety to secure a revenue, would confirm the tacked bills also.[4] In this, however, they overshot the mark.

While these events were happening in Jamaica, the English government in its difficulty turned to Sir Thomas Lynch and appointed him Governor of Jamaica.[5] This was a

[1] C. C. 1681–1685, p. 72.

[2] *Ibid.* p. 282.

[3] *Ibid.* pp. 121, 122, 137, 183, 184, 204.

[4] The instructions for the passage of a revenue law were issued in November of 1680, but the Assembly passed this bill only a year later. In order to force it to take action, the English government declared, in October of 1681, that all other laws passed by this Assembly should be null and void, unless a revenue bill were passed before the arrival of Lynch, who in the meanwhile had been appointed to succeed Carlisle as Governor. *Ibid.* p. 128; P. C. Cal. II, pp. 25, 26.

[5] C. C. 1681–1685, p. 87.

step well calculated to bring matters to an equitable settlement. Lynch had already displayed conspicuous ability in governing the colony; later, he had fearlessly opposed the attempt under Governor Carlisle to deprive the colonial Assembly of its customary powers. As a result, he enjoyed to the full the confidence of the colony. His instructions,[1] issued in September of 1681, were practically the same as those given to Carlisle the preceding year — to secure a revenue granted to the Crown in perpetuity or for at least seven years, and to assure the people that not only these funds, but the quit-rents as well, would be wholly devoted to the colony's public services. Until such a measure was passed, he was further instructed to refuse his assent to all other Acts of the legislature.

Lynch arrived in Jamaica in the early summer of 1682, but delayed taking any steps in this matter, until he should hear from the English government about the revenue bill passed the preceding year by Morgan's Assembly.[2] 'The people,' he wrote to the Lords of Trade, 'are well enough disposed, but by letters from England and evil designs here have been spirited into extraordinary distrusts and jealousies. So I conclude that they will do nothing till they hear from you, and but little after.' [3] When the Assembly met in the fall of 1682, although still without direct instructions from England on this point, Lynch tactfully pointed out the valid objections to their proceedings during the past year, and told them plainly that 'they must not expect the

___

[1] C. C. 1681–1685, pp. 113–115. [2] *Ibid.* p. 253. *Cf.* p. 282.
[3] *Ibid.* p. 282.

King to pass the laws while tacked to the Revenue Bill,
nor to allow Assemblies to be convened by their own acts.'[1]
He succeeded in inducing the legislature to pass a satisfactory revenue bill which, while free from the objectionable
features of the preceding measure, was likewise but of the
limited duration of seven years.[2]   On receipt of this news,

[1] Shortly after Jamaica had passed the revenue bill of 1682, the Lords
of Trade took under their consideration the Act of the preceding year.
They objected to the provisions of the Act, and to the fact that the other laws
had been tacked to it.   They decided that it should be disallowed, and that
if Jamaica ' refuse to pass a Revenue Act the Assembly is to be warned that
the laws of England empower the King to lay tonnage and poundage.'
C. C. 1681–1685, pp. 315, 316, 321, 322.   This threat involved an interesting
legal point.   The English subsidy of 1660 (12 Ch. II, c. 4) imposed import
and export duties in the realm *and its dominions*.   The addition of the
words in italics was probably due to carelessness ; at all events, no attempt
was made to collect these duties in the colonies.   In 1680, however, it was
suggested that the Jamaica difficulty could be solved by collecting these
duties there, but the expediency of this course was very doubtful, and nothing
was done.   C. C. 1677–1680, pp. 497, 498, 520, 521.

[2] C. C. 1681–1685, pp. 296–298, 300–303, 307–310.   For an interesting
contemporary account of the passage of this act, with valuable documents,
see A Narrative of Affairs. . . . Jamaica (London, 1683).   Lynch did not
think a perpetual revenue essential.   On Aug. 29, 1682, he wrote to the
Lords of Trade : 'You judged rightly for the King's honour that no short
Bill of Revenue should be accepted, but, with your leave, I think a perpetual
one against his interest.   For, without their Act, I doubt not to find enough,
after some considerable time, to pay the Governor, Chief Justice, and Auditor-General.   As to the fortifications and other contingencies, they are
the Island's concern and must be neglected at its peril.'   C. C. 1681–1685,
p. 282.   After the passage of the revenue bill, on Oct. 8, 1682, Lynch wrote
to the Lords of Trade : 'The revenue is for seven years, though I told the
Assembly that they might pass it for six if they would.   A perpetual bill
I would not suggest, as I could not put them into the train of rejecting my
proposals ; moreover, I thought that you will certainly send back their laws
(those tacked to the revenue bill of 1681), and that on receiving them they

the English government expressed great satisfaction, and confirmed nearly all the other Jamaica laws,[1] but at the same time they instructed Lynch to do his best 'to render the Act of Revenue perpetual, representing that the King may thus be ready to confirm their laws for more than seven years.'[2]

When the Jamaica Assembly met again in the fall of 1683, Lynch congratulated it on the success of its 'discreet behaviour,' and in reply the Speaker said that, 'after the King's gracious favour we shall have little more to do but every man to sit down under his own vine, studying to do our own happiness, and pray for His Majesty's long and happy reign.'[3] Despite this good feeling, Lynch encountered some difficulty,[4] but ultimately succeeded in having the revenue bill extended to a period of twenty-one years in all.[5]

This revenue arose from licenses for taverns and from an impost on spirituous liquors, and in addition the Crown definitely abandoned to the colony the quit-rents, which elsewhere were regarded as in the nature of a royal perquisite.[6]

will themselves offer it. It can never be done otherwise; pressing it is the certain way not to have it.' *Ibid.* p. 310.

[1] *Ibid.* pp. 369, 397–398, 400; P. C. Cal. II, pp. 46–48.

[2] C. C. 1681–1685, p. 386.

[3] *Ibid.* pp. 486, 487.

[4] The main opposition came from what Lynch called 'that little, drunken, silly party of Sir Henry Morgan's.' *Ibid.* p. 532.

[5] *Ibid.* pp. 487, 501, 506, 518, 522, 532. In return, the laws passed by this Assembly were, with one exception, confirmed by Order in Council for 21 years. *Ibid.* p. 487.

[6] In 1682, Lynch wrote to the Lords of Trade: 'I think that you should first see the rental of the quit-rents and consider whether the King should not be often thanked for so great a bounty.' *Ibid.* p. 310.

The moneys were received by a royal official, the Receiver-General, who was supervised by a Deputy-Auditor, also appointed from England, and the accounts were submitted to the Governor in Council.[1] Out of the revenue was paid the salary of the Governor,[2] the cost of keeping the forts in fit condition and other items.

At first the revenue was poorly managed,[3] but in the subsequent period, after the Revolution of 1688/9, it yielded an income adequate for these purposes. Henceforward Jamaica was no longer a burden on the English Exchequer. Thus in this colony, as in the other West Indies and in Virginia, the English government had ultimately succeeded in laying the basis of a permanently established revenue, out of which it could pay the salaries of its representatives in Jamaica, and thus prevent them from becoming dependent upon the colonial legislature.

In connection with the movement to reorganize the financial systems of the crown colonies and to place them on a permanent basis, there was created in 1680 a new imperial office, whose function was to audit their revenues and expenditures.[4] In that year William Blathwayt, an able official with considerable experience in colonial matters,

---

[1] C. C. 1681–1685, pp. 283, 473, 501.

[2] In 1684 this salary was £2000.   C. C. 1685–1688, pp. 407, 408.

[3] *Ibid.* 1681–1685, pp. 657, 683.

[4] In 1663 had been created the office of Receiver-General of the Revenues of the Foreign Plantations, but there is no evidence of any activity on the part of the patentees, Ross and Chiffinch.   C. O. 1/15, 60; C. C. 1661–1668, nos. 99, 100, 376, 435, 487, 488, 1527; Brit. Mus., Egerton MSS. 2395, ff. 370, 380.

was appointed Surveyor and Auditor General of all His Majesty's revenues in America.[1] His salary of £500 was charged to the royal provinces, Virginia paying £100 and the West Indies the balance.[2] From Blathwayt's jurisdiction was naturally excepted the plantation duties of 1673, because the Act of Parliament imposing them had specifically entrusted this matter to the Commissioners of the Customs. Thus this new official as such had no direct connection with the work of enforcing the laws of trade and navigation.[3]

Except in Virginia, where there was already an auditor appointed by the Crown,[4] Blathwayt was authorized and

[1] Blathwayt, Journal I, ff. 1–9; Va. Mag. IV, pp. 43–49; Mass. Col. Rec. V, pp. 521–526.

[2] Barbados and Jamaica each contributed £150 and the Leeward Islands £100. Later, when the number of royal provinces had increased, the Auditor's income was enlarged, as he was in several instances allowed a percentage on their revenues. In 1688, Randolph wrote from Boston to Blathwayt that he had proposed the allowance of a fee of 5 per cent, but that this was as yet not settled. He added, that Graham of the New York Council told him, that there they had settled £100 on Blathwayt. Goodrick, Randolph VI, p. 251. In 1682, Cranfield wrote to Blathwayt that an order had been passed in New Hampshire allowing him 2½ per cent of the revenue there. This revenue did not, however, exceed £100. Ibid. pp. 120, 122.

[3] He was solely interested in this matter, because the revenue that accrued to the Crown from forfeitures for violations of these laws was under his jurisdiction. Thus Blathwayt's deputy in Massachusetts, Randolph, was empowered "to inspect, examine, and state all accounts of all such rents, revenues, prizes, ffines, escheats, seizures, fforfeitures" etc. Mass. Col. Rec. V, pp. 526–529.

[4] In 1675, Nathaniel Bacon, Sr., had been appointed Auditor of the Virginia accounts in succession to Edward Digges. Bacon's rights were safeguarded in Blathwayt's patent, but it was provided therein that, on the

instructed to appoint deputies in the crown colonies. Those appointed by him as a rule occupied in addition some other colonial post. The Jamaica deputy, Reginald Wilson, was also the colony's Naval Officer, and the deputy in New England was the well-known Collector of the Customs, Edward Randolph.[1] These deputies audited the colonial accounts, which were then passed upon by the Governor and Council, and ultimately sent to Blathwayt,[2] who in his journals kept a careful record of these fiscal details. To a great extent, however, Blathwayt's work was perfunctory;

expiration of Bacon's grant, the Virginia office should be annexed to that of the Auditor-General. Despite this, in 1687, William Byrd was appointed by the English Treasury to succeed Bacon. The rights of these two Virginia Auditors were, however, attacked by Robert Ayleway, who in 1678 had obtained letters patent for this place. Owing to the opposition of Governor Culpeper, Ayleway was unable to enforce his patent against Bacon, but, on the appointment of Byrd in 1687, he revived his claim. Although the legal authorities could find no flaw in it, difficulties were put in his way, and he made terms with Byrd, to whom he assigned his grant. When Bacon was appointed Auditor, he was allowed 5 per cent for his work. At that time the revenue was received by a Treasurer, but the Governor and Council, believing this office to be superfluous, consolidated it with that of the Auditor and raised Bacon's fee to $7\frac{1}{2}$ per cent, as compensation for the extra work. Thus the Auditor acted as well as the Receiver-General of the provincial revenue, receiving it from the collectors and paying it out on warrants from the Governor and Council. Blathwayt, Journal I, f. 279; II, ff. 37–40; Va. Mag. XIV, pp. 270, 271, 368; Va. Hist. Register III, pp. 182, 183; P. C. Cal. I, p. 864; II, p. 136; C. C. 1689–1692, pp. 69, 70, 72, 77, 83; Cal. Treas. Papers, 1676–1679, pp. 806, 807; Chalmers, Opinions of Eminent Lawyers (Burlington, 1858), pp. 160, 161.

[1] Blathwayt, Journal I, ff. 74, 75, 88, 109, 238–240; Mass. Col. Rec. V, pp. 526–529.

[2] For the exact procedure in Jamaica, see C. C. 1681–1685, pp. 283, 473, 501, 502.

and necessarily so, since but slight control over the income and expenditure of the crown colonies could be exercised from so distant a centre as England. Everything depended upon the honesty and vigilance of the governors, deputy-auditors, and local treasurers. Hence Blathwayt's post of Auditor-General tended to, and ultimately did, become one of those sinecures of no public utility, which were the bane of the old administrative régime, and which, while not numerous in the colonial service, tended in a mild way to breed discontent in the colonies.

CHAPTER IV

CENTRAL AND LOCAL ADMINISTRATIVE MACHINERY

Parliament and Crown — The Privy Council and its Committees — The Secretaries of State — The Council for Foreign Plantations of 1660 — The Council for Trade of 1660 — Its revival in 1668 and that of the Colonial Council in 1670 — The Council for Trade and Plantations of 1672 — The Lords of Trade — The Admiralty and the Colonies — The Treasury and the Commissioners of the Customs — The Royal Governor — The naval officers — The collectors of the customs — The Surveyor-General of the Customs — Quarrel between Giles Bland and Governor Berkeley of Virginia — The colonial admiralty courts — The use of the navy to suppress illegal trading.

THE central fact in the history of the English Empire during the Restoration era was the creation of a comprehensive and symmetrical system regulating colonial trade. This commercial code was the work of Parliament, and marked the definite establishment of its claim to legislative power in imperial matters. The first Stuarts had succeeded in denying Parliament's competence in such questions,[1] but the collapse of the monarchy in the Civil War inevitably implied, at least for the time being, parliamentary jurisdictions over the American dominions. This result of the confusion and flux of the Interregnum decades was accepted without contest by the Restoration government, for Charles II tacitly waived his ancestors' claims to exclusive authority over the colonies. As a consequence, the Crown was deprived of some powers, but in reality its imperial duties and

[1] Beer, Origins, pp. 301, 302.

functions increased greatly during the Restoration era. For the work of Parliament was necessarily purely legislative, and the burden of enforcing the new commercial system, embodied in the half dozen fundamental statutes of the reign, fell upon the Crown. In addition, these laws of trade and navigation obliged the English executive to appoint royal officials within the confines of the proprietary and charter colonies, whose inhabitants had hitherto not been normally in direct relations with the organs of the home government. It was the colonial system enacted by Parliament, that forced the Crown to break in upon the feudal barricades created by the early colonial charters.

Another factor also considerably expanded the sphere of the Crown's activities in colonial administration. This was the great increase in the number of royal provinces. The fundamental trend in the constitutional development of the old Empire was the gradual substitution of crown colonies for those of the proprietary and charter type. Under the first Stuarts, Virginia was the only royal colony; in the "Old Dominion" alone did crown appointed officials direct the course of local self-government. The proprietors of the other colonies, whether corporations or individuals, enjoyed under certain broad restrictions, defined in their charters, virtually complete powers of government. Already under the first Stuarts, apart from the forfeiture of the Virginia Company's patent in 1624, distinct inroads had been made into this anomalous and unworkable system of semi-feudal independent jurisdictions.[1] Further steps

[1] Beer, Origins, pp. 328–333.

in this direction were taken during the Commonwealth, when a number of the colonies in the West Indies were forcibly seized from their proprietor in consequence of their overt espousal of the royalist cause.

This movement advanced at a greatly accelerated pace, when the English monarchy was restored in 1660. Barbados and the Leeward Islands were definitively organized as royal provinces on the Virginia model, and conquered Jamaica, hitherto governed on a military basis, likewise received the same political organization. In all of these colonies were firmly established balanced constitutions; the people were represented in the local assemblies, whose actions were controlled by royal governors, assisted by other officials likewise appointed from England. In addition, towards the end of the Stuart period, the number of Crown colonies was greatly enlarged. The Bermuda Company was deprived of the islands, which it had settled. All the New England colonies lost their charters and were joined in an artificial union with New York, which on the accession of James II had already by this very fact become a royal province.[1]

Thus the enactment of the laws of trade and navigation and the extension of the system of royal provinces added greatly to the work of the English executive. But apart from these general causes increasing the normal volume of colonial business after the Restoration, there naturally were at that very time an exceptionally large number of important colonial questions that pressed for immediate decision.

[1] The Jerseys were also included in this abortive arrangement.

After the widespread dislocation produced by the Inter-regnum, there had to be a settlement in the Empire, as well as in England, Ireland, and Scotland. A host of difficult questions crowded the government. In the first place, should Jamaica be restored to Spain, Charles's friend in misfortune, and, if retained, how should it be governed? Then, should Nova Scotia, which Cromwell had seized from France, be kept; and, if so, should the Temple charter of 1656 covering this territory be recognized as valid?[1] What attitude should be taken towards the Puritan colonies of New England, which all but in name were independent political entities, and looked askance at the restoration of the monarchy in England? What, if any, recognition should be given to the claims of the Kirkes to Newfoundland under the patent of 1637, which Cromwell had superseded when he appointed Commissioners to take charge of these fishing settlements?[2] Finally, what should be done with the Caribbee Islands, which the Commonwealth government had taken from the Earl of Carlisle, who had been their proprietor in virtue of the charter of 1627?

The ultimate decision in all these matters rested with the Crown, which still retained a large measure of its pre-rogative and was the source of all executive authority. Its work was performed primarily through the Privy Council, which was the centre of the administrative system. This

---

[1] C. C. 1574–1660, pp. 444, 447, 484, 496, 497 ; P. C. Cal. I, pp. 305, 316, 321-323.

[2] C. C. 1574–1660, p. 481. In addition, Lord Baltimore asserted his claims to Avalon in Newfoundland on the strength of the charter of 1623. *Ibid.* pp. 481, 482 ; C. C. 1675–1676, p. 157.

was a consultative and executive body, composed of the great state officials and of a varying number of men of exceptional prominence and standing, who fully enjoyed the royal confidence. Around the King and the Privy Council were grouped the great administrative departments, but as yet no special colonial office had been created. Hence this mass of colonial business naturally came before the Privy Council; and, in order to cope with it, recourse was had to the committee system that had already been developed under the first Stuarts. In 1660, a number of merchants and others interested in the West Indies and opposed to the Carlisle patent petitioned the King, that Colonel James Russell be continued in the government of Nevis. This petition was referred to the Privy Council and was read before it on July 4, 1660, a week after its receipt.[1] On the same day, in connection with this petition, which raised the entire question of the future disposal of the West Indies, an Order in Council was issued appointing a Committee of the Privy Council to deliberate thereon and further to meet every Monday and Thursday "to receive, heare, examine & deliberate upon peticons, proposicons, Memorialls, or other Addresses w[ch] shal be presented or brought in by any person or persons concerning the plantacons," and then to report to the Privy Council.[2] The members of this committee were in the main great officers of state, such as the Earl of Manchester, then

[1] C. C. 1574–1660, p. 482. A similar petition in favor of the retention of Governor Ward in St. Kitts was also received. *Ibid.*

[2] P. C. Register Charles II, I, f. 63; P. C. Cal. I, p. 295; N. Y. Col. Doc. III, p. 30.

Lord Chamberlain, the Earl of Southampton, then Lord Treasurer, the two Secretaries of State, Nicholas and Morice.[1] Among other matters, this body carefully investigated the question of reviving the Carlisle patent of 1627 covering the Caribbee Islands,[2] and also the Temple claim to Nova Scotia based on the charter of 1656.[3] In addition to this general committee, special committees of the Privy Council were also appointed for specific purposes. In September of 1660, the colonial committee was instructed to inform itself of the state of Jamaica and to report to the King; but, somewhat over a month later, a special committee was formed and the Jamaica business was entrusted to it.[4] In

[1] In 1661, Sir George Carteret, the Vice-Chamberlain, was added to this committee and to that for the affairs of New England. P. C. Cal. I, p. 309. In 1662, the Lord Chancellor Clarendon, the Earl of Portland, and the Earl of Sandwich were also appointed to serve on this body. P. C. Register, Charles II, III, f. 127; P. C. Cal. I, p. 336. Cf. C. C. 1661–1668, no. 847.

[2] On July 16, 1660, several Lords of the Council, sitting 'as a Committee touching the Plantations,' heard Lord Willoughby on his claims to the Caribbee Islands and Surinam, and also the merchants and planters opposing him. "It was ordered by his Matie, afterwards cominge & sitting in Councill," that Willoughby and the planters should "attend the Comittee for Plantacons" on July 26, and that the committee should report to the King. After this hearing, the committee stated that they could not make "any cleare or satisfactory Report to his Majestie or Councill," until they had further investigated the matter. On Aug. 2, the question was again considered, and on Aug. 20, 1660, the committee reported in favor of restoring Willoughby to his rights as leaseholder under the proprietor. C. O. 1/14, 20; P. C. Cal. I, pp. 296, 297; C. C. 1574–1660, pp. 483, 484, 486, 488, 489.

[3] C. C. 1574–1660, pp. 484–486, 488.

[4] P. C. Cal. I, pp. 298, 299. The original members of this body were the Duke of Albemarle, Arthur Annesley, and the Secretaries of State, Morice and Nicholas, of whom only the first was not a member of the larger committee. Subsequently, the Duke of York, the Earl of Sandwich, Sir George

1661, was constituted also a similar special committee for the affairs of New England,[1] and in the same year another committee was appointed to consider the French demand for the restitution of Nova Scotia.[2]

The work of the Privy Council and its various committees was mainly deliberative; its decisions were carried into actual effect by one of the Secretaries of State — at the outset, in 1661 and 1662, by Sir Edward Nicholas, to whose department the colonies were assigned. But Nicholas was by no means minister for the colonies in the modern sense. The Secretaries of State had as yet no clearly defined independent position, and were still attached and subordinate to the Privy Council. They were in the nature of its executive officers, and also served as intermediaries between it and the King. Nicholas brought petitions addressed to the King before the Privy Council, prepared the material for its consideration, kept rough minutes of its proceedings for his own use, and saw that its orders and those of the Crown, were executed.[3]

Obviously, the Privy Council and its committees could by no means do full justice to the many and intricate colonial questions that demanded more or less immediate settlement. Its active members, upon whom this duty devolved, were

Carteret, and Denzill Holles were added to it.　*Ibid.*　See also C. C. 1574–1660, pp. 491, 492;　C. C. 1661–1668, nos. 839, 847;　P. C. Cal. I, pp. 320, 384.

[1] P. C. Cal. I, pp. 308, 309, 344;　C. C. 1661–1668, nos. 88, 91.

[2] P. C. Cal. I, p. 316.　See also *ibid.* p. 305 and C. C. 1661–1668, no. 112.

[3] C. C. 1574–1660, pp. 489, 490;　C. C. 1661–1668, nos. 12, 19, 26, 37, 58, 76, 78, 83, 87, 91, 95, 133, 216, 222, 309.

at the same time the great officers of state, and had to super-
intend the extensive readjustment in English affairs that
followed inevitably in the wake of the restoration of the
monarchy. Immersed in this important work, which directly
affected so many vital national and private interests, they
naturally could not give adequate attention to colonial
matters. Moreover, no matter how much these statesmen
might be impressed with the importance of imperial problems, they unfortunately brought no detailed expert knowledge to their solution. Hence the demand immediately
arose that there be created an advisory body, composed
in part, at least, of experts, which should devote its entire
attention to colonial questions. Some tentative steps in
this direction had already been taken by the first Stuarts
and by the Cromwellian government.[1] The cumbersome
administrative machinery devised for this purpose during
the Interregnum was, however, far from satisfactory, and
the creation of "a select Councill solely dedicated to the
inspection, care and charge of America" was at that time
strongly advocated by a group of Englishmen interested
especially in the West Indies. These men, of whom the
chief were Thomas Povey and Martin Noell, renewed
their proposals very shortly after Charles's entry into
London.[2]

In view of the congestion of business, it is not surprising
that they met with a favorable response and, on December 1,
1660, was issued the formal commission creating a special

[1] Beer, Origins, pp. 307–316, 418–423.
[2] Brit. Mus., Egerton MSS. 2395, ff. 272–275. *Cf.* ff. 270, 271.

Council for Foreign Plantations.[1] In this body were represented various distinct groups and interests. Among
the statesmen were the Lord Chancellor Clarendon, the
Lord Treasurer Southampton, the Lord Chamberlain Manchester,[2] the two Secretaries of State, and Sir Anthony
Ashley Cooper, better known to fame as the first of the three
celebrated Earls of Shaftesbury. All of these men were
prominent members of the Privy Council; with the exception of Clarendon, who was the chief of Charles's ministers,
they were all members of its general Committee for Plantations. A second group comprised colonial administrators
and men already, or about to become, actively engaged in
colonial enterprises, such as: Lord Willoughby, the founder
of English Surinam and the leaseholder of the Caribbee
Islands; Lord Berkeley and Sir George Carteret, who were
to be among the future proprietors of the Carolinas and to
whom the Duke of York in 1664 granted the Jerseys;[3]
Berkeley's brother, Sir William, the experienced royalist
Governor of Virginia; John Colleton, about to be knighted,
one of the most prominent planters in Barbados[4] and
shortly to become a leading figure in the settlement of
Carolina.[5] Finally, there were included in the Council a

---

[1] C. O. 1/14, 59, ff. 1, 2; N. Y. Col. Doc. III, pp. 32–34; C. C. 1574–
1660, pp. 490, 492, 494. The Council was given power to appoint clerks,
messengers, etc., whose salaries were not to exceed £300 yearly. Philip
Froude was appointed as its secretary.

[2] Manchester was also the Governor of the Bermuda Company.

[3] C. C. 1661–1668, nos. 1095, 1169.

[4] Ibid. nos. 39, 60.

[5] Ibid. nos. 457, 558, 912.

number of experts in colonial matters, who in the main had acquired their knowledge from personal experience as traders or planters. Among these were Thomas Povey and Martin Noell, — to whose efforts was largely due the formation of the Council, — Sir James Drax, Thomas Kendall, and Edward Digges. With the exception of Digges, whose associations were with Virginia, virtually all these men were predominantly interested in the West Indies. This was a natural result of the high value attached to the sugar and tobacco trades and of the slight actual commercial importance of New England.

The commission of the Council stated that Charles II deemed its appointment necessary, in order that so many remote colonies, which had grown so greatly in wealth and population, should be brought under a uniform inspection and conduct for their future regulation, security, and improvement.[1] Annexed to the commission were detailed instructions defining the scope of the Council's work.[2] They were fully to inform themselves of the condition of each col-

---

[1] "They being now become a greate and numerous people whose plentifull trade and comerce verie much imployes and increaseth the navigacon and expends the manufactures of our dominions and exchanges them for comodities of necessary use, and bring a good accesse of treasure to our Exchequr for customs and other duties."

[2] C. O. 1/14, 59, ff. 3, 4; N. Y. Col. Doc. III, pp. 34–36; C. C. 1574–1660, pp. 492, 493; Alpheus H. Snow, The Administration of Dependencies, pp. 79–82. These instructions were based directly upon Povey's "Overtures touching a Councell to bee erected by his Ma^tle for the better regulating and improving of forreigne Plantations," which in turn rested upon a similar set of proposals, signed by Povey and Martin Noell. Brit. Mus., Egerton MSS. 2395, ff. 270–275.

ony in order to be able to give the King an exact account, so
that all could be regulated upon equal ground and principle.
Further, they were to apply themselves "to all prudentiall
meanes for the rendering these dominions usefull to England,
and England helpfull to them," and to introduce in the colonies a more uniform system of government.[1]   In addition,
they were instructed to take especial care that the recent Act
of Navigation should be strictly executed.   In order to carry
out these instructions the Council was authorized 'to advise
order settle and dispose of all matters relating to the good
government and improvement of the plantations,' and, if
further powers were needed, application was to be made to
the Privy Council.

Colonization and commerce were closely related and
overlapping spheres of activity, with no distinct lines of
demarcation.   From the standpoint of the supervising
government, the colonies were in the main commercial
enterprises designed to further English trade and shipping.
Hence, simultaneously with the foundation of the Council
for Foreign Plantations, a similar body was created to take
charge of commercial matters.[2]   In this case, also, the intent

[1] This section was copied directly from one in Povey's "Overtures,"
which reads: "This Councell is to apply itself to all prudentiall meanes for
the rendering these Dominions vsefull to England, and England helpfull
to them; and that the severall Peices, and Collonies bee drawn, and disposed into a more certaine civill, and vniforme waie of Government; and
distribution of publick Justice; in which they are at present most Scan-
dalously defective."   Brit. Mus., Egerton MSS. 2395, f. 273.

[2] The patent of the Council for Trade was issued Nov. 7, 1660, a
month prior to that of the Council for Foreign Plantations, which was
delayed by some belated additions to its membership.   Andrews, British
Committees, Commissions, and Councils of Trade and Plantations, pp. 66, 67.

was to bring to the aid of the government the expert knowledge and experience of men actually engaged in these pursuits.[1] This Council of Trade drew its membership from the same classes as did that for the colonies,[2] twenty-eight names being common to both.[3] Among its members were all of those just enumerated as belonging to the Council for Foreign Plantations, and also Sir John Wolstenholme and Sir George Downing, both of whom were skilled in financial and economic matters. In the main, this body was to devote its attention to English concerns, but in addition it was entrusted with some matters vitally affecting the colonics. The Council was instructed to consider the general state and trade of the colonies, and how far their future prosperity might be advanced by modifications of the existing English tariff in their favor. But in all matters, which concerned the colonies, they were directed to take advice from the Council appointed for their more particular inspection, regulation, and care.[4]

[1] The intention to constitute this body was expressed in a letter of the Privy Council to the Lord Mayor and Aldermen of London, stating that the Turkey Merchants, the Merchant Adventurers, the East India, Greenland, and Eastland Companies, and also the incorporated (*sic*, for unincorporated) traders for Spain, France, Portugal, Italy, and the West Indian colonies were each to present four names, of which the King would choose two, and then join to them experienced men and members of the Privy Council, who together should constitute "a Standinge-Comittee, to inquire into, and certify all thinges tending to the Advancement of Trade and Commerce." P. C. Register Charles II, I, ff. 131, 132; P. C. Cal. I, pp. 297, 298.

[2] The commission is in N. Y. Col. Doc. III, pp. 30–32.

[3] Andrews, *op. cit.* pp. 67, 68.

[4] Brit. Mus., Egerton MSS. 2395, f. 269. These instructions are also printed in Cunningham, *op. cit.* p. 915; Andrews, *op. cit.* p. 74. Early in

The first meeting of the Council for Plantations was held on December 10, 1660, and a month later, after the holidays, it organized for business, ordering its secretary, Philip Froude, to engage the necessary employees and appointing committees to investigate conditions in the various colonies and to write to them.[1] Letters, with general and detailed instructions for the separate colonies, were carefully prepared under the immediate supervision of Thomas Povey, to whom in especial, as "Clerk of the Council," this important work was entrusted.[2] Before being actually despatched, they had, however, to be submitted to the King for approval.[3] All the important colonial questions of the period came under the Council's consideration. Especial attention was devoted to the best means for furthering Jamaica's development, to the crisis in the Virginia and Maryland tobacco trade resulting from over-

1661, the Council for Foreign Plantations wrote to the government of Barbados, announcing its appointment and calling attention to the King's interest in the colonies as evidenced, not only by the creation of this Council for their inspection and management, but also "by the erecting a Generall Councell of Trade, wherein their Concernments in point of Manufactures, Navigation and Commerce are mingled and are otherwise provided for with the rest of his Maties Dominions." Brit. Mus., Egerton MSS. 2395, ff. 333 et seq. Cf. C. C. 1661–1668, no. 24. The colonial Council had been especially instructed to inform the colonies of the creation of this other body. C. C. 1574–1660, p. 492.

[1] The minutes of the Council are in C. O. 1/14, 59, ff. 1–57. They are somewhat incompletely abstracted in the pages of C. C. 1661–1668.

[2] C. O. 1/14, 59, f. 8; C. C. 1661–1668, no. 3. Povey's papers, in Brit. Mus., Egerton MSS. 2395, contain a mass of invaluable documents on the inception and activity of this body.

[3] Cf. Brit. Mus., Egerton MSS. 2395, ff. 333, 335; C. C. 1661–1668, nos. 24, 25.

production, and to the difficult problem arising from Puritan New England's independent spirit and disinclination to comply with the aims of English imperialism.[1] The charges of illegal trade between the tobacco colonies and the Dutch in New Netherland, in violation of the enumeration clauses in the Act of Navigation, likewise came before the Council, which recommended measures calculated to remedy this evil.[2] In addition, some minor details of administration were attended to, and some specific suggestions for fostering the economic development of the colonies were offered. The most far-reaching and pregnant political recommendation made by the Council was that Charles II should come to an agreement 'with all who have propriety in any of the Plantations, prevent same for the future, and take them all into his own hands.'[3]

The work of the Council was in the main done by its more or less expert members, such as Povey, Noell, Kendall, Drax, Digges, and Colleton. Their deliberations were as a rule presided over by one of their more conspicuously prominent associates, such as Lord Berkeley, Lord Ashley (better known as the Earl of Shaftesbury), or the Earl of Anglesey.[4] At the outset, in 1661, frequent meetings

[1] C. O. 1/15, 42, 47; Brit. Mus., Egerton MSS. 2395, f. 299.

[2] C. O. 1/14, 59, ff. 53–56.

[3] C. C. 1661–1668, no. 3.

[4] At the meeting of July 6, 1663, Lord Berkeley presided, and there were present Colleton, Noell, Kendall, and Digges. At the subsequent session, Dec. 7, 1663, Lord Ashley presided, and those attending were Lord Berkeley, Colleton, Noell, Digges, O'Neill, Crispe, Boyle, Waller, Shawe, and Jefferies. On Dec. 16, 1663, Ashley again presided, and those present were Lord Berkeley, Noell, Crispe, Boyle, Coventry, Povey, Middleton, and Howe.

were held and were well attended by the working members.[1] In the following years, the intervals between the sessions became longer and longer, and less activity was manifested. This was due primarily to the fact that the Council's work was predominantly advisory, and had to be passed upon by the King acting through the Privy Council and its committees.[2] Its chief function was to make preliminary examinations and to sift evidence, so that only matters of real importance would be brought before the Privy Council, where they could then be disposed of expeditiously.

This lack of responsibility and authority naturally lessened the interest of the members in their work, and tended to make its performance perfunctory. Then, as the years passed, some of the Council's important members, like Povey, were drawn into other lines of activity, which absorbed their time and energy. Finally, the acute stage which the economic quarrel with the Dutch reached in 1664, and the ensuing war which greatly increased the work

On Jan. 19, 1664, the Earl of Anglesey presided, and those attending were Lord Ashley, Colleton, Noell, Kendall, Digges, Crispe, Boyle, Waller, Povey, and Vernon. C. O. 1/14, 59, ff. 53–55.

[1] The great officers of state, whose membership was more or less of an *ex-officio* character, rarely attended the sessions. On one occasion, early in 1661, in connection with proposals for registering emigrants to the colonies, the Council requested such of its members as were Lords of the Privy Council to be present. C. C. 1661–1668, no. 32.

[2] May 20, 1661, Secretary Froude reported to the Council, that he had attended 'the Principal Secretary of State with the letter and report for New England, who gave answer that the letter for New England being a matter of State, the Lords of the Privy Council would take it into consideration, and to that purpose a committee of their Lordships was appointed for the management thereof.' *Ibid.* no. 91.

of all public officials, definitely put an end to the moribund Council's sessions. Its activities ceased virtually entirely towards the beginning of 1665.[1]

The course of the Council of Trade's active life ran parallel to that of the colonial body; for similar reasons it also expired toward the end of 1664. During its brief career, the Council investigated, and in a number of instances reported on, many important questions affecting English economic interests, such as the Swedish monopoly of pitch and tar, the East India trade, the erection of banks in England, the use of convoys to protect the merchant fleets, and the English sugar-refining industry.[2] Notwithstanding its instructions, apparently no purely colonial questions were handled, although some of the subjects just mentioned indirectly concerned the colonies. Like the colonial Council, this body did not fulfil the hopes anticipated from its appointment. According to Clarendon, the dominant political figure of these years, it "produced little other effect than the opportunity of men's speaking together, which possibly disposed them to think more, and to consult more effectually in private, than they could in such a crowd of commissioners.[3]"

These two Councils, during their four years of activity,

---

[1] The last recorded meeting in the minutes is that of Aug. 24, 1664, but there are indications of life as late as Feb. 24, 1665. C. O. 1/14, 59, f. 57; P. C. Cal. I, p. 384; C. C. 1661–1668, nos. 798, 833.

[2] Brit. Mus., Add. MSS. 25,115, ff. 3–103, 305 *et passim;* Cunningham, *op. cit.* appendix D, pp. 915–921; Cal. Treas. Books, 1660–1667, pp. 124, 245. George Duke was the secretary of this Council. *Ibid.* pp. 244, 513, 615.

[3] Clarendon's Autobiography (Oxford, 1827) II, p. 231.

had in the main acted in an advisory capacity to the Privy Council, which was also assisted in its final decisions by its own committees. When the Council for Plantations ceased to function, the colonial committee was obliged to undertake all the rough preliminary work of investigation and sifting. Its personnel, like that of the Privy Council, naturally changed with the vicissitudes of English political life, but, as in 1660, it continued to be composed of the chief ministers and leading statesmen of the day.[1] After the fall of Clarendon, in the late summer of 1667, the members of the "Cabal" took charge of affairs; and, early in 1668, the work of the Privy Council was reorganized and four standing committees were constituted — for foreign affairs, for military matters, for petitions and grievances, and for trade and plantations. This last committee consisted of Lord Robartes, the Duke of Buckingham, the Earls of Ossory, Bridgewater, and Lauderdale, Lords Arlington, Holles, and Ashley, Sir George Carteret, Sir Thomas Clifford, Sir William Morice and Sir William Coventry. They were ordered to meet every Thursday, or more often if necessary,

[1] In 1666, the Committee for Foreign Plantations was composed of the Lord Chancellor, Lord Treasurer, Lord Chamberlain, Lord Privy Seal, Earl of Anglesey, Lord Holles, Lord Ashley, Lord Arlington, the Vice-Chamberlain, and Secretary Morice. In 1667, Sir William Coventry and Sir John Duncombe were added; in 1668, the Earls of Bath and Carlisle. P. C. Register Charles II, VI, ff. 235, 554; VII, f. 111; P. C. Cal. I, pp. 421, 433, 434. In addition, the New England committee was also in existence. On Oct. 2, 1667, His Majesty in Council ordered that the Lords of the Council, "formerly appoynted a Committee for the Affayres of New England," should meet as often as necessary to make a "Re-view" of what had been done about those colonies. *Ibid.* p. 442.

and it was provided that nothing was to be decided by the Privy Council, until the matter had been first examined by some committee.[1] In addition, later in the year, this committee "calling vnto them his Majestys Attorney Generall or else his Majestys Advocate," was instructed to hear all causes that came by "way of appeale" from Jersey and Guernsey.[2] In this way originated the judicial committee, which in time came to be the ultimate court of appeal for the Empire.

The members of this general colonial committee were obliged to handle a number of detailed questions, such as those arising out of the territorial readjustments in America arranged in the Treaty of Breda of 1667.[3] At the same time, they were the leading politicians of the day in charge of domestic and foreign affairs, and could ill afford to spare the time demanded by such minor colonial questions. Hence again there arose a demand for an auxiliary council.[4] At this time, the chief promoters of this idea seem to have been

---

[1] Andrews, *op. cit.* pp. 88–90. In 1668, "to guarantee a more business-like administration, the Privy Council was reorganized in a number of committees, the most important being that for foreign affairs, an eminently practical system that had been disliked and long hindered by Clarendon." Cambridge Modern History V, p. 201.

[2] P. C. Cal. I, pp. 456, 457. In 1668 and 1669, some additions were made to this committee. *Ibid.* p. 457; P. C. Register Charles II, VIII, f. 317.

[3] C. C. 1661–1668, nos. 1712, 1769, 1770, 1824, 1883.

[4] Already on Sept. 23, 1667, the predecessor of this committee was instructed to take into its consideration the question of reviving the Council of Trade and uniting it with that for the colonies. The respective secretaries of these bodies were ordered to attend the committee with the council's commissions, instructions, *etc.* P. C. Register Charles II, VI, f. 594; P. C. Cal. I, pp. 434, 435.

Henry Bennet, Lord Arlington, and Lord Ashley, the future
Earl of Shaftesbury — the two "A"s in the "Cabal" min-
istry.   As Secretary of State, Arlington had been for some
time closely associated with colonial affairs; the bulk of
the correspondence from America was addressed to him,
and at some stage virtually every colonial question passed
through his hands or those of his efficient secretary, Joseph
Williamson.   Shaftesbury's connection with general colonial affairs was not quite so close.   As Chancellor of the
Exchequer, he was not officially concerned with their administration.   But he had been a prominently active member of the Council for Plantations of 1660, and was the
leading spirit in the colonization of Carolina.   Moreover,
he was a conspicuously strenuous exponent of the current
nationalism in economic policy.   Among his papers is
preserved an anonymous memorial, entitled "Some Considerations about the Comission for Trade," [1] whose
views agree perfectly with those expressed by Shaftesbury
on other occasions.   Therein it was contended that "that
which makes ye Consideration of Trade of farre greater
import now then ever is That ye Interest of Commerce
though formerly neglected is of late yeares Become an
Express Affayre of State as well with the French as w^{th}
ye Hollander and Swede.   And y^t Because it is understood
by latter experience to be more Conducing toward an uni-
versall Monarchy (eyther for ye gayning or preventing of
it) then eyther an Army or Territory though never so great,
of wch Instances out of severall Kingdomes might easily

---

[1] Shaftesbury Papers, Section X, no. 8, first paper.

be Produced, In regard It is Trade & Comerce alone that draweth store of wealth along with it and y^t Potency at sea By shypping wch is not otherwise to be had." Trade being thus well understood by our neighbors, the memorial continued, we must either lead in "this great & generall Affayre of State," or must be humbled under the power of them that are able to govern it. From these premises it naturally followed that the government should earnestly devote its best energies to the development of national trade.

In accordance with these views, there was appointed in October of 1668 a new Council of Trade, with instructions to take under its consideration colonial affairs, as well as England's foreign and domestic trades.[1] It included in its membership Lord Arlington, Lord Ashley, Lord Berkeley, Sir Thomas Clifford, Sir George Downing, Benjamin Worsley, and a number of London merchants.[2] This body exercised considerable influence on colonial administration. Among other matters,[3] it prepared a report in consequence whereof the privilege, which had been temporarily granted to Dutch ships to trade to New York, was rescinded.[4] It investigated the entire question of the execution of the laws of trade and navigation in the colonies, and upon its recommendations was based the order of January 20, 1669, providing measures for their better enforcement.[5]

[1] N. Y. Col. Doc. III, pp. 175, 176; F. R. Harris, Earl of Sandwich II, pp. 305, 306.

[2] C. C. 1661–1668, no. 1884.

[3] P. C. Cal. I, pp. 499, 517.

[4] *Ibid*. pp. 491, 492; N. Y. Col. Doc. III, pp. 176–178.

[5] C. C. 1661–1668, no. 1884; *ibid*. 1669–1674, p. 3; P. C. Cal. I, pp. 499–501.

In 1670, the special colonial Council was also revived. In July of that year a commission[1] was issued to the Earl of Sandwich, Lord Gorges, Lord Allington, Thomas Grey, Henry Brouncker, Sir Humphrey Winch, Sir John Finch, Edmund Waller, Henry Slingesby, and Silas Titus, constituting them a "Speciall and Select Counsill" to take charge of the colonies, to inform themselves of their present state — their trade, system of defence and government — and to report to the King, so that such orders should be given as might best conduce to the "Safety and Flourishing of those our Dominions." Of this body, Sandwich was appointed president and Henry Slingesby secretary. In addition to its ten official members, the Chancellor of the Exchequer, Ashley, the Lord Treasurer or Commissioners of the Treasury, and the Secretaries of State had not only access to its sessions, but also the right of speaking and voting. Two important facts differentiate this Council from its predecessor of 1660. Its size was much smaller, which was more in accord with Thomas Povey's original proposals, and the official members received salaries which gave somewhat greater authority to its work.[2]

[1] Shaftesbury Papers, Section X, no. 10, ff. 1–6; Bodleian, Rawlinson MSS., A 255, f. 140; N. Y. Col. Doc. III, pp. 190–193.

[2] The president received £700 yearly and the others £500. Shaftesbury Papers, Section X, no. 10, ff. 20–24. In addition, £1000 yearly was granted for incidental expenses, and £300 yearly was also allowed to Dr. Benjamin Worsley, who was a member of the Council for Trade, in consideration of past and future assistance from him in colonial affairs. Thus the total annual cost of the Council was £6500. Cal. Treas. Books, 1669–1672, pp. 769, 772, 847, 1177, 1360; C. C. 1669–1674, p. 135; W. R. Scott, Joint-Stock Companies III, p. 531.

Annexed to the commission were carefully prepared instructions,[1] based upon those issued to the Council of 1660, but modified naturally by the experience of the intervening decade. In general, the Council was to apply itself "by all prudentiall wayes and Meanes so to Order, Governe, and Regulate the Trade of our whole plantations, that they may be most serviceable one unto another, and as the whole unto these our kingdomes so these our kingdomes unto them." With this object in view, they were to make a study of the economic and industrial conditions in the colonies and to suggest improvements. Naturally they were specifically instructed to see that the laws of trade were obeyed.[2]

One special line of investigation was enjoined upon the Council, which admirably illustrates the stress placed upon colonies as sources of supply that should free England from dependence on her rivals in the race for commercial supremacy. At the outset of the movement of colonization, it had been confidently anticipated that New England would take the place of the Baltic countries as a source of naval stores. These expectations had, however, come to nought,[3] but the idea was now revived. The commissioners were

[1] Shaftesbury Papers, Section X, no. 10, ff. 9–15; Bodleian, Rawlinson MSS., A 255, f. 145; C. O. 389/4, 5.

[2] This board of commissioners did not wholly supersede the colonial work of the Council of Trade. They were instructed to write to the colonial governors of the King's signal care towards the colonies "and of our erecting not only a generall Councill for Trade, that might take cognizance of such things as may be their concerne But of our appointing this Councell in particular which is employed only for the better care and conduct of them."

[3] Beer, Origins, pp. 56, 65, 75, 76, 279, 280.

ordered to consider especially if masts, ship-timber, flax, hemp, pitch, and tar could not be obtained from America, and "also where Mills might be most conveniently placed and encreased for the sawing of Timber, and planke, and how best we may ease the charge and promote the building there of great Shipping."[1] This view of the economic value of colonies was also illustrated in the additional instructions issued to the Council in August of 1670.[2] Herein the commissioners were ordered to recommend to the colonies the production of saltpetre, so that England should not be obliged to import it from the East Indies, and further, as it seemed probable that the colonies could produce more drugs, gums, and dyeing materials than they did, and even spices and other products of the East Indies, Turkey, and the Spanish and Portuguese colonies, they were also to investigate this subject, and to encourage the colonial planters in such undertakings.

It was the purpose of the government to make this a very influential body. With the object of adding greater weight to it, in 1671, a number of the most prominent noble-

---

[1] "And in regard whatsoever Conduceth to the Increase of Shipping must equally Conduce to ye safety and Strength of these Nations, and that not only Masts, butt all other Materialls, as well for ye building as fitting out of ships of great Burthen may, as wee are informed, be plentifully furnished from some of our Plantations, if care here unto were more especially used. You are therefore more particularly to advise about this matter with the severall Governours and Colonies of New England, and to propound to them or receive their Opinion what Methods and Course might bee most fitt for ye produceing Flax, Hemp, Pitch, and Tarre, in those Countryes in most plenty."

[2] Shaftesbury Papers, Section X, no. 10, ff. 17–19; Bodleian, Rawlinson MSS., A 255, f. 150.

men and statesmen — the Duke of York, Prince Rupert, the Duke of Buckingham, the Duke of Ormonde, the Earl of Lauderdale, Lord Culpeper, and Sir George Carteret — were appointed non-official members.[1] At the same time, the diarist Evelyn was made a salaried official commissioner, "a considerable honour," so runs his account of the incident, "the others in the Council being chiefly noblemen and officers of state." [2] Some indication of the Council's status is also given by the fact, noted by Evelyn, that proper arrangements were made "that his Majesty might come and sit amongst us, and hear our debates." [3]

In the following year, it was decided to transfer the Council of Trade's work to this far more active commission in charge of purely colonial affairs. In all probability this step was primarily due to the appreciation of the fact that these two subjects were closely related and could be advantageously handled together, as was already done by the Privy Council's committee. Accordingly, in September of 1672, a commission to this effect was issued, creating a Council for Trade and Plantations.[4]

---

[1] Shaftesbury Papers, Section X, no. 10, ff. 25–27; N. Y. Col. Doc. III, pp. 190–193; C. C. 1669–1674, p. 178.

[2] Evelyn, Feb. 28, 29, and March 10, 1671.

[3] *Ibid.* June 26, 1671. Evelyn states that, on May 26, 1671, the oaths were administered to him and to Buckingham, Lauderdale, Culpeper, and Carteret by the Earl of Sandwich, as president, and that "it was to advise and counsel his Majesty, to the best of our abilities, for the well-governing of his Foreign Plantations, &c., the form very little differing from that given to the Privy Council."

[4] Shaftesbury Papers, Section X, nos. 8 and 10. Under Sept. 1, 1672, Evelyn writes: "Now, our Council met at Lord Shaftesbury's (Chancellor

Some important changes in its membership were made. That "incomparable person," as Evelyn devotedly calls him, the Earl of Sandwich, one of the old Cromwellian guard, who had been recently killed in a naval engagement with the Dutch,[1] was succeeded in the presidency by Ashley, now Earl of Shaftesbury. Lord Culpeper was made vice-president, and as secretary was appointed Dr. Benjamin Worsley, who had been prominent in the Council of Trade, and, as an expert on the economic possibilities of the colonies, had in 1670 been attached to the Council of Plantations as "assistant" with a salary of £300.[2] Among the clerks was Shaftesbury's friend and adviser, the philosopher John Locke, who in 1673 succeeded Worsley as secretary.[3] The salaried official members included Evelyn, Slingesby, and Brouncker; and, in addition, the most important members of the Privy Council, such as the Lord Chancellor, the Lord Treasurer, the Secretaries of State,

of the Exchequer) to read and reform the draught of our new Patent, joining the Council of Trade to our political capacities." See also Evelyn, Oct. 13, 1672, and C. C. 1669–1674, p. 407.

[1] Evelyn, May 31, 1672.

[2] Cal. Treas. Books, 1669–1672, p. 769; *ibid.* 1672–1675, p. 173; C. C. 1661–1668, nos. 1299, 1822; *ibid.* 1669–1674, p. 135; Evelyn, May 31, 1672.

[3] Evelyn, Oct. 24, 1672, Sept. 16, 1673, Oct. 15, 1673. Under the last date, he notes: "To Council, and swore in Mr. Locke, secretary." Worsley's salary of £500 as secretary ceased on June 24, 1673, and Locke's began on that day. In addition, the president received yearly £800, the vice-president £600, each of the salaried members £500, and about £1000 was allowed for contingent expenses. Cal. Treas. Books, 1672–1675, pp. 14, 126, 172, 173, 419, 426, 460, 476, 579, 602, 710. Locke's accounts as secretary and treasurer are in the Public Record Office Declared Accounts, Pipe Office, Roll 2967.

were authorized to attend the Council's sessions and to join in its proceedings by voice and vote.[1]

The Council for Plantations and its enlarged successor had together a joint life of somewhat over four years, during which short period they greatly improved the entire system of imperial control. They held formal meetings on an average of at least twice a week,[2] and in addition considerable work was done by its members on committees or as individuals. On one occasion, when complaints of "many indiscreet managements" were brought against Sir Charles Wheler, the Governor of the Leeward Islands, Evelyn wrote that "this business staid me in London almost a week, being in Council, or Committee, every morning."[3] The Council examined carefully the mass of petitions, complaints, and memorials emanating from colonial sources, and also demanded detailed information from the colonial authorities on local conditions to aid it in its work. Former officials, colonial planters, and others conversant with conditions in the colonies were freely called upon for information. Upon the exceptionally full knowledge of the facts thus acquired were based its reports to the Privy Council. In addition, the Council prepared the preliminary drafts of the com-

[1] The instructions were virtually the same as those issued to the two separate Councils, which it superseded. Shaftesbury Papers, Section X, no. 9.

[2] Professor Andrews has carefully compiled a list of these meetings from various sources, but mainly from the colonial calendar and from Evelyn's Diary. Andrews, *op. cit.* pp. 101 *et seq.* In addition to the state papers abstracted in the calendar, there is available for a study of this Council an entry book of letters written by it, containing also reports and other important documents. This is C. O. 389/10.

[3] Evelyn, Nov. 14, 1671.

missions and instructions to the various colonial governors, which were then submitted to the Privy Council for approval.[1] Furthermore, this board carefully scrutinized the legislation in the different colonies to see if it were not detrimental to English or imperial interests.[2]

In addition to systematizing this routine work of colonial administration, the Council investigated and reported on every special colonial question of these years. Among other matters, considerable attention was devoted to the awkward situation created by New England's recalcitrant attitude; this was handled with the necessary delicacy and tact.[3] They also formulated the rule that during the Dutch war ships homeward bound from the colonies should sail only in fleets or under convoy.[4] Spain's protest against the Jamaica logwood trade in Campeachy likewise came before the Council,[5] and also the question of making a separate government of the Leeward Islands, hitherto annexed to Barbados.[6]

Despite this Council's zealous and conscientious activity, and its marked efficiency when contrasted with any similar preceding board or committee, it did not wholly escape

[1] C. C. 1669–1674, pp. 300, 301, 539, 540, 545, 567–571, 575, 619, 625, 626.

[2] Ibid. pp. 360, 361. Evelyn "was of the Committee with Sir Humphrey Winch, the chairman, to examine the laws of his Majesty's several plantations and colonies in the West Indies, &c." Evelyn, Nov. 8, 1672.

[3] Ibid. May 26, June 6, July 4, Aug. 3, 1671, and Feb. 12, 1672.

[4] Ibid. Feb. 12, 1672.

[5] Ibid. April 19, 16; 2.

[6] Ibid. March 1, 1672.

criticism. Like the later Board of Trade,[1] it was charged with neglecting to communicate sufficiently with the colonial governors. At this time, the Lieutenant-Governor of Jamaica, Sir Thomas Lynch, was an exceptionally efficient public official, and like some of his successors in similar posts elsewhere, such as the Earl of Bellomont and William Shirley, he was a most frequent and indefatigably voluminous correspondent. Apart from occasional letters addressed to the Lord Keeper, the Master of the Ordnance, the Lords of the Treasury, Sir John Trevor, one of the Secretaries of State,[2] Lynch wrote regularly to Arlington and his secretary, Williamson, as well as to the Council for Plantations and its secretary Slingesby.[3] Lynch was especially anxious to receive from the government explicit instructions about the Jamaica logwood trade to Campeachy. But as this question threatened to involve England in war with Spain, the subject had to be carefully considered, and there was naturally considerable delay in answering Lynch's frequent and urgent appeals. On January 27, 1672, Lynch wrote to Williamson : "I would beg you once more for God's sake to move my Lord (Arlington) in this (the logwood trade question) and what else may be of moment, and be pleased more frequently to give me his Lordship's orders when he is not pleased to write them himself, or let me know whether I must not apply myself to, or follow the

---

[1] *Cf.* O. M. Dickerson, American Colonial Government, 1696–1765, pp. 66–69.

[2] C. C. 1669–1674, p. 387.

[3] See *ibid.* in the index a list of Lynch's letters.

orders of my Lord President Sandwich, or Mr. Secretary Slingesby."[1] Six months later, Lynch wrote to the Council, complaining that his many letters had not been acknowledged and adding that 'one of his great discouragements is that he must act according to the reason of things here, which at court may be understood according as one has success or friends there.'[2] At the same time, he wrote to Williamson that the Council had 'at least 100 sheets of paper of his before them, but not even from the meanest of their clerks has he had a syllable; at which he wonders.'[3] When finally, in October, the government had completed its examination of the logwood trade question, the Council's secretary sent the desired instructions to Jamaica, stating at the same time that he had been directed to acquaint Lynch that, 'through the war, but chiefly by reason of the unhappy death of the late President, the Earl of Sandwich, their Lordships have not written so frequently as he might possibly expect, yet . . . such care will be taken in future for supplying him with advice as that he shall not need to fear any discouragement for want of it.'[4]

[1] C. C. 1669–1674, pp. 322, 323. Lynch also wrote to Sir Charles Lyttelton, who ten years before had been the executive head of Jamaica, to use his influence in this matter. *Ibid.* p. 324.

[2] *Ibid.* pp. 385, 386.

[3] *Ibid.* p. 387. On Nov. 5, 1672, Lynch wrote to Secretary Slingesby that his letter of July 23 had arrived, and that this was the first one he had received since his assumption of the government the preceding year. He added, that he hoped that, in the future, Slingesby would have leisure more frequently to give the Council's commands. *Ibid.* pp. 425–428.

[4] *Ibid.* p. 417.

In view of the gravity of the case, this delay in the government's decision was inevitable,[1] and although Lynch's impatience is comprehensible, the Council cannot be charged with neglecting the colonies. This episode, however, emphasizes one defect that was inherent in the council system. Lynch was at loss where to turn for instructions, whether to the Council for Plantations or to the Secretary of State, Lord Arlington, who carried into effect the decisions of the King and Privy Council. The Council for Plantations' authority and effectiveness were necessarily impaired by the fact that it was a purely advisory body without executive authority. Among the papers preserved by Thomas Povey is an anonymous memorial written at the time, which plainly laid bare this defect and suggested a remedy.[2] This clear-sighted critic pointed out that "whatsoever Council is not enabled as well to execute as advise must needs produce very imperfect and weake effects. It being by its subordition and impotency obliged to have a continual recourse to Superiour Ministers, and Councils filled with other busnes, wch oftentimes giues great and prejudicial delays, and usualy begets new or slower deliberations, and results, then ye matter in hand may stand in need of." Hence, he concluded, such a council necessarily becomes weak and ineffective.

[1] The main delay was caused by Sir William Godolphin, the English Ambassador in Spain. Arlington wrote to him about this matter in October of 1671, but his reply was received only eight months later. Arlington's Letters (London, 1701) II, pp. 336, 373.

[2] Brit. Mus., Egerton MSS. 2395, f. 276.

In all probability, this was the underlying cause that led to the revocation of the Council's commission on December 21, 1674.[1] But, in addition, there were certain more specific and personal reasons, connected with the changed political situation in England. In 1673, Shaftesbury was dismissed from office, and shortly thereafter Arlington also resigned his post of Secretary of State; the two chief patrons of the Council could thus no longer protect it. The rising power in the political world was Sir Thomas Osborne, who in 1673 secured Clifford's place of Lord Treasurer, and in 1674, as Earl of Danby, became Charles's chief minister. Evelyn relates that, when Danby succeeded Clifford, the Council for Trade and Plantations "went in a body to congratulate the new Lord Treasurer, no friend to it, because promoted by my Lord Arlington, whom he hated."[2] Danby's hostility to the Council was probably due also to less personal motives. It was an expensive body, costing about £7000 yearly, and the Exchequer was chronically depleted. Though open to criticism on other counts, Danby fully realized the necessity for strict economy; he "was the first man of his time to apply himself systematically to the problems of finance that underlie all administration." [3]

Whatever may have been the exact reasons for the dissolution of the Council, in consequence thereof 'all matters under their cognizance were left loose and at large.' The

[1] N. Y. Col. Doc. III, pp. 229, 230; C. O. 391/1 (preceding f. 1).
[2] Evelyn, June 23, 1673.
[3] Pollock, in Cambridge Modern History V, pp. 214, 215.

Privy Council's Committee for Trade and Plantations, upon whom devolved all this work,[1] could not cope with it, unless it were completely reorganized. The anonymous critic[2] of the council system, quoted above, had suggested that, since English practice did not admit of plenary authority being vested in any but the highest Council, "it remains only as ye best expedient, That Com^{rs} be appointed out of ye Privy Council, under ye Great Seal," who should hold regular meetings every week to consider colonial affairs and should be empowered to act and order with as ample an authority as the Commissioners of the Admiralty did. Furthermore, it was urged that these Commissioners should have a permanent secretary who should devote all his time to colonial matters. He should correspond with the governors and other colonial officials, should collect and preserve all documents relating to these affairs, and in general should keep himself informed of everything that concerned both the English and the foreign colonies.[3] A device very similar to this was adopted by the government.

[1] The petition of Mason and Gorges against Massachusetts was referred to this committee on Jan. 13, 1675, with orders for it to meet the following day. Similar action was taken with the Newfoundland question on Feb. 12, 1675. P. C. Cal. I, pp. 616, 617, 619. The Journal of the Lords of Trade begins with a session on Feb. 9, 1675, and further meetings were held on Feb. 11, 12, 23, 25, and 27. C. O. 391/1, ff. 1–6.

[2] Brit. Mus., Egerton MSS. 2395, f. 276.

[3] "The want of such a necessary and settled Officer, among many other inconveniencys, having bin ye occasion that scarce any Record, Testimonial, Letters or papers of Consequence haue bin to be found in any place, wch may informe and assist his Ma^{ts} Councels, And may shew and justify ye original Right and progres of the Settlements of many of our most considerable Colonies, and of those under other States."

On March 12, 1675,[1] Charles II formally committed those matters, that had been under the "Inspection and Management" of the dissolved Council, to the Privy Council's Committee for Trade and Foreign Plantations, and designated as members of it over a score of the state officials and great noblemen, of whom nine, especially named, were entrusted with "the immediate Care and Intendency of those Affaires in regard they had been formerly conversant and acquainted therewith."[2] This Committee was instructed to meet at least once a week,[3] and Sir Robert Southwell, one of the Clerks of the Privy Council, was ordered constantly to attend it.[4]

This Committee, generally known as the Lords of Trade, differs in important respects from its predecessors. It was a permanent standing body with its own clerks, who systematized its business and its archives. A formal journal of the proceedings was carefully kept, and a satisfactory system was devised for classifying and filing the growing mass of colonial documents. This work was instituted by Sir

---

[1] C. O. 389/11, f. 1; *ibid.* 324/4, f. 7; *ibid.* 391/1, ff. 8, 9; P. C. Register Charles II, XI, f. 395; P. C. Cal. I, p. 619; No. Ca. Col. Rec. I, p. 222; C. C. 1675–1676, p. 182.

[2] These nine were the Lord Privy Seal, the Earls of Bridgewater, Carlisle, and Craven, Viscounts Fauconberg and Halifax, Lord Berkeley, the Vice-Chamberlain, and the Chancellor of the Exchequer. In June of 1675, the Earl of St. Albans was added to the committee. P. C. Register Charles II, XI, f. 450.

[3] Originally five members were to constitute a quorum, but in May of 1675 this number was reduced to three. P. C. Cal. I, p. 620.

[4] The Committee decided to meet regularly on Thursdays in the forenoon, and oftener as occasion should require. C. O. 391/1, f. 8.

Robert Southwell,[1] one of the Clerks of the Privy Council, a position of far greater dignity than the name seemingly indicates. He was efficiently assisted in this work by William Blathwayt, who had entered this service on September 29, 1675.[2] In May of 1676, as Southwell, on the score of ill health, had asked to be relieved from constant attendance on the Committee, it was ordered that such of the Clerks of the Privy Council as so might desire — there were four in all [3] — should in rotation assume these duties for six months at a time; and that Blathwayt, whose ability had quickly gained recognition, should be continued as "an Assistant" to these Clerks with a salary of £150 a year.[4] It was in this humble capacity that Blathwayt began his long and intimate official connection with the colonies. After some years of assiduous attention to this work, his unquestionably great business ability and his unrivalled

[1] When in 1676 Southwell asked to be relieved from this work, the Lords of Trade were ordered to decide upon a suitable reward for his services "in putting the many Papers depending before their Lordships into very good method, which were in some disorder when delivered up by the late Councill of Plantations." P. C. Cal. I, p. 658.

[2] Cal. Treas. Books, 1676–1679, p. 249.

[3] In 1679, they were Sir John Nicholas, Sir Robert Southwell, Sir Phillip Lloyd, and Sir Thomas Doleman. Ibid. p. 1231.

[4] P. C. Cal. I, pp. 658, 664, 665. In 1677, on the strength of a report from the Committee that his "Diligence is very great," Blathwayt's salary was raised to £250. Ibid. p. 743. The Clerks of the Privy Council were paid for this work at the rate of £400 yearly. In addition, two clerks were employed, and there were various incidental expenses, among which may be mentioned the cost of books, maps, and treaties purchased for the Committee's use. The total disbursements were about £1300 yearly, while the superseded Council had cost £7000. Cal. Treas. Books, 1676–1679, pp. 249, 282, 299, 642, 740, 802, 898, 969, 1075.

knowledge of these matters brought him the position of Secretary to the Lords of Trade and made him the most influential person in the colonial administrative system.

For somewhat over twenty years the Lords of Trade governed the colonies. The Committee's personnel changed with the passing years,[1] but its active members were always the chief state officials.[2] Hence its decisions were virtually invariably accepted. As a result, colonial affairs were administered with a directness and lack of delay hitherto unknown, and not again encountered until a hundred years later, when a special Secretary of State for the Colonies was created. The Lords of Trade corresponded with the colonial governors and prepared their instructions; they demanded and received detailed reports from the colonies and carefully watched the course of their development — economic, fiscal, and political. Every colonial question came before them, and the policy adopted was in nearly every instance an expression of their views.

These various boards and committees, together with the Privy Council and the Secretary of State entrusted with

[1] For the membership in 1679, see P. C. Cal. I, pp. 819, 820; C. C. 1677–1680, p. 355. In 1686, this Committee consisted of 40 members, and in 1688 James II ordered all the Lords of the Privy Council to be a standing Committee for Trade and Plantations. *Ibid.* 1685–1688, pp. 219, 489; C. O. 391/6, ff. 123–125.

[2] For instance, the meeting of May 3, 1677, was attended by the Lord Treasurer, the Lord Privy Seal, the Duke of Albemarle, the Earls of Craven, Bath, and Bridgewater, the Lord Chamberlain, the Speaker, and by the Secretaries of State, Williamson and Coventry. On Nov. 8, 1677, were present the Lord Privy Seal, the Earl of Craven, Secretary Williamson, and the Chancellor of the Exchequer. *Ibid.* 391/2, ff. 31, 145.

colonial affairs, were the principal organs of the central administrative system, by means of which the colonies were governed.   One of their main duties, if not the chief one, was to see that the laws of trade and navigation were effectively executed, for these laws embodied the essence of English colonial policy.[1]   In addition, two other administrative departments participated actively in this specific work, the Admiralty and the Treasury.[2]   Both of these

[1] The government used all its resources to this end, even the diplomatic service.   England's representatives, especially those in Holland, were continually on the lookout for illegal trade between the colonies and the countries to which they were accredited, and the Dutch government was even asked to assist in its suppression.   In 1662, Sir George Downing advised the government that several ships had arrived in Holland directly from Barbados.   P. C. Register Charles II, III, f. 101 ; P. C. Cal. I, pp. 334, 335.   In 1668, Sir William Temple, the English Ambassador at the Hague, was instructed as follows : "You must make it your business to be inform'd very particularly of Three Merchant Ships, fitting now at *Amsterdam*, for the *Barbadoes*, with several manufactures for their lading ; and if you have an opportunity then, to advertise the Governour thereof, that he may seize them, because it is a great breach of the Act of Navigation, and yet so acceptable to the People, upon that Island, that it may contribute much to the debauching of them, at least from their dependance upon England." This inquiry was to be made as fully and as privately as was possible. Arlington's Letters (London, 1701) I, pp. 360, 361.   In 1685, the English Envoy, Bevil Skelton, presented to the States-General a memorial, to the effect that many English vessels came directly from the English colonies to the Netherlands and requesting them to pass an act, whereby their Admiralty would be enjoined to assist the English consuls in preventing this.   B. T. Commercial Series I, 6, A 31.   In this year, the Lord High Treasurer, Rochester, authorized the Commissioners of the Customs to pay Mr. Nodges's bill for expenses in viewing several ships from the English colonies in the River Maas and at Rotterdam.   Treas. Books, Out-Letters, Customs 10, f. 27.

[2] A description of the administrative side of the system of imperial defence is not germane to the purpose of this work.

departments and their subordinate boards, respectively the Navy and the Customs, were prominently concerned in carrying into effect the laws of trade and navigation.

The English admiralty jurisdiction had already at an early date been extended to America, but until the Commonwealth no extensive use had been made thereof. It was then not only employed to condemn vessels seized as prizes in the Dutch and Spanish wars, but also foreign ships caught trading to the West Indian colonies in violation of the Navigation Acts of 1650 and 1651.[1] After the Restoration, James, Duke of York, was appointed Lord High Admiral of England, and, by a supplementary commission issued in 1662, he was granted the same extensive powers over the colonies.[2] Not only was the Admiralty entitled to specific dues, such as those arising from condemned prizes, but in addition vessels seized for violating certain clauses of the commercial code were triable in the admiralty courts. In order to carry these powers into effect, the Lord High Admiral appointed deputies in the crown colonies, and admiralty courts were erected in them. Furthermore, towards the end of the period, the ships of the navy were especially instructed to seize all illegal traders and some were stationed in the colonies for this specific purpose.

The English Treasury's jurisdiction over the colonies was more extensive and intimate. In addition to its interest in securing the Crown's share of condemnations in the colonies for violation of the Acts of Trade, the Treasury was

[1] Beer, Origins, pp. 334–337, 391.
[2] C. C. 1661–1668, no. 245.

directly concerned in the strict enforcement of these laws, in so far as their provisions tended to increase the English customs revenue. Moreover, the enforcement of the enumeration clauses was to a large extent under the direct control of the English customs officials. They issued the bonds to vessels sailing from England, and it was in such ships that most of the enumerated goods were exported from the colonies.[1] These English officials were responsible that no ship departed from England without having given such bonds, and, in case any eluded their vigilance, they ordered their seizure upon arrival in the colonies.[2] In such instances, the coöperation of the authorities in the colonies was required, but where the bond had been actually given in England, its enforcement depended solely upon the home government. Besides, by the Act of Navigation of 1660, the colonial governors were required to send twice a year copies of the bonds taken by them to the Custom-House in London.[3] Naturally

[1] Naturally such bonds would be issued only to ships qualified to trade to the colonies, and hence these officials also kept unfree ships out of this trade.

[2] In 1672, the Lords of the Treasury wrote to the Governors of Barbados, Virginia, and Jamaica that they had reason to believe that six ships, specifically designated, had sailed for the American colonies without having given bonds, and ordered them to seize any or all of these ships upon arrival. Cal. Treas. Books, 1669–1672, p. 1232.

[3] 12 Ch. II, c. 18, § xix. On Sept. 6, 1663, Governor Charles Calvert wrote to Lord Baltimore that he had received two letters from the London Custom-House about the Act of Navigation, which he would answer by these ships and that he would "send Copys of This yeares bonds to yᵗ Lopp & not to them." Calvert Papers I, p. 245. This custom was kept up by Calvert, and the papers were delivered by Lord Baltimore to

the enforcement of such bonds, which, however, covered only a small portion of the total quantity of enumerated goods exported, devolved mainly upon the colonial authorities. Even though the copies of these bonds were not regularly sent to London, the English government had other sources of information,[1] and, while not argus-eyed, kept a close watch on the course of colonial trade. Wherever fraud was suspected, the colonial governors were instructed by the Treasury to prosecute the offenders.[2]

Thus the enforcement of the policy of enumeration was from the outset largely in the hands of the Treasury and its subordinate officials. Their duties were greatly expanded when, in 1673, Parliament imposed the plantation duties and entrusted their management to the Commissioners of the Customs. This board's work in enforcing that law and the enumeration clauses quickly spread to the other provisions of the system, until ultimately the whole commercial code

the Treasury and by them to the Customs. *Ibid.* pp. 263, 264, 279, 295; Cal. Treas. Books, 1669–1672, p. 1101.

[1] By Order in Council of Aug. 15, 1662, the Lord High Treasurer and the customs officials were ordered to take care that the enumeration clauses were observed, as Sir George Downing had sent advice "that divers English Shipps laden in Barbadoes are lately arrived in Holland without touching in England." P. C. Register Charles II, III, f. 101; P. C. Cal. I, pp. 334, 335.

[2] On Jan. 14, 1673, Treasurer Clifford wrote to the Governors of Massachusetts, Virginia, Antigua, Montserrat, and Nevis, mentioning specific ships — nine in all — that had laden within their respective jurisdictions enumerated goods, which were then exported directly to Ireland. He stated, that he assumed that bonds had been taken from these vessels, and ordered the Governors to prosecute them. Cal. Treas. Books, 1672–1675, p. 35.

was under its direct supervision. In 1686, the Commissioners of the Customs stated that the entire body of these laws was under their care and control and that it was their business to maintain a uniform and efficient system.[1] At this time, the board was looked upon as the special guardian of the system's integrity. The detailed instructions issued for the guidance of the local officials were prepared by them,[2] and at times orders were even sent by them or by the Treasury directly to the colonial governors.[3] On all questions requiring detailed fiscal or economic knowledge, the government sought the advice of these Commissioners. They sedulously watched the working of the system and recommended measures calculated to secure its greater efficiency. Thus, in 1683, they advised that the Irish customs officials be instructed to send returns of the ships clearing for the colonies in that kingdom and entering from them.[4] Shortly thereafter, they proposed that England's representatives in France, Spain, the Netherlands, Denmark, Sweden, and the Hanse towns be instructed to use all diligence to discover ships arriving there directly from the colonies with the enumerated products.[5] In 1685,

---

[1] C. O. 324/4, ff. 213–218; C. C. 1685–1688, pp. 187, 188.

[2] C. O. 324/4, ff. 151–166; ibid. 5/904, ff. 329–332; ibid. 1/58, 73, 73 i; C. C. 1685–1688, pp. 77, 258, 270.

[3] In 1684, the Privy Council ordered that a letter be written and sent by the Commissioners of the Customs to the colonial governors, requiring them to examine into the performance of the conditions of the enumerated bonds given there and to prosecute in all cases of non-fulfilment. P. C. Cal. I, p. 71.

[4] C. C. 1681–1685, pp. 477, 478.

[5] Ibid. p. 563.

they recommended that the ships of the navy be again instructed to seize all foreign vessels trading to the colonies.[1] These are but a few instances of this board's multifarious activities in colonial administration.

Each of these three departments of the central administrative system — the Privy Council with its committees and the boards of trade and plantations more or less directly responsible to it, the Admiralty, and the Treasury — had its own distinct representatives in the royal provinces. In these colonies, the chief local agent charged with the execution of the laws of trade was the governor, who was appointed by the Crown and was immediately accountable to it and to the Privy Council. His duties in this regard were statutory. By the Acts themselves the governor was obliged to take an oath to obey the law, and any neglect thereof made him liable to dismissal and to the payment of a heavy fine of £1000. In addition, he was also charged with the clerical duties involved in carrying them into effect.[2] The Acts made no distinction between the royal provinces and the proprietary and charter colonies, and hence these duties were by law also imposed upon the governors of the latter colonies. But the executive heads of these jurisdictions were in no sense of the word agents of the central administrative system. They were not responsible to, nor could they be controlled by, any department of the English government, but were appointed by the proprietors or chosen by the people

[1] C. O. 324/4, ff. 142, 143; C. C. 1685–1688, pp. 26, 27.

[2] 12 Ch. II, c. 18, §§ ii, xix; 15 Ch. II, c. 7, § viii; 22 & 23 Ch. II, c. 26, § xii.

of these semi-independent jurisdictions. Notwithstanding this fact, since the Acts so provided, the English government naturally instructed both the royal governors[1] and the authorities in the other colonies carefully to enforce the law. In 1663,[2] letters were written to the royal governors and also to the authorities in Maryland and New England, reciting the provisions of the Navigation Act and their serious obligations under them, and stating that information had been received that the law was violated, "through the dayly practises and designes sett on foote, by trading into forrain parts from Virginia Mariland, and other his Majesties Plantations, both by Land and Sea as well unto the Monados, and other Plantations of the Hollanders, as unto Spaine, Venice, and Holland." This state of affairs was attributed to the neglect of the governors, both in not seeing that the vessels arriving had certificates that they were qualified to trade in the colonies, and also in not taking bonds before the ships with enumerated commodities on board were allowed to depart. The governors were accordingly instructed to repair their neglect, and to send copies of these bonds twice a year to the Custom-House in London, together with accounts of all vessels taking in cargoes in the colonies.

As no method was devised for obliging the proprietary ✝ and charter governors to take the statutory oaths to obey

[1] For the instructions to Barbados and Virginia in 1661 to 1663, see Brit. Mus., Egerton MSS. 2395, ff. 333 *et seq.;* P. C. Cal. I, p. 359; Va. Mag. III, pp. 15–20; C. C. 1661–1668, nos. 24, 368.

[2] P. C. Register Charles II, III, ff. 450, 451; P. C. Cal. I, pp. 365–367; N. Y. Col. Doc. III, pp. 44–46.

the laws of trade, it depended mainly upon their own voli-
tion; and, in general, but the scantest attention was paid
by these colonies to this section of the law. Moreover,
for some time no regular system was adopted for securing
these oaths from the royal governors. In 1668, the Council
of Trade reported that several of the governors had been
remiss in this respect,[1] and four years later, the House of
Commons requested the King to see that these oaths were
taken.[2] During the following few years, the attention of
the English government was forcibly directed to this subject
by Massachusetts' recalcitrant attitude, which threatened
to disrupt the entire colonial system. In 1675, the Commissioners of the Customs reported in detail on illegal
trade in the colonies, and urged the necessity of all the
governors taking these oaths.[3] On the Lords of Trade
requesting full information as to the exact situation concerning these oaths, the Commissioners, however, replied that
they could not furnish it, since this matter was not within
their cognizance.[4] This information was then sought from
the Secretary of State's office.[5] This lack of essential
knowledge indicated an unsatisfactory state of affairs, both
in England and in the colonies, and demanded action.

[1] C. C. 1661–1668, no. 1884.
[2] Com. Journals IX, p. 244.
[3] C. O. 1/34, 74, 75; C. C. 1675–1676, p. 231.
[4] C. O. 324/4, f. 22; C. C. 1675–1676, pp. 235, 287, 296.
[5] On Jan. 10, 1676, by command of the Lords of Trade, Sir Robert
Southwell wrote to William Bridgeman to inquire which of the governors
"have taken or not taken the oaths they ought, that accordingly they may
be written to for the better execution of the said Acts." Cal. Dom. 1675–
1676, p. 505; C. C. 1675–1676, p. 309.

Accordingly, in 1676, a circular letter enjoining strict obedience to the laws of trade was sent to the colonial governors;[1] and, at the same time, the Attorney-General was instructed to prepare a commission for administering to them the statutory oaths.[2] To him was also entrusted the preparation of the form of the oath to be taken; and, after his work had been approved by the government, the oath was formally administered to the royal governors in 1677 and 1678.[3]

The multifarious duties of these governors, apart from the high dignity of their position, would not permit them to attend in person to all the minor details involved in enforcing the laws of trade.[4] Hence this work was entrusted by them to a subordinate clerk, who in time became known as the clerk of the naval office, or simply as the naval officer.[5] Though not directly mentioned in any of the laws of trade and navigation prior to the administrative statute of 1696, the naval officer early became a prominent feature of the local administrative system.[6] During the course of the

[1] C. O. 324/4, ff. 37–39; C. C. 1675–1676, pp. 369–371, 381.

[2] C. O. 324/4, ff. 49 et seq.; C. C. 1675–1676, pp. 374, 378, 379.

[3] C. O. 324/4, f. 53; P. C. Cal. I, pp. 633, 664, 740, 741; No. Ca. Col. Rec. I. pp. 227, 228; C. C. 1675–1676, pp. 385, 389, 390; ibid. 1677–1680, pp. 174, 204, 266, 354; Cal. Treas. Books, 1676–1679, pp. 170, 227.

[4] In 1663, Governor Calvert of Maryland wrote to Lord Baltimore that he had received the Staple Act of that year and would observe it diligently, but he wanted to know if every cargo had to be searched in detail for foreign goods, as this would be "an Endlesse trouble both to the Officers and Mast' & Owners of such goods." Calvert Papers I, p. 242.

[5] See the report of the Commissioners of the Customs to the Treasury on this officer, dated Feb. 16, 1694. Brit. Mus., Add. MSS. 22,617, ff. 141 et seq.

[6] In 1665, Sir Thomas Modyford wrote that he had "settled ye Nauall Office" in Jamaica. C. O. 1/19, 27.

Restoration period, such officers were appointed in a number of the crown colonies.[1] He was the personal representative of the Governor and was entrusted by him with the detailed work of enforcing the commercial code: the giving of bonds, the examination of ships' papers and cargoes, and the entrance and clearance of vessels. The English government had frequently insisted that full accounts of all such details should be regularly forwarded to England,[2] but the governors had only most intermittently complied with these instructions. Shortly before 1680, however, the naval officers in the West Indies began to send with fair regularity to England detailed accounts, known as naval office lists, giving more or less full particulars of all vessels arriving and departing as well as of their cargoes.[3] Later, this custom was introduced in the continental colonies.

[1] In 1682, Massachusetts established naval offices at Boston and Salem, and in the same year Rhode Island also created such an office. C. O. 1/48, 34; Mass. Col. Rec. V, p. 337; R. I. Col. Rec. III, pp. 108–110, 119. Such officers do not, however, belong to the same category as do those appointed by the royal governors. After the revocation of the New England charters and the establishment of royal government, Andros appointed a naval officer in this jurisdiction. Goodrick, Randolph VI, p. 253.

[2] In 1672, for instance, the King wrote to the Governors of Barbados, Montserrat, Antigua, Nevis, St. Kitts, and Jamaica: "We require you to send to Lord Treasurer Clifford in England a list of all bonds that you shall so cause to be taken, with an account of all ships, their burthen, masters' names, and to what place belonging that shall lade in your government yearly." Cal. Treas. Books, 1672–1675, pp. 15, 16. See also the instructions issued to the Earl of Carlisle in 1678. *Ibid.* 1676–1679, pp. 928, 929.

[3] C. O. 33/14 contains such naval officers' statements from Barbados for the years 1679 to 1709. *Ibid.* 33/13 are parallel accounts from the collectors of the customs of the same colony. *Ibid.* 142/13 contains similar statements from Jamaica, covering the years 1685 to 1705. Some earlier

As any neglect of these naval officers to perform their duties made the governor liable to severe penalties, it was only fitting that they should be appointed by him. Yet, at a comparatively early date, these officials in the West Indies began to be appointed in England, and gradually this custom spread to the continent until, towards the middle of the eighteenth century, all these places in the crown colonies were in the gift of the Secretary of State. This practice originated first in Barbados, and in a manner which throws considerable light on the administrative methods of the day.

In 1676, one of the minor positions in Barbados, which

accounts must have been sent from Jamaica, for in 1676 the Governor, Lord Vaughan, wrote to the Lords of Trade that he had instructed the Naval Officer to send them every six months, and in 1682 Governor Lynch wrote that he also had given the same orders. C. C. 1675–1676, p. 412; *ibid.* 1681–1685, p. 283. In 1681, Governor Stapleton of the Leeward Islands was notified that the officers in the colonies had been remiss in forwarding exact accounts of their trade, and he was instructed to direct the naval officer to keep particular accounts of all exports and imports, with full details, and to send them to the Lords of Trade. 'If fit officers for the duty be wanting,' he was ordered to appoint them. *Ibid.* 1681–1685, p.141. There are available a number of such accounts of the trade of these islands from 1680 on. One statement, giving an account of the vessels arriving at St. Kitts from June of 1677 on, refers to a previous account sent to England. C. O. 1/46, 38; *ibid.* 1/47, 32; *ibid.* 1/49, Part I, 18; *ibid.* 1/53, 87; *ibid.* 1/54, Part I, 9; *ibid.* 1/64, 134. The existence of many gaps in this set of documents, is due in the main to the fact that the original statements were, as a rule, sent directly to the Custom-House in London and, with its other archives, they were subsequently destroyed by fire. The Lords of Trade wanted these accounts used in the preparation of a detailed annual schedule of imperial trade, but the Commissioners of the Customs reported in 1679 that it was "a Worke of Great Difficulty & Charge if not wholly impracticable to extract all goods imported & exported." Treas. Books, Out-Letters, Customs 5, f. 110. See also *ibid.* 8, ff. 4, 66–71.

prior thereto had been at the disposal of the Governor, was filled by a crown appointee. The Governor, Sir Jonathan Atkins, was of a fearless and independent character and strenuously objected to this diminution of his prerogative. In reply to his protest, the Secretary of State, Sir Henry Coventry, wrote that in future, before any such appointments were made in England, he would investigate whether or no the place were patentable, and, further, that he would try to persuade the King to establish a settled rule about all the offices in the colonies.[1]   While this correspondence was proceeding, one Abraham Langford was appointed by the Crown as Naval Officer of Barbados, with permission to act by deputy.[2]   Atkins naturally again objected, and unwisely even refused to admit Langford to the office.[3]   On November 28, 1676,[4] Secretary Coventry addressed a sharp letter of rebuke to Atkins, and ordered him to recognize Langford's patent of appointment. He added, that he had been 'just to his word' about this general subject of appointments, and "had not only Spoken to his Majesty, and as I thought very well prepared him towards it," but the late address of

[1] Coventry wrote : "On the one side should all Governours and Generalls bestow all places, there would be but little left for the King to oblige, or indeed to create or make Dependants, so on the other side what you say is very true, it is hard when a Governor hath according to former Presidents placed a Man of Honour in an Imployment, that he should be by an Extraordinary Command put out." Brit. Mus., Add. MSS. 25,120, ff. 90, 91, 112, 120; C. C. 1675–1676, pp. 332, 449, 450.

[2] *Ibid.* p. 379. On June 14, 1676, Coventry wrote to Atkins that he should admit Langford into this office. *Ibid.* p. 403.

[3] Brit. Mus., Add. MSS. 22,617, ff. 141, 142.

[4] *Ibid.* 25,120, ff. 96–99.

Barbados against the enumeration of sugar and the affront offered to Langford's patent "make the Conjuncture at present improper." Atkins perforce had to submit, and Langford enjoyed his patent for this office until his death several years thereafter.[1] His case was used as a precedent, and his successors in the office at Barbados continued to be appointed by the Crown.[2] At about the same time, in Jamaica also, the naval officer began to be nominated in England.[3] Although so appointed, these officials were,

[1] In 1677, Coventry wrote to Atkins about this general subject, and the latter's expressed opinion "that it is prejudiciall to Government to have Officers nominated here," stating that "his Majesty and Councill are of another Opinion, and that it concerneth his Majesty to be a little better acquainted with those that bear Offices in his Plantations then of late he hath been, for till some late Orders of the Councill, his Majesty hardly knew the Lawe or the men by which his Plantations were governed. The Governor was the only person known to him, but his Majesty was resolved to be better acquainted with them and let them know, they are not to govern themselves, but be governed by him." He further added that "some late Stubborn Carriage in the Plantations" would occasion a stricter inquiry into "their Comportments," than hitherto had been made. Brit. Mus., Add. MSS. 25,120, f. 120.

[2] In 1682, shortly before his death, Abraham Langford petitioned that his son, who had acted as his deputy, might be his successor. Sir Richard Dutton, the Governor, also sought the place for his brother. C. C. 1681–1685, pp. 279, 293, 340, 382, 474. Neither received the appointment. The actual nominee was apparently one Thomas Gleave, who, under James II, was succeeded by Archibald Carmichael. Brit. Mus., Sloane MSS. 2441 f. 22b; Add. MSS. 22,617, ff. 141, 142; C. O. 33/13 passim.

[3] In 1681, one Reginald Wilson applied for a patent as Naval Officer of Jamaica. Sir Thomas Lynch, who had governed the colony ten years before, supported this petition, stating that at that time he had established this office 'to inspect all bills of lading and cocquets that I might not be surprised, but that the several Acts of Trade and Navigation might be exactly complied with according to my oath and duty.' He had appointed this Wilson,

however, not paid by the English Exchequer, but were supported by fees levied on the vessels trading in the colonies.

At a very early date, it was seen that the royal governors and their subordinate officials were not able to secure a strict enforcement of the laws of trade. At the same time, it was also fully realized that, as there were no imperial officials of any description in the proprietary and charter colonies, the laws were apt to be ignored by the local authorities in these semi-independent jurisdictions, whenever their local interests were to any extent adversely affected. Hence arose the demand that special officials be appointed by the English government to secure the execution of the laws of trade in the colonies. In 1662 and 1663, the chief violation complained of was the illegal shipment of tobacco directly to New Netherland and Europe.[1] The Council for Foreign Plantations devoted considerable attention to this matter, but could devise no more effective remedy than the despatch of special instructions to the colonial governors.[2] Further action was demanded by the Farmers of the Customs, who were directly interested, in so much as this illegal trade diminished the

who had performed his duties very exactly, but had subsequently been dismissed by the Earl of Carlisle to make room for a man of his own selection. As Lynch's recommendation was so unqualified, Wilson received the appointment. C. O. 1/47, 53; C. C. 1681–1685, pp. 107, 147, 148; P. C. Cal. II, p. 26. On Wilson, see also C. C. 1681–1685, pp. 267, 305, 306; Bodleian, Rawlinson MSS., A 171, f. 199; Brit. Mus., Sloane MSS. 2724 (Earl of Carlisle's answer to charges of Sam. Long).

[1] P. C. Register Charter II, III, ff. 101, 450, 451; P. C. Cal. I, pp. 334, 335, 365–367; N. Y. Col. Doc. III, pp. 44–46; Va. Mag. III, pp. 18, 19.

[2] C. C. 1661–1668, nos. 345, 357; N. Y. Col. Doc. III, pp. 44–46; C. O. 1/14, 59, f. 53.

English customs revenue. They complained [1] that the colonial and English traders did, "both by land & water carry & convey greate quantities of Tobacco to the Dutch whose Plantations are contiguous, the Custom whereof would amount to tenne thousand pounds p. ann. or upwards, thereby eluding the late Act of Navigation and defrauding his Matie." As a remedy, the Farmers proposed to send at their own expense officials to the various colonies to prevent such illegal practices. The Council for Foreign Plantations approved of this suggestion, and, after deciding upon the powers of these proposed officials, early in 1664, recommended its adoption. [2] The government ratified this recommendation, and by an Order in Council of April 22, 1664, the Farmers of the Customs were empowered at their own charge to send officers to the colonies to see to the execution of the Navigation Act. [3] In the meanwhile, however, the international situation had reached a critical phase. The determination of the English government to attack the Dutch colony of New Netherland and the successful outcome of this expedition rendered it largely unnecessary to send these customs officials to America, since this centre of the illegal trade was now an English possession.

Illegal trade, however, by no means disappeared. To some extent it was even facilitated by the Dutch war, for the temporary dispensation of certain clauses of the Naviga-

[1] C. O. 1/14, 59, ff. 53, 54; N. Y. Col. Doc. III, p. 47; C. C. 1661–1668, no. 597.

[2] C. O. 1/14, 59, ff. 54–56; N. Y. Col. Doc. III, pp. 48–50; C. C. 1661–1668, nos. 605, 644, 649.

[3] P. C. Register Charles II, IV, f. 79; P. C. Cal. I, pp. 377, 378.

tion Acts was used to cover violations of the provisions that still remained in force.[1] In some more or less sporadic instances, the enumerated products were sent directly to Europe and European supplies were imported directly into the colonies from places other than England.[2] On December 4, 1668, the Council of Trade reported to Charles II that several of the colonial governors had been remiss in the following respects: in not taking the oaths to enforce the laws of trade as enjoined by statute; in allowing unqualified ships to trade; in not obtaining bonds before the enumerated goods were shipped. As the chief remedy, they proposed that the Farmers of the Customs should maintain an officer in each colony to administer the oaths to the

[1] In the Leeward Islands, the distress caused by the war induced the local authorities to suspend these laws temporarily. In 1667, the Governor, Council, and Assembly of Nevis, considering the great scarcity, ordered that a liberty of trade be granted to two ships of Hamburg, on condition that this should not be used as a precedent. C. C. 1661–1668, no. 1631. See also no. 1669. In 1668, was registered a complaint to the effect that the Governor of Antigua had allowed the French and Dutch to trade there. Cal. Treas. Books, 1667–1668, pp. 439, 440.

[2] On Oct. 29, 1667, the Treasury wrote to Sir John Finch, the English resident at Florence, in reply to his letters concerning an English ship that had arrived at Leghorn with part of her cargo from Barbados, instructing him in future to arrest any such vessel. Cal. Treas. Books, 1667–1668, p. 198. A few weeks later, the Treasury wrote to the colonial governors, stating that several ships had gone directly from the colonies to Tangier, to the Mediterranean ports, and to other places, and enjoining upon them greater care in the enforcement of the laws. Ibid. pp. 201, 202; Treas. Books, Out-Letters, Customs I, ff. 49–51. Although an English possession, Tangier was not placed within the barriers of the colonial system, and the enumerated goods were not allowed to be shipped there directly. On this illegal trade from the colonies to Tangier and the attempt to legalize it, see P. C. Cal. I, pp. 486, 499; Cal. Treas. Books, 1667–1668, p. 449.

governors, that only vessels whose papers this officer had seen should be allowed to trade, and that no bond or security be accepted without his approval.[1] This report was favorably endorsed by the Privy Council, and early in 1669 the Farmers of the Customs were ordered to send to the colonies or to select in them, and to maintain at their own charge, one or more persons in each plantation, "whom his Majesty shall Approve and Authorise," to administer the oaths to the governors and to see that the law was obeyed. At the same time, letters were despatched to the Governors of Virginia, Maryland, New York, and the island colonies, ordering them to take the statutory oaths and to assist these officers.[2]

It is not quite clear to what extent the Farmers of the Customs used this authority. In Virginia, they named Edward Digges, a prominent citizen of the colony, as their representative,[3] and probably in some of the other colonies also officers were appointed.[4] But, in general, no extensive change in the local administrative machinery was, or could be, made in the short space of time during which the system

[1] C. C. 1661–1668, no. 1884. On Oct. 5, 1668, in connection with a complaint from the Farmers of the Customs about ships trading directly from Barbados to Tangier, the Treasury had passed a resolution that the Farmers should have liberty to have an officer in each colony to see that all ships traded according to the law. Cal. Treas. Books, 1667–1668, p. 449.

[2] P. C. Register Charles II, VIII, f. 179; P. C. Cal. I, pp. 499–501.

[3] See warrant of Aug. 25, 1669, approving the appointment of Edward Digges by the Farmers of the Customs. C. C. 1669–1674, p. 40; Va. Mag. XIX, pp. 350, 351.

[4] In 1670, Secretary Ludwell of Virginia referred to a letter from "Mr. Delavell the farmers Comiss'r at New Yorke." Va. Mag. XIX, p. 354.

of farming the revenue was continued in England. In 1671, this method was abandoned, and the Commonwealth precedent was followed in appointing Commissioners of the Customs, at whose head was placed Sir George Downing.[1]

Like the Farmers whom they had superseded, this board was mainly intent upon securing as large a customs revenue as was possible; and, as the only branch of illegal trade in the colonies that might seriously interfere with this purpose was an extensive evasion of the enumeration of tobacco, they concentrated their attention on Virginia and Maryland. On October 31, 1671, a warrant was issued, appointing Edward Digges "Agent at Virginia," with extensive powers of control over the colony's trade. His salary of £250 was made payable by the Receiver-General of the Customs in England.[2] No provision was made for a similar officer in Maryland, because its Governor, Charles Calvert, was

[1] Cal. Treas. Books, 1669–1672, p. 935; Atton and Holland, The Kings Customs, p. 103.

[2] Digges was instructed to see that the enumeration bonds were taken and to send copies of them, together with detailed accounts of all ships arriving and departing, to the Commissioners of the Customs. Simultaneously with his appointment, a letter was sent to Governor Berkeley, informing him of the new method of collecting the English customs revenue, "whereof the duty on the tobaccos of Virginia are a considerable branch," and stating that information had been received of many evasions of the enumeration of to-bacco. Berkeley was ordered to prevent these frauds and strictly to enforce all the laws of trade, and he was further instructed that the security of all enumeration bonds taken by him had to be approved by Edward Digges, "whom we have appointed to take care of same and to transmit copies of said bonds to the Customs Commissioners in London." Cal. Treas. Books, 1669–1672, p. 1126. Cf. p. 948.

already very methodical in enforcing the laws and regularly sent to England copies of the bonds taken by him, as well as accounts of the colony's exports. In view of the salary paid to Digges in Virginia, Lord Baltimore, however, thought that his son, the Governor, was also entitled to some remuneration for his zeal, and secured for him a salary of £200 from the English Treasury.[1] This system of employing surveyors — this was the technical designation used by the Treasury — in Virginia and Maryland remained in effect only a short time, for in 1673 Parliament imposed the plantation duties and specifically entrusted their management and collection to the Commissioners of the Customs. It thus became the statutory duty of this board to appoint customs officials in all the colonies.

Shortly thereafter, in the fall of 1673, the Commissioners of the Customs proceeded to act upon their new powers and appointed collectors of the customs in all the colonies except New England, North Carolina, New York, and New Jersey.[2] In 1674, appointments were also made in these last three

---

[1] The warrant for this salary was issued only in November of 1672, but it was paid from Christmas of 1671 on. This salary was to be paid to Calvert until he should "appoint some one to receive same: same to be for the encouragement of said Calvert so long as he shall continue to perform the said service." On June 2, 1673, Calvert wrote to Baltimore, thanking him for procuring this salary and stating that, as instructed, he would appoint a person to receive it. The salary was, however, always paid to him. Cal. Treas. Books, 1669–1672, pp. 1101, 1137, 1345; Calvert Papers I, pp. 263, 264, 279, 295, 300.

[2] Cal. Treas. Books, 1672–1675, pp. 424, 427. No provision naturally was made for the rudimentary settlements in the Bahamas, nor for Newfoundland, which was not considered a colony.

colonies,[1] and finally, in 1678, a collector for New England was chosen in the person of Edward Randolph.[2]   Apart from Randolph, there were several men among these original appointees of 1673, and those shortly thereafter succeeding them, who played a prominent part in colonial politics.[3] Digges and Calvert were naturally not continued in their former positions, and their exceptionally large salaries were stopped,[4] but they were appointed collectors in their respective colonies.   Digges was Auditor of Virginia and a member of the Council, and, possibly on account of the pressure of other work or because of ill-health — he died shortly afterwards — but more probably in consequence of the withdrawal of his salary, he declined the position.[5]   In his stead, early in 1675, was appointed Giles Bland,[6] who was destined to a short, but turbulent and tragic, career in Virginia politics. In Maryland, Governor Calvert accepted the office and continued in it until the death of his father, Lord Baltimore, when he succeeded to the proprietorship.   In his place shortly thereafter, in 1676, was appointed Christopher Rousby,[7] who, like Bland in Virginia, was to meet an untimely and violent

[1] Cal. Treas. Books, 1672–1675, pp. 498, 501, 521, 522.

[2] *Ibid.* 1676–1679, p. 1023.   In 1678, on the recommendation of Governor Andros of New York, a Collector and a Comptroller were also appointed at Pemaquid.   *Ibid.* p. 1018.

[3] For these appointments up to 1679, see *ibid.* 1672–1675, pp. 613, 667, 866; *ibid.* 1676–1679, pp. 288, 312, 641, 1018, 1093, 1211.

[4] *Ibid.* 1672–1675, pp. 437, 452, 456.

[5] *Ibid.* p. 667; Va. Mag. XIV, p. 270.

[6] February 1, 1675, warrant from Treasurer Danby to the Customs board to appoint Giles Bland.   Cal. Treas. Books, 1672–1675, p. 667.

[7] *Ibid.* 1676–1679, pp. 229, 230, 373.

death. In addition to Calvert, there was on the original list one other proprietary Governor, Sir John Heydon of the Bermudas, and also Joseph West, the former Governor of South Carolina.[1] Among the subsequent noteworthy appointments were Edwyn Stede in Barbados,[2] who later was Deputy Governor of that island, and Thomas Miller,[3] whose activities caused a miniature political upheaval in North Carolina.

As a rule, one collector was appointed for each colony, with authority, however, to designate such deputies as might be required.[4] But in Virginia, where there were no regular ports of entry, the agents of the colony induced the government in 1676 to appoint seven collectors — among whom were such prominent colonials as Nicholas Spencer, John Washington, and Ralph Wormley — to act in the four principal rivers of the colony and on "the Eastern Shore."[5]

---

[1] In 1674, Philip Carteret, the Governor of East New Jersey, was also appointed to be the Collector there, with authority to appoint a deputy. Cal. Treas. Books, 1672–1675, pp. 521, 522.

[2] Ordered appointed Sept. 14, 1674, in place of Robert Bevis, Bevin, or Beven. *Ibid.* p. 580. This was evidently Robert Bevin who, jointly with Stede, acted as agent of the Royal African Company in Barbados. C. C. 1669–1674, pp. 363, 364, 544; P. C. Cal. I, pp. 572–574.

[3] Ordered appointed Nov. 16, 1676. Cal. Treas. Books, 1676–1679, p. 373.

[4] In the Leeward Islands, a joint-collector was appointed for Nevis and St. Kitts, but Antigua and Montserrat each had its own collector. *Ibid.* 1672–1675, pp. 427, 451, 452.

[5] *Ibid.* 1676–1679, pp. 346, 347. At the same time, Captain Philip Lightfoot was appointed Comptroller and Surveyor General of the colony. *Ibid.* Nicholas Spencer and John Washington held the joint-collectorship on the Potomac, but in 1679, after the death of the latter, Spencer was appointed sole collector. Treas. Books, Out-Letters, Customs 5, f. 8. This

Similarly, nine years later, Maryland was divided into two districts with separate collectors.[1]

In addition to these collectors, the Commissioners of the Customs appointed in nearly every one of the colonies an official called the Comptroller and Surveyor General, who, while subordinate to the Collector, acted as a check upon him and countersigned the accounts that he sent to England.[2] None of these officials, except Nicholas Bad-

warrant from the Treasury to the Customs, ordering Spencer's appointment, is printed in Atton and Holland, The King's Customs, p. 462.

[1] In the beginning of 1685, Nehemiah Blackiston, the Comptroller and Surveyor in Maryland, was appointed Collector, in succession to Christopher Rousby, who had been murdered. But on Sept. 24, 1685, John Rousby was appointed Collector at Patuxent River, and Blackiston's duties were restricted to the Wicomico and Pocomoke rivers. He was obliged, however, to officiate only at the Wicomico, and George Layfield, the colony's Comptroller and Surveyor, was authorized to act as his deputy on the Pocomoke, with power to appoint deputies to perform his own duties as Comptroller on the Patuxent and Wicomico rivers. Treas. Books, Out-Letters, Customs 10, ff. 9, 51. See also C. O. 5/739, f. 78; C. C. 1685–1688, pp. 6, 286. In 1687, John Payne was appointed to succeed John Rousby in the Patuxent River district. Treas. Books, Out-Letters, Customs 11, f. 36.

[2] On April 30, 1673, Treasurer Clifford wrote, apparently to the Customs, that he approved of their proposals for executing 25 Ch. II, c. 7, and of the appointment of collectors in each of the plantations, but added: "That there may be a check over the action of the Collectors I think fit a Surveyor should also be appointed at each Plantation to be allowed a sixth part of the salary proposed for the Head Collectors," the remaining five-sixths to go to the collectors for their pains and " the charge of under officers." Cal. Treas. Books, 1672–1675, p. 126. For the surveyors appointed, see *ibid.* pp. 427, 596, 866, 708; *ibid.* 1676–1679, pp. 288, 312, 641, 755, 1019, 1119. For the system of control over the collectors, see *ibid.* 1676–1679, pp. 728, 729. In the Bermudas and in Montserrat, on account of their small trade, no comptrollers were appointed, and the collectors were granted the entire allowances

cock and Nehemiah Blackiston in Maryland [1] and Timothy Biggs in North Carolina,[2] were at all prominent in the controversies, in which the collectors became so frequently involved.

As this corps of customs officials was of considerable size, experience showed that it would be advisable to appoint a superior official to inspect and control their work. In 1683, William Dyre, who had been Collector of the New York provincial revenue,[3] was appointed Surveyor General of the Customs in the American colonies.[4] In the spring of 1683, Dyre was in Barbados on official business and unearthed some abuses there.[5] Towards the end of the year, he appeared in

established for the imperial customs officials in these colonies. *Ibid.* 1672–1675, pp. 427, 499.

[1] The warrant for Blackiston's appointment was dated Jan. 16, 1683. Treas. Books, Out-Letters, Customs 8, f. 182. The appointment of Badcock was authorized on June 23, 1680. *Ibid.* 5, f. 230.

[2] The warrant for Biggs's appointment was dated Sept. 28, 1678. Cal. Treas. Books, 1676–1679, p. 1119.

[3] In 1674, Dyre had been appointed Collector of the New York revenue, and in 1681 he was tried in the colony 'as a false traitor' for collecting customs duties that had not been, as was claimed, duly authorized. On Dyre denying the competence of the New York court, he was sent for trial to England, where the charges against him were held to be groundless. C. C. 1681–1685, pp. 81, 259, 304, 555; Conn. Col. Rec. III, p. 344 n. See also Mrs. Schuyler Van Rensselaer, History of the City of New York II, pp. 232–242. On Dec. 2, 1682, Dyre was ordered appointed Collector of the Customs in Pennsylvania and the Jerseys, and a month later he secured the post of Surveyor General. Treas. Books, Out-Letters, Customs 8, f. 172.

[4] For Dyre's commission and instructions of Jan. 4, 1683, see C. O. 140/4, f. 32; Mass. Col. Rec. V, p. 530; Conn. Col. Rec. III, p. 344.

[5] Treas. Books, Out-Letters, Customs 8, f. 239; C. C. 1685–1688, p. 58; Toppan, Randolph IV, p 5.

Jamaica, where, after some hesitation on the part of the local authorities, he was permitted to exercise the powers of his commission.[1] In 1684, he was in New England, where his family had been residing for several years.[2] Dyre's career in New York had already made him unpopular in Massachusetts,[3] and his commission as Surveyor General was regarded with considerable distrust.[4] While there, he participated in, and claimed the credit for, the seizure of a notable pirate.[5] In 1685, Dyre investigated conditions in Pennsylvania and New Jersey, and complained of the illegal trade carried on there.[6] In New Jersey, he seized a ship for trading without entering, and although, so he alleged, the case was absolutely clear, yet the jury found against him and charged him with a long bill of costs, for refusing to pay which he was arrested. It was on the strength of this complaint that the Privy Council ordered the Attorney-General to institute proceedings against

[1] C. O. 140/4, f. 32; C. C. 1681–1685, p. 572.

[2] Toppan, Randolph IV, p. 5.

[3] The verses, written on Randolph's return to New England as Collector in 1679, contained the following lines : —

> "He that keep a Plantacon Custom-house,
> One year, may bee a man, the next a Mouse.
> Y^r Brother *Dyer* hath the Devill played,
> Made the New-Yorkers at the first affraide,
> Hee vapoured, swagger'd, hector'd (whoe but hee ?)
> But soon destroyed himself by Villanie."

Ibid. III, pp. 61–64.

[4] *Ibid.* I, pp. 155, 235; III, pp. 339, 340. In 1686, Governor Dongan of New York stated that, according to report, Dyre was "the worst of men." Goodrick, Randolph VI, p. 166 n.

[5] C. C. 1681–1685, pp. 684–686.

[6] House of Lords MSS. II (1695–1697), p. 465.

the Jersey charter.[1] In 1686, we find Dyre using his authority to appoint customs officials in the Bermudas and in Connecticut, and complaining of the illegal importation of European goods in the latter colony.[2] In November of 1685, Patrick Mein was appointed to succeed Dyre as Surveyor General and assumed his duties in 1686.[3] Towards the middle of the year, he was in New York and New Jersey investigating conditions there. A few months later, he appeared in Maryland, where the customs service was in an unsatisfactory state, and reported upon the conditions in that colony. He likewise visited Virginia, where at this time also there was considerable trouble about the administration of the laws. While in the " Old Dominion," he issued detailed instructions to the customs officials established there.[4] After having completed his survey of the continental colonies to the satisfaction of the Commissioners of the Customs, Mein was ordered to proceed to the West Indies, with instructions

[1] C. C. 1681–1685, pp. 61, 106; House of Lords MSS. II (1695–1697), p. 465; P. C. Cal. II, p. 89.

[2] C. C. 1681–1685, p. 295; Conn. Col. Rec. III, p. 344.

[3] On Jan. 15, 1685, the Customs Board was authorized to appoint William Carler to succeed Dyre, but apparently no action was taken, and on Nov. 17, 1685, Mein's appointment in succession to Dyre was authorized by the Treasury. Treas. Books, Out-Letters, Customs 9, f. 90; 10, f. 73.

[4] C. C. 1685–1688, pp. 209, 253, 277, 280, 305; House of Lords MSS. II (1695–1697), p. 465; C. O. 5/739, ff. 72–75; ibid. 1/62, 20xi; Goodrick, Randolph VI, p. 199. The instructions issued by Mein on Dec. 24, 1686, to the Virginia collectors carefully described their duties under the five fundamental statutes of the Restoration Parliament, and ordered them to correspond with the Commissioners of the Customs in England and to obey their instructions. He further enjoined upon them not to engage in trade, either directly or indirectly. C. O. 1/59, 34.

to inspect the management of the 1673 plantation duties and the four and a half per cent revenue, and also the execution of the laws of trade and navigation, and especially to prevent ships from leaving these islands unless they had given satisfactory enumerated bonds.[1]

Thus there was established in the colonies a comprehensive system of customs officials, who not only were absolutely independent of the authorities in the charter and proprietary colonies, but also were in a great measure free from control by the royal governors, since they were directly responsible to the higher authority of the Commissioners of the Customs. Moreover, apart from the fees occasionally allowed them for entering and clearing vessels, these officials were absolutely independent of the colonial governments, because their salaries were derived from the Exchequer or from funds under the exclusive control of the English Treasury. When these collectors and comptrollers were first appointed in 1673, it was arranged that they should receive as compensation a fixed portion, varying in the different colonies, of the 1673 duties collected by them.[2]   As this revenue was very small and the shares thereof allotted to the collectors were at the outset not large, they had in most instances to be increased, so that ultimately considerably over one-half of the income from this source went to those

---

[1] Treas. Books, Out-Letters, Customs 11, f. 177.

[2] At the beginning, it was determined to allow one-eighth in Virginia and Maryland, one-fifth in Barbados, one-third in Jamaica, Nevis, and St. Kitts, and one-half in Montserrat, Antigua, and the Bermudas. Of these amounts, the collector was to receive two-thirds and the comptroller and surveyor one-third.   Brit. Mus., Add. MSS. 28,089, ff. 30–32.

collecting it.[1] Thus, already in 1675, the Virginia and Maryland collectors were authorized to retain one-half and the comptrollers one-quarter of the gross amount of these duties collected there.[2] This arrangement could not, however, be applied to New England, because only insignificant quantities of the enumerated goods were exported thence to the other colonies, and, besides, it was doubtful if the law could be adequately enforced there. Accordingly, when in 1678 Randolph was appointed Collector of New England, Treasurer Danby ordered his salary of £100 to be inserted in the English customs establishment until further orders, which, he wrote: "I intend to give when a revenue shall arise in that country out of which it may be paid."[3] Needless to say, such orders were never issued. In addition, the Surveyor General was paid by the

[1] Already on Dec. 12, 1673, it was ordered that the former allowance of one-eighth in Virginia and Maryland should be increased to one-half, of which the collectors were entitled to two-thirds and the surveyors to one-third. The same arrangement was made in 1674 for New York and North Carolina. Cal. Treas. Books, 1672–1675, pp. 437, 456, 498, 522. In 1677, the proportion allowed in Jamaica was raised to one-half and, in 1679, that in Barbados to one-fourth. *Ibid.* 1676–1679, p. 641; Treas. Books, Out-Letters, Customs 5, ff. 12–18.

[2] This order was issued by Danby on the strength of a report of the Commissioners of the Customs to the effect that, in view of the fact that Digges formerly had received £250 yearly and Calvert £200, this work was now inadequately compensated and, as the object of these duties was "to turn the course of a trade rather than to raise any considerable revenue to His Majesty," the proportions allowed to the customs officials in these colonies should be increased to one-half and one-quarter of the amount collected. Cal. Treas. Books, 1672–1675, pp. 705.

[3] *Ibid.* 1676–1679, p. 1142.

Exchequer, Dyre and Mein each receiving twenty shillings a day for their services.[1]

When, in 1684, the system of farming the four and a half per cent export duties in Barbados and the Leeward Islands was discarded, the Treasury was obliged to create an elaborate staff of officials to take charge of this revenue. The allowances formerly granted to the collectors and comptrollers were discontinued, and the collection of the 1673 duties, as well as the enforcement of laws of trade and navigation, was entrusted to these new officials. In Barbados, Edwyn Stede (the former Collector of the Customs) and Stephen Gascoigne were appointed Chief Commissioners of this four and a half per cent revenue with salaries of £200 apiece. Under them were a score of minor officials — several collectors, a comptroller, as well as clerks, searchers, waiters, watermen — each with a fixed salary. The aggregate cost of this entire staff, including the two chiefs, was £1455, which was paid out of the four and a half per cent duties.[2] In the Leeward Islands,

[1] Treas. Books, Out-Letters, Customs 8, f. 239; 9, f. 90; 10, f. 73.

[2] This amount was reckoned equivalent to 2328 hundredweight of muscovado sugar, figured at 12s. 6d. Separate accounts were ordered kept of this revenue and that arising from the plantation duties of 1673. The accounts of the 4½ per cent revenue were ordered to be sent regularly to the Commissioners of the Customs and to William Blathwayt, the Auditor-General. Such goods as were received in payment of these duties were to be shipped to England, except rum, lime-juice and molasses, which would "sell to the least advantage in England." Hence, all the salaries of these officials were ordered to be paid "out of the Receipt of these Commodities, either by converting them into Muscovado Sugar, money or otherwise, as is most convenient," and, in case these receipts were not sufficient for the entire salary list, the deficiency was to be made good "out of other Vents of Goods." These elaborate instructions were issued on Sept. 2, 1684. Treas. Books,

where the revenue was comparatively insignificant, a much less elaborate staff was required. As head commissioners or collectors were appointed Henry Carpenter and Richard Nagle, with salaries of £100 apiece. Their station was Nevis, and for each of the other islands — St. Kitts, Antigua, and Montserrat — separate collectors were appointed. Subordinate to them were a number of searchers and waiters, and the total charge of the entire service was roughly £650 yearly.[1]

The establishment of this colonial customs service was not effected without considerable friction. The charter and proprietary colonies naturally looked askance at these officials, who were the sole direct representatives of the imperial authority within their jurisdictions. Moreover, in the crown colonies also, difficulties arose from the extensive authority conferred on the collectors of the customs. By the statutes, the governor was the colonial official primarily responsible for the execution of the laws of trade and

Out-Letters, Customs 9, ff. 43–48. On Oct. 4, 1684, a more careful method of auditing the accounts was prescribed and Blathwayt's deputy in the colony was authorized to inspect all the books and accounts of these officials. *Ibid.* f. 55. During the subsequent five years, various changes were made in this staff. *Ibid.* ff. 57, 72; 10, ff. 21, 28; 11, ff. 56, 85, 95, 152. The only noteworthy change was that, in 1687, Edward Cranfield, who had unsuccessfully tried to govern New Hampshire, was upon his own petition appointed one of the Commissioners, in succession to Gascoigne, "supposed to be cast away in his passage hither." He was also at the same time appointed Collector of the Customs. *Ibid.* 11, f. 6.

[1] *Ibid.* 9, f. 54. During the following five years, several changes were made in this staff. *Ibid.* f. 63; 10, ff. 27, 132, 143; 11, f. 95. In 1685, the salaries of Carpenter and Nagle were raised to £150, and, in 1686, Thomas Belchamber was appointed to succeed Nagle, lately deceased. *Ibid.* 10, ff. 33, 143.

navigation, and, according to a strictly literal interpretation of the law, the work of the collectors should have been confined solely to matters connected with the 1673 duties. But, in addition to this, the collectors were from the very outset instructed also to see in general to the enforcement of the entire commercial system. They were ordered not only to collect the plantation duties, but to secure the execution of all the other trade laws — to see that ships arriving from England had given bonds there and that in other cases proper bonds were given in the colonies, to seize all vessels violating the Staple Act of 1663, and not to allow any "to unlade before handing in a report and manifest." [1] It was but natural that, in trying to exercise these broad powers, the collectors should meet with some opposition from the colonial governors and their subordinate officials, to whom hitherto this work had been wholly entrusted.

In Virginia, this opposition culminated in a serious quarrel between Governor Berkeley and Giles Bland, who was appointed Collector of the Customs in 1675.[2] He was the son of a London merchant of extensive and varied activities, John Bland, who is mainly remembered on account of an incisive criticism of the purely economic features of the newly created colonial system. Towards the end of the sixties, Giles Bland was in Tangier, of which his active father was the Mayor,[3] and, a few years thereafter, he came to

[1] Cal. Treas. Books, 1672–1675, pp. 451, 452; Brit. Mus., Add. MSS. 28,089, ff. 30–34.

[2] Cal. Treas. Books, 1672–1675, p. 667.

[3] E. M. G. Routh, Tangier, pp. 120–123.

Virginia to take charge of his father's extensive landed estates there.[1] In 1674, as a result of a personal quarrel with the colony's Secretary, Thomas Ludwell, during which he was held to have affronted the "Grand Assembly" and insulted the Council, Bland was fined £500 by the Virginia authorities. Thus, already before his appointment as Collector of the Customs, he was in bad odor with the oligarchy governing the colony, and soon thereafter he became involved in an acrimonious dispute with the autocratic Governor, Sir William Berkeley, about the enforcement of the laws of trade.[2] In the main, the trouble arose from the fact that Berkeley and the local officials wished to restrict Bland's authority to the collection of the plantation duties of 1673, and hampered him when he tried to carry out his broad instructions to supervise the execution of the entire body of the laws of trade. In the course of a long letter [3] on the obstructions encountered by him, Bland pointed out to Governor Berkeley how impossible it was for him to enforce the laws, as the trading vessels refused to enter and clear with him, but continued as heretofore to do so solely with the collectors of the provincial revenue. In ignoring him, Bland continued, these vessels "slight his Ma[ts] Authority & Comands," and are encouraged to do so by the local officials. As a result, he further claimed, considerable illegal trade was carried on, which he had no means of checking. In consequence of these so-called scan-

---

[1] Va. Mag. XX, p. 238.

[2] Brit. Mus., Egerton MSS. 2395, f. 496; Va. Mag. XX, pp. 238, 239; C. C. 1669–1674, pp. 609, 624; *ibid.* 1675–1676, pp. 231, 232, 379.

[3] September 16, 1675. Brit. Mus., Egerton MSS. 2395, ff. 511 *et seq.*

dalous charges, the Virginia authorities suspended Bland from his post until the King's pleasure should be made known.[1] Shortly thereafter began the disturbances culminating in Bacon's rebellion, in which Bland took a prominent part, naturally on the side of the insurgents. It was presumably for this reason, rather than on the merits of his special controversy with Berkeley, that the Commissioners of the Customs were ordered on August 21, 1676, to present a fit person to succeed Bland, "whom his Majesty has commanded to be removed from that employment."[2] A few months later, Bland fell victim to Governor Berkeley's vindictive spirit and was hanged for his participation in the rebellion.

It is obvious that the collectors of the customs could not secure the enforcement of the laws of trade unless vessels were obliged to enter and clear with them. Bland was fully justified in making this contention.[3] But it is equally plain

[1] Brit. Mus., Egerton MSS. 2395, f. 515; C. C. 1675–1676, pp. 298, 299; Va. Mag. XX. p. 242.

[2] Cal. Treas. Books, 1676–1679, p. 308. Bland's letter of April 28, 1676, to Williamson, embodying his own specific grievances and those of the party opposed to Berkeley, was endorsed as having been received in June. C. O. 1/36, 54; C. C. 1675–1676, pp. 385, 386. On July 28, 1676, the Virginia agents were called to account, because Bland had been dismissed without first making application to the Treasury. In reply, they asserted that he had been restored to his office. On this occasion, these agents claimed that Bland's powers extended only to collecting the 1673 duties and 'that the Governor is under a penalty of 1000 l. for entering and clearing of all ships that come for England or go elsewhere.' Cal. Treas. Books, 1676–1679, p. 67.

[3] Bland wrote to Berkeley: "As touching ships coming from England wch yor Hon^r will not Admitt y^t I should take any cognizance of," how can I find out if they really came from England if they do not enter with me. Brit. Mus., Egerton MSS. 2395, f. 513.

that, unless this work were likewise performed by the subordinate officers of the governor, he could not perform his statutory duties of enforcing the colonial system.[1] Consequently it gradually became the established custom for both the collectors and the naval officers to examine the ships' papers at arrival and departure. Formal instructions to this general effect were in 1683 sent from England to the royal governors.[2] The work of these two sets of officials was thus largely the same,[3] and one acted as a check on the other. This dual system,[4] which was largely unique, was found to be fairly effective, and hence was retained by the continental colonies when they secured their independence from Great Britain, and is still a characteristic feature of the customs administration of the United States.

The Crown and the Privy Council with its attendant committees and boards were represented in the colonies by the governors and the naval officers; the Treasury agents

---

[1] In most of the colonies, the local revenue was in part raised by customs duties, and hence ships had also to enter and clear with the purely provincial revenue officials. Thus three sets of officials were directly concerned in the same work. In practice, however, the system was not so cumbersome, as in some of the colonies the same man held two offices.

[2] C. O. 5/904, ff. 330–332; *ibid.* 1/52, 60; C. C. 1681–1685, pp. 477, 478, 549, 564, 565. See also C. C. 1685–1688, pp. 289, 291.

[3] The collectors also saw to the payment of the 1673 plantation duties, in which the naval officers had no concern. Similarly, it was the special duty of the naval officers to take bonds from such vessels shipping the enumerated commodities as had not already given security in England.

[4] The Commissioners of the Customs wanted the collectors appointed by them to be also the naval officers, but, as they reported in 1694/5, although they had on many occasions recommended this step, they had "very rarely prevailed therein." Brit. Mus., Add. MSS. 22,617, ff. 141, 142.

were the surveyors general and the collectors of the customs. Similarly, the third of the English administrative departments directly concerned in the execution of the laws of trade, the Admiralty, likewise had its personal representatives in America. These agents of the Admiralty were of two distinct classes: the Vice-Admirals and the officials of the admiralty courts, which had cognizance of specific violations of the commercial system; the captains and other officers of the royal navy, who were authorized under the Navigation Act to seize vessels violating certain of its provisions.

The Navigation Act of 1660 not only authorized, but "strictly required," all officers of the Royal Navy to seize as prizes any foreign ships trading to the colonies and to deliver 'them to the Court of Admiralty for trial.[1] In case of condemnation, one-half of the proceeds of such seizures was to be allotted to the officers of the Navy concerned therein, and the balance to the Crown. But if the offending vessel were seized in the colony by civil officials, then the trial was to be held "in any court of record," while, on condemnation, the proceeds were to be equally divided between the Crown, the Governor, and the informer or

---

[1] The statute is not quite clear, and might have been interpreted to mean that the trial should take place in the English High Court of Admiralty. This doubt was voiced by the Council of Barbados, which in 1661 wrote that they would 'prosecute the late Act of Navigation, but begged that the King's ships might not carry off ships lying in their ports to the Admiralty Court in England, but should have them tried before the courts of record here.' C. C. 1661–1668, no. 84. Whatever the intent of the legislature was, the English government interpreted this clause to mean the colonial admiralty courts.

seizer.[1] Similarly, the penalties for violations of the enumeration clauses were made recoverable in the courts of record.[2] It was a matter of continuous discussion, which apparently could never be absolutely settled, whether the admiralty and vice-admiralty courts were courts of record. The weight of legal opinion and also that of current practice were, however, against this contention, and in general it was assumed that by this term was meant solely the common law courts.[3] Less ambiguous than the Act of 1660 was the Staple Act of 1663, which provided that seizures for violations thereof could be condemned in any of the colonial courts or in any court of record in England.[4] Thus these two fundamental statutes gave an exclusive jurisdiction over certain seizures to the admiralty courts, while in other cases such power was conferred on the courts of record, and again in a third class these two kinds of courts were given concurrent authority.

[1] 12 Ch. II, c. 18, § i.

[2] *Ibid.* § xviii.

[3] Towards the end of 1688, a Dutch ship suspected of illegal trading was seized by the civil authorities in Jamaica. Evidence was offered that the vessel belonged to Dutch owners, that nearly all the seamen were Dutch, "and that they had both bought and sold here contrary to the Acts of Navigation." Before proceeding with the case, "Mr. Magragh, the King's Counsell moved the Board (the Jamaica Council) for directions how to proceed against the Dutch Shipp lately Seized for breach of the Acts of Navigation," stating that he believed there was "Evidence sufficient to prove Shee has Traded contrary to Law but that they cannot try her in the Admiralty by reason the Statute of the 12th of King Charles, the Second directs the Tryall to be in a Court of Record." He prayed for a special commission for the speedy trial of this seizure, which was granted, and shortly afterwards it was condemned. C. O. 140/4, ff. 256–257; C. C. 1685–1688, p. 621.

[4] 15 Ch. II, c. 7. See also 22 & 23 Ch. II, c. 26, §§ x, xi.

During the Interregnum, admiralty courts had been erected
in some of the West Indian colonies and had been used for
condemning both prizes of war and also foreign ships
found trading to the English colonies.   The prolongation of
the Spanish War after 1660 and the provisions of the Navigation Act of that year made it necessary to continue this
jurisdiction in America.   In 1661, Edward Doyley, the
Governor of Jamaica, was instructed to settle 'Judicatories
for civil affairs and admiralty,'[1] and in 1662 the Duke of
York's powers as Lord High Admiral were extended to
England's foreign possessions in Africa and America.[2]   Accordingly, when in this year Lord Windsor was appointed
Governor of Jamaica, he was instructed by the Crown to
cause to be held courts of admiralty by such judges as
should be commissioned for that purpose by the Duke of
York.[3]   But in the following year, when Lord Willoughby
was appointed Governor of the Caribbee Islands, the Crown
gave him authority 'as High Admiral to constitute courts
for marine causes,' together with 'powers of Vice-Admiral
to execute martial law and expel by force all intruders.'[4]
This commission unquestionably infringed upon the authority previously granted to the Duke of York as Lord High
Admiral of the colonies, and led to some difficulties.

[1] C. C. 1661–1668, no. 22.

[2] *Ibid.* no. 245.

[3] *Ibid.* no. 259; C. O. 1/16, nos. 35, 36.

[4] C. C. 1661–1668, no. 478.   In the preceding year, 1662, when Lord
Willoughby received a grant of the Caribbee Islands, 'the office of High
Admiral of said islands, with the jurisdictions, liberties, and profits thereto
belonging," had been specifically excepted.   *Ibid.* no. 387.

Shortly after his arrival in Barbados, Willoughby wrote to the Secretary of State, Sir Henry Bennet, that he had heard that the Duke of York had appointed Colonel Barwicke his Vice-Admiral, which he could only conceive to be some mistake, as his own commission from the King created him Vice-Admiral in those seas with power to hold courts of admiralty. He then added that he would desist from acting under his commission until receipt of further orders, and that he had written to the Duke of York, praying for a commission from him and craving pardon for his neglect in not having made this request before.[1] At the same time, Lord Willoughby also wrote to Clarendon, entreating his favor with the Duke of York on account of the gross mistake that he had made in not taking a commission as Vice-Admiral from him as well as from the King, and exculpating himself on the ground that he did not know of the enlargement of the Duke of York's powers until he had arrived in Barbados.[2] Accordingly, in future, the authority of the Duke of York was specifically recognized in the commissions issued by the Crown to the royal governors. Therein they were appointed Vice-Admirals with power to establish admiralty courts, but this authority was to be exercised according to such commissions, directions, and instructions as they should receive from the Duke of York.[3] He issued separate commissions appointing the colonial governors his Vice-Admirals.[4]

[1] *Ibid.* no. 617.   [2] Bodleian, Clarendon MSS. 81, ff. 5, 6.

[3] See the instructions and commissions of Sir Thomas Modyford in 1664 and of Sir Thomas Lynch in 1671. C. C. 1661–1668, nos. 656, 664; C. O. 1/18, 20; C. O. 138/1, ff. 88–95.

[4] See, *e.g.*, the Duke of York's commission of Jan. 26, 1667, constituting

Except naturally in the case of New York,[1] which was the Lord High Admiral's proprietary dominion, this authority was granted only to the royal governors, and not to the officials of the proprietary and charter colonies. Nor was any attempt made at this time to extend the English admiralty jurisdiction over these semi-independent communities and to give its agents authority within them.[2] Whenever courts of this nature were erected within these colonies, the power to do so was based upon the vague provisions of the original colonial charters, which in some cases might be construed as conferring upon the patentees jurisdiction in admiralty matters. In Maryland, his "Lo^{pps} Admirall" exercised such authority as was vested in Lord Baltimore by virtue of the charter of 1632.[3] In Massachusetts, the General Court ordered in 1674 that all admiralty cases should be determined by the Court of Assistants without a jury, unless the court should see cause to the contrary.[4] The

William, Lord Willoughby, Vice-Admiral of the Caribbee Islands. C. C. 1661–1668, no. 1389.

[1] When Governor of New York, Andros had a commission as Vice-Admiral, but the Duke of York reserved the right to appoint the judge, registrar, and marshal of the admiralty court. In 1678, Andros was given authority to appoint these three officials. In the same year, Andros stated that the admiralty jurisdiction had been exercised by special commission or by "the Court of Major and Aldermen at New-Yorke." C. O. 155/1, ff. 18–33, § ii; N. Y. Col. Doc. III, pp. 260–262, 268; C. C. 1677–1680, pp. 237, 238.

[2] In 1680, Randolph urged the necessity of issuing an admiralty commisson covering Massachusetts, on account of the number of prizes brought there. C. C. 1677–1680, pp. 487–490; Toppan, Randolph III, pp. 56–61.

[3] Calvert Papers I, pp. 268, 269, 279, 287.

[4] Mass. Col. Rec. IV, Part II, p. 575. In 1680, Governor Bradstreet stated that this court had jurisdiction in admiralty cases "without a Jury according to the Sea Laws." C. O. 1/44, 60i.

exercise of this jurisdiction, Randolph claimed, was one of the many instances in which Massachusetts had exceeded the authority granted by the charter.[1] In addition, some of the other colonies of this group also occasionally used the admiralty jurisdiction.[2]

Thus the English Admiralty confined its authority to the crown colonies. Admiralty courts were at this time erected in all of these governments, except Virginia. In answer to the query of the English authorities about the existence of such a court there, Governor Berkeley stated in 1671: "In Twenty Eight yeares There has been neuer one prize brought into theis Country. Soe that there is noe neede of

---

[1] Toppan, Randolph III, pp. 229, 230, 232–235; C. C. 1681–1685, pp. 440, 441, 445, 446.

[2] In reply to the English government's query on this point, Governor Peleg Sanford of Rhode Island stated in 1680: "Wee have made provision to act according to the Lawes of England as neare as the constitution of our place will bear, havinge but little occasion thereofe." C. O. 1/44, 58 i; C. C. 1677–1680, pp. 523, 524. On the same occasion, Governor Leete of Connecticut stated that they had little traffic abroad and hence had "small occasion" for an admiralty court and so had none, but that such cases were left to the Court of Assistants. Conn. Col. Rec. III, pp. 294, 300, 301; C. C. 1677–1680, pp. 576–578. At this time also, Governor Winslow of New Plymouth wrote: "Wee doe not find Admiralty jurisdiction granted us," nor have we presumed to erect a court of admiralty, though we have sometimes occasion for it on account of the prizes brought into our harbors. In these cases, he said, they took bonds to bring the cause to a speedy trial in some court of admiralty established by the King in England or elsewhere. C. O. 1/44, 55 i; C. C. 1677–1680, pp. 522, 523. In the Bermudas, under the Company's rule, there was no court of admiralty, but the Governor and Council determined maritime causes when the occasion presented itself. Lefroy II, pp. 332, 429, 433; C. C. 1677–1680, pp. 393, 394. An Admiralty Court was also erected in South Carolina. C. C. 1685–1688, pp. 451, 452.

a pticular Court for that concerne."[1] Prior to 1688, there was no special admiralty court in this colony, and cases involving breaches of the laws of trade were tried by the General Court and also by the county courts.[2] Until toward the end of the Restoration period, up to the time when the charters of the New England colonies were revoked, the English admiralty jurisdiction was practically exclusively exercised in the West Indian colonies. It was upon the experience and precedents of the past twenty years in those colonies that admiralty courts were then erected in New England.[3] When the government of New Hampshire was taken over by the Crown, its Governor, Edward Cranfield, was appointed Vice-Admiral and an Admiralty Court was established.[4] The same authority was vested in the representatives of the Crown in Massachusetts and, on July 5, 1686, was held the first session of the royal Admiralty Court there.[5]

Shortly after the Restoration, admiralty courts were es-

[1] C. O. 1/26, 77 i.

[2] Although the Governor of Virginia, Lord Howard of Effingham, had a commission as Vice-Admiral, the seizures for illegal trading made in 1686 by the officers of the navy were tried with juries by the General Court or by the county courts.   C. O. 1/62, 20 ii, vi, viii.   See also P. A. Bruce, Institutional History of Virginia I, pp. 697–700.

[3] On the New York Admiralty Court at this time, see C. C. 1685–1688, pp. 228, 261, 306, 461, 467; Toppan, Randolph IV, pp. 96–98, 125, 126.

[4] C. C. 1681–1685, pp. 200, 307, 368, 369, 698.

[5] Letter-Book of Samuel Sewall in Mass. Hist. Soc. Coll. 6th Series I, p. 34.   After the revocation of the Bermuda charter, such a court was also established there.   In 1687, Governor Robinson wrote to Blathwayt that he had appointed as its Judge one Green, "a pretended Lawer yᵉ best I could provide."   C. O. 1/60, 88; C. C. 1685–1688, pp. 392, 393.

tablished in Jamaica [1] and in Barbados [2] by their respective
Governors, in virtue of the authority vested in them by the
Duke of York. When the Leeward Islands were separated
from Barbados, their Governor was appointed Vice-Admiral,
and a similar court was established in that jurisdiction.[3] As
a general rule,[4] the governors appointed the officials of these

[1] In 1662, the Governor of Jamaica, Lord Windsor, established a Court
of Admiralty, of which William Michell, one of the Council, was appointed
Judge. C. C. 1661–1668, nos. 355, 379, 810. The early records of this
Court are preserved in the Public Record Office, Admiralty Court, Miscellanea 959. See also C. O. 1/19, 271; C. C. 1661–1668, no. 942.

[2] In addition to the Court of Admiralty, there was in existence in Barbados a Court of Exchequer for the trial of revenue cases. In 1669, a
vessel was tried in this Court for illegal trading. C. O. 1/24, 42; C. C.
1669–1674, p. 15. In 1681, although not so instructed, the Governor,
Sir Richard Dutton, revived this Court of Exchequer. The Lords of
Trade approved of this step. C. C. 1681–1685, pp. 179–181, 216.

[3] Sir Charles Wheler, the Governor, so reported in 1671. C. O. 1/27,
52; C. C. 1669–1674, pp. 288, 291. But his successor, William Stapleton,
wrote in 1672 that there was no court of this nature because, although he
had been constituted Vice-Admiral, he had not received "any orders or
instructions from his Royal highnesse high admirall of England." C. O.
1/29, 141; C. C. 1669–1674, p. 392. In 1676, Stapleton made the same
report. C. O. 1/38, 65; C. C. 1675–1676, pp. 497–502. In 1677, the desired
commission from the Duke of York was sent, and shortly thereafter admiralty courts were erected, when required, in the separate islands under
his government. C. C. 1677–1680, pp. 152, 244, 245; C. O. 155/1, ff. 4, 5.

[4] There were a few isolated exceptions in which the appointment was
made in England. Such was Barwicke's in Barbados under Lord Willoughby, which has already been mentioned. C. C. 1661–1668, no. 617;
Bodleian, Clarendon MSS. 81, ff. 5, 6. In 1665, Sir Thomas Modyford,
the Governor of Jamaica, appointed George Reid Advocate-General in the
Admiralty, 'in pursuance of an order bearing date at Whitehall 20th day of
February 1665.' C. C. 1661–1668, no. 1662. Cf. no. 1092. In 1680, Governor Atkins of Barbados complained that the Registrar of the Admiralty
had been appointed by patent in England. C. C. 1677–1680, pp. 532–536.

courts — the judges, registrars, marshals, and advocates;[1] and, in some instances, they even sat as judges themselves.[2]

During the period under consideration, there was no regular appeal to England from the decisions of these courts. This led to occasional injustice, as the colonial tribunals were decidedly lacking in legal knowledge and experience.[3] The only method of seeking redress was to petition the King and to trust to the Privy Council ordering a reversal of the colonial sentence. Thus, in 1671, the ship of one Rabba Couty, a Jewish resident of New York, although provided

---

[1] The Governor of the Leeward Islands, Sir William Stapleton, appointed the Deputy-Governors of the separate islands to be Judges of the Admiralty. C. O. 1/57, 51; C. O. 1/58, 83 i.   Governor Modyford of Jamaica appointed his brother, Sir James, Chief Judge of the local Admiralty Court.   C. C. 1661–1668, no. 1689.

[2] In 1666, Governor Willoughby of Barbados wrote that he had erected a Court of Admiralty and 'himself sat as judge.' C. C. 1661–1668, no. 1246.   In 1682, Sir Richard Dutton, the Governor, also sat as Judge in this Court.   C. C. 1681–1685, pp. 334, 417–419, 552.

[3] Already at this time these courts and those of the common law engaged in disputes as to the extent of their respective jurisdictions.   Such altercations had been common in England and were later, after England had extended the admiralty jurisdiction over all the colonies, of frequent occurrence in the continental colonies.   W. T. Root, The Relations of Pennsylvania with the British Government, pp. 96 et seq.   In 1679, the Barbados Assembly wrote to their agents in London that the admiralty jurisdiction should be regulated, as this Court assumed "power to determine of things done upon land, & even to proceed upon penall Statutes to the Great Discouragement & terror of people tradeing to this place." C. O. 31/2, ff. 339–341; C. C. 1677–1680, p. 352.   In 1680, the Governor of Jamaica, Lord Carlisle, was instructed to see that in future no parish should extend into the sea beyond the high-water mark, because by former laws the parishes were so bounded as to encroach on the admiralty. C. O. 138/3, ff. 447 et seq.; C. C. 1677–1680, pp. 624, 625.

with a pass from Governor Lovelace of that colony, was condemned by the Jamaica Admiralty Court on the ground that Couty was not a denizen. Couty's complaint to the English authorities was in due course referred to the Council for Trade and Plantations, which reported strongly against the legality of the sentence, and accordingly the King ordered that the confiscated property be restored.[1]

The question of allowing such appeals arose on several other occasions, but was opposed by the colonies as subversive of their government;[2] and, on their side, the English authorities as a rule cautiously refrained from interfering with decisions of the colonial courts.[3] Toward the end of this period, however, a system of appeals was being informally established. In 1686, one Thomas Cook of Ireland petitioned the King, stating that his ship, the *O'Brien*, had been seized by Captain St. Lo of H.M.S.

[1] C. C. 1669–1674, pp. 434–436, 453.

[2] In 1673, on the Governor of Jamaica putting the question whether there should be allowed an appeal from the Admiralty Court to the King or the Court of Delegates in England, the Jamaica Council unanimously decided 'that it would prove of ill consequence and tend to the subversion of the Government if once admitted, and that there never had been any such precedent of an appeal allowed, either in this island or any of his Majesty's dominions beyond the seas.' C. C. 1669–1674, p. 527.

[3] In 1675/6, the English Court of Admiralty in part reversed the sentence of the Jamaica Admiralty Court, but on an appeal being taken, the Commissioners of Appeals in Cases of Reprisals ruled against this decision, stating that they conceived they had nothing before them but "to take Care that what had been Judicially done in Jamaica might not be overthrowne by the Proceedings here," and that they had left "all the proceedings of that Island in their full force and Validity; And the rather because no Regular Appeale had been brought or entred against those Proceedings." P. C. Cal. I, pp. 648–650.

Dartmouth, and on trial had been unjustly condemned in the Nevis Admiralty Court.[1] This petition was referred to the Lords of Trade, who in turn sought the opinion of Sir Thomas Exton, the English Admiralty Judge. He reported [2] that in his opinion the seizure was not warranted by law,[3] and "altho there may not in Strictness of Law Ly any appeale, yet *ex speciali gratia* of his majesty, he may admitt ye complaynants to except ag^t this Judgment: and with sub-

[1] C. C. 1685–1688, p. 257.

[2] C. O. 1/58, 83 viii.

[3] At the trial held in the Nevis Admiralty Court, Captain St. Lo demanded the condemnation of the vessel on the ground that it was not free and qualified to trade to the colonies. The evidence was undeniable that the ship was foreign-built, that her destination was Jamaica, that part of the cargo consisted of 60 chests of candles which could not legally be imported directly from Ireland, and that the owner had ordered the sale of the vessel and cargo in Jamaica. C. O. 1/57, 51; *ibid.* 1/58, 83 i. Exton based his opinion that the condemnation was illegal on the fact that the seizure had been made nearly 1000 miles from Jamaica and out of sight of any of the colonies and that, as no goods had been imported, consequently no law had been transgressed. *Ibid.* 1/58, 83 vi, viii. Other English authorities agreed with Exton as to the illegality of the condemnation. *Ibid.* 1/58, 83 ii–vii. At the same time, this Nevis court also tried another seizure of St. Lo's, the *Ester* of Dublin. St. Lo first charged that the vessel was unfree, but it was established to the satisfaction of the Court that it had been built in Ireland and that no alien owned any part of it. This complaint was dismissed, and then St. Lo claimed that the vessel had imported candles directly from Dublin in violation of the Staple Act of 1663. In ans er, the captain of the seized ship stated that the vessel had been seized on the high seas, and that, as no importation had been made, the law had not been violated. The Court sustained the captain and freed the ship. *Ibid.* 1/57, 51; *ibid.* 1/58, 83 i. It should be remembered that, while in this case there might have been some doubts as to the intent to trade to the English colonies, in the former case not only was there none, but in addition the vessel was unfree.

mission to your Honors for ye security of navigation and trade it may seem necessary, for when those Admiraltyes find there is a superior power to inspect their sentences & so to confirme or reuerse, they wilbe more carefull to follow the rules of Law and so administer justice impartially." Exton further added that he had seen judgments of the other colonial admiralty courts which seemed to him very unjust, but which he could not redress, "there lying no appeale hither." In such cases, he had advised the injured parties to petition the King, and he now advised that appeals from the colonial admiralty courts be received, calling attention to the fact that even from the English High Court of Admiralty could an appeal be taken. On the strength of this report, it was decided that the appeal in this case should be heard by the King in Council.[1] Ultimately in the following year, after both sides had been heard, the appeal was dismissed and the judgment of the Nevis court was confirmed.[2] In other cases also at this time, if it appeared on investigation that the facts warranted it, an appeal was allowed from the colonial courts.[3]

---

[1] *Ibid.* 153/3, ff. 232, 233; C. C. 1685–1688, p. 268. According to the usual procedure in appeals from colonial courts to the Privy Council, which still is maintained, the petitioner had to deposit security, in this case £1000.

[2] C. O. 153/3, f. 233; C. C. 1685–1688, p. 390.

[3] In 1687, Captain Talbot, R.N., was by Order in Council allowed to appeal from the decision of the Jamaica Admiralty Court in the case of the *Swallow*, which had been seized by him, but then acquitted "as a Ship free to trade to all parts within the Tropicks." C. O. 1/60, 40, 40i; C. C. 1685–1688, p. 365. In 1687, the ship *Good Intention*, which had been seized by Captain St. Lo and subsequently condemned in the Antigua Admiralty Court, was on arrival in England arrested by its former owner John Kir-

These West Indian admiralty courts were largely used for condemning prizes seized from the enemy. Jamaica was the centre of a large number of lawless privateers — the buccaneers of romantic glamour — who, often under the protection of legal commissions issued for this purpose, preyed upon Spanish commerce. In many instances they brought their booty for condemnation to the Jamaica Admiralty Court.[1] Later, during the Dutch and French wars, these courts were used for the trial of more legitimate prizes.[2] But, in addition, a not inconsiderable number of seizures for illegal trade were tried in these courts.[3] There was considerable uncertainty and a number of disputes about the scope of their jurisdiction in this respect, and the practice varied in the different courts. Unfree ships — that is, vessels not conforming as to crew, build, and ownership to the provisions of the Navigation Acts —

wan. The case was tried in the English Admiralty Court, which decided in favor of Kirwan, but, as it was not a court of appeal, this decree was ineffective. Kirwan then petitioned the King for permission to appeal, which was granted. After a careful investigation of the facts by the Lords of Trade and a hearing of the arguments of counsel, the Privy Council confirmed the sentence in favor of St. Lo.   C. C. 1685–1688, pp. 378, 381, 382, 384, 398; C. O. 153/3, ff. 275, 276.

[1] Of these condemnations the Crown was entitled to one-fifteenth and the Lord High Admiral to one-tenth.   C. C. 1661–1668, nos. 446, 1062.

[2] Cf. Cal. Dom. 1675–1676, p. 8.

[3] Some of these have already been referred to. Such a case evidently also came before the Jamaica Admiralty Court, when Sir Charles Lyttelton was Judge, on Jan. 25, 1664. Public Record Office, Admiralty Court, Miscellanea 959. See also the instructions issued to Governor Lord Windsor in 1662 in C. C. 1661–1668, no. 259, and the cases referred to in C. C. 1685–1688, pp. 99, 204.

when seized by officers of the navy, were by the statute made triable in the admiralty courts. But the question arose, whether or no such courts had jurisdiction, if the seizure had been made by the navy within a port and not on the high seas.

The governors not infrequently preferred that in such instances the trial should be in the common law courts, in which case on condemnation they would be entitled to one-third of the proceeds, whereas nothing would accrue to them if the verdict were rendered by the admiralty courts. On the other hand, apart from any other reasons, the officers of the navy preferred the admiralty courts as, in case of condemnation there, they received one-half of the proceeds, instead of the third to which the informer or seizer was entitled from the common law courts.[1] Furthermore,

[1] In 1686, after trial of the case, John White, Judge of the Jamaica Admiralty Court, ordered the dismissal of the *Swallow*, an unfree vessel seized in port by Captain Talbot, R.N., partly on the ground that the Admiralty had jurisdiction only over seizures made at sea. Lieutenant-Governor Molesworth wrote to William Blathwayt that Talbot had lost the case because he had libelled the ship in the Admiralty, "as if she had been taken at Sea," whereas she was taken in port, and also because he had not positively asserted the time of seizure. 'On this nicety' judgment was given against Talbot, Molesworth said, and then added that the case should have been tried in a common law court with a jury. A few months later, Molesworth again wrote to Blathwayt on this subject, stating that Talbot would not have lost the case had he proceeded correctly, but 'whether it was that he scorned to bring himself forward as an informer, or coveted a larger share than belonged to him, I cannot say, but certain it is that though the ship was taken in harbour, he libelled her as if taken at sea, thereby pretending unto half forfeit for himself and half for the King. Judgment was given against him, whereas had he brought his action at Common Law with a *tanquam* for the King and Governor as well as for himself, he would

in some instances, seizures made by the civil authorities were also tried in these courts.[1]

In general, the prosecuting officials greatly preferred to try seizures in the admiralty courts, as they were much more likely to find for the Crown. In cases of this nature,[2] they acted without juries, which in the common law courts were prone to be over-lenient toward illegal traders. Some of the jurymen might be engaged in the same devious pursuits. Moreover, the social conscience of the colonies was apt to omit smuggling from the list of the crimes. As a result, there was slowly developing the opinion that, in order to secure the effective enforcement of the colonial system, it would be necessary to establish admiralty courts in all the colonies and to give them jurisdiction over all breaches of the laws of trade and navigation. In 1680, Sir Henry Morgan[3] sent the English government the details of the trial by the Jamaica Admiralty Court of a vessel condemned for evading the local revenue laws. This verdict was com-

have had no difficulty.' *ibid.* 1/58, 64, 64i; *ibid.* 138/5, ff. 326–333; C. C. 1685–1688, pp. 303, 356, 357. For another interesting case at Nevis, in 1671, see C. C. 1669–1674, p. 233.

[1] *Cf.* C. C. 1669–1674, pp. 434, 435; C. C. 1681–1685, pp. 334, 417–419, 552; C. C. 1685–1688, pp. 525, 530.

[2] In 1680, in connection with a trial in the Nevis Admiralty Court for riot and murder at sea, the Governor, Sir William Stapleton, as Vice-Admiral, appointed the Judges, the indictment was made by a grand jury, and the prisoner was acquitted by a petty jury. C. O. 155/1, ff. 1–23; C. C. 1677–1680, pp. 570, 571.

[3] He was Judge of the Jamaica Admiralty Court, but when, at this time, as Deputy-Governor, he assumed charge of the government, he appointed John White to preside in his place. C. C. 1675–1676, pp. 342–344; C. C. 1681–1685, pp. 5, 6.

plained of bitterly, and strenuous efforts were being made to have it reversed in England.[1] Morgan insisted that the trial had been conducted fairly, and added that without the Admiralty Court 'the Acts of Navigation cannot be enforced, for it is hard to find unbiassed juries in the Plantations for such cases.' As an example, he cited the case of a vessel that had come directly from Ireland to Jamaica with several casks of Irish soap, on account whereof it was seized. The case was tried in the common law court, and the jury brought in a verdict for the defendant on the evidence of one witness, who testified under oath that soap was a food-stuff upon which a man could live for a month and that, as it could be considered under the category of provisions, it could legally be imported directly from Ireland under the Staple Act of 1663.[2] When such fantastic fictions and tortuous evasions [3] could impress a jury, it is not surprising that the imperial officials placed greater reliance on the admiralty courts. It was the futility of attempting to secure a verdict from a jury in even the clearest of cases that ultimately led to the extension of the admiralty courts throughout all the colonies.

The royal governors, in their position as vice-admirals,

[1] On this case, see C. C. 1677–1680, pp. 343, 344, 487, 552, 567, 568, 581, 627, 631, 639; P. C. Cal. I, p. 864; Brit. Mus., Stowe MSS. 2724, ff. 198, 200; C. O. 138/3, f. 292.

[2] C. C. 1677–1680, p. 487.

[3] In the case of the *Ester*, which was tried in 1686 in the Nevis Admiralty Court for importing candles directly from Ireland, the defence claimed that there was "an adjudged Case in Jameco that Candles Should bee taken as provision and the Ship Bringing them acquitted from her Seizure." C. O. 1/57, 51; *ibid.* 1/58, 83 i.

and the courts established in virtue of the authority thus vested in them were the direct agents of the English Admiralty in enforcing the laws of trade. In addition, as has been seen, the Admiralty was represented in the colonies by the officers of the men-of-war stationed there. Under the Navigation Act of 1660, it was their duty to seize unfree ships trading to the colonies.[1] Occasionally in the West Indies such seizures were made by them,[2] but no especial activity was displayed until the eighties, when the independent course of the New England traders threatened to make ineffective the carefully devised commercial code. The grave difficulties experienced at this time with Massachusetts gave an exaggerated significance to any reports of illegal trade in the other colonies. In 1682, the Commissioners of the Customs recommended that the ships of the navy, especially those sent to the colonies, should have instructions to seize vessels violating the Navigation Act;[3] and, in 1685, on the strength of a letter from Captain Jones of H.M.S. *Diamond* at Barbados, wherein was mentioned "an instance that contrary to Law foreign Vessels are per-

---

[1] In 1668, the Council of Trade suggested, among other means for suppressing illegal trade, that directions be given to the ships of the navy and to merchant vessels to arrest any ship trading to the colonies contrary to law. After looking into the matter, the Privy Council (the King being present) declared, early in 1669, that "his Majestys Shipps Of Course" have such commissions and that, if any merchant ships should desire them, "upon giueing Security (with other usuall formalityes)," the Duke of York was authorized to grant them. C. C. 1661–1668, no. 1884; *ibid.* 1669–1674, p. 6; P. C. Cal. I, p. 501.

[2] See, *e.g.*, C. C. 1669–1674, p. 233.

[3] *Ibid.* 1681–1685, p. 529.

mitted to trade there," they urged that such instructions be again sent.[1] Accordingly, Samuel Pepys, the Secretary of the Admiralty, was directed by an Order in Council to instruct the commanders of the ships of the navy on all the colonial stations to seize foreign vessels found trading there.[2] Immediately thereafter, the authority of these officers was considerably amplified, for they were also specifically instructed to seize as well such vessels as were found violating the other provisions of the trade laws.[3]

These renewed and extended orders led to considerable activity. In the West Indies, Captain St. Lo of H.M.S.

---

[1] C. O. 1/55, 75; *ibid.* 324/4, f. 141. The abstract in C. C. 1685–1688, pp. 26, 27 greatly exaggerates the statement of Jones. In consequence of information sent by Governor Stapleton of the Leeward Islands, Danby intended already in 1678 to speak to Secretary Pepys about procuring instructions for the men-of-war in the Leeward Islands and other colonies to assist the governors in seizing ships that kept out of their reach and loaded without making entry. Cal. Treas. Books, 1676–1679, p. 976.

[2] C. O. 324/4, f. 142; C. C. 1685–1688, p. 27; P. C. Cal. II, p. 81.

[3] P. C. Cal. II, pp. 85–88. In 1685, Henry Guy, on behalf of the Treasury, also wrote to William Blathwayt, requesting that copies of the detailed trade instructions issued to the governors might be forwarded to the Admiralty for distribution to the captains of ships serving in the colonies. C. C. 1685–1688, p. 77. In 1686, Captain St. Lo complained that the people in Boston, Massachusetts, would not "suffer any of the Kings Commanders to make Seizure of Shipps or goods for false, or irregular importacon or Exportacon unless they can assigne it as a Breach of the Act of ye 12th of his late Ma[ty] or have warrants from hence for making such Seizures." The Commissioners of the Customs reported that deputations from them, in pursuance of warrants from the Treasury, to such officers of the navy were "sufficient authority to seize by vertue of all the Plantacon Laws." Treasurer Rochester accordingly instructed them to issue such deputations to the ships of the navy in the colonies. Treas. Books, Out-Letters, Customs 10, f. 186.

Dartmouth was particularly conspicuous in such work.   On
one occasion, in 1686, three vessels seized by him were tried
in the Nevis Admiralty Court.[1]   At the same time, Captain
Talbot of H.M.S. *Falcon* was similarly occupied on the
Jamaica station.[2]   But this use of the navy was by no
means confined to the island colonies.   In 1683, Lord
Howard of Effingham, who had just been appointed
Governor of Virginia in succession to Lord Culpeper,
urged the necessity of sending a frigate to protect the
colony and to suppress pirates and illegal traders.   In
this connection, the Commissioners of the Customs reported to the Lords of Trade[3] that they had already
in 1682 advised the use of ships of the navy for this purpose, and that they favored the appointment of a ketch
to be permanently stationed in Virginia.[4]   The Lords of
Trade accordingly accepted Effingham's recommendation;
and, in 1684, the ketch *Quaker* under Captain Allen was sent
to Virginia on this service.   On her arrival, the Secretary
of Virginia wrote that he hoped she would protect the colony

[1] C. O. 1/57, 51; *ibid.* 1/58, 83 i.   Of these, one was proven to be free
and was condemned for violating the Staple Act of 1663.   The question of
St. Lo's authority to seize such an offender was not raised; it rested purely
on his instructions, not upon the statutes.

[2] *Ibid.* 138/5, ff. 199–219; C. C. 1685–1688, pp. 356, 357.

[3] C. C. 1685–1688, p. 529.

[4] Said vessel, they said, should receive instructions from them, and should
be under the orders of their customs officials in Virginia and Maryland,
subject naturally to the superior authority of the governors of these colonies.
In addition, they advised that a ketch be likewise sent to the West Indies,
and that the men-of-war at Jamaica should assist their officials in that
colony.

and would prevent the frauds too often practised there by the New England traders.[1] Captain Allen was, however, not only zealous, but somewhat over-punctilious in the execution of his duties, and soon found himself unpopular in a society not accustomed to a meticulously strict interpretation of the law. On December 29, 1685,[2] he wrote to the English authorities that the Virginians were very angry at his staying there and claimed that he had spoiled their trade, because he would not let them cheat the King. They called him, he added, 'old rogue and old dog,' and when they saw his ship, they said: "Here comes the devil's ketch."

In 1686, H.M.S. *Deptford* under Captain Crofts was sent to assist Captain Allen in preventing illegal trading to Virginia and Maryland.[3] His over-zealousness in seizing vessels on purely technical charges, when no fraud had been intended, together with apparently justified charges against him of attempts to levy blackmail on innocent traders,[4] quickly brought him into conflict with the local authorities. In 1687, Governor Howard registered with the English government formal charges, of which Pepys wrote, "I doubt many of them too justly brought;" and Crofts was ordered home to answer them.[5] The Governor was sustained,[6] and,

---

[1] C. C. 1681–1685, pp. 531, 557, 572, 658, 659.

[2] C. O. 1/60, 60 i; C. C. 1685–1688, p. 465.

[3] C. C. 1685–1688, p. 240.

[4] Regarding one of these charges of extortion, the Surveyor General, Patrick Mein, wrote in 1686 to Lord Howard, that he believed Crofts was guilty. C. O. 1/62, 20 xi.

[5] *Ibid.* 1/61, 60i; *ibid.* 1/62, 20, 20i–xv; C. C. 1685–1688, pp. 240, 372–374, 387, 388, 417, 444, 465–467, 495.

[6] C. C. 1685–1688, p. 555.

in 1688, Thomas Perry replaced Crofts as commander of H.M.S. *Deptford*. On December 31, 1688, Effingham issued to him detailed instructions about enforcing the laws of trade and navigation.[1] Perry was to inform himself of the statutes in question and was to procure for his own use a copy of the book of rates containing them; he was strictly to examine and search all ships that he might meet " in Cruseing or Saileing from Port to Port within his Ma^tys Dominion of Virginia or Province of Maryland "; and, while in port, he was to allow no ship to depart or enter without a permit from the Collector of the Customs.

In one of its phases, this quarrel between Crofts and Lord Howard illustrates a serious defect in the established administrative system. The fact that three of the great English executive departments were represented in the crown colonies by distinct and separate agents implied a division of authority, which inevitably led to disputes impairing the smooth running of the machinery. Legally, the royal governor was the supreme executive authority in the colony, but occasionally it was only after considerable difficulty and delay that he could make his will effective. The Treasury and Admiralty officials in the colonies at times thwarted his wishes and acted independently, trusting to secure the support of their immediate superiors in England, to whom they were directly responsible and whose influence would naturally outweigh that of the governor. In so far as the customs officials were concerned, such incidents were rare in the royal colonies. These officials were usually over-

[1] C. O. 1/63, 92.

awed by the superior status and dignity of the Governor, and hesitated to disobey him. But the officers of the navy were, in general, of much higher social rank than the customs officials and occupied posts of greater importance. Consequently they were much more independent, and friction between them and the governors was not an infrequent occurrence. Ships of the navy on colonial stations were placed under the orders of the royal governors,[1] but the captains at times refused to respect them, while the governors on their part occasionally arrogated to themselves greater authority than was warranted by their commissions.[2]

Captains Allen and Crofts, while on the Virginia and Maryland station, were subject to the commands of Governor Howard of Virginia. During the course of their bitter disputes, some of Crofts's officers complained to the Governor of ill usage on the part of their captain. Whereupon Lord Howard summoned Crofts to appear before him to decide these differences, and, on Crofts refusing to heed the summons, threatened to send him home in irons.[3] Crofts was supported in his refusal by his superior officer, Captain Allen, who claimed that Lord Howard had no authority to summon a naval officer before the Council at Jamestown. 'Such differences,' he claimed, 'should be submitted to the King, or tried by Court-martial,

---

[1] C. C. 1681–1685, pp. 757, 763.

[2] See, e.g., the claims of Governor Lynch in Jamaica. C. C. 1681–1685, pp. 428, 491–493, 597; nos. 1433, 1480–1484, 1711, 1935, 2032, 2044, 2051, 2055, 2060, 2063.

[3] Ibid. 1685–1688, pp. 372–374, 387, 388, 444, 465.

for I do not think the Council here competent to deal with affairs of the Navy.' [1]

Such quarrels, which cropped up every now and again, hampered the efficiency of the administrative system and interfered with the enforcement of the laws. They were a direct result of the triple system of control in England and the absence of an absolutely supreme central authority in the colony, which could make its will immediately effective. If such difficulties existed in the royal provinces, it is not surprising that far graver obstacles were encountered in the charter and proprietary governments. For in these quasi-independent jurisdictions there was no royal governor, and the local authorities viewed with suspicion and dislike all agents of the imperial government. They were over-prone to look upon every act of the customs officials and of the officers of the navy as an invasion of the liberties guaranteed by the colonial charters. The resulting friction,[2] while far more serious, was similar in its manifestations to that in the royal provinces. But it proceeded from a radically different cause. In the one case, the trouble was due to a defect in the administrative machinery, which could have been remedied by a slight readjustment. In the other, it was due to what was regarded by these self-governing communities as the intrusion of an alien authority within their limits;

---

[1] C. C. 1685–1688, pp. 466, 467. The Duke of Albemarle's commission as Governor of Jamaica gave him powers as Vice-Admiral to suspend the officers of the royal navy. *Ibid*. p. 293.

[2] This friction, especially in Massachusetts and Maryland, will be treated subsequently when describing the development of these colonies under the laws of trade and navigation.

and for this there was no corrective other than a revolutionary change in their political status. The difficulty in the crown colonies was superficial and largely personal; that in the charter and proprietary colonies was fundamental and in the fullest sense of the word political.

CHAPTER V

THE SLAVE-TRADE AND THE PLANTATION COLONIES

Classification of the colonies according to their imperial value — The demand for slaves in the West Indies — The English African Company — Dutch opposition to its trade — The complaints of Barbados against the Company — Its reorganization in 1672 — Opposition of the West Indian colonies to the Royal African Company — Its attempts to supply Spanish America — The interlopers.

THE English colonies of the Restoration period form themselves into varying groups depending upon the canon of classification that may be adopted. The geographical standard would roughly divide them, according to their configuration and location, into island and continental colonies; or, applying the more discriminating physiographic tests of climate, soil, and natural resources, would further separate them into a number of subdivisions. Obviously, such a classification would differ radically from one based upon the nature of their internal political organization. From this standpoint the colonies fall into three distinct groups: the royal provinces with their elective assemblies and crown-appointed governors; the proprietary colonies whose political organization was on a monarchical basis and closely resembled that of the crown colonies, the fundamental distinction being that the proprietor, not the King, appointed the governor; and thirdly, the charter colonies, which were in essence completely self-governing communities of a more or less democratic type. When judged, not by the character of their local political institutions, but from the standpoint of imperial public law and administration, the colonies again grouped themselves somewhat differently into two classes; first, the royal provinces, and secondly, the charter and proprietary colonies. In the former, the executive directly represented the Crown and brought the imperial government into immediate contact with the inhabitants. In the latter, this relationship was mediate, as the colonial charters interposed a proprietor or a corporation between the Crown and its subjects in these colonies. This was the general broad classification adopted by the English government in its routine work of colonial administration. Colonies so different institutionally as Connecticut from Pennsylvania, or as Rhode Island from Maryland, were placed together in one comprehensive group called the Proprieties.

For the purposes of this work, no one of these various classifications is available. In a study, which lays stress upon the economic features of the old Empire, and whose aim is to describe the commercial, not the political, system, the subdivision must necessarily be based upon different characteristics if it is to be at all significant. English colonial policy was dominated by economic considerations, and as has been pointed out, one of the chief advantages, if not the main one, anticipated from the movement of expansion, was the development of new sources of supply in America that would serve to free England from dependence upon foreign nations. The somewhat vague, yet clearly discernible, comprehensive aim of the English statesmen was to mould the colonies into a self-sufficing commercial Empire, of which each section should supplement the economic activities and resources of the others. Some of the colonies developed into such complementary economic units, while others equally conspicuously failed to answer this fundamental purpose of English policy. There were various gradations of complete and partial failure or success, but, in general, according to this canon the colonies divide themselves into two distinct groups.

The colonies, which in part or virtually completely failed to correspond with the aims and ideals of English policy, were those on the continent north of the line to be drawn later by Mason and Dixon. Conspicuous among them were the New England settlements which, owing to climate and resources similar to those of England, instead of supplementing the economic life of the metropolis, closely paralleled it in many phases of its activities. The same was true, and scarcely to a less extent, of New York, the Jerseys, and Pennsylvania. In general, these northern continental colonies with their temperate climate could not produce the exotic commodities desired in England. With the noteworthy exception of furs, the products of their fields, forests, and waters could as a rule not be profitably shipped for sale to the English markets; and, even if they could so have been, in many instances they were decidedly not wanted there as they competed with the interests of the landed class, then the predominant political force in England.

The other group consisted of such colonies, whose economic activities, instead of competing with those of England, supplemented and stimulated them. It was composed of the island colonies and of some on the continent. Occupying an isolated position in this group, and one so unique that it might be placed in a subdivision by itself, was Newfoundland. Neither in law, nor in practice, was Newfoundland as yet a full-fledged colony, although England exercised sovereignty over the southeastern section of the island. Apart from some rudimentary permanent settlements having no regular form of government, it consisted of a series of fishing stations, where the fishermen from the West of England gathered yearly during the summer months to procure their cargoes of cod-fish for the markets of Catholic Europe. It, however, well answered the aims of the English government; as a valuable nursery of seamen and as a source of sea power, it was from the imperial standpoint a valuable economic asset. Conspicuous among the other colonies of this group were the West Indies—Barbados, Jamaica, and the Leeward Islands—whose chief crop, sugar, was one of the mainstays of English commerce. In this group also may be placed the Bermudas and the Bahamas. Their economic importance was limited by their scant natural resources, but they were being valued more and more for their strategic position on main-travelled trade-routes. The colonies on the continent comprised in this group were especially Virginia and Maryland, whose staple product, tobacco, entered very largely into England's foreign trade. The settlements to the south of Virginia were still in a formative state and had as yet not found the path that brought them prosperity in the eighteenth century, when the rice of South Carolina and the tar and pitch of North Carolina formed important elements in England's colonial trade.

One feature of the economic structure of these sugar and tobacco colonies, which distinguishes them sharply from the northern continental communities, was that ultimately their resources were in varying degrees, yet to a predominant extent, developed by means of African slave labor. In Virginia and Maryland this outcome was witnessed only in the following century, but already at this time in the West Indies the large plantation cultivated by negroes was establishing itself as the normal type of production. In the sugar fields of Barbados at a most rapid pace, and more gradually elsewhere in the West Indies, white labor was being displaced by the negro slave.[1] The prosperity of these colonies was considered to depend upon this sytem of labor, and their demands for a cheap and abundant supply of African slaves

[1] In 1667, it was estimated that in 1643 there were in Barbados only 6400 negroes, as against more than 50,000 in 1666. (C. C. 1661–1668, no. 1657.) In his Description of Barbados, John Scott stated that in 1645 the colony had 5680 slaves and in 1667, 82,023. (Brit. Mus., Sloane MSS. 3662, ff. 54[a/b] of the volume reversed.) In 1668, Governor Willoughby stated that the total population was 60,000, of which 40,000 were negroes. (P. C. Cal. I, pp. 521, 522; C. C. 1661–1668, no. 1788.) Nicholas Blake in 1669 also estimated the slave population at 40,000. (C. C. 1699, pp. 589 et seq.) At this time, the number of negroes in the other colonies was far less. According to Governor Willoughby, in 1668 there were in Antigua only 700 and in Montserrat 300. (Ibid. 1661–1668, no. 1788; P. C. Cal. I, pp. 521, 522.) In 1670, it was estimated that Jamaica had 2500 negroes. (C. C. 1669–1674, pp. 52, 53.) In 1671, Governor Berkeley stated that Virginia had 2000 negro slaves. (C. O. 1/26, 77 i; Hening II, pp. 511–517.)

became increasingly insistent. The negroes were deemed, to use a contemporary expression, 'the strength and sinews of this western world.'[1] Their scarcity, according to Sir Thomas Lynch,[2] was 'the grand obstruction' in Jamaica and 'without them the Plantations will decline and the people be discouraged.' 'These settlements,' wrote Lieutenant-Governor William Willoughby of Barbados in 1666, 'have been upheld by negroes and cannot subsist without supplies of them.'[3] As the prosperity of the most valuable colonies was based upon the negro slave, the English government felt it incumbent to follow the lead of the other colonizing nations — of these, the country of Torquemada and Alba alone did not engage in this demoralizing trade — and to take steps that the colonial planter should not be dependent upon foreign traders for his essential supply of labor. Such dependence, it was logically held, would jeopard the entire imperial structure. The measures taken to obviate this apparently grave peril constituted an important feature of English colonial policy. The regulation of the African trade was an integral and organic part of the colonial system, and hence some account thereof is an essential preliminary to an examination of the development of the plantation colonies during this period.

The Portuguese and Spanish had made extensive use of this system of labor in developing their American dominions. Thanks to the negro's brawn and toil, tropical and sub-tropical America, where the climatic conditions debarred

[1] C. C. 1661–1668, no. 577.   [2] *Ibid*. no. 934.
[3] *Ibid*. no. 1281.   *Cf*. nos. 618, 756.

the Caucasian from strenuous physical labor, did not remain
an uncultivated desert.   These negroes were obtained from
West Africa, whose life until the abolition of the slave-trade
in the nineteenth century was intimately connected with
that of the plantation colonies in the New World. Up to
that time, in so far as Europe was concerned, "West African
history was the complement of West Indian." [1] In that
pestiferous region, slavery was a time-hallowed institution,
"bound up with the whole social and economic organization of West African society." [2]   The Europeans were thus
responsible only to the extent that they made use of an
already existing obnoxious system and aggravated its
inherent evils.   At times there were cases of kidnapping,
but the trade had its well-charted channels; and, as a
general rule, the slaves were procured by the European
traders from African dealers in barter for merchandize. [3]
By the middle of the seventeenth century the traffic was
on a firmly established and well-organized basis.   It scarcely
aroused any moral opposition and was generally regarded
as an unquestionably legitimate branch of commerce.   In
1684 was published anonymously a bitter attack on the
methods of the slave-trade and the treatment of the negroes
in the English West Indies, which was so comprehensive
and convincing in character as to amount to a condemnation of the institution of slavery itself. [4]   Four years later, a

[1] Lucas, Historical Geography, West Africa (2d ed.), p. 39.

[2] J. A. Tillinghast, The Negro in Africa and America (Am. Economic
Assoc. 1902), p. 88.

[3] Lucas, West Africa, pp. 70, 71.

[4] Philotheos Physiologus, Friendly Advice to the Gentlemen-Planters

similar protest was made by the Pennsylvania Quakers,[1] but these isolated voices called forth no echoing response from a completely unsympathetic and largely uncomprehending world.

Ever since the days of Henry VIII, the English had intermittently engaged in trading to Africa.[2] Elizabeth's Guinea Company had been followed by two others of Stuart creation,[3] but the main object of these early enterprises was to procure gold, ivory, wax, gum, and other African commodities. Until the successful introduction of the sugar cane in Barbados, Englishmen were but slightly concerned in the slave-trade. With the advent of the sugar industry there arose an insistent and steady demand for negro slaves,[4] which naturally greatly altered the nature of England's African trade. But slight success, however, was attained until the Restoration,[5] when a determined effort was made to obtain an important share of this lucrative commerce. Two objects were held in view. In the first place, the aim was to secure an adequate supply of slaves for the English colonies, thus freeing them from the danger of having to

of the East and West Indies, printed by Andrew Sowle in 1684. Sowle printed a number of books and pamphlets for the Quakers. A. C. Myers, Narratives of Early Pennsylvania, etc., p. 224.

[1] W. H. Smith, A Political History of Slavery I, p. 6; W. E. B. Du Bois, The Suppression of the African Slave-Trade, pp. 20, 21; E. R. Turner, The Negro in Pennsylvania, pp. 65, 66.

[2] W. R. Scott, Joint-Stock Companies to 1720, II, pp. 3–11.

[3] Beer, Origins, p. 220 n.; Certain Considerations Relating to the Royal African Company of England (London, 1680), p. 3.

[4] Beer, Origins, p. 415.

[5] W. R. Scott, op. cit. II, pp. 15–17.

rely upon foreign traders and also making the English Empire more self-sufficient. Furthermore, the purpose was to compete with the Dutch and other slave-traders in supplying the insatiable demands of Spanish America. The familiar economic arguments of the mercantilistic type were used to prove the national advantage of the trade.[1]

Owing to the intrenched position of the Dutch on the slave-coast and the peculiar conditions surrounding the trade, it could be carried on successfully by private individuals only if they were extensively supported and protected by their government. The sole other alternative was a monopolistic company with large resources. Outside of European waters armed commerce was still the rule, and there was scant likelihood that the Dutch would allow unprotected private merchants to trade peacefully on the slave-coast. Moreover, in order to facilitate commerce, trading stations had to be established, and forts also had to be erected to repel European enemies and to defend the traders against the savage tribes that sold the weaker enslaved races to the Europeans. Short of abandoning the traffic entirely to foreigners, the trade to Africa could have been left free and open to all Englishmen only if the government were to undertake its entire regulation and defence, sending out convoys to protect the traders and building and maintaining forts and stations. Such a course would have necessitated the assertion and maintenance of English sovereignty over portions of West Africa and would have led to

[1] Certain Considerations Relating to the Royal African Company of England (London, 1680), pp. 1–5.

interminable disputes and conflicts with the European powers interested in the slave-trade. Moreover, the finances
of a seventeenth-century government could not stand the
strain of so extensive an understanding. Even so restricted
as was then the scope of governmental activities, the expenditures were wont to exceed the income. Parliament
was chary in its grants, and the taxpayer was keenly sensitive to any additional burdens. Hence, as was customary in
such instances, recourse was had to the device of a privileged
company, to which was granted a monopoly of trade in
return for the great expense and risk necessarily involved
in an undertaking of this nature.[1]

Towards the end of 1660, the first African Company of
the Restoration era was formed with the Duke of York
at its head.[2] Charles II personally invested in this enterprise, which was energetically carried on.[3] But events soon
showed that the resources of a much more powerful and
wealthy organization were needed if England were to secure
a firm foothold in West Africa. The English Company was
bitterly opposed by the Dutch, who, during their protracted
war of independence from Spain, had succeeded in ousting
the Portuguese from West Africa and, as their successors,

[1] In 1663, the English African Company stated that in 1660 the trade
was carried on by individuals, who were a constant prey to the Dutch, 'and
were quite tired out of the trade by their great and frequent losses. . . .
So if his Majesty had not established a company the nation had probably
by this time been quite driven out of it.' C. C. 1661–1668, no. 618. See
also Beer, Origins, pp. 220–225.

[2] C. C. 1661–1668, no. 408.

[3] Ibid. nos. 120, 206. In 1662, the Company agreed to deliver 300 negroes
in Jamaica. Ibid. no. 287.

now claimed the slave-trade as their exclusive national preserve.[1] They treated all other European traders, even at unoccupied points on the West African coast, as intruders, and did not hesitate to use violence in expelling them. The first conspicuous act of aggression came, however, from the English. In 1661, Captain Robert Holmes, in command of a small naval force, seized some Dutch trading stations, to which England had a more or less valid claim.[2] In their turn, the Dutch stirred up the natives against the English and forcibly interfered with their commerce. In 1661 and 1662, two English ships were seized on the African coast by the Dutch and another was prevented from trading with the natives.[3] In order to cope with the powerful Dutch West India Company, England obviously needed a far stronger Company than that of 1660. Accordingly the patent of 1660 was surrendered; and, on January 10, 1663, a new charter was issued to the Company of Royal Adventurers trading to Africa, granting to it all of Africa from Sallee to the Cape of Good Hope and forbidding all other Englishmen to trade there.[4] Among the patentees, besides the Queen and other members of the royal family as well as a number of great noblemen, were the leading men occupied in colonial enterprises and their administration, such as Lord Berkeley, Sir George Carteret, Sir John Col-

---

[1] C. C. 1661–1668, nos. 467, 553.

[2] *Ibid.* nos. 177, 304, 316, 338. See also H. L. Schoolcraft, The Capture of New Amsterdam, in English Hist. Rev. XXII, pp. 684–686.

[3] C. C. 1661–1668, nos. 205, 383; P. C. Cal. I, pp. 328–330.

[4] C. C. 1661–1668, no. 408. See also Clarendon's Autobiography (Oxford, 1827) II, pp. 231–234.

leton, Sir Martin Noell, and Thomas Povey. The fact that the same group of men were prominent both in this Company and in the work of colonial expansion significantly shows how closely related were these two spheres of activity. The English African Company had the full support of the government, for not only were Charles II and his immediate family financially interested in its fortunes,[1] but it was regarded, not as a mere private enterprise, but as a quasi-public undertaking whose success was a question of grave national concern.

This enlarged company immediately proceeded vigorously to engage in the slave-trade, with the twofold purpose of supplying the English colonies and also Spanish America. In the way of the latter object stood serious difficulties. Cromwell's war with Spain had been inherited by the Restoration government, and desultory fighting still continued in the West Indies. Moreover, apart from the existence of an informal state of war, Spain strictly prohibited foreign vessels from trading to her colonies. The English government was anxious to settle the outstanding differences in order to gain admission to the Spanish colonial trade. But the means adopted were scarcely those best calculated to attain this end. In 1662, the Governor of Jamaica, Lord Windsor, was instructed to endeavor to obtain and preserve good correspondence with the Spanish colonies; but, if their governors refused his overtures, he was somewhat inconsistently authorized to settle such trade by force and by such acts as should seem most proper to oblige the

[1] C. C. 1661–1668, nos. 504, 508.

Spaniards to admit them to a free trade.[1]   As the governors
of Porto Rico and San Domingo absolutely denied such
intercourse, the Jamaica Council in 1662 determined to try
force.[2]   During the autumn of that year, an armed expedition from Jamaica successfully surprised the city of Santiago
in Cuba; and, early in 1663, another force captured and sacked
Campeche on the mainland.[3]   In great indignation Spain
protested against these assaults, and, to relieve the tension,
Sir Charles Lyttelton, upon whom the government of
Jamaica had devolved on Lord Windsor's departure, was
instructed in the future to forbid such undertakings.[4]
However effective in other ways exploits of this nature
might be, they assuredly were not likely to open the Spanish
colonial ports to English traders.

But if the English were not allowed access to the Spanish
dominions, this proposed trade in slaves might still be carried
on, provided the Spaniards were permitted to come to the
English colonies and to buy there the slaves that they
required.   On receipt of the above-mentioned royal orders
to desist from further hostilities, Lyttelton wrote to the
Secretary of State that he hoped soon to establish trade
relations with the Spaniards, especially in negro slaves,
which they could fetch from nowhere else so easily as from
Jamaica.[5]   Against such intercourse, however, stood the

[1] C. C. 1661–1668, no. 278.

[2] *Ibid.* no. 355.

[3] Heathcote MSS. (H.M.C. 1899), pp. 34, 35.   For full details, see C. H.
Haring, The Buccaneers in the West Indies, pp. 104–110.

[4] Heathcote MSS. pp. 88, 89; C. C. 1661–1668, nos. 441–443.

[5] C. C. 1661–1668, no. 566.

Navigation Act, which expressly prohibited foreign ships from trading to the English colonies. In 1662, some Spaniards had come to Barbados to procure negroes and were allowed to trade by the acting Governor despite the opposition of the Council.[1] In order to legalize such intercourse, recourse was now had to the Crown's disputed prerogative to dispense with Acts of Parliament. In 1663, Charles II issued orders permitting Spanish ships to trade to the English West Indies for the purpose of purchasing negroes.[2] In Barbados, some slight use was made of this permission,[3] but nothing could be effected in Jamaica, which was most conveniently located for this purpose.

In 1664, Sir Thomas Modyford, a prominent colonial,

[1] *Ibid*. no. 417.

[2] C. O. 1/17, 13; *ibid*. 389/4, ff. 1 *et seq.*; P. C. Register Charles II, III, ff. 336–338; P. C. Cal. I, pp. 345–349; C. C. 1661–1668, nos. 414–417, 425, 426. See also the instructions issued to Willoughby in 1663. C. O. 1/17, 49; P. C. Cal. I, p. 360; C. C. 1661–1668, no. 489. It was ordered that every negro so exported, except such as had already been contracted for in England with the African Company, should pay a duty of ten pieces of eight, of which each was reckoned equivalent to four shillings. In 1663, the African Company stated that they had sent a ship with 160 negroes to the Spanish Main, and complained to Whitehall that Lord Willoughby had exacted £320 on these slaves from their factors in Barbados. Willoughby was ordered to make restitution, and he was instructed that the duty of ten pieces of eight should be levied only on 'negroes bought upon the place by Spanish subjects or others, to be transported into foreign dominions, and not otherwise.' C. C. 1661–1668, nos. 583, 585.

[3] In September and October of 1662, and again in May of 1663, the President of the Council, Humphrey Walrond, allowed some Spaniards to trade, receiving from them in return comparatively large sums of money, which he agreed to hand over to Governor Willoughby on the latter's arrival in Barbados. C. C. 1661–1668, nos. 417, 434, 569; C. O. 31/1, f. 78.

was appointed Governor of Jamaica with instructions to preserve good correspondence with the Spaniards and to do
everything to encourage the trade of the African Company,
whose interests he had represented in Barbados.[1] Modyford
accordingly opened negotiations with the Governor of San
Domingo.[2] At first, favorable answers to these overtures
were received,[3] but ultimately they were rejected.[4] The
difficulties in the way were well described in a despatch
of one of the ablest of the Restoration colonial officials to
the English Secretary of State. On May 25, 1664,[5] the President of the Jamaica Council, Thomas Lynch, wrote that
it was not in the power of the Spanish governors to allow
the English to trade in their colonies, 'nor will any necessity
or advantage bring private Spaniards to Jamaica, for we
and they have used too many mutual barbarisms to have a
sudden correspondence. . . . Nothing but an order from
Spain can gain us admittance or trade, especially while
they are so plentifully and cheaply supplied with negroes
by the Genoese, who have contracted to supply them with
24,500 negroes in seven years.'[6] Even if this bitter antagonism of the Spaniards — the inevitable fruit of the
exploits of the lawless Jamaica buccaneers — could have

---

[1] C. C. 1661–1668, no. 664.   [2] Ibid. no. 739.   [3] Ibid. no. 762.
[4] Ibid. no. 744.   [5] Ibid.

[6] At this time it was also said : 'The fortune of trade here none can guess,
but all think that the Spaniards so abhor us, that all the commands of
Spain and necessity of the Indies will hardly bring them to an English port ;
if anything effect it, negroes are the likeliest.' C. C. 1661–1668, no. 811.
For an account of the Assiento of these two Genoese, Grillo and Lomelin, see
Georges Scelle, La Traite Négrière aux Indes de Castille I, pp. 495–549.

been overcome, no extensive trade relations could have been established at this time, because, as a result of the inveterate opposition of the Dutch, the English African Company was scarcely able to obtain enough negroes to satisfy the demands of the English colonies.

The African Company planned to procure three thousand negroes yearly for the English colonial market, which they offered to sell in lots, "as hath been customary," at £17 the head.[1] This method of selling in lots [2] was not adapted to the requirements of the tobacco colonies, where there was not sufficient capital available for such wholesale purchases,[3] and hence the relations of the Company were at the outset confined solely to the richer sugar colonies, whose demands were far greater. Already in December of 1662, the chief of these colonies, Barbados, petitioned the King that the trade to Africa should be free, or else that they might be furnished with negroes by the Royal Company at the same

[1] Declaration of the Company of Royal Adventurers of England trading into Africa (London, 1667), pp. 8, 9. The buyer had the option of paying these £17 in Spanish pieces of eight, which were valued for this purpose at four shillings, or in colonial produce — sugar, cotton, and indigo. Twenty-four hundred pounds of muscovado sugar was computed as equivalent to £17.

[2] In her novel, Oroonoko, or the Royal Slave, Mrs. Aphra Behn, who had lived in Surinam, has left a vivid description of this system. Works (London, 1871) V, p. 82.

[3] In 1663, Governor Charles Calvert of Maryland wrote to Lord Baltimore: "I haue endeauored to see if I could find as many responsable men that would engage to take a 100 or 200 neigros euery yeare from the Royall Company at that rate mentioned in y^r Lo^{pps} letter but I find wee are nott men of estates good enough to vndertake such a buisnesse, but could wish wee were for wee are naturally inclin'd to loue neigros if our purses would endure it." Calvert Papers I, p. 249.

prices as they had been by the private merchants.[1] Circumstances completely beyond the control of the Company prevented it from satisfying the colonial demand.

When, in the summer of 1663, the English ships arrived on the African coast, they had to encounter the determined hostility of the Dutch. The native chiefs were bribed not to trade with the English and even to attack them.[2] The Dutch, so ran the complaint to the English government,[3] 'have endeavoured to drive the English Company from the coast, have followed their ships from port to port, and hindered them coming nigh the shore to trade. . . . Had it not been for the countenance of some of his Majesty's ships, to give the Company a respect in the eyes of the natives and preserve their forts, the Company had ere this been stripped of their possessions and interest in Africa.' The English Envoy to the United Provinces, Sir George Downing, was instructed to demand full and speedy satisfaction for these injuries and also assurances that they would not be repeated.[4] As no redress could be obtained, Captain Robert Holmes with a small squadron was sent by the government to Africa to protect the English trade. During the opening months of 1664, he captured a number of the Dutch Company's

---

[1] C. C. 1661–1668, no. 392.

[2] *Ibid*. no. 507.

[3] *Ibid*. no 618. See also Heathcote MSS. (H.M.C. 1899), pp. 146, 149, 150.

[4] C. C. 1661–1668, no. 545. On Sept. 25, 1663, the African Company wrote to Downing that they were "extreamly Sensible" of their obligation to him for prosecuting their complaints against the Dutch. Brit. Mus., Add. MSS. 22,920, f. 19.

important forts and inflicted severe damage.[1] He then sailed across the Atlantic to attack the American possessions of the Dutch West India Company, of which the chief, New Netherland, was destined shortly to become an English colony. During his absence, the famous Dutch admiral, De Ruyter, arrived with a strong force on the African coast and, in addition to quickly nullifying the acts of Holmes, he captured with one exception all the English posts as well.[2] Thus events were gradually bringing about another armed struggle between England and the United Provinces. In reality a state of war existed already in 1664, but, pending abortive negotiations for a peaceful solution, it was not declared until the following year.

This war was only one manifestation of the deep-seated economic rivalry between the English and Dutch nations and, fundamentally, it was due to the fact that the Dutch blocked many of the paths over which England had to pass in order to attain her full economic development. More specifically, the immediate cause of the war was the determination of the United Provinces to maintain inviolate their monopoly of the slave-trade and to prevent the English from establishing themselves in West Africa.[3]

[1] C. C. 1661–1668, nos. 646, 697, 737, 829. Under date of Sept. 29, 1664, Pepys recorded: "Fresh news come of our beating the Dutch at Guinny quite out of all their castles almost, which will make them quite mad here at home sure. And Sir G. Cartaret did tell me, that the King do joy mightily at it."

[2] Lefèvre Pontalis, John de Witt I, p. 316.

[3] On Dutch interference with England's African and East Indian trades, see Sir George Downing, A Reply (London, 1665), pp. 19, 21, 42, 43; and A Catalogue of the Damages for which the English demand Reparation

Finally in 1667, after some memorable fighting, famous in the annals of naval warfare, peace was concluded at Breda on the general basis of each power retaining its conquests. Thus, in America, Lord Willoughby's colony of Surinam was ceded to the Dutch and New Netherland became part of the English Empire. In West Africa, the English lost Cormantine, but instead gained Cape Coast Castle. Far more important, however, was the Dutch renunciation of their exclusive claims in this region. In the future, the English Company could pursue its course unhampered by the continuous prospect of violent opposition from the Dutch.[1] Just as the first Dutch war under Cromwell had put an end to the exclusive claims of that trading nation in the Far East and allowed England to develop her East Indian trade,[2] so this second armed conflict opened up the unoccupied points of the West African coast to the English merchants.

(London, 1664). From Paris, April $\frac{7}{17}$, 1664, Lord Holles, the English Ambassador, wrote to Downing: "I looke for lesse kindnes from your Minheers that you deale with, who vse vs very coursely euery where as all my intelligence from England tells me, refusing vs y^e restitution of Poleron, & denying vs trading in all y^e coast of Guinee (wch can Signify nothing else but that they meane to quarrell $\dot{w}^{th}$ vs) & vpon all occasions falling foule vpon y^e English." Brit. Mus., Add. MSS. 22,920, f. 35.

[1] The ninth clause of the treaty provided that "whereas in countries far remote, as in Africa and America, especially in Guinea, certain protestations and declarations, and other writings of that kind, prejudicial to the liberty of trade and navigation, have been emitted and published on either side by the governors and officers in the name of their superiors," it is agreed that all the aforesaid claims shall be henceforth null and void. Chalmers, A Collection of Treaties (London, 1790), p. 136; Dumont, Corps Universel Diplomatique (Amsterdam, 1731) VII, Part I, p. 45.

[2] Beer, Cromwell's Policy in its Economic Aspects, in Political Science Quarterly, Vols. XVI, XVII.

The English Company was, however, in no condition to avail itself of this opportunity. It had suffered heavy losses during the war and the preliminary hostilities in West Africa.[1] Its original capital of £122,000 had almost entirely disappeared, and its credit was at so low an ebb that loans to secure the indispensable fresh resources could not be negotiated.[2] Moreover, it had become involved in a serious controversy with the chief English slave-holding colony, Barbados, which complained bitterly of the high prices and the inadequate number of slaves shipped there. In 1668,[3] Governor Willoughby wrote to Charles II that the colony would be ruined unless the trade to Africa were made free, so that they might be supplied as plentifully as formerly. Slaves, he claimed, were so excessively dear and scarce that the poor planters would be forced to emigrate to foreign colonies in order to gain a livelihood.[4] In the same year, formal charges against the Company were brought before the House of Commons, in the form of a petition signed by a number of men, among whom were Sir Paul Painter and Ferdinando Gorges, who were prominently identified with Barbados.[5]

To the first charge that formerly, under free trade, the colonies were well and cheaply supplied, and that forts in

---

[1] C. C. 1661–1668, nos. 902, 903.

[2] W. R. Scott, op. cit. II, p. 18.

[3] C. O. 1/21, 89; C. C. 1661–1668, no. 1539.

[4] At the same time, the Barbados Assembly petitioned the King to the same effect. Ibid. no. 1563.

[5] The charges and replies are in the Answer of the Company of Royal Adventurers of England trading into Africa, published in 1667.

West Africa were not necessary, the Company replied that without such forts England would lose the African trade, and the merchants would be at the mercy of every enemy; and further, that the colonies had never been more cheaply and plentifully supplied than immediately prior to the Dutch war.   Secondly, it was charged that the Company was in bad credit and heavily in debt, and being thus unable to find the capital required for its trade, had "lately taken up an unknown way of granting their Licences to others of his Majesties good Subjects to fetch *Negroes* from Guiny, exacting for the same two, three, four and five Hundred pounds a Ship."   In reply, the Company admitted that it was greatly in debt as a result of the heavy losses inflicted upon it by the Dutch, but pointed out that on the other hand the colonies owed it £90,000.   Furthermore, they said that they had been forced to adopt the licensing system in order that the colonies might be supplied, and that the fees so obtained were devoted to the maintenance of the forts.[1]   The third charge was that the Company had contracted to furnish thousands of negroes yearly to the Spanish colonies, while the English colonies were not only poorly supplied, but in addition had to suffer from the competition of the products raised by this labor in Spanish America.   The Company admitted the Spanish contract; otherwise, they said, the Dutch would have secured it, but stated that never in any year had more than 1200 negroes been delivered on its

---

[1] These fees, they said, were "3*l.* *per* Ton, or 10 *per Cent* on the *Cargo,* which is less then the Company pays in proportion upon their whole Trade" towards the maintenance of the forts.

account, while at the same time the English colonies had been furnished by them with over 6000 slaves in a single year. Further, they asserted that the colonies themselves sold many negroes to the Spaniards, and that such slaves were employed in the mines and in domestic service, and hence did not raise products competing with those of the English colonies. Finally, it was charged that the negroes were formerly sold in the colonies at from £12 to £16 a head,[1] and that of late the price had been £25 and had even risen to £30.[2] In reply, the Company stated that before they had received a charter the average price of negroes in the colonies was £17 or 2400 pounds of sugar, and that at the outset they had instructed their agents to sell at this figure,[3] but that on account of the Dutch war the price had inevitably risen, and might recently have been as high as £30.[4]

Early in 1668, the Secretary of the Company, Sir Ellis Leighton, also issued a formal answer to the complaints that had come directly from the colony.[5] He especially emphasized the absolute necessity of carrying on this trade

[1] Or 1600 to 1800 lbs. of sugar.

[2] It was also claimed that the best negroes were at the same time sold to the Spaniards for £18. The Company, however, denied that the best negroes were delivered to the Spaniards and only the "refuse" ones sold to the English colonies.

[3] " The Company alwayes did order them to be sold in Lotts according to the custome of the Countrey."

[4] Before the Restoration, the best male slaves were sold in Barbados for £30, and the female for £25 to £27. Richard Ligon, A True and Exact History of Barbados (London, 1657), p. 46. Already in 1661, Barbados complained of the great rise in the price of negroes. C. C. 1661–1668, no. 85.

[5] C. O. 1/22, 21; C. C. 1661–1668, no. 1680.

by means of a privileged company, saying sarcastically that
'open markets and free trade are best for those that desire
them is certain, and so it is to buy cheap and sell dear, and
most of all to have commodities for nothing, and if all his
Majesty's dominions and plantations were made only for
Barbadoes it might be expedient; but since it is conceived
that his Majesty will have regard to what may preserve
the trade of the nation, and not only to what will gratify
Barbadoes, they think their desire of free trade will prove as
impracticable and pernicious to themselves as destructive to
all other public interests.' Leighton then carried the war into
the enemy's camp, stating that Barbados was greatly in debt
to the Company, and praying the King to write to the Governor to assist them in recovering these outstanding sums.

During the following year Barbados renewed its complaints, but the government decided not to allow trading
in violation of the Company's charter.[1] The colony's case
had been greatly prejudiced by the fact that the financial
difficulties of the Company were in part due to its inability
effectively to collect its outstanding debts in Barbados
under the existing local laws. Already in 1663, before
Lord Willoughby had assumed the government of the
colony, the local authorities had issued an order "obstructing all proceedings at law against any planters there for
their debts." [2] In response to some complaints of the merchants and traders,[3] the Council for Foreign Plantations in-

---

[1] P. C. Cal. I, pp. 518–520.
[2] *Ibid.* p. 354; C. C. 1661–1668, no. 459.
[3] C. C. 1661–1668, no. 462.

vestigated the matter and reported that this order was without justification, as there was an excellent prospect for a plentiful crop, and that there was good cause to suspect that "the said President and some of the Councill being deeply indebted did take hold of the said Petition (praying for the measure in question) aswell to avoid the payment of their owne debts as to gratify the Petitioners." They added that this order for a stay in proceedings for the recovery of debts was unprecedented and of so evil a consequence that, if not immediately prevented, it would tend to the ruin not only of Barbados, but of all the other colonies as well; and advised Charles II to rescind it and to forbid such orders in the future.[1] Accordingly, Lord Willoughby was directed to give effectual and speedy redress to this grievance;[2] but as he had to act with the advice of the members of his Council who, being planters, "carry it in favour of their brethren," this instruction could not be fully executed.[3] In 1664, the African Company stated in a petition that they had supplied Barbados liberally with slaves and had given long credits to the planters who owed them £40,000, yet they were very much abused "by the intollerable delayes of Payment amongst the most of the Planters, against which the present Form of Judiciary proceedings in that Island afford no Remedy, but what is worse than the disease." [4]

This was merely an instance of the friction that inevi-

[1] P. C. Cal. I, pp. 352–354; C. C. 1661–1668, no. 470.
[2] P. C. Cal. I, p. 355.   [3] C. C. 1661–1668, no. 689.
[4] P. C. Cal. I, pp. 381–383.

tably exists between all debtor and creditor communities, and which played an important part in the politics of the old Empire. Without any conscious moral turpitude, there was a constant tendency on the part of the colonial planters to scale down their debts by inequitable currency and bankruptcy legislation. Against such measures the English merchants had to protect themselves as best they could. Accordingly, when the African Company in 1668 met the demands of Barbados and agreed to sell negroes at the old price of £17, it stipulated that good security had to be given for their payment.[1] No satisfactory arrangement could, however, be made, nor would Barbados amend its law for the recovery of debts. In reply to the orders of the English government that the lands, as well as the goods, of a defaulting debtor should be liable, the Speaker of the Assembly wrote in 1670[2] that their laws were in every way as effectual for the recovery of debts as those of England, and that they had much more reason to complain than had the Company, in that it had not complied with its proclamation to furnish negroes at £17, but had sold the best to the Spaniards, and the refuse to them at nearly double this figure.[3]

[1] C. O. 1/22, 22; C. C. 1661–1668, no. 1681.

[2] C. C. 1669–1674, pp. 133, 134.

[3] In 1669, the Royal African Company complained "that the Creditors of the said Company living in Barbados refuse to pay their Debts, and that the iniquity of proceedings, and the ill constitution of the Lawes in that Island is soe great, that as these Lawes have already ruyned the said Company, so in a little time they will infallibly ruyne the Inhabitants themselves." After a hearing of the interested parties, the Privy Council ordered that henceforth lands, as well as goods, in Barbados should be liable to be sold by "an out Cry" for debts, and that the Governor should cause a law to this

In the meanwhile the financial condition of the Company had been going from bad to worse, and in 1671 bankruptcy was imminent. The English Exchequer itself was on the brink of insolvency and could not stand the additional burden of providing and maintaining the forts in West Africa so that this commerce might be open to all. Hence again, the only alternative to losing the trade entirely was a drastic reorganization of the insolvent Company and the formation of a new one with ample capital to continue its work. It was proposed that the stockholders of the old Company, whose capital had amounted to £122,000, should receive ten per cent in new stock, while the creditors holding claims amounting to £57,000 were offered forty per cent, of which the bulk was in cash. The plan went through, and in 1672 the Royal African Company was incorporated with a capital of £100,000, of which £35,000 was applied to satisfying the claims of the stockholders and creditors of the old Company.[1] Among the numerous patentees were the statesmen, officials, men of affairs, and merchants interested in large colonial and commercial enterprises, such as the Duke of York, Prince Rupert, Shaftesbury, Arlington,

effect to be passed by the Barbados legislature. P. C. Cal. I, pp. 528, 529, 532. A year later, Governor Willoughby, who was in London, wrote to the Speaker of the Assembly that, although he had 'justified their laws to be authentic enough for the recovery of just debts,' yet this complaint of the African Company had prejudiced them, and that it would be advisable to alter their laws. C. C. 1669–1674, pp. 81, 82. In reply, the Speaker wrote the letter quoted in the text.

[1] The capital was shortly thereafter increased to £111,100. W. R. Scott, *op. cit.* II, pp. 19, 25; C. C. 1661–1668, no. 407. In Professor Seligman's library is one of the original prospectuses of this reorganization.

Williamson, Berkeley, Sir Peter Colleton, Thomas Povey, Ferdinando Gorges and Josiah Child. To them, as to their predecessors, was granted the exclusive right to trade in Africa between Sallee and the Cape of Good Hope.[1]

The new Company proceeded vigorously to engage in the African trade. For nearly two years after the issue of the charter its activities were hampered by the war with the Dutch and the embargoes laid in consequence thereof, yet the Company despatched during this period seven ships with soldiers and ammunition to preserve the forts in Africa and to carry negroes thence to America. In 1674, fifteen ships were sent and in 1675, twenty.[2] Acting energetically and skilfully, the Company established itself firmly at various points in West Africa, especially on the Gold Coast and on the Gambia, and by means of its numerous forts and trading stations was able to secure an ever increasing share of the trade with that region. English manufactures were bartered for the native produce — gold, ivory, redwood, wax — but especially for the slaves demanded by the planters of the New World.[3] Thanks to the settlement of the difficulties with the Dutch, the financial history of the new Company differed radically from that of its predecessor. Up to the Revolution of 1688/9, the stockholders had every reason to be satisfied with the returns on their investment. From

[1] C. C. 1669–1674, pp. 409–412; Va. Hist. Soc. Coll. New Series VI, pp. 37–53.

[2] C. C. 1675–1676, p. 388.

[3] African Co. Papers 10, ff. 1, 2. The average yearly exports from England to Africa during the nine years 1680 to 1688 were £70,000. Report of the Committee of the Privy Council (London, 1789) II, Part IV, no. 5.

1676 to 1688 high dividends were paid at irregular intervals; in both 1676 and 1677, the stockholders received about twenty-two per cent, while the average rate annually for the entire period was roughly eight per cent.[1] This success was attained despite obstacles encountered in many quarters. Abuses were committed by the Company's servants, difficulties with the colonies were a serious handicap, and thirdly, its monopoly was invaded by private traders.

The Company's affairs in Africa and in the colonies were necessarily managed by agents and servants, upon whose honesty depended the success of the enterprise. In those days of infrequent and slow communications efficient control from so distant a centre as London was impossible, and ample opportunity was afforded for unscrupulous actions. As a result, the Company suffered, and also the colonies, since the cost of their indispensable labor was thereby raised. One great item of loss was the terrific mortality of the negroes during their transportation from Africa to the West Indies,[2] which at this time averaged roughly twenty per cent.[3] Obviously, since the slaves were very valuable, it

[1] Scott, *op. cit.* II, pp. 33, 34. Despite this, the Company stated in 1683: 'We are envied for our advantages, yet our members have not had so much as interest on their money, though no stock has been managed with more faithfulness and care.' C. C. 1681–1685, p. 526.

[2] This was not a peculiarity of the English trade. In 1670, *La Justice*, sailing for the French West Indies with 434 negroes, arrived with about 310, and *La Concorde* at the same time brought over safely only 443 out of 563. S. L. Mims, Colbert's West India Policy, pp. 169–171, 286.

[3] In 1679, the Royal African Company asserted that 25 per cent was the usual mortality, but as this statement was made in order to prove that the price of negroes sold by them in Jamaica could not be lowered, it cannot be

was in the interest of the Company that this mortality should be as low as possible; their original cost in Africa was considerable, the expenses of their transportation were high, and they commanded a big price in the colonies. Thus, apart from any humanitarian considerations, mere self-interest would have dictated the best possible treatment. Unfortunately, but little was understood of even rudimentary hygiene; and, furthermore, in some instances virulent diseases attacked the ships and literally converted them into charnel-houses.[1] In other cases, the negroes proved refrac-

accepted without some question. C. O. 391/3, ff. 228 *et seq.* In 1707 was prepared a report by the Royal African Company for the Board of Trade, showing that, in the nine years from 1680 to 1688, 60,783 negroes were shipped from Africa, of which 46,396 were delivered in Barbados, Jamaica, and the Leeward Islands. What became of the other 14,387 is not stated. C. O. 388/10, H 108. In 1789 was published a governmental report on the slave-trade, giving the same figures and stating that they were derived from the Board of Trade's books, but further adding that the 14,387 unaccounted for were lost in transportation. Report of the Committee of the Privy Council (London, 1789) II, Part IV, no. 5.

[1] In a letter dated Dec. 2, 1678, the Company's agents in Barbados reported the arrival of the *Martha* with 385 of the 447 negroes embarked in Africa, and also that of the *Arthur* with 329 out of 417 taken on at Arda, of whom many were small and some weak, old, and very sickly. African Co. Papers 1, ff. 6, 7. In 1681, a vessel arrived in Barbados with 130 out of the original 232 negroes.

VESSEL'S NAME	NUMBER OF NEGROES ARRIVED	NUMBER ORIGINALLY EMBARKED
Golden Fortune	226	258
Mary	474	507
Delight	169	171
Robert	235	350
Bonadventure	256	320
Unity	180	200
Prosperous	580	610
Return	170	330
Daniel	428	530
Unity	306	397
Total	3024	3673

African Co. Papers 16 *passim.*

tory and rebellious, and as the small white crew could not cope with them if at liberty, they were kept in confinement and weighed down with irons.[1] Such factors would not, however, completely account for this great mortality. The horrors of the middle passage were greatly accentuated by an abuse that was the bane of nearly all the great commercial companies, namely, the unauthorized private trading of their employees. It appears that at times the captains of the slave-ships bought negroes for their own account, and callously overcrowded their ships to the grave detriment of their human cargo's health.[2] Of one such vessel, which had

Ibid. f. 119. The list here printed of slave-ships arriving in Barbados between Jan. 27, 1683, and April 21, 1684, shows that in about one-half of these ships the mortality was comparatively low, about 7 per cent, while in the others it averaged about 28 per cent.

[1] In 1680, a vessel arrived in Barbados with 180 out of the original 213. The agents reported that they conceived "many of the men are much the worse for being soe loaded with Irons as they have bin all the Voyage," because they were unruly and the captain feared an uprising. African Co. Papers 1, f. 62. The horrors of the middle passage were graphically described by a contemporary writer who said: "For no sooner are they arrived at the Sea-side, but they are sold like Beasts to the Merchant, who glad of the booty puts us aboard the Ships, claps us under Deck, and binds us in Chains and Fetters, and thrusts us into the *dark noisom* Hold, so many and so close together, that we can hardly breathe, there are we in the hottest of Summer, and under that scorching Climate without any of the sweet Influences of the Air, or briezing Gale to refresh us, suffocated, stewed, and parboyled altogether in a Crowd, till we almost rot each other and ourselves." Philotheos Physiologus, Friendly Advice to the Gentlemen Planters of the East and West Indies (1684), Part II, pp. 82, 83.

[2] At a later date, it was said: "The covetnous of most Commanders to Carry many to advance their Freight (for they are generally Paid by the Head) as it hath occasioned unanswerable abuses; so the death of abundance which should be prevented if possible." John Pollexfen, A Discourse of Trade (London, 1697), p. 130.

arrived in Barbados in 1679, the agents there wrote to the Company that its appalling condition was due to such overcrowding, and that they presumed that those owning these negroes had not been deterred by any fear of the consequences, because they had resolved, "if soe many remained a Live in ye Ship as they pretended to, they would have no Loss, ye Living being still theirs, & ye Dead the Comp^{as}." [1] According to Sir William Wilson Hunter, the annals of the East India Company afford no counterpart of the sixteenth century "Portuguese commodore of two royal ships, who lost one by overloading it with a double cargo, while he freighted the other with his own goods." [2] The African Company can supply this undesired deficiency, for here certainly is a close, and if anything a more ghastly, parallel.

In addition, the Royal African Company was handicapped by continuous disputes with the colonies. A few weeks after its incorporation, in December of 1672, a declaration was issued by the Duke of York, as Governor of the Company, offering to contract in London for the delivery of negroes in the colonies at prices in lots, ranging from £15 for Barbados to £18 for Virginia, and reserving to itself the right to sell at the best price obtainable in the colonies those negroes

[1] Barbados, June 10, 1679, Edwyn Stede and Stephen Gascoigne to the Royal African Company. Regarding this ship's condition, they wrote: "It doth most certainly appeare to us the great mortality of negroes that was in y^t ship from Callabar hither & here was occasioned by ye ships being crowded & pestred wth ye supernumerary Negroes taken into y^t ship, not having roome to stow or cleane them, for wee never saw soe nasty foule and stincking Ship in our Lives." African Co. Papers 1, f. 23. On this private trade, see also *ibid.*, ff. 38, 43.

[2] Hunter, History of British India II, p. 167.

for which no contract had been made prior to their arrival.[1] Immediate cash payment was not demanded, but liberal terms were allowed to purchasers.[2] As Barbados had not as yet complied with the royal orders to amend its unsatisfactory debtor law, the Company inherited its predecessor's controversy with the colony on this score. This friction was further intensified by the fact that, during the first two years of the Company's existence, England was at war with the United Provinces and, consequently, considerable difficulty was experienced in supplying the colonial demand.

The English government had several times already instructed Barbados to amend its debtor laws,[3] and in 1673, when Sir Jonathan Atkins was appointed Governor, these orders were renewed. He was instructed to endeavor to get the Assembly to pass a satisfactory law and to acquaint it, 'how sensible his Majesty is, what great prejudices are brought upon the trade of that island by the difficulty men find in recovering their just debts.'[4] Accordingly, when the Barbados Assembly met late in 1674, Atkins laid stress on 'the great clamour in England of the injustice of the Island

---

[1] The negroes were to be between the ages of 12 and 40, and the price was fixed at £15 for Barbados, at £16 for the Leeward Islands, at £17 for Jamaica, and £18 for Virginia. C. O. 1/29, 60; *ibid*. 1/60, 34; C. C. 1669–1674, p. 444.

[2] The slaves contracted for in London were to be paid for in three equal instalments, respectively two, four, and six months after delivery.

[3] In 1671 and 1672, the Governor was instructed to assist with the utmost care the agents of the Company in recovering its just debts. P. C. Cal. I, pp. 572–574; S. P. Dom. Charles II, Entry Book 31, ff. 92, 93; C. C. 1669–1674, pp. 363, 364.

[4] C. C. 1669–1674, p. 543.

to their creditors,' and recommended that their antiquated and inequitable legal methods be thoroughly overhauled.[1] To some extent this unquestionable grievance — so staunch a friend of the colony as was Governor Atkins termed it a 'great scandal' — was redressed by the Assembly.[2] In its turn then, the colony proceeded to complain of the inadequate supply of negroes furnished by the Royal African Company.[3] Their prosperity, they said, depended upon a plentiful supply, which was not forthcoming, and in addition the prices demanded were claimed to be excessive.[4]

On being summoned by the Lords of Trade to answer these complaints,[5] the African Company stated[6] that during the first two years after their incorporation, though much obstructed by the Dutch war, they had sent four ships with slaves to Barbados, and that, in 1674, six of their vessels had delivered about 2000 negroes in that colony, while 3000

[1] Full information about these legal details may be found in the extant records. See especially C. C. 1669–1674, nos. 1183, 1191. A careful summary is available in E. D. Collins's Studies in the Colonial Policy of England, 1672–1680, in Am. Hist. Assoc. Report 1900, pp. 159–162.

[2] C. C. 1675–1676, pp. 166–168, 174, 180, 193; C. C. 1677–1680, p. 7.

[3] C. O. 31/2, ff. 165, 172, 177–182, 183; C. C. 1675–1676, pp. 193, 206–208, 210; C. C. 1677–1680, pp. 6, 7.

[4] At this time, in 1675, the price of negroes in Barbados was claimed to be £20 to £22, which they said they could not afford to pay, "our Lands being worne out, our Commodities being lowe & Great Dutyes vpon them." Regarding the offer of the Company to furnish negroes in lots at £15, they stated that it was less advantageous than to pay £20 to £22 for good negroes. C. O. 31/2, ff. 178, 179. On Sept. 20, 1675, Governor Lord Vaughan of Jamaica wrote to Secretary Williamson that the Company had of late supplied them plentifully, but at extraordinary rates, no negroes being sold under £22 for ready money. C. C. 1675–1676, p. 192.

[5] *Ibid.* p. 373.   [6] *Ibid.* pp. 387, 388.

had been ordered sent in 1675. As regards the allegation that they had sold their negroes for £20 to £22, they asserted that an examination of their books would show that the selling price averaged about £15.[1] The Lords of Trade then questioned the official representative of the colony in England, Colonel Thornborough, who admitted that Barbados was then and had for some time been plentifully supplied, and that the complaint referred to the time when the Dutch war had created a scarcity.[2] Accordingly, a severe letter of censure was sent to Governor Atkins, in whom the colony had found a zealous advocate, for continuing these complaints after their cause had been removed.[3]

But in 1679 the Barbados Assembly again instructed Sir Peter Colleton and Colonel Henry Drax of the Committee

[1] The Company further said that the colony already owed them £25,000 and would owe £70,000 more for the 3000 negroes sent in 1675.

[2] C. C. 1675–1676, p. 388. Between March and June, 1676, there had been sold by the Company in Barbados 1372 negroes; 224, which could not be disposed of there, had been shipped to the other colonies. *Ibid.* p. 481.

[3] C. O. 1/38, 31; P. C. Cal. I, pp. 676–679; C. C. 1675–1676, pp. 484, 485, 488, 489. On July 14, 1676, Atkins had written that he did not believe that since his arrival in Barbados, somewhat less than two years prior thereto, 2500 negroes had been imported, although three times as many could have been sold. C. C. 1669–1674, p. 615; *ibid.* 1675–1676, p. 422. In reply to the letter of censure, he wrote to Secretary Williamson that, for some time before his arrival and for a year thereafter, the Company had sent very few negroes. He added that since then the colony was fully supplied and could take 2000 to 3000 slaves yearly. *Ibid.* 1677–1680, pp. 6, 7. In 1677, a vessel, which had arrived in England from Barbados, reported that the colony was very prosperous and that several Spanish ships were trading there for their "refuse" negroes. One of these vessels had taken away 300, paying about £25 apiece for them. Cal. Dom. 1677–1678, p. 263.

of Gentlemen Planters in England to complain that the island was poorly supplied and that the negroes delivered there by the Company were poor and useless.[1] This complaint was not without some justification, for though the number of negroes was not inadequate,[2] their quality was unquestionably poor.[3] It was, however, not disingenuous and had a covert purpose, being intended to prejudice the Company in the abortive campaign which Barbados was then inaugurating against its monopolistic privileges.[4] As there was no

[1] C. O. 31/2, ff. 339–341; C. C. 1677–1680, p. 352.

[2] In the twelve months beginning Dec. 1, 1678, the Company sold in Barbados 1425 negroes for £20,520, valuing the sugar received in payment at 10s. a *cwt*. On Jan. 5, 1680, were received 484 more, which were sold for £7050. C. C. 1677–1680, p. 510. In addition, at this time a considerable number of negroes were sold in the colony by interlopers. On Dec. 2, 1678, the agents in Barbados wrote to the Company: "Wee feare ye many Negroes soe lately imported (by the interlopers) will be a means of making ye Comp{ys} Slaves" not sell so quickly as otherwise. African Co. Papers 1, ff. 6, 7.

[3] On Aug. 18, 1680, the agents in Barbados wrote to the Company: "Wee doe assure the Company both these Last Ships brought as many Miserable Poore Old Lame Blind and Bursten Negroes as ever any two Ships of Like Numbers brought Since wee have been here. . . . And indeed what ever the matter is wee know not but within these two or three yeares the negroes have generally proved bad and come in Ill Condition in Respect of what they did before." African Co. Papers 1, ff. 63, 64.

[4] At the same time that this complaint was forwarded to England, the Gentlemen Planters there were instructed to see 'whether the Royal African Company cannot be divided into sundry and separate stocks and jurisdictions.' C. C. 1677–1680, p. 352. On Dec. 2, 1678, the agents of the Company in Barbados, Edwyn Stede and Stephen Gascoigne, wrote to London that Colonel Christopher Codrington was a great favorer of interlopers, and that he, Drax, and Sharpe had bought the chief negroes from the last private trader at very low prices. If this be true, they added, it was done with the design of prejudicing the Company by enabling them to

change of success, this design was soon dropped, and the specific complaint about an inadequate supply was not pressed.

During the following ten years the English government was not further bothered with the examination of such grievances from Barbados. The Company delivered there yearly on an average 2400 negroes,[1] which, with those secured surreptitiously from the private traders in violation of the Company's monopoly, amply filled the wants of the colony. But this interloping trade, which at this time had assumed considerable proportions, was strongly favored by the colony and equally firmly opposed by the Company. Its efforts to suppress the interlopers led to constant friction in Barbados and more than kept alive the colony's antagonism to the privileged Company.

The relations of the Royal African Company with the other West Indian colonies were essentially similar. The Leeward Islands had suffered severely during the Dutch and French War, which was concluded in 1667, and had virtually to begin their economic life anew. A fundamental requirement was a large number of slaves to develop their resources. The Governor, Sir Charles Wheler, reported in 1671 that

say when they arrive in England that they can buy more cheaply of interlopers than from the Company, and then to use this as an argument for an open trade. African Company Papers 1, f. 7.

[1] C. C. 1681–1685, p. 71. Between September of 1682 and August of 1683, the Company consigned to Barbados 18 ships with 6380 negroes. *Ibid.* p. 486. The total number of negroes delivered by the Company in Barbados during the nine years from 1680 to 1688 was 21,521. C. O. 388/10, H 108.

4000 were needed;[1] and, in 1676, Governor Stapleton stated that the islands were in a position to take and pay for 1000 negroes yearly.[2] The slave population had greatly increased during these years. In 1678, it amounted to 8500.[3] Despite occasional complaints, the wants of these islands as a whole seem to have been adequately filled.[4] Yet there was unquestionably some friction on this score between the Royal African Company and the separate islands,[5] and this was increased, as in Barbados, by certain provisions in the local laws which interfered with the effective collection of debts.[6]

---

[1] C. O. 1/27, 52; C. C. 1669–1674, pp. 287–292.

[2] C. O. 1/38, 65; C. C. 1675–1676, pp. 497–502. In 1672, Stapleton said that during the past seven years no slaves had been brought by the Royal African Company, but that 300 had been imported into Nevis by licensed ships and 300 into Montserrat and Antigua. C. C. 1669–1674, pp. 392, 393.

[3] St. Kitts 1436, Nevis 3849, Montserrat 992, Antigua 2172. C. C. 1677–1680, p. 266.

[4] In the nine years from 1680 to 1688, the Company delivered in the Leeward Islands 6073 negroes. C. O. 388/10, H 108.

[5] In 1680, the Council of St. Kitts complained to the Lords of Trade that the Royal African Company did not supply their wants and stated that it was 'as great a bondage for us to cultivate our plantations without negro slaves as for the Egyptians to make bricks without straw.' They admitted that a large number of negroes had been sent to Nevis, whence they might have been supplied, but they claimed that in this manner they got only the poor negroes and these at immoderate rates. C. C. 1677–1680, pp. 571–574. See also C. O. 391/3, ff. 231, 232; C. C. 1677–1680, p. 629.

[6] Though united under one government and at this time occasionally holding a federal General Assembly, each of the four chief islands had its separate legislature and insisted upon passing its own laws. C. C. 1681–1685, p. 530. In 1683, some London merchants trading to the Leeward Islands stated in a petition that 'a law has lately been made at St. Chris-

In Jamaica, similar disputes and controversies took place. After the conclusion of peace with Spain in 1670, the colony was able to develop its agricultural resources, which hitherto had been neglected on account of the large profits derived from privateering. As a result, the slave population of the island grew apace. In 1670, the colony had but 2500 negroes, while five years later their number was said to have been 9000.[1] At this time, the Governor, Lord Vaughan, wrote that the Royal African Company had of late supplied Jamaica very well, though at extraordinary rates, no negro being sold for less than £22 cash.[2] The following year, however, Peter Beckford — a forefather of Chatham's well-known supporter — as Secretary of the Colony, wrote to Sir Joseph Williamson[3] that the people were 'much dissatisfied with the Royal Company.' He claimed that, as they were

tophers which, in effect, leaves the debtor at liberty to pay, or not to pay, his debts at will, and we have reason to fear that the inhabitants of the other Islands will try to obtain a like Act to the ruin of petitioners.' *Ibid.* p. 528. At the same time, the Royal African Company complained against this law, stating that, according to it, the property of the debtor was appraised by three of his neighbors and had to be taken by the creditor at this valuation, and any surplus over his claim had to be paid to the debtor. 'It is plain,' they said, 'to what frauds such a law gives opening.' *Ibid.* pp. 538, 539. Accordingly, the law in question was repealed by an Order in Council. *Ibid.* pp. 569, 774. Governor Stapleton, however, wrote to the Lords of Trade that until recently there had been no complaint against this Act and a similar one in Nevis, and that the merchants had always been treated fairly. *Ibid.* p. 585. The question was then reopened, and the Lords of Trade decided that a clause should be added to the Act, compelling the appraisers to take the property at the valuation set by them. *Ibid.* p. 714.

[1] C. C. 1669–1674, pp. 52, 53; *ibid.* 1675–1676, pp. 314, 315.
[2] *Ibid.* 1675–1676, p. 192.   [3] *Ibid.* pp. 411, 412.

so inadequately furnished with negroes, it had become a good trade to buy slaves in Barbados for £17 with the object of selling them in Jamaica for £24. In order to expedite the settlement of Jamaica, it was even suggested at this time that special permission be granted to this colony to trade to Africa for negroes, provided security were given not to carry them elsewhere.[1] The average number of negroes imported during this decade was 1500 annually, but the island demanded more.[2]

In 1679, the Jamaica legislature petitioned the Duke of York to intercede with the African Company for a sufficient supply of negroes at moderate rates.[3] In due course this petition was carefully investigated by the Lords of Trade, who held a hearing, at which were represented the interested parties.[4] On behalf of the Royal African Company, it was stated that Jamaica owed them £60,000 for negroes and that upon the arrival of this year's ships the amount would be increased to £110,000. It was contended that the negroes cost originally in Africa £5, that the expense of their transportation was only somewhat less than this sum, to which further had to be added twenty-five per cent which "they lose by the vsual mortality of ye Negros," while in addition the Company spent yearly for maintaining the forts in Africa £20,000.

In their turn, the representatives of the colony stated[5]

[1] C. C. 1675–1676, pp. 515, 516. [2] Ibid. 1677–1680, p. 344.
[3] Ibid. p. 436. [4] Ibid. pp. 625, 626; C. O. 391/3, ff. 228 et. seq.
[5] These statements were embodied in a memorial, which was read by the Committee on Nov. 4, 1680, the day of this hearing. C. O. 1/46, 32; C. C. 1677–1680, pp. 626, 627.

that Jamaica would buy yearly 3000 to 4000 negroes, provided the price were £16 or £17 in lots containing 'no refuse negroes' and a credit of six months time were allowed. 'If the Company,' they said, 'objects that the Island has always had more than it could pay for, then it is truly answered' that this is due to the extortionate prices demanded, and that 'the Islanders are under no great obligation to the Company for biting and devouring them by such unreasonable and unconscionable dealing.'

With a view to a compromise satisfactory to both parties, the Lords of Trade thereupon asked the Company whether they could furnish Jamaica with negroes at £18; and, upon the receipt of an affirmative answer, they advised the King to order the Company to send there yearly 3000 'merchantable' negroes to be sold at £18 a head in lots on six months credit, provided good security were given. The Committee further reported that the Company should also be obliged to send constant supplies of negroes to the other colonies and to take particular care that Montserrat and St. Christopher (which had also forwarded complaints of a great scarcity) should be well stocked in the future.[1] This report was adopted and its recommendations were embodied in an Order in Council, dated November 12, 1680.[2]

The Company's agents in Jamaica complied with the terms of the order, although to some extent violating its spirit by making up lots of a poorer average equality than

[1] C. O. 391/3, ff. 231, 232; C. C. 1677–1680, p. 629.
[2] P. C. Cal. II, p. 12; C. C. 1677–1680, p. 639.

had been customary. But even if the average were poorer, the price of £18 was so low that competent judges thought the private traders would be driven from the Jamaica market.[1] Instead of this result, the Company found that under the prevailing conditions it could not make money at this price, and hence the number of negroes stipulated was not sent to Jamaica, and the field was left free to the increasing number of interlopers.[2]

[1] On June 27, 1681, Hender Molesworth and the other agents in Jamaica wrote to the Company: "Wee preseeded wth an equall respect to the Order of Councill & your Interest (in the Sale of Bills Negroes) Soe that making our Lotts accordingly (wth a mixture of more Ordinary Negr^s) wee Sold at £18 p head Six m^{ts} & £17 ready money. After wch rate the diffrence vpon the whole is not considerable from what it would have been if wee had only putt choice negroes in Lotts as formerly & Sold at £22." They then added that the interlopers could not sell profitably at this price and would be ruined. African Co. Papers 1, f. 116. On June 13, 1681, the Deputy-Governor of Jamaica, Sir Henry Morgan, wrote: 'I doubt not that the interloping commerce would fall of itself if the Company would keep the Island sufficiently supplied with negroes at the present rates.' C. C. 1681–1685, pp. 72, 73. Shortly thereafter, he wrote that the Company had, in accordance with the royal commands, sold the negroes in the last ship at £18 a head, 'which proves a great help and ease to the country.' Ibid. p. 82.

[2] On Aug. 29, 1682, the new Governor, Sir Thomas Lynch, wrote to the Lords of Trade: 'I think the Company has imported about fifteen hundred since I came, which were sold for ready money in a day; and many men that had money went away without any slaves.' A month later, he wrote that Jamaica was inadequately supplied. The date of Lynch's arrival was May 14, 1682. Ibid. pp. 231, 286, 301–303. On May 6, 1683, Lynch wrote that during the preceding six months the Company had sent none. Ibid. p. 427. See also pp. 486, 525, 532. These statements, and those made in the above references, do not fully agree with the official report of the Company, giving the number of negroes delivered by it in Jamaica during the nine years from 1680 to 1688: —

Early in 1683,[1] the Royal African Company petitioned the King, recapitulating the events leading up to the order in Council of November 12, 1680, and stating that the price of £18 therein stipulated had been embodied in a Jamaica law, which further made 'the planters judge in their own cause as to what negroes are merchantable, to our great prejudice.' In addition, they asserted that they were injured by the fact that Spanish money was legally current in Jamaica at rates greatly in excess of its intrinsic value[2] and, furthermore, that the competition of the interlopers in Africa had raised the price of negroes there by one-third. As a consequence, they claimed that their trade to Jamaica could not be continued, and prayed as a remedy that the

1680 .	1371	negroes
1681 .	1576	negroes
1682 .	1452	negroes
1683 .	2919	negroes
1684 .	2066	negroes
1685 .	3327	negroes
1686 .	3094	negroes
1687 .	595	negroes
1688 .	2402	negroes
Total .	18,802	negroes

C. O. 388/10, H 108.

[1] C. C. 1681–1685, p. 370.

[2] They said that light Spanish money passed in Jamaica without any determined weight and that, as the prices of the colony's produce were in consequence high, they lost one-third on their returns from Jamaica. The Jamaica law of 1681 provided that Peru pieces of eight should pass at 4s. and Mexico Seville at 5s. C. O. 139/8 (Printed Acts of Jamaica, 1681–1737), pp. 27, 28. In reply, the Jamaicans stated that 'the lightness of money' did not prejudice the Company, and that it had been current at these rates for years. C. C. 1681–1685, p. 378.

Order in Council of November 12, 1680, be rescinded and that the Jamaica law limiting the price of negroes be not confirmed.

The representatives of Jamaica in England, in reply, contended that the Company's troubles were due to mismanagement and that light money might be refused. They further pointed out that the interloping private traders found it profitable to sell at £18.[1] Pending further information as to the merits of the case, the government decided that the Jamaica Act fixing the price of negroes should not be confirmed, but should remain in force only during the King's pleasure.[2] Upon receipt of the news of these proceedings in England, Governor Lynch, who was especially anxious to develop a trade in negroes from Jamaica to Spanish America, wrote to the Lord President of the Privy Council: 'We were surprised to hear that our friends contended so violently for keeping up the Negro Act. I gave no such directions, and the people will be quite content with the King's order. It is the failure to provide negroes that is the ruin of all.'[3] In his speech to the Assembly in the fall of 1683, Lynch also spoke against the colony's law fixing the price of negroes, saying "it's against the reason and nature of commerce to put a perpetual or standing price on goods we need, for trade ought to have all liberty and encouragement."[4]

In the meanwhile, further investigations were being made

---

[1] C. C. 1681–1685, p. 378. See also pp. 383, 384.
[2] *Ibid.* p. 386; P. C. Cal. II, pp. 46–48.
[3] C. C. 1681–1685, p. 427.   [4] *Ibid.* p. 487.

in England. The representatives of the colony complained bitterly that the Royal African Company had suspended shipping negroes to the island, and asserted that as a result 5000 would be needed the first year and 3000 annually thereafter. They further said that they had no authority to consent to an abrogation of the agreement of 1680, but, if this were done, they prayed that the Company be obliged to furnish the numbers mentioned above, as otherwise, the price being no longer limited, 'it will simply feed the market with just enough to keep the prices at a ruinous height.'[1] On its behalf, the Royal African Company begged for a release from the agreement of 1680, because the change in conditions during the intervening three years had made its terms impossible.[2] Finally, in November of 1683, the Lords of Trade advised the repeal of the agreement of 1680, as well as that of the Jamaica Act embodying its terms; and recommended that the African Company be obliged to furnish this colony with 5000 negroes the first year and 3000 annually thereafter.[3] The final decision was somewhat delayed by further complications,[4] but in the spring of 1684 the government adopted this recommendation, and orders to this effect were issued.[5] A short time thereafter, Governor Lynch in-

[1] *Ibid.* 1681–1685, pp. 512, 513.

[2] *Ibid.* pp. 471, 525, 526. They claimed that the colonies owed the Company £130,000 for negroes delivered.

[3] *Ibid.* p. 536.

[4] *Ibid.* pp. 544, 570, 579, 580, 598.

[5] *Ibid.* pp. 601, 602, 612; P. C. Cal. II, p. 63. On Feb. 28, 1684, before the issue of the Order in Council giving effect to this arrangement, Lynch wrote to the Lords of Trade that he had acquainted the Assembly with their decision, 'with which they seemed satisfied, and desired to thank

formed the English authorities that the Royal African was beginning to supply them well, but that they would not want the large number of negroes agreed upon, unless the Spaniards should come to Jamaica to procure slaves for their colonies.[1]

It was not alone the colony's own needs, but also the desire to gain a share of the slave-trade to Spanish America, that caused the Jamaica merchants at this time to insist upon so large a number of negroes. As has already been pointed out, the various African companies of this period were designed both to supply the wants of the English colonies and also to secure a portion of the lucrative Spanish trade. With this latter object in view, the provisions of the Navigation Act had even been relaxed. The continuance of hostilities between the English and the Spanish in the West Indies had, however, frustrated this scheme; but, after the conclusion of a definitive peace in 1670, renewed hopes were entertained. In 1672, Sir Thomas Lynch, then for the first time in charge of Jamaica, wrote to Secretary Arlington that he had had expectations of entering into a trade with the Spaniards, but that they were more cautious than ever since the peace, and hence only a few straggling negroes could be sold to them.[2] This failure was mainly due to a fresh international dispute caused by English traders cutting logwood in Yucatan, which Spain insisted was an unwarranted

your Lordships.' C. C. 1681–1685, p. 593. Shortly after its adoption, this settlement was slightly modified. *Ibid.* pp. 632, 636.

[1] *Ibid.* p. 656.

[2] *Ibid.* 1669–1674, p. 335. See also pp. 339–341.

invasion of her colonial dominions. During the following years, Spain seized a large number of English colonial vessels engaged in this trade, and incidentally also some others not implicated in it, while in reprisal the English took several Spanish ships.[1] Despite these more than sporadic hostilities, further attempts were made during this decade to sell negroes to the Spaniards,[2] but nothing of importance could be accomplished until that energetic supporter of the Spanish trade, Sir Thomas Lynch, again assumed the administration of Jamaica. In 1682, shortly after his arrival in the island, the new Governor wrote that there was an excellent opportunity for a trade in negroes to Spanish America, but unfortunately the colony's supplies were inadequate.[3] Several months thereafter, Lynch reported that, as a Spanish vessel had been unable to procure negroes from the Royal African Company's agents in Jamaica, he had permitted it to buy about one hundred from an interloper,[4] and that two or three thousand could have been sold to the Spaniards during the preceding half year, had such numbers been available.[5]

At this time, comparatively few negroes were being delivered in Jamaica for the account of the Royal African Company, as the price of £18 fixed by law did not allow a sufficient margin of profit; but, in 1684, after this matter had been adjusted, the supply of negroes became adequate. As a result, fairly large purchases were made by the Span-

---

[1] See *post*, Vol. II, pp. 67–71.
[2] See Brit. Mus., Egerton MSS. 2395, f. 501.
[3] C. C. 1681–1685, pp. 301–303. [4] *Ibid*. p. 393.
[5] *Ibid*. p. 427. See also pp. 594, 597.

iards in Jamaica.[1] But just when this difficulty was being removed, another obstacle presented itself. In 1677, at the request of the Royal African Company, which had made an arrangement with the Spanish authorities, the English government had instructed Governor Atkins of Barbados and Governor Vaughan of Jamaica to allow Spanish ships to purchase negroes there, provided the laws of trade and navigation were not infringed.[2] Acting on these instructions, two Spanish ships had been allowed to trade at Jamaica in 1677.[3] In the meanwhile, however, the English government made belated inquiries as to the legality of the orders issued by it. The Solicitor-General reported that this trade was illegal, since negroes should be esteemed goods or commodities, which, according to the Navigation Act, could not be exported from the colonies in foreign ships.[4] Accordingly, early in 1678, the Lord of Trade decided that this trade ought not to be permitted.[5] Apparently, however, no orders to this effect were sent to the colonies, and it was on the strength of the instructions sent to Lord Vaughan in 1677 that Lynch permitted Spanish vessels to come to Jamaica. In 1684, the legality of this trade was again questioned. A Spanish vessel engaged in taking negroes from Jamaica to the Spanish Main was seized as an offender against the Navigation Act. Lynch, who was the chief sponsor of the trade and also financially

---

[1] C. C. 1681–1685, pp. 594, 682–684, 721, 748.

[2] *Ibid*. 1677–1680, p. 84.   [3] *Ibid*. p. 169.   [4] *Ibid*. p. 120.

[5] *Ibid*. pp. 175, 209, 210. See also pp. 85, 134, 135. In 1680/1, a Spanish vessel remained at Jamaica for a considerable time, waiting for the slave-ships. *Ibid*. 1681–1685, pp. 5, 6.

interested in it, claimed that this action was purely vexatious, refused to countenance the proceedings, and the ship
was released.[1] The men responsible for this seizure then
complained to England,[2] where the matter was referred to
the Commissioners of the Customs. They reported in
favor of continuing the order of 1677 permitting the Spanish negro trade.[3] Accordingly, specific instructions to this
effect were sent on November 30, 1684, to Hender Molesworth, who as Lieutenant-Governor had assumed charge of
the island on Lynch's death a few months prior to this.[4]

[1] C. C. 1681–1685, pp. 593, 629, 636, 637, 656.
[2] Ibid. pp. 641, 645, 740, 749.   [3] Ibid. pp. 677, 719, 728, 733.
[4] Ibid. p. 739. This order led to suggestions for a further relaxation
of the laws of trade. In 1685, Molesworth wrote that an attempt had
been made to seize the ship Saint Antonio belonging to Nicolas Porcio,
the agent of the Assiento. The act, he added, seemed to be malicious,
but he begged for an explanation of the King's orders in favor of this Spanish
trade. 'Is the liberty of buying and exporting our English manufactures
comprehended, though not expressed, within the intention of the order?
My construction is that it is so,' but the Jamaica Council was in doubt.
Molesworth then argued that such sales of English manufactures would be
very advantageous and would not lead to the illegal exportation of the
island's produce in violation of the enumeration clauses. He further added
that such importations of English manufactures into the Spanish colonies
were prohibited, 'yet the danger is easily avoided, by making up the goods
in small parcels and so covering them as to protect them from rain. These
are landed in some wood near the port to which they are bound, and left
with a man to watch them till they can be brought into town by night.
This cannot be done with our Island produce, through its nature, weight,
and bulk; moreover, it is of no value there.' Ibid. 1685-1688, pp. 19, 20.
In 1685 also, the holders of the Assiento requested permission to import
Spanish fruits directly into Jamaica. The Commissioners of the Customs
reported adversely; but, at the request of the Royal African Company, the
Lords of Trade decided to instruct the Governor of Jamaica to favor this
petition so far as he legally could. Ibid. pp. 54, 55, 64. In 1686, the

Molesworth, who had been one of the African Company's factors in Jamaica, naturally followed Lynch's policy of encouraging this trade. The Dutch merchants, who had contracted with the Spanish government for its supply of negroes, sent an agent to Jamaica,[1] and several ships with slaves purchased there were sent on account of this Assiento to the Spanish colonies. Such ships, as in Lynch's time, were despatched under the convoy of the English man-of-war stationed at Jamaica.[2]

There quickly developed in the colony considerable opposition to this Spanish trade. The Jamaica planters, as distinct from the merchants, had always opposed it,[3]

Assiento's agent in Jamaica petitioned for permission to export some of Jamaica's products — principally sugar, which was cheaper than in Cuba — on payment of the same duties as were collected in England. Being illegal, this was refused, but the Council asked Molesworth to recommend this suggestion to the King. *Ibid.* p. 357.

[1] For the early history of the Assiento, see J. de Veitia Linage, The Spanish Rule of Trade to the West Indies (trans. by John Stevens, London, 1702), pp. 154–159. According to Lynch, the Dutch firm of Quayman (Coymans) Brothers made a contract in 1683 with Spain to furnish 18,000 negroes in seven years and appointed Nicolas Porcio as their agent in the West Indies. C. C. 1681–1685, pp. 594–596. In 1685, one Beck (Béque) arrived in Jamaica as the representative of Coymans, and requested the delivery of Porcio's effects. On the disputes about this matter, see *ibid.* pp. 44, 76, 77, 142, 143. A detailed and authoritative account of the various contracts with Spanish government has been written by Georges Scelle, who gives full details of Coymans, Porcio, Balthazar Béque, Santiago del Castillo, and the legal wrangles in Jamaica. Unfortunately, he made no use of the English colonial state papers, which would have added considerable additional information. Scelle, La Traite Négrière aux Indes de Castille (Paris, 1906), I, pp. 641–675.

[2] C. C. 1681–1685, pp. 593, 752, 755; *ibid.* 1685–1688, pp. 82, 83, 142, 143.

[3] Brit. Mus., Egerton MSS. 2395, f. 501.

fearing both that the best negroes would be sold to the Spaniards and also that the price of their own labor supply would
be raised by the increased demand. The political party in
the island, which had been opposed to Lynch, availed itself
of this hostility and tried in various ways to thwart the
policy of Molesworth.[1] They attacked Molesworth because he, like Lynch,[2] was receiving large fees for permitting this trade and for the protection afforded to it by the
English men-of-war.[3] These payments were customary and
were made openly; they were not regarded as illegitimate
perquisites, though the not over-sensitive political morality
of the day was beginning to regard them with suspicion.
Molesworth did not deny the facts; but, strangely obtuse
to the principle involved, vehemently defended himself,
writing to the Earl of Sunderland in a tone akin to righteous
indignation that the 'premios, with which the Spaniards
had rewarded my services, are envied by my opposers, who
magnify the same above all measure, and would make that

[1] In 1684, Molesworth wrote to Blathwayt that the future well-known
Governor of Massachusetts, William Phipps, then Captain of H.M.S. *Rose*,
'being egged on by ill-wishers to the trade,' had insulted the Spanish at
Jamaica and was driving them away. C. C. 1681–1685, p. 729.

[2] C. O. 1/54, Part II, nos. 108, 114; C. C. 1681–1685, pp. 595, 722,
748.

[3] C. O. 138/6, ff. 287–294. This English trade with the Spaniards
centred at Jamaica, but some also was carried on in Barbados. One of
the charges brought in 1683 against Sir Richard Dutton, the Governor, was
that he had demanded six dollars a head for allowing 1000 negroes to be sold
to the Spaniards. Dutton admitted receiving the sum, but said that it had
been given to him after the conclusion of the business, and stated that such
payments had been customary under former governors. C. C. 1681–1685,
pp. 552, 559–561.

appear criminal which is really meritorious.'[1]   In addition, this party in 1686 tried to obstruct the trade by passing laws imposing duties on negroes exported and on goods imported in foreign bottoms, but Molesworth refused to give his assent to them.[2]

During the midst of this controversy, in December of 1687, the Duke of Albemarle — the unworthy son of the great Monck -- arrived as Governor of the colony. He allied himself with Sir Henry Morgan and the other leaders of the party opposed to Molesworth and his policy.[3]   With his consent, the Assembly in 1688 passed an act raising the value of the coin current in the island, which was equivalent to scaling down the debts of creditors, and called forth justifiable complaints from the Royal African Company.[4]   Shortly thereafter, however, death brought to a close the Duke of Albemarle's intemperate career, and Molesworth, who had been in England convincing the government of his rectitude, was again restored to office, while all the appointments of Albemarle were cancelled.[5]   These steps could not, however, do away with the opposition of the planters to the Spanish trade, or with their resentment towards their chief creditor, the Royal African Company; and thus, when the Revolution of 1688/9 drove James II from the throne, there were outstanding a number of unsettled difficulties between the slave-trading Company and Jamaica.

---

[1] C. C. 1685–1688, pp. 180, 181. *Cf.* pp. 278, 407, 408.
[2] *Ibid.* pp. 212, 213, 277, 278.   [4] *Ibid.* pp. 516, 523, 573, 622.
[3] *Ibid.* pp. 480, 514–516.   [5] *Ibid.* pp. 619, 620.

At various times and in varying degrees, all the sugar colonies were involved in similar controversies with the Royal African Company. Such disputes were, however, confined to the West Indies. In the tobacco colonies, the negro had not as yet to any marked extent displaced the white laborer. In 1671, Governor Berkeley estimated that Virginia had 2000 negro slaves,[1] and ten years later Lord Culpeper stated that, out of a total population of between 70,000 and 80,000, 15,000 were white indentured servants and only 3000 negro slaves.[2]   Thus, at this time, Virginia's slave population was just equal to the number that the Jamaica merchants insisted should be shipped to their colony every year. Conditions in Maryland were essentially the same. At so late a date as 1705, the slave population of this province numbered only 4475.[3] The slow expansion of slavery was due to the fact that the tobacco planters were not so prosperous as their fellows engaged in the West Indian sugar industry, and did not have the comparatively large capital required for the extensive purchase of negroes.[4]

During the seventies, the decade in which the Royal African Company received its charter, tobacco was greatly depressed in price; and, in addition, Virginia was disorganized by serious political disturbances. As a consequence,

---

[1] C. O. 1/26, 77 i; Hening II, pp. 511–517.

[2] C. C. 1681–1685, p. 157.   [3] C. O. 5/715, G 15.

[4] "The institution of slavery played there [Virginia] but an insignificant part in the course of the greater portion of this century, not because the African was looked on as an undesirable element in the local industrial system, but because the means of obtaining the individuals of this race were very limited." Bruce, Economic History II, p. 57.

this colony afforded a poor market for negroes. Some slaves were, however, imported by the Company,[1] which had its representative here as in the island colonies.[2] By 1679, however, this small supply was already in excess of the effective demand, for a few months later the Company was informed that "now good negroes are soe plenty that few will buy bad though at Low Prizes."[3] Two years later, Governor Culpeper, after commenting on the disastrously low price of tobacco, wrote: 'Our thriving is our undoing, and our purchase of negroes, by increasing the supply of tobacco, has greatly contributed thereunto.'[4] Yet, during the following years preceding the Revolution of 1688/9, Virginia continued to purchase negroes, though on a small scale when compared with the numbers landed in the West Indies. In part these slaves were procured from the island colonies, and in part also from interloping private traders.[5] Presumably some negroes were also obtained from the Royal African Company, as it continued to have an agent in Virginia to look after its affairs.[6] These interests were,

[1] C. C. 1669–1674, p. 552; ibid. 1675–1676, p. 202; Va. Mag. XIV, p. 198.

[2] On Feb. 17, 1679, John Seayres wrote from Virginia to the Company that as their agent, Mr. Skinner, had died, the Governor had honored him with this employment. He added some information about one of the Company's ships that had arrived in Virginia from Africa, and stated that 46 of the choicest negroes had been sold before entry to various men. African Co. Papers 1, f. 9.

[3] Virginia, June 25, 1679, Nathaniel Bacon and Edward Jones to the Company. Ibid. f. 19.

[4] C. C. 1681–1685, p. 156.   [5] Bruce, Economic History II, pp. 80–85.

[6] In 1686, Christopher Robinson was the agent. African Co. Papers 12, f. 149.

however, as yet of marked insignificance when contrasted with those in the West Indies.[1]

In addition to the friction arising from the causes already described, the Royal African Company complained constantly about the favor manifested towards interlopers by the West Indian colonies. The charter of the Royal African Company prohibited all other Englishmen from engaging in trade to West Africa,[2] and in return for this monopoly the Company was expected to build and to maintain forts and trading stations out of its own funds. It was generally admitted that such forts were necessary, partly in order to control the savage tribes with whom the trade was established, partly because the rivalry of the European commercial nations was so unbridled in non-European regions that short shrift would have been allowed to any unprotected trader.[3] The annual expenditure of the Royal African

[1] An abstract of the letters received by the Company from 1683 to 1698 shows scarcely any from Virginia. *Ibid.*

[2] The penalty for violating this prohibition was confiscation of the ship and cargo, of which one-half went to the Crown and one-half to the Company. C. C. 1669–1674, p. 412.

[3] *Cf.* Certain Considerations Relating to the Royal African Company of England (London, 1680), pp. 6, 7. The proclamation of 1674 enjoining respect for the Company's monopoly stated that "it is found by experience, That Traffique with Infidells & Barbarous Nations not in Amity with vs and who are not holden by any League or Treaty cannot bee carried on without the Establishment of Forts and Factoryes in Places convenient, The mainteynance whereof requires so great and constant expense that itt cannot bee otherwise defreyed" than by managing the trade by a joint stock company. C. O. 1/31, 80; C. C. 1669–1674, p. 626; British Royal Proclamations, 1603–1783 (Am. Antiqu. Society, 1911), p. 120.

Company on account of these forts was between £15,000 and £20,000,[1] which amounted to from £2 to £3 a negro. Thus the private trader, who was not burdened with these charges, had a considerable initial advantage in competing with the Company.   It was stated at the time that the colonies might possibly, during peace, be supplied at ten per cent lower rates by the Dutch traders and the English interlopers, but it was pointed out that no negroes could be secured from these sources during war.[2]   It might further have been argued that, without these forts, the English would have been virtually excluded from West Africa, and that the interloper was able to ply his trade in comparative safety only because of the protection indirectly afforded to all of English nationality by the Company's establishments. Hence, the more successful and numerous the private traders, the weaker would become the Company.   If this were the line of development, the ultimate result would be that the English would be driven from Africa, since the public finances of the day and current practice in such matters would not allow the government to assume the burden of maintaining the necessary forts.   The plantation colonies would then have been at the mercy of their French and Dutch rivals, and there can be but little doubt that the English West Indies under such conditions would

---

[1] In 1680, the Company on one occasion stated that this charge was about £15,000, and on another £20,000.   P. C. Cal. II, p. 8; C. O. 391/3, ff. 228 et seq.;   C. C. 1677–1680, pp. 625, 626.   In a pamphlet published the same year, this amount was also stated to be £20,000.   Certain Considerations Relating to the Royal African Company (London, 1680), pp. 6, 7.

[2] Brit. Mus., Egerton MSS. 2395, f. 466.

have had to pay exorbitant prices for their labor supply. It was, however, unreasonable to expect that the individual planter or merchant in the colonies, even if he realized the possibly fatal effects of encouraging the interlopers, would as a rule be public-spirited enough to sacrifice his own immediate interests by refraining from dealing with them. Consequently these private traders always found in the West Indies a ready, though clandestine, market for their human wares.

In 1674, the Royal African Company stated in a petition to the government that they had advice that several ships from New England and the other colonies and also Dutch and other foreigners were, with the consent of some of the governors, importing directly into the colonies negroes and African products, and prayed the King to issue a proclamation against such practices.[1] A proclamation[2] to this effect was accordingly issued, and explicit letters were also written to the colonial governors enjoining strict obedience to its terms.[3]

The enforcement of this proclamation depended mainly upon the activity of the governors;[4] and in Barbados, where

[1] P. C. Cal. I, pp. 614–615.

[2] C. O. 1/31, 80; C. C. 1669–1674, p. 626.

[3] P. C. Cal. I, p. 616. In reply, Governor Leverett of Massachusetts wrote that none of their adventurers were engaged in this trade, but that some from England and Barbados, who had been on this voyage, had come to New England to have their vessels repaired. C. C. 1675–1676, pp. 274, 275.

[4] In 1679, the agent in Virginia, John Seayres, wrote to the Company that the best way to prevent interloping was to "gett yor affaires Perticularly recommended by the Comiss.^{rs} of his Maties Customes to the severall

the interlopers were most conspicuous, the chief magistrate at this time was Sir Jonathan Atkins, who, uncritically accepting all the colony's complaints, failed to support the Royal African Company in enforcing its monopoly. In 1675, the Company's agents in the colony wrote: "Wee cannot yet find a meanes to prevent the presumption of Interlopers who in defiance of his Maties Com̄ands, and all wee can doe thereupon brave vs & the Authority here." [1] The following year, when one of these agents, Edwyn Stede, had seized such an interloper, a suit was brought against him for the recovery of treble damages under James I's Statute of Monopolies.[2] On this specific score, and on the general ground that the Governor did not give the Company adequate support in maintaining inviolate its privileges, a complaint against him was registered in England. In due course, during 1676, the government took up the matter, and Governor Atkins was severely rebuked for allowing such legal proceedings,[3] and was instructed in the future to secure the Royal African Company in its privileges and to take

Collectors and Officers of the Customes in this Collony to whom they Yearly send new Orders or else by a particular comānd from the Councell board to ye Governor and all other Publique Officers here to wch they must give obedience Although they haue divers ways to evade the comands of ye Proclamation."   African Co. Papers 1, f. 13.

[1] C. O. 1/35, 19; C. C. 1675–1676, pp. 278, 279.

[2] C. C. 1675–1676, p. 496; 21 Jac. I, c. 3, § iv; W. H. Price, The English Patents of Monopoly, pp. 135–141. On the difficulties encountered by the agents, see also E. D. Collins, op. cit. in Am. Hist. Assoc. Report, 1900, pp. 173, 174.

[3] The legal advisers of the government all held that there was no ground for such action under this statute of James I.   George Chalmers, Opinions of Eminent Lawyers (Burlington, 1858), pp. 580, 581.

care that no such actions at law in contempt of its charter were permitted.[1]

At the same time, similar instructions were sent to the other colonial governors, including Lord Vaughan of Jamaica, whence a like complaint had reached England. In 1676, an interloping vessel with three hundred negroes had been seized at the request of the Royal African Company's agents in Jamaica and then libelled in the local Court of Admiralty. The Judges, however, dismissed the case, claiming lack of jurisdiction, which action Dr. Richard Lloyd, the English expert in admiralty law, asserted was without any legal justification.[2]

Despite these imperative instructions, the interdicted trade could not be suppressed. Even the utmost vigilance on the part of the colonial officials would not have been able to cope with the schemes devised by the self-interest of the planters and merchants. As Governor Atkins of Barbados said in 1677, all the diligence in the world could not prevent the clandestine landing of negroes at night.[3] But, in addition, a number of the colonial officials were personally interested in this trade. In 1677, the agents in Barbados wrote to the Royal African Company of the arrival of an interloping vessel with ninety-eight negroes, stating that

[1] C. C. 1675–1676, pp. 359, 496, 497, 504, 509–511; P. C. Cal. I, pp. 655, 656, 680, 681; C. O. 324/2, ff. 103–106. In his defence, Atkins wrote early in 1677 to Secretary Williamson that he had never encouraged the interlopers, and that, while he had the King's frigate at Barbados, he had seized all of them. C. C. 1677–1680, pp. 6, 7.

[2] *Ibid.* 1675–1676, pp. 368, 369, 416, 418, 419.

[3] *Ibid.* 1677–1680, p. 63. *Cf.* p. 94.

among its owners were the Chief Judge and one of the
revenue officials.   This, they added, encouraged other people to engage in this trade, since they saw 'those that sit
in great places and live by the King's Commissions presume
to act as they do.'[1]   Occasionally a vessel was seized and
condemned,[2] but negroes still continued to be landed
in Barbados by the private traders.[3]   In the beginning of
the eighties, there also developed a trade of bringing negroes
from Madagascar.[4]   But, as this island was not within the
limits of the Company's charter,[5] its legal privileges were
not violated thereby, although its interests were adversely

---

[1] C. C. 1677–1680, p. 93.   On the interest of prominent Barbadians
in this trade, see African Co. Papers 1, f. 7; C. C. 1681–1685, pp. 145,
146.

[2] *Ibid.* 1677–1680, p. 183.

[3] On the trade of the interlopers in Barbados, Jamaica, and the Leeward
Islands during the years from 1677 to 1681, see African Co. Papers 1, ff.
1, 12, 26, 28, 41, 46, 48, 52, 53, 64, 75 *et passim*.   On some of the methods
employed by these illicit traders to evade the English customs regulations,
see P. C. Cal. I, pp. 685, 686, 691.

[4] Already in 1676, Randolph reported that there were in Massachusetts
some slaves that had been brought in the colony's ships from Madagascar.
In 1679, Robert Holden stated that a ship had just returned to Boston
from Madagascar, after landing some negroes in Jamaica.   The following
year, Governor Bradstreet said that no negroes were imported into Massachusetts, except that two years before a vessel had brought 40 or 50 from
Madagascar.   Toppan, Randolph II, pp. 225–259; C. O. 1/43, 71; *ibid.*
1/44, 61 i.

[5] In 1686, a vessel from Madagascar with negroes and merchandise was
permitted to enter by the New York Collector of the Customs, Lucas San-
ten.   Governor Dongan and the Surveyor General of the Customs, Patrick
Mein, insisted, however, that security be given to answer any claims of
either the Royal African or the East India Company.   C. C. 1685–1688,
pp. 220, 230–232, 253.

affected.[1] In 1681, Sir Richard Dutton, the Governor of Barbados, reported that the Royal African Company had imported during the preceding seven years about 2000 negroes annually, and that many had also been brought from Madagascar and by the interlopers.[2] Dutton, himself, was not sufficiently zealous in checking the interloping trade, and as a result, in 1683, the English government judged it necessary to admonish him to observe strictly the instructions already issued and to use greater diligence in the future.[3]

In the other colonies also, the interlopers were assured of a good reception from the planters and merchants. Even in a colony where slavery had as yet attained so insignificant an extension as in Virginia, some negroes were sold by these illicit traders.[4] In the Leeward Islands, naturally, this trade was more considerable. In 1680, serious complaints were received from the African Company that violence had been offered to their agent in Nevis.[5] Two years later,

[1] On April 9, 1681, the Barbados agents wrote to the Company: "Wee are apprehensive the Trade that is of Late drove to Madagascar for Negroes wch they bring hither may in time be some Inconvenience to the Companys trade; And as it is noe small quantitie have been imported being between 900 & 1000 that have been brought & sold here in about 2 mo^s time, soe that if noe remedy be found they and the Int^r lop^rs will give a full supply of negr^s to this place." African Co. Papers 1, f. 88.

[2] C. C. 1681–1685, pp. 70–72.

[3] The instructions referred to had been issued in 1680 to Governor Atkins. P. C. Cal. II, p. 8; C. O. 29/3, f. 75; C. C. 1681–1685, pp. 73–75, 145, 146, 332–336, 480.

[4] C. O. 5/1308, 13; African Co. Papers 12, f. 149; Bruce, Economic History II, p. 85.

[5] C. C. 1677–1680, pp. 570, 571, 579, 580, 583, 584.

an interloper was seized at St. Kitts by a ship of the navy, but as the illegal traffic still continued, peremptory instructions had to be sent in 1683 to Governor Stapleton to use his utmost efforts to suppress it.[1] From 1685 on, the ships of the navy on this station were active in hunting down interlopers, several of which were seized and condemned.[2] At this time, some of the chief men in Nevis and St. Kitts proposed to buy negroes from the Dutch in St. Eustatius, arguing that this would be legal, provided the slaves were imported in English vessels, since the Company's charter merely prohibited private trading by Englishmen to Africa. The agents of the Company in Nevis wrote to England about this scheme, pointing out that it would be most prejudicial, since it might lead to the Dutch establishing a magazine for negroes at St. Eustatius, whence the English colonies could draw their supplies.[3] The African Company forthwith laid the case before the government; and, in response to their complaint, the Lords of Trade in 1687 instructed the Governor, Sir Nathaniel Johnson, not to countenance this trade.[4] These importations into Nevis could not, however, be totally stopped.[5]

[1] C. C. 1681–1685, pp. 243, 480.

[2] *Ibid.* 1685–1688, pp. 86, 125, 147; C. O. 155/1, ff. 43–53. In 1688, an interloper from Bristol was seized and condemned at Montserrat. Blathwayt, Journal I, f. 304.

[3] C. C. 1685–1688, p. 216.

[4] *Ibid.* pp. 362, 398, 404.

[5] In 1688, Governor Johnson wrote to the Lords of Trade that one Crispe was represented by the officers of the customs and by those of the African Company 'as a persistent smuggler of negroes and sugar to and from the Dutch islands.' *Ibid.* p. 552. See also *ibid.* pp. 505, 553.

In Jamaica also, the Company had to contend with the interlopers.[1] As in the other colonies, careful instructions were issued against trading with them,[2] and occasionally an interloping vessel was seized by the ships of the navy stationed at Jamaica and then condemned in the Admiralty Court.[3] It was admitted in 1681, however, that some interlopers had managed to escape the vigilance of the officials and to land their negroes.[4] In one of his despatches of that year, Sir Henry Morgan wrote that, during the temporary absence of the frigate, four such ships had in two weeks successfully landed their prohibited negroes.[5] The comparatively large extent of the trade at this time was due to the fact that the island was then poorly supplied by the Royal African Company. Morgan predicted that 'the interloping commerce would fall of itself,' if this condition were remedied.[6] In this he was undoubtedly correct. But until 1684, when the colony's dispute with the Company about the price of negroes was adjusted, interlopers came not infrequently to Jamaica. In fact, Governor Lynch even permitted the sale of negroes from this source to the

[1] In 1674, when the Dutch war was interfering with the Company's operations, Jamaica had even passed a law allowing the free importation of negroes in ships qualified under the Act of Navigation. This law, naturally, was not confirmed in England. C. C. 1669–1674, p. 564; E. D. Collins, *op. cit.* pp. 163, 164.

[2] For the instructions issued by the governors to their subordinate officials, see Brit. Mus., Sloane MSS. 2724, f. 1; *ibid.* 2728 B, f. 193.

[3] C. C. 1681–1685, pp. 5,

[4] *Ibid.*

[5] *Ibid.* pp. 21, 22.

[6] *Ibid.* pp. 72, 73.

Spanish traders.   Thereafter, however, despite occasional complaints,[1] there was relatively little trouble on this score.

As a result of the clandestine nature of the interloping trade, it is naturally impossible to state in precise quantitative terms its proportion to that of the Royal African Company.   But the data available unquestionably warrant the conclusion that the illicit importations were far less than those of the privileged Company, and apparently a ratio of one to four would be a fairly close approximation to the truth.   Yet the Company suffered severely from the competition of the private traders, mainly because their activities greatly raised the original price of the negroes in Africa.[2] In 1679, it was stated in a letter to the Company from Cape Corso Castle that there were a great number of interlopers on the Gold Coast, who "gave such extravagant rates for Slaves (and there is so few upon the Coast)." [3]   As a result, the Company was not able to furnish the colonies with slaves at the prices set by the English government.   Moreover, the higher prices secured were, towards the end of the eighties, showing a diminishing margin of profit.   Already at this time were evident signs of the financial difficulties that later beset the Company.[4]

---

[1] C. C. 1685–1688, pp. 157, 216, 299, 300, 339.

[2] African Co. Papers 1, f. 119; C. C. 1681–1685, p. 370.

[3] African Co. Papers 1, f. 50.

[4] In 1686, the Company stated that they had struggled under great difficulties to support the great expense of maintaining their forts and factories, whereby they had kept the African trade from falling wholly into the hands of the Dutch; but that they had gained little for themselves, owing to the interlopers who, in spite of the orders issued by the government, succeeded

From the standpoint of public policy, however, the Royal African Company had accomplished its purpose. It had firmly established English interests in West Africa and had become an influential factor in the slave-trade. The English colonies were no longer dependent upon foreigners for their labor supply, and, in addition, some share of the valuable Spanish-American trade had been secured. But these results had been attained only at the cost of considerable friction with the West Indian colonies. These colonies constantly owed the Company large amounts[1] and, as is usual in the case of the habitual debtor, were prone to regard their creditor as an unconscionable oppressor. The English government firmly supported the Company as the organ which was to carry into effect an important national policy. The colonial governors were placed in a delicate position, because their imperative instructions from England ran diametrically counter to public sentiment in the colonies. According to a contemporary writer, if the Governor were "zealous for the Company, hee loses the Country, and if hee favour the Country, to which hee is necessitated by his interest, hee as certainly loses the Company and is slander'd, as one guilty of Tricks, w[ch] destroys him at Court."[2] Thus in 1677, Sir Jonathan Atkins, the Governor of Barbados, complained to the Lords of Trade that the merchants upon the Exchange and the Guinea

in landing their negroes in remote ports and creeks. C. C. 1685–1688, p. 257.

[1] Certain Considerations Relating to the Royal African Company of England (London, 1680), p. 5.

[2] Brit. Mus., Egerton MSS. 2395, f. 466.

Company took it upon themselves in some measure to be Governors of Barbados, and that, having so many masters, he knew not whom to please.[1] It was not only in this case, where Atkins was clearly at fault,[2] that the government decided in favor of the Company; but, in general, its privileges were vigorously supported in England. The colonies were, however, not placed at its mercy, for the government was ready to listen to all complaints and saw to it that negroes were furnished in adequate quantities and at reasonable prices. So persistent, however, was the opposition to the Company that, in order to secure its privileges, it was found necessary to appoint its agents in the colonies to important positions. Without some official voice in the administration of the colonies, the Company would have been most inadequately supported. Thus one of the Company's agents, Robert Bevin, was appointed in 1673 to be the first Collector of the Customs in Barbados;[3] and, the following year, Edwyn Stede, another agent, succeeded him in this post.[4] In 1684, Edwyn Stede and Stephen Gascoigne, the two representatives of the Company, were appointed the commissioners of the four and a half per cent revenue and were entrusted with the enforcement of the laws of trade.[5] Towards the end of this period, as Deputy-Governor, Stede was for a time in complete charge of affairs. Similarly, before his appointment as Governor of Jamaica, Sir Thomas

---

[1] C. C. 1677–1680, p. 150.   [3] Cal. Treas. Books, 1672–1675, p. 427.

[2] *Ibid*. pp. 206, 207.   [4] *Ibid*. p. 580.

[5] Treas. Books, Out-Letters, Customs 9, f. 43.   Similarly, the commissioners of this revenue in the Leeward Islands, Carpenter and Belchamber, were also the agents of the Company.   C. C. 1685–1688, p. 505.

Modyford had represented the African Company's interests in Barbados. Moreover, one of the agents in Jamaica, Hender Molesworth, was appointed Lieutenant-Governor of the colony. On the death of Sir Thomas Lynch, he became the acting chief magistrate; and, in 1689, he was appointed Governor of the island.[1]

[1] C. C. 1689–1692, f. 69.